A MODERN INTRODUCTION TO LOGIC

A MODERN INTRODUCTION TO LOGIC

BY

L. S. STEBBING, M.A.

READER IN PHILOSOPHY IN THE UNIVERSITY OF LONDON
SOMETIME FELLOW OF GIRTON COLLEGE, CAMBRIDGE

"A Science which hesitates to forget its
founders is lost.   To this hesitation I ascribe
the barrenness of logic."—A. N. WHITEHEAD.

THOMAS Y. CROWELL COMPANY
PUBLISHERS   NEW YORK

PRINTED IN GREAT BRITAIN

To
VIVIAN S. SHEPHERD

PREFACE

THE science of logic does not stand still. Mr. Bradley, writing in 1883 the *Preface* to the first edition of his *Logic*, said ' Logic is not where it was, and cannot remain where it is '. The statement is applicable to the development of logic to-day. It is true that the recent developments of logic have not tended in a direction of which Bradley would have approved, but there can be no doubt that ' logic is not where it was '. During the last half-century greater advances have been made than in the whole of the preceding period from the time of Aristotle. But the introductory text-books now being used in British Universities show no trace of these developments ; in the main they follow the traditional lines, differing chiefly in the accuracy with which they follow Aristotle himself, and with regard to the exclusion or inclusion of a certain amount of metaphysical discussion.

Books on logic may be regarded as falling into four main groups, to be distinguished according as the approach is traditional, metaphysical, pragmatic, or mathematical. The line of approach is determined by the conception of the nature and scope of logic. The most widely used English text-books belong to the first group. Traditional Logic is based upon the doctrines of Aristotle, of the schoolmen, and the *Port Royal Logic*. Aristotle founded the science of logic when he realized the importance of the form of a proposition and was thus led to recognize that all deduction is formal. This achievement should surely constitute sufficient title to fame. But the ' Father of Logic ' has been venerated after the fashion of a Victorian parent ; his authority has been unquestioningly accepted even when his doctrines have been felt to be erroneous. Thus Leibniz, for instance, was hindered in his attempt to create symbolic logic because he was unable to admit that Aristotle could be mistaken. This veneration of the authority of the Master is contrary to the spirit of Aristotle himself. He would assuredly have been surprised had he foreseen the failure of his disciples to develop the science which he founded. Nothing in the whole course of human speculation is more astonishing, or in its way more depressing, than the contentment of the traditional Logicians with the restriction of the forms of propositions to the fourfold schedule.

This restriction was due to Aristotle's failure to carry his analysis far enough. This failure also resulted in the traditional doctrine that every proposition ascribes a predicate to a subject. Respect for Aristotle blinded the traditional Logicians to these defects, and prevented them from criticizing the unsatisfactory assumptions upon which his logical doctrine rests.

The phrase "traditional Logicians" is here used to describe those writers on Logic who have not sought to go beyond the logical doctrines of Aristotle but have contented themselves with the elaboration of technical details. These include—to adopt a phrase from Lewis Carroll—'the writers and editors of Logical text-books which run in the ordinary grooves'.[1] Common to these Logicians is the acceptance of the subject-predicate doctrine, of the traditional schedule of propositions, and the restriction of deduction to the syllogistic form. The traditional 'Formal Logic' is based upon these views. The 'Inductive Logicians', of whom J. S. Mill is the foremost example, have made no attempt to remedy the deficiencies of the traditional Formal Logic.

The metaphysical Logicians were dissatisfied with the traditional Logic only in so far as it was 'formal'. They protested against the 'severance' of 'Logic' from 'Reality'; they made central the doctrine of judgement, and were concerned with the relation of the knowing mind to what it knows. Their chief representatives in this country are Bradley and Bosanquet. To the latter is due the conception of Logic as 'the morphology of knowledge'. To Bradley the attempt to develop a formal science seemed to rest upon a 'sheer illusion'. The views of these writers have nothing in common with the conception of logic which underlies this book. Neither Bradley, nor Bosanquet, nor any of this school of Idealist Logicians, has ever succeeded in making clear what exactly is meant by the principle of identity-in-difference upon which the metaphysical logic of the Idealists is based. Their logic ends in 'shipwreck', as one of them, Mr. Joachim, pointed out in his important book *The Nature of Truth*.

Discontent both with the traditional and the metaphysical Logicians inspired the revolt of the Pragmatists. They sought to 'humanize' logic, to relate reasoning to other human activities, and thus to base logic upon psychology. In agreement with the metaphysical Logicians, they have decried the study of 'formal logic', whilst at the same time they have vigorously protested

---

[1] *Symbolic Logic*, p. 163. Whately, Bain, and Fowler may be cited as typical nineteenth-century examples of such writers. It may safely be said that every elementary text-book in logic now in use in this country falls under the description of traditional Logic. I have followed Lewis Carroll in giving the traditional Logicians the dignity of a capital 'L'.

against the Idealist theory of truth. Certain of the pragmatists, notably Mr. Alfred Sidgwick, have made valuable contributions to the 'art of thinking', but they have not advanced the science of logic.

The fourth line of approach is determined by the conception of logic as essentially formal, which results in the identity of pure logic and abstract mathematics. This is the conception that underlies this book. A new impetus has been given to the study of logic by the work of the symbolic, or mathematical, logicians. The expression "symbolic logic" requires some explanation.[1] The use of symbols for the expression of logical principles is an accidental convenience; their use is no doubt psychologically indispensable, but it is not logically necessary. The importance of a special symbolism is that it makes possible the revelation of form. Symbolic logic is formal. It is now recognized that the ideal of logic is to exhibit form. The rigorous analysis of mathematical "proofs" has shown that such "proofs" are *demonstrative* only when they are completely formal. Hence, mathematics is the science of pure form. It follows that the achievement of the ideal of logic makes it indistinguishable from pure mathematics. It might be supposed that the science of logic thus conceived has nothing in common with Aristotle's conception of logic. But that would be a mistake. There are considerable grounds for supposing that, in recognizing that the ideal of logic is the exhibition of form, the mathematical logicians are carrying on the work which Aristotle himself initiated. In Chapter XXV an attempt is made to indicate the nature of this development, and throughout the book emphasis is laid upon the continuity of some of Aristotle's doctrines with those of the mathematical logicians.

This continuity of development is of itself a sufficient justification for the inclusion of a chapter on the Traditional Syllogism. But there is another reason why the elementary student should be initiated into logic through the syllogism. There can be no doubt that the syllogism is a form very often exemplified in our ordinary reasoning; moreover, it is psychologically the simplest form, so

---

[1] There is considerable divergence in the terminology used by modern logicians. "Symbolic logic" is often used as a synonym for "mathematical logic"; sometimes the term "logistic" is preferred. The use of the name "logistic" to denote what is usually called "symbolic logic" was suggested at the International Congress of Philosophy held at Paris in 1904, and it has generally been adopted by continental logicians, but English and American writers usually prefer the name "symbolic logic". It is desirable not to use these names as exact synonyms, but to confine "symbolic logic" to the study of special types of deductive systems, using "mathematical logic" as a synonym for the "science of pure form". The expression "an algebra of logic" will then be appropriately used to denote a special set of postulates and primitive concepts, such as the Schroeder system.

that syllogistic arguments provide the easiest means of enabling the student to apprehend form as such and to realize that the validity of reasoning depends upon its form. But it must be admitted that many of the technical traditional developments of the syllogism are nothing but elaborate trivialities. So, too, are the technicalities of the traditional doctrine of immediate inference. An endeavour has been made to reduce the consideration of these technicalities to the minimum required to enable a student to pass elementary examinations in logic. It is to be hoped that the time is not far distant when University examiners will no longer require proficiency in these technical dodges, but will seek to test the student's grasp of logical principles. But that time has not yet arrived. Its date must doubtless be postponed until there are sufficient text-books written from a more modern point of view. It is difficult to break through the vicious circle constituted by the dependence of examiners upon the text-book, and by the dependence of the text-book upon the requirements of University examinations.

The conditions of examinations apart, some knowledge of Aristotle's logical doctrines ought to form part of the equipment of an educated man. These doctrines and the terminology in which they are expressed have entered so deeply into the structure of Western thought and language, that an understanding of them is necessary for the proper appreciation of much great literature as well as of Western philosophy. Certainly the student who intends to read philosophy would be seriously hampered in his understanding of the great metaphysical systems were he completely ignorant of Aristotelian logic. But it is *Aristotelian* logic that he should study, not the accretions due to the traditional Logicians.

The plan of this book requires some explanation. Its intention is to provide a text-book suitable for students reading for the first examinations for University degrees, and also for first-year work for *Honours* examinations. This double purpose has made a certain amount of repetition unavoidable. This is regrettable, but is rendered necessary by the present transitional state of the teaching of logic. A 'Note to Students', following this *Preface*, suggests the order in which the chapters should be read by those having no previous knowledge of the subject.

It has not been my intention to take the student very far into mathematical logic, but only to enable him to realize that the principles of symbolic logic are not peculiar to a special kind of study but are principles exemplified in everyday reflective thinking no less than in mathematical deductions. I have not sought to write an *introduction to symbolic logic* ; my purpose has been to emphasize the connexion between Aristotelian logic and symbolic logic, and thus to write a text-book which will include as little as possible

that the student has subsequently to unlearn, or for the teaching
of which the modern logician feels it necessary to apologize.

In writing this book I am conscious of having learned most from
Professor A. N. Whitehead, Mr. Bertrand Russell, Professor G. E.
Moore, and Dr. C. D. Broad. The numerous footnote references to
their writings do not sufficiently indicate the extent of my obliga-
tions to them. I have also learnt much from Mr. W. E. Johnson.
In personal discussion I owe more than I can say to my friend,
Miss E. M. Whetnall. She has read nearly the whole of the book
in manuscript, and has discussed most of the chapters with me in
detail. In consequence of her extremely helpful criticism at least
some serious mistakes have been avoided. I am also greatly
indebted to my friends, Mrs. Roberts (Susan Miles) and Miss Helen
M. Smith, who have read some of the chapters and have made
valuable criticisms. For help in the correction of the proofs I am
indebted to various friends, and in the compilation of the *Index*
to the students of my advanced logic class. I am especially
indebted to Mr. A. F. Dawn for his help in the final revision of
the proofs. To all of these and to some other friends, whom I
have not named but who in different ways have helped and encouraged me in the writing of this book, I desire to record here
my grateful thanks.

L. SUSAN STEBBING

LONDON,
July, 1930

NOTE TO STUDENTS

The student who is quite unfamiliar with logic is advised to read the chapters in the following order :

Chapters I–VIII, § 2.

Chapter XII, §§ 1–3.

Chapters XIII–XV, § 5.

Chapters XVI–XXII, § 3.

Chapter XXIV.

Chapters VIII, § 3–XI.

Chapter XXII, § 4.

Chapter XII, § 4.

Chapter XV, § 6.

Chapter XXIII.

Chapter XXV.

ABBREVIATIONS

Anal. Priora . . . . Aristotle : *Analytica Priora*. (*O.U.P.*)

Anal. Post. . . . . Aristotle : *Analytica Posteriora*.

F.L. . . . . . J. N. Keynes : *Formal Logic*.

Introd. . . . . . H. W. B. Joseph. *Introduction to Logic*. (2nd Ed.)

Int. Math. Phil. . . B. A. W. Russell : *Introduction to Mathematical Philosophy*.

W. E. J. . . . W. E. Johnson : *Logic*.

Proc. Arist. Soc. N.S. . *Proceedings of the Aristotelian Society*. *New Series*.

CONTENTS

xv

A MODERN INTRODUCTION TO LOGIC

A MODERN INTRODUCTION TO LOGIC

PART I

CHAPTER I

REFLECTIVE THINKING IN ORDINARY LIFE

'Only connect.'—E. M. Forster.

LOGIC, in the most usual and widest sense of the word, is concerned with reflective thinking. We all constantly use the words 'thinking' and 'thought'. So long as we are not asked to define them we feel confident that we know what these words mean. But we do not always use the word 'thinking' in the same sense. Sometimes we contrast "I think of " with "I am now seeing ". In this sense we are using "think " to denote our awareness of something not directly presented to sense. Thus anything that 'passes through our heads' is called a *thought*. For example, lying on the sea-shore on a hot sunny day, in an idle mood, we may have a train of thoughts, a set of more or less disconnected ideas passing through our minds. These thoughts may be intimately bound up with our present sense-impressions—the heat of the stones, the sound of the waves, the call of the sea-gulls. In such a mood we do not connect one thought with another; we are at the mercy of any sense-impression that may break in upon us. Suppose now that the idler on the rocks is aroused by such loud, insistent shouting that he recognizes 'in a flash', as we say, that *this* shouting has some peculiar significance for him. His reverie ended, he jumps up and looks around. Let us suppose that he now sees the water breaking on the rocks just below. He turns round to find that the rock on which he is standing is completely cut off from the shore in front. Behind is a steep, overhanging cliff, which he could not scale. The tide will soon completely cover the place where he has been lying. He cannot swim. What is he to do? He supposes that the people on the cliff, who shouted to him, have probably realized his situation. He wonders whether they can help him. Looking up he sees that some one is pointing to the face

1   1

of the cliff. Does that mean that there are footholes ? He looks, but can find none. Then he observes above his head a narrow projection of cliff. If he could clamber on to that perhaps he would be out of reach of the incoming tide. Would that be so ? Again he looks, and sees that just below the ledge there is the dark brown discolouring of the rocks that is the mark of high tide. That ledge, then, will be safe, if he can reach it.

In the above situation we have a concrete illustration of the contrast between unreflective and reflective thinking as the latter occurs in ordinary experience. At first the man was not attending to his sense-impressions ; nor was his thinking consciously controlled. But as soon as he was conscious that the situation was one of danger he was confronted with a problem to be solved. Consequently, he was forced to think *about* the situation so as to alter it in accordance with his practical needs. He becomes aware of the sea as *menacing* ; he not only *sees* the water near his feet, he *sees it as a sign of danger* because he interprets it as signifying ' retreat to shore cut off '. Similarly, he not only hears people shouting ; he *interprets* their shouts as having special *meaning* for him. He not only *sees* the various shades of brown on the face of the cliff, he *interprets* them as signs of high tide level. Suppose now that he asks himself the question whether the tide is likely to rise above the normal level to-day. He considers that last night the moon was in its first quarter ; therefore, it will be a neap tide ; hence, if he can reach the ledge he will be safe. In this last stage of his reflective thinking he is obviously relying upon previous knowledge of facts relevant to the situation. He *remembers* that the moon was at its first quarter the night before ; he *knows* that a neap tide is connected with the moon in that position, he infers that the tide will not rise high to-day. In this process of thinking directed to a practical end it is unlikely that the thinker will consciously use words. He may have merely a visual image of the appearance of the moon as he saw it yesterday, and pass directly to the reflection—' a neap tide ', and thence, to the conclusion : " So *that's* all right." The remembered appearance of last night's moon is thus directly interpreted as signifying what he wanted to know.

Suppose that, once he is perched on the ledge, the man looks about him to distract his thoughts. He sees on the other side of the cove, some way up in the side of a rocky headland that juts into the sea, a wide opening, not previously noticed, or taken to be a natural cleft in the rock. Now that his attention is directed to it, he sees that the opening is not the entrance to a cave, for he can discern bricks cemented together. Taken in itself there is nothing startling in a brick wall, but in this situation its discovery suggests the question how a brick wall came to be *there*. It can't be the remains of a house, for it is about half-way up in the side of a steep cliff below which the tide never goes out. The headland is seen to be connected with the mainland by a narrow ledge of rock more than a hundred feet high. He knows that on the top of the headland are the ruins of a castle which is supposed to have been King Arthur's. Perhaps the brick wall was once right inside the rock, the face of which has now fallen away. That is a reasonable supposition, for it is a stormy coast and rocks that have evidently fallen are piled below. In that case, however, the bricked chamber would have had no outlet to the light. Perhaps it is a secret chamber, or a dungeon. In that case it is probable that there will be some connexion with the mainland—perhaps a secret underground passage. At this point of his reflection, he must perforce cease his questioning. In his present position he has no means of testing his suppositions. Next day he may proceed to test the correctness of his theory with regard to the brick wall. On investigation of the headland he finds a disused shaft which he calculates to be in the right position to connect with the chamber. He discovers a not unsimilar shaft on the main cliff, near the church. He reflects that a passage running from the one shaft to the other would pass beside the brick wall, and connect the underground chamber with the church. At this point he will feel that he has accounted for the brick wall in the cliff.

Simple as these two illustrations are, they suffice to show how thinking essentially consists in solving a problem. The first was a practical problem, namely, how to reach a place of safety. The second was a problem arising out of the perception of something unexpected in a familiar situation. In this case the solution of the problem was sought merely for its own sake, in order to answer the question, " Why is *so-and-so such-and-such* ? "—a question asked only when *the such-and-such* has features that would not be expected to occur in the given situation. The occurrence of these unexpected features is felt to be explained as soon as they are related to a situation in which their occurrence would not be unexpected. The explanation consists in finding intermediate links that connect the brick wall and the cliff. It is reached as a process of reflective thinking in which each link, *brick wall, disused shaft, castle, church*, is attended to not for its own sake but as being a sign of something else. Such a process of reflective thinking is known as *inferring*. In this case there was a passage from something sensibly presented to something not presented but inferred, which may, or may not, be the case. To determine whether it is the case, or not, the inference must be further tested. Such testing may be carried out in two widely different ways. The inferred conclusion may admit of direct inspection. In this case, the test would consist in verifying the conclusion by direct observation of something presented to sense. Clearly it is not always possible to perform such a test as, for example, in our illustration, which was concerned with a question about a state of affairs in the past. In such cases the conclusion is tested by its power to connect together various observable items which, apart from the *supposed* connexions, would remain disconnected.

We have spoken of 'directly observing something'. But what we *directly* observe, see with our eyes, for instance, is a very small part of what we observe when we say that we are perceiving so-and-so. Thus, for example, in looking at a puzzle picture where a man's head is suggested by the lines drawn to indicate the leaves of a tree, we *suddenly* discover the head. Knowing what we are in search of we attend to some only of the lines drawn and actively connect them with others, finally making out of the set of lines attended to the representation of a man's head. No hard and fast line can be drawn between what is actually seen and what is suggested by what is seen. We see what we have a mind to see. In the situations of everyday life our senses are being constantly stimulated by a variety of sense-impressions amongst which we have learnt to pay attention to some as being specially *significant*, that is as being signs of something else in which we are interested. When one thing signifies another, there is between them that connexion which enables us to pass in thought from the one to the other. The sun setting in a bank of clouds may be noticed merely for its shape and colour, and appreciated for its beauty. But it may also be apprehended as signifying *wet day to-morrow*. Again, waving a flag may be a sign of high spirits, or of a certain state of mind called patriotism.

Thinking, we have seen, essentially consists in solving a problem. The ability to think depends upon the power of seeing connexions. Reflective thinking consists in pondering upon a given set of facts so as to elicit their connexions. " I didn't think " often means " I failed to connect ", that is, " I didn't recognize that given *that*, I must have *this* ". There are various kinds of connexion from the bare juxtaposition of *this* and *that* to the essential connexion of an X with a Y which must be if X is.[1] The mere addition of one fact to another would be of little value for reflective thinking. It is unlikely that we ever have *mere* additions, even in the idle reverie of day-dreaming. In day-dreams one idea follows another with no apparent connexion ; they are said to occur 'at random'. Yet modern psychologists say that there are 'reasons' why this idea follows that. Freud, for instance, has attempted to *explain* these

---

[1] Compare, for instance, the connexion implied in
'A rainbow and a cuckoo's song
May never come together again,'
with the connexion implied in ' All equilateral triangles are equiangular '.

occurrences, i.e. to set out the conditions upon which the succession of ideas is consequent although the day-dreamer himself may not be aware of any connexions. When, however, we contrast day-dreaming, taken as it occurs, with directed thought, even of such a simple type as in our two illustrations, we seem to be moving on a different plane. Directed thought is thought directed to the solution of a problem ; it originates in a *felt* difficulty and is controlled throughout by the initial apprehension of the conditions of the problem.

Without some degree of direction there is nothing in our mental processes which merits the name " thinking ". Day-dreaming must, therefore, be excluded since, in so far as it is directed, it is directed by factors which lie outside the course of the reverie itself. In the widest sense of the word " thinking " every one thinks. In the strictest sense, in which " to think " means " to think logically ", some people never think, and no one is always thinking even when he appears to be doing so. It may be doubted, for instance, whether Mrs. Nickleby ever thought. Consider the following extract :

' I think there must be something in the place ', said Mrs. Nickleby, who had been listening in silence ; ' for, soon after I was married, I went to Stratford with my poor dear Nickleby, in a post-chaise from Birmingham—was it a post-chaise though ! ' said Mrs. Nickleby, considering ; ' Yes, it must have been a post-chaise, because I recollect remarking at the time that the driver had a green shade over his left eye ;—in a post-chaise from Birmingham, and after we had seen Shakespeare's tomb and birthplace, we went back to the inn there, where we slept that night, and I recollect that all night long I dreamed of nothing but a black gentleman, at full length, in plaster-of-Paris, with a lay-down collar tied with two tassels, leaning against a post and thinking ; and when I woke in the morning and described him to Mr. Nickleby, he said it was Shakespeare just as he had been when he was alive, which was very curious indeed. Stratford—Stratford¸', continued Mrs. Nickleby, considering. ' Yes, I am positive about that, because I recollect that I was in the family way with my son Nicholas at the time, and I had been very much frightened by an Italian image boy that morning. In fact, it was quite a mercy, ma'am ', added Mrs. Nickleby, in a whisper to Mrs. Wititterly, ' that my son didn't turn out to be a Shakespeare, and what a dreadful thing that would have been ! '

An examination of Mrs. Nickleby's mental processes, as revealed in this passage, shows no sign of direction to an end. Clearly Mrs. Nickleby could observe, and she was able to recollect what she had observed. But her recollections were at the mercy of random associations ; there is a connexion but it is the connexion of temporal contiguity. What happened is remembered and recorded *as* it happened. There is no selection, no omission under the influence of an explicit relevant interest. What she observes does not signify anything beyond itself ; hence, its suggestive power is confined to what happened next, and then to what happened after that, and so on. There is no thinking here, for there is no direction to a conclusion. Presumably Mrs. Nickleby would stop for lack of breath or of listeners. There is no train of thought that, having worked itself out to a conclusion, comes to a natural end.

Contrast now Boswell's report of a conversation with Samuel Johnson :

'Mr. Langton told us that he was about to establish a school upon his estate, but it had been suggested to him that it might have a tendency to make the people less industrious. JOHNSON : " No, Sir. While learning to read and write is a distinction, the few who have that distinction may be the less inclined to work ; but when everybody learns to read and write, it is no longer a distinction. A man who has a laced waistcoat is too fine a man to work ; but if everybody had laced waistcoats, we should have people working in laced waistcoats. There are no people more industrious, none who work more than our manufacturers ; yet they have all learnt to read and write. Sir, you must not neglect doing a thing immediately good, from fear of remote evil ;—from fear of its being abused. A man who has candles may sit up too late, which he would not do if he had not candles ; but nobody will deny that the art of making candles, by which light is continued to us beyond the time that the sun gives us light, is a valuable art, and ought to be preserved." BOSWELL : " But, Sir, would it not be better to follow nature ; and go to bed and rise just as nature gives us light or withholds it ? " JOHNSON : " No, Sir ; for then we should have no kind of equality in the partition of our time between sleeping and waking. It would be very different in different seasons and in different places. In some of the northern parts of Scotland how little light is there in the depth of winter." '

In this conversation each statement is connected relevantly with the next and the whole is directed by the initial suggestion. Although Johnson passes from the consideration of the advisability of educating the people to a reflection with regard to the length of a winter night in northern Scotland there is no abrupt break. The transition is effected for the purpose of adducing relevant examples. In each example there is the selection of a characteristic that bears upon the conclusion, whilst those that are irrelevant are ignored. Reflective thinking is essentially selective, and thus involves abstraction. The characteristic that is abstracted from a total situation may be by no means obvious.

Consider, for instance, the following passage :

'A rope suggests other ropes and cords, if we look to the appearance ; but looking to the use, it may suggest an iron cable, a wooden prop, an iron girding, a leather band or bevelled gear. In spite of the diversity of appearance, the suggestion turns on what answers a common end. . . . We become oblivious of the difference between a horse, a steam-engine, and a waterfall, when our minds are engrossed with the one circumstance of moving power. The diversity in these had, no doubt, for a long time the effect of keeping back their first identification ; and to obtuse intellects, this identification might have been for ever impossible. A strong concentration of mind upon the single peculiarity of mechanical force, and a degree of indifference to the general aspect of the things themselves, must conspire with the intellectual energy of resuscitation by similars, in order to summon together in the view, three structures so different. We can see by an instance like this, how new adaptations of existing machinery might arise in the mind of a mechanical inventor.' [1]

This example affords a good illustration of the way in which an unobvious characteristic may be abstracted by the thinker in order to further a relevant interest. The similarity between objects having many differences that would be important in *other* connexions may be noted because it is relevant in *this* connexion. Hence the importance of abstraction. Without abstraction there can be no recognition of similarity ; without the recognition of similarity there can be no advance in knowledge. Every human being is capable of some degree of abstractness in thinking, that is, of imaginatively selecting some one character out of a complex situation so that it may be attended to in isolation. There is an effort of abstraction required in the case of the puzzle picture mentioned above. So long as the observer sees the line as constituting part of the foliage of the tree, he will fail to see it as part of the face he is trying to discover. In a way strictly analogous to this, the scientific genius selects from a mass of facts characteristics that are ignored by the ordinary man. In the practical affairs of everyday life we normally attend only to stimuli that are insistent and striking. Familiarity with a complex situation enables us, we say, to ' take it in at a glance '. But this rapid glance may fail to reveal features that are of significance in certain connexions. Moreover, our reactions to situations rapidly become habitual and are not modified in response to small variations in the situation itself. Undoubtedly rapidity of habitual response is necessary in order that life may be preserved and its ordinary business successfully carried out. But the success of habitual response checks the impulse to wonder and is thus inimical to the development of reflective thinking. A situation that seems perfectly familiar fails to arouse inquiry ; it is accepted at its face value. Accordingly, it does not become the occasion of investigations designed to lead to the acquirement of fresh knowledge. The familiar use of language which enables us to refer, sometimes by a single word, to a complex situation, may hinder us from noting unexpected features that are nevertheless present. For instance, if a doctor observing a set of symptoms were to label the disease from which the patient was suffering as " influenza ", and were then content to treat the diagnosis as complete, he might be led into serious error. It might be necessary for him to look for some symptom not commonly associated with the other set, which would lead him to make a fresh diagnosis. What seemed to be influenza may turn out to be typhoid. We shall see later how the advance of knowledge

---

[1] Bain, *The Senses and the Intellect*, p. 521.

is dependent upon the ability to attend to what is unusual and to observe its connexions with what is already familiar.

Reflective thinking is, then, relevant thinking. What is relevant in a given situation depends upon its connexions. The detection of relevant factors presupposes a large fund of knowledge bearing upon the situation, which may not all be consciously present in the process of reflection. In ordinary life we often possess a considerable amount of knowledge relevant to the situations within which we are called upon to act. We take for granted a number of generalizations that can be directly applied to a given case. We say, " It will rain to-morrow, because the sun has set in a bank of clouds ", " Don't wear that dress at the seaside, for it will fade ". If we were asked, " Why will it fade ? " our reply might be, " Oh ! that is the shade of blue that always does fade in sea air ". This latter statement is an empirical generalization, that is, an assertion that a certain set of characters have in our past experience been found to be conjoined on an indefinite number of occasions, with the implication that they will continue to be so conjoined. If, however, the reply were : " Because that blue colour is due to a dye that is chemically unstable, so that it becomes unfixed under the influence of strong sea air ", a beginning would have been made in analysing the factors contained in the total situation *blue dress and sea air*, and thus in connecting one relevant factor with another. This process of analysis and subsequent synthesis plays an important part in the process of discovering true generalizations with regard to what happens in the world. This process is sometimes known as induction, with which we shall be later concerned. At present, it is sufficient to notice that we constantly make generalizations going beyond what has been observed, which we proceed to apply to particular cases. Thus a certain character m comes to be recognized as a sign of another character p ; whereupon, we conclude that, since *this S* has m, it has p.

Were it not the case that we find in experience that characters are constantly conjoined in such a way that one may be taken as the sign of another, reasoning would be impossible. Thus, whenever we reason we recognize that a certain state of affairs is the case because it is signified by some other state of affairs. The latter is said to be the ground upon which our belief in the former is based. This belief is the conclusion of the reasoning. The conclusion is a *reasoned* conclusion because it is based upon evidence ; something is taken as the sign of something else. A mistake may be made on both counts. What *is* may not be what we have taken it to be ; or it may be *that*, and yet may not be connected in the way we have supposed. Even in such a case, however, the conclusion would be a *reasoned*, though a faulty, conclusion.

To sum up. We have distinguished between reflective thinking and idle reverie. We have further distinguished between directed thinking, which alone merits the name of thinking, and reminiscent thinking of the kind indulged in by Mrs. Nickleby. We have seen that reflective thinking originates in a problem to be solved and is throughout controlled by the conditions of the problem and is directed to its solution. Hence, reflective thinking has a natural end, the conclusion of the reflection. The various stages in this process are related to the conclusion as the grounds upon which it is based. These grounds may be called *premisses*. Relatively to the conclusion the premisses are taken for granted. The premisses may be obtained by means of direct observation or as the result of a previous process of reasoning. In either case the apprehension of the premisses depends upon a considerable amount of relevant knowledge which does not enter explicitly into the reflective thinking. There are various relations that may hold between premiss and conclusion ; these will have to be distinguished. They are, however, all various modes of signifying. Wherever a relation such as that of *signifying* holds, there is a basis for reasoning.

CHAPTER II

LANGUAGE

'God, having designed man for a sociable creature, made him not only with an inclination and under a necessity to have fellowship with those of his own kind, but furnished him also with language, which was to be the great instrument and common tie of society.'—*John Locke.*

§ 1. LANGUAGE AND SIGNS

WE use language because we desire to communicate our thoughts, feelings and desires to others. Whatever may be the historical origin of spoken language, there can be no question that its motive lies in the desire of man to affect those with whom he is in contact. Language is a social phenomenon. Men speak in order that they may be *heard* ; they desire to be heard in order that they may express themselves to others and thereby influence them. Hence, men use language in order to be *understood*. To understand anything is to apprehend it in its connexions or to apprehend it as a sign of something else. We saw in the last chapter that one thing may be a sign of another, e.g. the sun setting into a bank of clouds may be the sign of a wet day to-morrow. It is a *sign* only for the spectator who has learnt from past experience to associate the one occurrence with the other. There is no sign without an interpreter. Hence, *to signify* requires (1) what is signified, (2) the signifying sign, (3) the interpreter of the sign as signifying.

The man stranded on the rock, in the illustration in the first chapter, interpreted the gestures of the people on the cliff as signifying *something* connected with his own safety. On investigation he correctly interpreted the signs as meaning " that ledge will be safe ". This is an example of a demonstrative gesture interpreted as signifying something visibly presented. But what the man *saw*, and what the sign *meant*, was something more than was visually apprehended. He saw not merely a projecting ledge of rock but a place out of reach of the rising tide. Had he been completely ignorant of the phenomena of tides he could not have interpreted the sign as he did. All the signs we are capable of interpreting occur in this way, namely, in a context of experience which alone can make these signs *significant*. Throughout the discussion of logical method we shall see how the ability to connect, hence to interpret the occurrences

10

of nature, depends upon the power to recognize certain occurrences as significant of other happenings.

It is impossible to think without using signs, for to think is to go beyond what is sensibly presented. This is not to say that thinking is impossible without words, for words are only one kind of signs. In the widest sense of the word "language" we use language whenever we deliberately use something as the sign of something else. A sign *consciously* designed to stand for something will be called a *symbol*. We should not say that "the sun setting into a bank of clouds" *symbolizes* "wet day to-morrow"; we should, however, say that the printed marks just read and understood by the reader *symbolize* what they served to call up in his mind. It is not possible to draw a hard and fast line between "sign" and "symbol" as these words are here used. Were that possible there would be less doubt as to the historical origin of languages. But in the developed language in which this book is written, the difference between sign and symbol is quite unmistakable. How does this difference come about? As has just been indicated, only an approximate answer to this question can be given.

Signs may be natural or artificial, i.e. conventional. The simplest kind of language, that is, the simplest system of consciously devised signs, is gesture language. A gesture language is one in which the signs are either demonstrative, that is, consist simply in pointing to what is to be indicated; or imitative, that is, a sign which imitates or copies what it signifies. For example, if a man indicates that he is thirsty by going through the movements he would make in raising a cup to his lips, he is employing an imitative gesture as a sign. Such signs are called "natural signs" owing to the fact that, since they resemble the thing or action signified, they are the most natural means of indicating what we want to indicate. These signs can be so used as to draw attention to something not actually present, and are thus fitted to fulfil one of the most important functions of language. Sounds can be used as imitative signs, as when one signifies a certain bird by "cuckoo", or a certain game by "ping-pong". As, however, most things have not a characteristic sound, a language based wholly upon imitative sounds could not progress very far. A conventional sign is one that is neither a demonstrative gesture nor an imitative sound or gesture; it is deliberately devised to stand for something and has thus acquired a relatively fixed significance so that it can be understood as referring to something definite and the same on each occasion of its use. Gesture language may involve the use of conventional signs, when, as the result of past experience, the beginning of an imitative movement is taken to stand for the whole movement, or when a schematic representation of it suffices for the sign to be understood. In the same way picture writing, which begins by being pictorially imitative, develops, whilst still remaining ideographic, into conventional signs. Such signs have to be learnt before they can be understood and such learning does not form part of the common experience of the human race. Thus Europeans have to learn Egyptian hieroglyphic and Chinese ideograms just as they have to learn any other foreign language, although such writing began with imitative signs.

As an instrument of thinking natural signs suffer from two serious defects. First, the number of recognizably different sounds that the human voice is capable of making and the number of different gestures that the human body can perform are definitely limited and are fewer than the ideas it is desired to convey. Secondly, there is need to represent not only what is not actually present but also what is incapable of being sensibly presented, namely, general characteristics of things, that is to say abstractions, e.g. *strength, purposiveness, inferiority in numbers*, and so on. Consequently, in order that thought should be developed there is need of an arbitrarily devised set of signs that are in no sense imitative. Such a set of signs constitutes a non-representative language.

The reader of this book is so thoroughly familiar with his own language, so steeped in its normal associations, so familiar with the context supplied by its social use, that he will probably find it difficult to think of these English words as *merely* conventional signs. Yet the word " man ", for instance, is a shape (as here printed) or a sound, if it be spoken aloud, that is arbitrarily devised to stand for something with which the reader is familiar. It is well known that primitive people, not excluding some of the Greeks, have been apt to assume that a word has an inherent fitness to represent what it signifies. Heraclitus, for instance, regarded words as sensibly embodying the nature of things. Thus Mr. F. M. Cornford says that for Heraclitus " The Logos is revealed in speech. The structure of man's speech reflects the structure of the world ; more, it is an embodiment or representation of it ".[1] It is, moreover, well known that many primitive peoples are reluctant to tell strangers their names lest power over them should be acquired. It is probably some relic of this belief that has led many to attempt to trace all language to an onomatopoeic origin.[2] Aristotle, however, clearly

---

[1] Cornford, *From Religion to Philosophy*, p. 45.
[2] Cf. de Morgan, *Formal Logic*, pp. 246–7. ' If all mankind had spoken one language, we cannot doubt that there would have been a powerful, perhaps a universal school of philosophers who would have believed in the inherent connexion between names and things ; who would have taken the sound *man* to be the mode of agitating the air which is essentially communicative of the ideas of reason, cookery, bipedality, etc. The writers of whom I speak . . . treat words as absolute images of things by right of the letters which spell

recognized that spoken and written words, language *par excellence*, are conventional and not imitative. Thus he says that a noun is " a sound significant by convention " and he adds : " The limitation ' by convention ' was introduced because nothing is by nature a noun or a name—it is only so when it becomes a symbol."[1]

How, then, does a word become a symbol ? That is to say, how does a written mark, or a spoken sound, become a conventional sign of something quite unlike itself ? To answer this question fully would be to write a history of the growth of languages, and a study of the child's development in using and understanding language. But it will be sufficient for our purpose, if we can indicate the way in which a new word comes to have meaning for us. The reader of this book is not a child and is probably unversed in the psychology of language, but he can readily recall from his own experience how some word which he did not understand came to have meaning. Suppose, for instance, that he had not met the word " triforium ", but that, being in the Church of *Notre Dame* at Paris, some one had said to him : " That is a triforium ". He would then know that the verbal symbol " triforium " stood for an open gallery above the arches of a church. Again, suppose he did not know what " saxophone " meant. If some one showed him one of these musical instruments and told him that it was called a *saxophone*, he would understand the word, that is to say, he would know the object to which it refers. There is another way in which its meaning might be conveyed to him. He might be told : " A saxophone is a musical instrument something like a U-shaped trumpet ". This somewhat inadequate description might enable him to recognize a saxophone, supposing that he already knew what a trumpet was. If, on subsequently seeing a saxophone, he were able to give its name, it would be clear that he understood what " saxophone " means.

A word, then, has meaning for us when we know what it is *to which* the word refers. We saw that, in order that anything should be a sign, there must be : (1) the sign, (2) the thing signified, (3) an interpreter. We shall find it convenient to use the word " referend " to stand for *that which is signified*.[2] A word is the special kind of sign called a " symbol ". A word is understood when it is recog-

them. " The French ", said the sailor, " call a cabbage a *shoe* ; the fools ! Why can't they call it a cabbage, when they must know it is one ? " '

[1] *de Interpretatione*, 16a, 20, 25.

[2] It is perhaps unfortunate to have to introduce new terminology, but the word " object " is not suitable for the purpose for which I use the technical term " referend ". The referend is *that which is being referred to*. Messrs. Ogden and Richards have suggested the word " referent ". (*The Meaning of Meaning*, p. 13.) But " referent " is already in use among logicians as a technical term in the logic of relations. (See p. 111 below.) Cf. Susan Miles, " Intuition," *The Monist*, July, 1925.

nized as a sign signifying a referend. Thus, for instance, we understand " horse ", if we can interpret it rightly as applying to those animals that are horses; we understand " whatnot " if we can interpret it rightly as applying to those articles of furniture called by that name, and so on. It is possible to understand a given word when we are provided with a correct description of its referend, or with a definition of it in words, the referends of which we know. It is in this way that we come to understand such technical terms as " polygon ", " diapason ", " marling-spike ". But we may understand a word although we cannot describe the referend in other words, still less be able to *define* the word. The reader would probably hesitate were he asked, " What does the word ' table ' mean ? ", but he would be right in saying that he *knows* what " table " means.[1]

It is important to notice that in the strict sense of " understand " —with which we are here concerned—*what* we understand is always a symbol. People sometimes talk vaguely about " understanding the universe ", or " understanding life ", or " understanding a person ". In these phrases, " understand " is used loosely to signify " knowing certain facts about " or " having certain attitudes to " or " capable of making certain responses to ", or all of these at once. But this is not a use of the word that is suitable to logic. Only signs can be understood, and to understand a sign is to know what it signifies. Hence, to understand a verbal symbol is to know what it refers to, i.e. to know the referend for which it stands. The word *symbolizes* the referend. It should now be clear that the relation of " symbolizing " is fundamentally different from the relation of " imitating " or " copying ". In the case of onomatopoeic words, e.g. splash, ping-pong, cuckoo, the symbols are themselves imitative, but *as symbols* they simply *stand for* what they symbolize. There is no need to dispute that onomatopoeia has played a part in the historical origin of languages. But in a developed language, recognized as such, i.e. as a system of *arbitrary signs*—what Aristotle called " sounds significant by convention—it has no place. But it must not be forgotten that the earliest use of language is to stimulate actions and evoke responses, not to communicate thoughts and to indicate properties.[2]

§ 2. THE HEARER-SPEAKER ATTITUDE

In language used for the purpose of communication two persons are involved, the hearer and the speaker. For convenience we shall

---

[1] We shall see later that the word " means " is extremely ambiguous. There are different ways in which symbols can *mean*. (See Chap. VIII.) But it is a word in constant use and is sufficiently, though vaguely, understood to be clear in this context.

[2] See § 3 below.

LANGUAGE 15

symbolize the hearer by B and the speaker by A. In order that
A should communicate something to B, A must know something
that B does not know. Nevertheless, A and B must know something in common ; there must be some basis of common experience
which forms, as it were, the context within which the communication
occurs. Let us at present confine ourselves to that form of communication in which A is giving information to B. Then A makes
a statement which B is to accept or to reject. Such a statement,
offered for acceptance or rejection, is a *proposition*. This proposition
may itself be the answer to a question originally asked by B. Suppose B, confronted with an unfamiliar object, were to ask, " What
is that ? " A replies : " That is a set of bagpipes ". Here " that "
indicates something of which they are both directly aware ; it thus
affords the basis from which the communication can proceed. " Is
a set of bagpipes " is the information given by A to B. This is the
simplest kind of communication, in which the risk of the hearer's
misunderstanding the speaker is at a minimum. Let us now suppose that A and B are in Trumpington Street, Cambridge. A says :
" That Church is very large". B replies: "That is not a Church,
it is the Pitt Press Buildings ". Here B is aware of the referend
pointed to by A, but refuses to accept the description implicit in
the phrase " That Church " which A uses to indicate the referend.
The phrase " That Church " is what Prof. Whitehead calls a " demonstrative phrase ".[1] If A now retorts, " It looks like a Church ",
here " *it* " simply demonstrates, and a descriptive phrase, which
may be correct, is applied to what is demonstrated.

The distinction between a demonstrative phrase and a descriptive
phrase is very important.[2] But the distinction is apt to be obscured
by the elliptical nature of our ordinary conversation which successfully takes a great deal for granted. A demonstrative phrase is
like a bodily gesture ; it points out something for consideration.
A descriptive phrase ascribes characteristics. But a demonstrative
phrase, though intended simply to demonstrate, nearly always includes an element of descriptiveness, as in "That Church".[3] We
may then accept the demonstration and reject the descriptive element.

[1] A. N. Whitehead, *The Concept of Nature,* p. 7. The whole passage (pp.
6–12) might be read with advantage. The word " demonstration " in this
passage has the same meaning as in " demonstrative pronoun ".
[2] The nature of this distinction may become clearer after Chapter III has
been read. It is a fundamental distinction of great importance for the understanding of much work in modern logic and metaphysics. The exact nature
of a descriptive phrase of the form " A Gothic Church ", and so on, will be
discussed in Chapter IX. The distinction between demonstrative phrases and
descriptive phrases will be seen to throw light upon the analysis of certain
propositions whose verbal expression is complicated.
[3] Cf. Chap. XXII, § 1 below.

Thus, in the example given, A succeeded in demonstrating (i.e. pointing out) what he intended to indicate, since his demonstrative phrase was understood by B.   But B rejected the descriptive element whereupon A substituted a purely demonstrative " it " so that he might demonstrate without any element of descriptiveness.   It is almost impossible to achieve simple demonstration by means of language.   We constantly attempt to achieve such demonstration but cannot succeed unless verbal language can be supplemented by demonstrative gestures.   Even then, our demonstration occurs within a context that gives significance and thus prevents the demonstration from being *purely* demonstrative.

In complex situations we are constantly confronted with the question :   " But what do you *mean* by saying so and so ? "   The answer can again be given only in words.   In replying A must find symbols which (1) correctly symbolize the referend he *intends* to symbolize, (2) will call up in B's mind the *same* referend.   It is obvious that the risk of B's misunderstanding, i.e. *mis*taking the symbols, will be the greater the less there is of (i) experiences common to A and B, (ii) community of language available for referring to those experiences.   Hence, the force of the metaphorical expression used by people who have failed to establish contact : " We did not even understand each other's language ".

§ 3.   THE TWO USES OF LANGUAGE

We have so far spoken as though the main function of language were to communicate information.   This is no doubt a most important function.   For science it is its *sole* function.   For this reason a science, in proportion as it becomes what we call " scientific " finds it necessary to devise a *terminology*, i.e. a set of technical terms which aim at precision, i.e. *uniqueness of reference*.   A scientific statement is, *qua* scientific, precise.   It is important not to confuse *science* with *scientists*.   For even a scientist is a " whole man " who does not always achieve—even in his published writings—that impersonality of thought which is necessary for exactness of statement.   Moreover, no thinker, not even the physicist, is wholly independent of the context of experience provided for him by the society within which he works.[1]   Nevertheless, his aim is so to use his verbal sym-

---

[1] Thus Cornford, writing of Greek religion and philosophy, reminds us that ' there is an inalienable and ineradicable framework of conceptions which is not of our own making, but given to us ready-made by society—a whole apparatus of concepts and categories, within which and by means of which all our individual thinking, however original and daring, is compelled to move. . . . It is different for every age in history, for every well-marked group in the intellectual chart of mankind, and even within such groups in a minor degree, for every nationality.   Hence, the error of supposing that human nature is much the same at all times, and that since non-human nature is

bols as to achieve uniqueness of reference, and thus to use language in order to communicate information that is exact and precise.

Many statements are made, however, not for the sake of conveying information, but in order to arouse in the hearer a certain response, to create in him a certain state of mind. That this is an important, as well as a proper, function of language will be admitted by every one capable of responding to literature. Every good literary critic has realized that the poet uses language not mainly to express statements that are true, or false, but to express what is neither true nor false. When Shelley says,

> ' Life, like a dome of many-coloured glass,
> Stains the white radiance of eternity.
> Until Death tramples it to fragments,'

he is neither talking nonsense, nor making an assertion that must be accepted or rejected as true, or false. The question of truth and falsity does not arise. Shelley is using language for an entirely different purpose from that of the scientist who says, " The specific heat of air at constant pressure is 0·2734 ". This statement simply expresses what the scientist believes to be true. He would call it " a fact ". The difference between these two uses of language is not difficult to apprehend yet they are seldom clearly distinguished. To mark the distinction Mr. I. A. Richards has suggested the convenient terminology " the scientific use of language " and " the emotive use of language ".[1] When language is used simply in order to refer to a referend its use is *scientific*. When it is used in order to arouse an emotional attitude in the hearer, to influence him in any way other than by that of giving him information, then its use is *emotive*. The most unmistakable examples of the emotive use of language can be found in literature, just because it is not the function of literature to instruct. A writer in a recently published book has put the point well when he says : " When words are selected and arranged in such a way that their meaning either arouses, or is obviously intended to arouse, æsthetic imagination, the result may be described as *poetic diction* ".[2] He adds, " the same sounds

much the same too, the Greek philosopher of the sixth century B.C., studying his outer and inner experience was confronted with the same problems seen in the same light as the English philosopher of to-day. The difference—the immense difference—between the two lies in their several inheritances of collective representation. It is a difference that comes home to any one who has to "translate" (as it is called) from Greek into English. He will soon discover that, when once we go beyond the names of objects like table or trees and of simple actions such as running and eating, no Greek work has an exact equivalent in English, no important abstract conception covers the same area or carries with it the same atmosphere of association.' (Op. cit., p. 45.)

[1] *The Principles of Literary Criticism*, Chap. XXXIV. See also *The Meaning of Meaning*, pp. 226–9, 255–60, 271–5.

[2] Owen Barfield, *Poetic Diction : A Study in Meaning*, pp. 13, 14.

2

of an English railway a few years ago. A precise word, we may say metaphorically, is one that is sensitive to small differences in the objects to which it refers. " Religious " is a word that, as ordinarily used, is clearly very vague. It refers to various different emotional and intellectual attitudes and may be used indiscriminately to apply to various intellectual and emotional levels of development. For many purposes we do not need to distinguish these various meanings by using precise words to distinguish them. If we wish to be clear we add phrases making the reference more precise. Such words as " Conservative ", " politician ", " humorous " are obviously vague. They refer indefinitely to many objects which for certain purposes would have to be distinguished. We attempt to make our references less vague, in such cases, by adding qualifying phrases, such as " a rigid Conservative ", " a party politician ", and so on. If on leaving a village concert hall A says to B, " The room was very full but there were very few villagers there ", he is making a vague statement. If he says, " The seats were all occupied but there were not above a dozen villagers there ", he is making a less vague statement. If he proceeds to specify the number of villagers as, say, " ten ", he is less vague still. It may be said that in this case he is as precise as the ordinary resources of language permit and as the practical purposes of life require. Clearly a vague statement is more likely to be true than a precise statement. To make statements that are both precise and true is difficult. Otherwise, we might all be scientists. A long process of analysis and reflective thinking is necessary in order to get rid of the vagueness that infects our language. But, we have insisted, vagueness is a matter of degree. It is neither possible nor desirable wholly to get rid of it. For, in the first place, our experiences are only more or less common. A word that is not quite precise has what William James called a " fringe of meaning ", which enables us to communicate with others without intolerable prolixity. Secondly, the speaker's referends are by no means always clear to himself. He knows more or less what he wants to talk about. Thus Newton's vagueness as to what he was referring to by the word " force " did not prevent his formulating the laws of motion, nor did it hinder his discovery of the law of gravitation.[1] Beyond a somewhat uncertain degree precision is not necessary to ordinary life and may even be a hindrance to progress at a certain stage of scientific development. Where precision is necessary, it is necessary to invent a symbolism *which has no other purpose in view than uniqueness of reference*. If language were to achieve the ideal of demonstration, wit would be at an end.

    In ordinary conversation it is impossible to draw a sharp line

[1] See p. 315 *n*.

between what is communicated by spoken language (i.e. expressed in verbal symbols) and what is communicated by intonation, gesture, facial expression. Who does not know the expressiveness of a Frenchman's shrug of the shoulders ? By such means we succeed in reducing the number of occasions when we need to ask : " But what do you *mean* ? " In printed language, we resort to such devices as italics, exclamation marks, periphrases, but always with some risk of being misunderstood.

Ambiguity is to be carefully distinguished from vagueness. Whereas the latter serves a useful purpose, ambiguity is a serious defect. A word is ambiguous when it stands for different referends on different occasions. Thus ambiguity is largely a matter of context. A word in a given context may be quite unambiguous, but in another context it may suffer from considerable ambiguity. Many words are both ambiguous and vague, e.g. Conservative, politician, artist, ridiculous, and so on.

The traditional Logicians were in the habit of calling attention to words which they said were " equivocal " or " ambiguous ", since they were used in various senses. They gave examples such as, " *vice* " (standing for a moral disposition, and a carpenter's instrument), " *fair* " (standing for the colour of a person's complexion, and for a just bargain). But these words are not *ambiguous;* they are *different words*. When Shakespeare says,

'Not on thy sole but on thy soul, harsh Jew,
Thou makest thy knife keen,'

he is not saying something ambiguous ; he is simply making a pun. There cannot be ambiguity unless we are using the *same* word in more than one sense. Complete ambiguity would be complete nonsense. Reference to the context within which the word is being used is necessary in order to ascertain whether a word is ambiguous or not. No word in isolation is properly ambiguous. In one sense the demonstrative " it " may be said to be ambiguous since it stands for a different referend on every occasion of its use. Since, however, it is precisely its function to do so, it would be better to say that words such as " it " are indeterminate in reference. Ambiguity arises when, in communicating with B, the language used by A refers B to a referend other than that which A intended, or when B (and possibly A) is led on to extend to one referend what is true only of another, without realizing that a transition has been made. Coleridge's well-known story of the two theological students who, discussing the attributes of God, ended with the conclusion : " I see. Your 'God' is my 'Devil '," affords a good illustration of ambiguity. One of the main purposes of defining words is to get rid of harmful ambiguities. But it is a mistake to suppose that all words of which we know the definition are unambiguously used.

CHAPTER III

ACQUAINTANCE AND DESCRIPTION

'SOCRATES. I know, Meno, what you mean; but just see what a tiresome dispute you are introducing. You argue that a man cannot inquire either about that which he knows or about that which he does not know; for if he knows, he has no need to inquire; and if not, he cannot; for he does not know the very subject about which he is to inquire.'—*Plato.*

§ 1. THE AMBIGUITY OF 'KNOWING'

WHEN we use the word "know" we do not always use it in the same sense. Sometimes we say that we know some one or some thing; sometimes we say that we know that so-and-so is the case. For example, a man might say, "I know him and I know that he went to France last week." Some one else might say, 'I don't *know* him, but I know to whom you are referring." In these two sentences the word "know" has been used in three different senses. "I know him" would ordinarily be understood to mean "I am acquainted with him". The words "that he went to France last week" express something that is true *about* him, and which the speaker claims that he *knows*. What he is claiming to know is a *fact*, viz. the fact *that he went to France last week*. We must distinguish carefully between knowledge of things (or of persons) and knowledge of facts. The latter is expressed in true propositions. In English we use the same word 'know' both with regard to *things* and with regard to *facts*, but some languages have a pair of words which to some extent, but not precisely, recognize the distinction. Thus in Latin there are *noscere* and *scire*; in Greek, γνῶναι and εἰδέναι; in French, *connaître* and *savoir*; in German, *kennen* and *wissen*. Once this distinction is pointed out it is easy to see that these two senses of 'knowing' are quite different. There is, however, a third sense of 'know' which is more confusing. The second speaker reported above disclaims acquaintance but asserts that he 'knows to whom' reference is being made. It seems, then, that there are two ways in which we may know persons or things. These must now be distinguished.

In ordinary life we are said to be acquainted with a person to whom we have been introduced. In this sense a man is acquainted with his wife, with the friend with whom he lives, with his barber.

No one now living is acquainted with Julius Caesar, if we mean by 'Julius Caesar' the man who wrote *de Bello Gallico*, who crossed the Rubicon, and was killed by Brutus on the Ides of March. It is not possible to define *acquaintance*. It is an unanalysable relation in which a knower stands to something. This relation is one with which we are all familiar. We are acquainted with that of which we are directly aware.[1] For example, we can be acquainted with the colour of the table at which we are looking, and with the noise made by a passing motor-car. It must be carefully noted that in saying that there is acquaintance with the noise made by a passing motor, the reference is simply to the noise. If we were to assert that the noise was made by a motor we should be asserting something about the noise, we should not be claiming acquaintance with the motor. As we are here using the word, then, 'acquaintance' means that relation in which a knower stands to something that is directly presented to him. By a convenient extension of the term we can say that we are acquainted with what has been directly presented to us but which is not now being presented. This is the sense in which we might say that we are acquainted with some one to whom we have been introduced but who is not now present. It is doubtful whether, in the strictest sense of the word 'acquaintance', we ever are *acquainted with* persons.[2] It is only necessary to contend here that we must distinguish between knowing a person whom, as we say, we have met personally, and knowing some one in some other way.

Every one understands what is meant by such a statement as 'I am not acquainted with Stanley Baldwin, but I know who it is you are discussing'. What we have now to consider is what *exactly* it is we are knowing when we say that although we are not acquainted with Stanley Baldwin we know who it is you are discussing. Suppose that we are at a public meeting that is to be addressed by Mr. Baldwin. At a given moment the Chairman rises and announces that he is to have the pleasure of 'introducing Mr. Baldwin'. The chairman at that moment, we will suppose, makes a demonstrative gesture pointing out a certain individual seated beside him. Baldwin is then introduced to us. We may already have known him as *being the Prime Minister of Great Britain in* 1928, or as *being the chief speaker at a certain meeting*, or as *being the politician that smokes a pipe, is fond of pigs and makes good after-dinner speeches*, and so on. These are characteristics that may, or may not, belong to the man who has just been introduced to us. The phrases by means

---

[1] The phrase 'directly aware' is used here in its ordinary sense. It is the directness of the relation that is important.

[2] If, as seems not improbable, a person is a logical construction, then we could not be acquainted with a person. (See Chap. IX.)

of which we refer to such characteristics are descriptive phrases, e.g. " the politician that smokes a pipe ", " the Prime Minister". We know also that the name " Stanley Baldwin " applies to the individual to whom we believe these characteristics belong. Just as we say that the name " Stanley Baldwin " applies to an individual, so we can say that these descriptive phrases apply to the individual that possesses the characteristics expressed by the phrases. We can understand these descriptive phrases and can use them significantly before we are acquainted with the individual whom they describe. It is important to emphasize the fact that our understanding of a descriptive phrase is independent of any acquaintance with the object described.

There are, then, two different ways in which we can know things. We can know a thing by being acquainted with it. The only things with which we can be acquainted are things of which we are directly aware. We can also know a thing by knowing its characteristics. In the latter case we must know both what the characteristics are and that these characteristics belong to this thing. We are then said to know the thing by description. Thus we know Baldwin by description when we know, for example, that the characteristic of *being Prime Minister in* 1928 belongs to him. It is possible both to know a thing by description and to be acquainted with it. Most of our knowledge of things is knowledge by description. If our knowledge were confined to acquaintance we could know very little. The descriptive knowledge that we can have of things may be more or less determinate. Our knowledge of an object is more determinate in proportion as it is more precise and comprehensive. The more characteristics that we know to belong to an object, the more determinate is our knowledge of that object. When we say " I know a great deal about that object " we usually mean " I know a great many characteristics that belong to that object ". It is in this way that our knowledge of an object may develop, so that we are able to ask questions about something which, in one sense, we already *know*. This distinction between determinate and indeterminate knowledge relates only to knowing by description. Acquaintance does not admit of degrees.[1]

---

[1] This distinction between *acquaintance* and *knowledge by description* was first clearly drawn by Mr. Bertrand Russell. (See *Problems of Philosophy*, Chap. IV, and the references given in Chap. IX below.) It has often been confused with the distinction drawn by William James between *acquaintance* and *knowledge about*. (See *Principles of Psychology*, I, p. 221.) But this is quite a different distinction ; it is concerned with what we have called the distinction between determinate and indeterminate knowledge, whereas *acquaintance* and *description* relates to the way in which *symbols are used*. The analysis of descriptions will be given in Chap. IX. Cf. also Chap. II, § 2.

§ 2. PROPER NAMES AND DESCRIPTIVE PHRASES

We have seen that a descriptive phrase ascribes characteristics. These characteristics may, or may not, belong to some object. If there is any object to which these characteristics belong, then the descriptive phrase applies to that object, or objects. For example, if there is no individual who is both *honest* and a *politician*, then " honest politician " is a descriptive phrase that describes nothing. If there are several individuals who are honest and are also politicians, then " honest politician " applies to each one of them. We can certainly understand what is meant by " honest politician " even if there are none. That is to say, we can understand a descriptive phrase without knowing whether there is anything that is described by it, and we could use it significantly even if we believed that there was nothing to which the phrase applied. The reason why we can thus understand and use descriptive phrases, even when there is nothing to which such phrases apply, is that their meaning is independent of the context within which on any given occasion they may occur. That is to say, their significance does not depend upon a *given* situation. Descriptive phrases are thus to be sharply distinguished from demonstrative symbols. A symbol that simply demonstrates, or points out an object, has no significance apart from the object which it demonstrates ; it indicates an object without ascribing characteristics. A demonstrative symbol would be meaningless were there nothing for which it stood.[1]

These two kinds of symbols may be defined as follows :

A demonstrative symbol is a symbol which stands for an object with which we are directly acquainted.

A descriptive phrase is a symbol which ascribes characteristics and is such that it has significance independently of the context within which it is being used.

A demonstrative symbol may be regarded as a logically proper name, since it symbolizes an object with which there is acquaintance, and which is thus immediately given. We do not mean to suggest that a demonstrative symbol is what would ordinarily be called a proper name. On the contrary, if we attempt to find an example in accordance with the above definition, we shall find that our examples are very unlike ordinary proper names. If, fixing your attention on something sensibly presented to you, e.g. a patch of colour, you were to say " *this* ", then " this " is a demonstrative symbol or logically proper name. What " this " stands for depends upon the context within which it occurs. It means different objects on different occasions of its use, i.e. it stands for different referends. That is to say, the referend of " this " is determined by its use on every occasion ; it is equivalent to a demonstrative gesture.

[1] Cf. Chap. II, p. 15.

made by Mill between connotation and denotation. The variation
in terminology is due to the difference in the point of view from
which the distinction has been conceived.

The *intension* of a word is commonly said to be all that we
intend to mean by it.[1] This definition suggests an unfortunate
intrusion of psychology into logic. It is perhaps for this reason
that the idealist Logicians, who approach logic from the side of
psychology and metaphysics, prefer to use " intension " instead of
" connotation ". But what we intend to mean is vague and variable.
Dr. J. N. Keynes has usefully distinguished three different meanings
of " intension ", which may be briefly summarized here :[2]

(1) *Conventional intension*, i.e. those attributes which are commonly
regarded as constituting the definition of the word, such that if any
of these were lacking the word could not be applied. The philosopher
John Locke, for instance, raises the question whether a certain
kind of shape is to be included in the definition of " man ", and
he points out that, if so, certain abnormal persons must be refused
the name of " man ". Conventional intension corresponds to some
extent to what Mill meant by connotation.

(2) *Subjective intension*, e.g. those attributes which the use of a
word calls up in the mind of a person using it. This has sometimes
been called the psychological meaning of a word. For example,
the word " home " calls up different ideas in different people's
minds, so that its subjective intension may vary considerably from
one individual to another. This is a notion that is quite useless
for the purposes of logical thinking.

(3) *Objective intension*, i.e. *all* those attributes which are in fact
possessed in common by *all* the objects to which the word applies.
Dr. Keynes uses the word *comprehension* as equivalent to objective
intension. As we never know *all* the attributes possessed by an
object, this notion is not of much utility.

Extension, as used in relation to intension, is an extremely
ambiguous word. The traditional treatment of this topic is very
unclear owing to the fact that quite different notions have been
confused and the topics connected with each of them have been
dealt with together. These confusions run throughout the traditional Logic, which is based upon the metaphysical theories implicit
in Aristotle's theory of logic. We shall constantly be concerned
with difficulties that would not have arisen had it not been for these
deep-rooted confusions. They can be cleared up only as we proceed.
One very important confusion may, however, be dealt with at once.

The relation of a class (e.g. *Frenchmen*) to a wider class within

---

[1] See Joseph, *Introd.*, Chap. VI, p. 121. " The intension of a term verbal
is what we intend by it, or what we mean by it when predicated of any
subject."   [2] *F.L.*, Pt. I, Chap. II.

which the former is contained (e.g. *Europeans*) is quite different from the relation of an individual (e.g. *Napoleon*) to a class of which this individual is a member (e.g. *Frenchmen*). These different relations were not distinguished by the traditional Logicians, who treated them both as examples of extension. Thus the class *Europeans* was said to " extend over " or to " include in its extension " the class *Frenchmen* ; also, the class *Frenchmen* was said to include in its extension all individual Frenchmen, e.g. Napoleon, Mazarin, Villon, Bossuet, etc. To use one word to express both these relations was bound to lead to difficulties. The confusion was increased by the attempt made by some logicians to include in the extension of *Frenchmen*, not only all those Frenchmen who have lived, are living, and will live, but also all French characters in fiction, e.g. *Jean Valjean* (in Victor Hugo's *Les Miserables*), *M. Paul Emmanuel* (in *Villette*), and so on. If extension be used in this third sense it is the correlative of subjective intension rather than of connotation. Dr. Keynes accordingly proposes to call it " subjective extension ", which he understands to mean " the whole range of objects real or imaginary to which the name can be correctly applied ". This, however, raises quite a different problem from the problem of distinguishing psychological meaning from conventional intension, so that Keynes' terminology is not helpful. We shall be concerned later with the difficulties due to this third interpretation of extension.

We have, then, distinguished two quite different senses in which " extension " is used and two different interpretations of the latter sense. Thus " extension " is said to mean :

(1) The relation of a class to the sub-classes it includes ; (2) the relation of a class to the individual members which compose the class, these individuals being understood to be *either* (*a*) all those which may be said to *exist*, in the ordinary meaning of the word " exist ", or (*b*) all individuals real and imaginary.

Neither (1) nor (2) corresponds exactly to what Mill meant by denotation but (2*a*) approximates to it.

The interpretation of " extension " in sense (1) has been held to involve what has been called " the inverse variation of extension and intension ". What this means can best be made clear by means of an example. If we consider the classes : *squares, rectangles, parallelograms, quadrilateral figures*, we see that they fulfil the following conditions : (1) each class (taken in order from first to last) includes fewer individual members than the succeeding classes (since, e.g., all squares are rectangles, but not all rectangles are squares) ; (2) each class has a greater number of characteristics than the succeeding class. Thus, for example, if we know that a given plane figure is a *square* we know a greater number of characteristics with regard to it than if we only knew that it was a *rectangle*.

or London, or England are names which signify a subject only. Whiteness, length, virtue signify an attribute only. But *white, long, virtuous*, are connotative. The word white denotes all white things, as snow, paper, the foam of the sea, etc., and implies, or in the language of the schoolmen, *connotes*, the attribute *whiteness* '.[1] Thus Mill so defined " connotative name " that it follows that if a name is connotative it *must apply to* something—which is what Mill meant by *denoting*. But, as we have seen, a descriptive phrase which is, of course, connotative may have no application, e.g. ' glass mountain ', ' circular square ', ' consistent philosopher ', ' impeccable statesman '. It is clear, then, that " connotation " cannot be defined as Mill defined it. A word, a name, or a phrase is connotative when it means, or stands for, a characteristic or set of characteristics such that anything that possesses these characteristics is denoted by the word, or the name, or the phrase. Thus connotation determines denotation provided that the connotative word does apply to something ; but a connotative word need not denote. A word, a name, or a phrase is non-connotative when it does not stand for any characteristic but simply demonstrates its referend. Hence a non-connotative word is a demonstrative symbol. To understand a non-connotative word we must be acquainted with its referend. This is, we have seen, the case with logically proper names such as " this ". The words that stand for simple qualities, such as " red ", " sweet ", " loud ", are non-connotative words which denote simple qualities. In order to understand what " red " means, we must have seen something red. Thus " red " demonstrates the quality for which it stands.

To sum up this discussion. The distinction between *describing* and *applying to* is important, and is the basis of the traditional distinction between connotation and denotation. But it is a mistake to suppose that all words, or names, must both describe and apply to something. Hence, we must reject Mill's definition of connotation and the traditional treatment of intension as alike offering confused accounts of the distinction. We conclude that : (1) some names have no connotation, e.g. demonstrative symbols, logically proper names and names of simple qualities ; (2) there are different kinds of names, or words, that have connotation, viz. ordinary proper names and descriptive phrases ; (3) some names have no denotation, e.g. descriptive phrases which describe nothing, e.g. ' glass mountain ', ' centaur '. With regard to the distinction between two kinds of connotative words it is to be observed that the connotation of descriptive phrases determines the denotation, whereas the denotation of ordinary proper names determines their restricted connotation within the context in which they are used.

[1] Loc. cit.

CHAPTER IV

PROPOSITIONS AND THEIR CONSTITUENTS

'Only the proposition has sense; only in the context of a proposition has a name a meaning.'—*Wittgenstein.*

§ 1. THE PROPOSITION

WHEN we attempt to analyse an example of reflective thinking—such as the examples given in Chapter I—we find that it consists of propositions either asserted to be true, or supposed to be true, from which propositions other propositions can be inferred. Thus the unit of logical thinking is the proposition. This must now be precisely defined :

A proposition is anything that is believed, disbelieved, doubted, or supposed.

Not every sentence expresses a proposition but only those sentences which express what is either true or false.[1] For example, Phaedrus having listened to Socrates' prayer to Pan says : ' Let me also share in this prayer ; for friends have all things in common '. The first sentence expresses a request ; the second sentence, " for friends have all things in common ", expresses a proposition. It is asserted by Phaedrus as being true, and, as the conjunction " for " shows, it is offered as a ' justification ' for his making the request. In order that a proposition may be communicated, it must be expressed. The expression of a proposition involves symbols. These symbols may be, though they need not be, words. We have seen that words are a special kind of symbols, or signs, peculiarly adapted to express what we ordinarily think about. The verbal expression of a proposition is a sentence. Although words are symbols we sometimes make a distinction between propositions expressed in words and propositions expressed in symbols. In that case we should mean by a symbol a *non-verbal symbol* deliberately devised for a special purpose. At present we shall be mainly concerned with propositions expressed in sentences. But we want to consider

[1] Cf. Aristotle, *De Interpretatione,* 17*a*, 1. ' Yet every sentence is not a proposition, only such propositions as have in them truth or falsity. Thus a prayer is a sentence, but is neither true nor false.'

It is clear that commands, requests, exclamatory sentences and expressive sighs are not propositions.

3

doubts that so-and-so is the case. A fact is not an event. It does not occur *at* a time, although some facts are facts with regard to a particular time. It is a fact that Charles I was defeated at the battle of Naseby. This is a fact with regard to Charles I and the battle of Naseby. If I now judge that Charles I was defeated at the battle of Naseby, there is another fact, namely, *that I am now judging that Charles I was defeated at the battle of Naseby*. If on some subsequent occasion I again judge that Charles I was defeated at the battle of Naseby, there is another fact with regard to another and a later time. We are not here primarily concerned with judging, believing, etc., but *with what is judged, believed, etc.*, i.e. with *propositions*. Although it is not easy to define a " fact ", we see that it is not difficult to understand what " fact " means. Nor shall we attempt to discuss what precisely is meant by saying that a proposition is true, or that a proposition is false. Every one knows what he means when he says that the proposition *The moon is smaller than the earth* is true, and that the proposition *The sun is smaller than the earth* is false. If I judge that it will be wet to-morrow, and it *is* wet the next day, then I judged truly ; if it is *not* wet the next day, then I judged falsely. What I am judging on each occasion is that something is the case. A fact is anything that is the case. For example, that these words are printed in black ink is the case ; that is, it is a fact that these words are printed in black ink. It is this fact that makes the proposition *These words are printed in black ink* true, and that also makes the proposition *These words are printed in red ink* false. When I judge truly, *what* I judge is a fact. Facts simply *are* ; they are neither true nor false. Only propositions can be true, or can be false, and their truth or falsity depends upon their relation to facts.[1]

Common sense is accustomed to distinguishing between *things* and the *qualities and relations* that things may have. For example, *this table* is a thing ; it has the quality of *being brown* ; it stands in a certain position in a certain room at a certain time, that is to say, it has spatial and temporal relations to other things. Again, *Charles I* is a thing ; he has the quality of *being an unfortunate man*. Regarded as things, *Charles I, this table, the Tower of London, my pen*, are simple. *That the Tower of London is admired by Americans* is a fact. *That Charles I is unfortunate* is a fact. These facts are clearly not simple in the sense in which the common-sense *things* we have been considering are simple. Each of these facts consist of two or more constituents. The fact *that Charles I was unfortunate* consists of two constituents—a thing (*Charles I* [2]) and

---

[1] See G. E. Moore, *Facts and Propositions*, and cf. Chap. XIII, § 5 below.
[2] " Charles I " is here used as a logically proper name, i.e. as standing for something with which we might be acquainted. It is not necessary to

a quality (*being unfortunate*). *That Charles I married Henrietta Maria* is a fact consisting of three constituents—two things (*Charles I*) and (*Henrietta Maria*) and a relation that relates them (*marriage*). Such facts as these are simple facts and the propositions which express these facts are simple propositions.

Two or more simple propositions may be combined so that out of them a single proposition is constructed. For example, *Charles I married Henrietta Maria and the Catholics were pleased* is a single proposition constructed out of the two simple propositions *Charles I married Henrietta Maria* and *The Catholics were pleased*. A single proposition constructed out of simple propositions will be called a compound proposition.[1] That such a compound proposition is a single proposition is shown by the fact that if either of the two constituent propositions which are connected by *and* is false, the proposition is false, even though the other proposition is true. For example, *Columbus was a great sailor and he sailed round the world* is false, if, as is in fact the case, the constituent proposition, *He sailed round the world* is false, though the other proposition, *Columbus is a great sailor* is true. There are various different ways in which simple propositions may be combined so as to construct compound propositions. The examples so far given are of the simplest kind.

The first distinction, then, to be made between different kinds of propositions is between simple propositions and compound propositions. Each of these kinds can be further subdivided.

(A) SIMPLE PROPOSITIONS

We have already seen reason to dissent from the traditional view that every proposition consists of a subject and a predicate that is attributed to the subject. This is only one of the various kinds of simple propositions that we must now distinguish.

The most primitive proposition is the *subjectless proposition*, sometimes called the exclamatory proposition, e.g. *Fire !* ; sometimes called the impersonal proposition, e.g. *it rains, it thunders*. Although *it rains* has a grammatical subject, it may be doubted whether it has a logical subject. *Fire !* may be thought to have a subject and no predicate. But this would be a mistake. Such a proposition has neither subject nor predicate. The analysis of subjectless

contend that *Charles I* (or any of the other examples) is in any ultimate sense a thing. It may be that we never reach absolutely simple things. But we are not here concerned with questions of ultimate analysis.

[1] Mr. Bertrand Russell, F. P. Ramsey and other modern logicians use the term " atomic propositions " for simple propositions of this kind, and " molecular propositions " for compound propositions. I have used the terminology of Dr. J. N. Keynes and Mr. W. E. Johnson.

times put it, belongs to a class. Thus *Socrates* is said to be a member of the class philosophers. *That dog* is said to be a member of the class *fox-terriers*. It is important to distinguish these propositions from such propositions as *All Athenians are Greeks, Some dogs are fox-terriers*. Although they are of fundamentally different logical forms, they have frequently been confused.[1] The distinction between these two forms was first stated by a German logician, Frege, about the year 1879, and a little later, independently, by an Italian logician Peano. Propositions of the form *Socrates is a philosopher* have not received a distinctive and generally accepted name. It will be convenient to call them *class-membership propositions* to distinguish them from propositions of the form *All Athenians are Greeks, Some dogs are fox-terriers*. They must also be distinguished from propositions of the form *Socrates is wise*, i.e. from *subject-predicate* propositions.[2]

So far we have considered only affirmative propositions. Any proposition can obviously be denied. For example, *Baldwin is honest* is denied by *Baldwin is not honest*. The notion of denial, or negation, expressed by " not " is difficult to analyse, but it is perfectly familiar. We all understand what is meant by the denial of the proposition " Baldwin is honest ". The word " not " has been frequently used in the preceding pages and has so far presented no difficulty to the reader. We shall, therefore, take " not " as understood.[3]

(B) COMPOUND PROPOSITIONS

There are two main divisions of compound propositions. Mr. W. E. Johnson has introduced a convenient terminology to distinguish these and their various subdivisions, which will be adopted here.[4] For the sake of brevity and clearness we shall now use p, q, r, to stand for propositions. Thus instead of writing a simple proposition, e.g. *William married Mary*, or *This dog is affectionate*, we shall write p. That is to say, " p " will represent any simple proposition we might choose to assert ; " q ", " r ", will represent any *other* simple propositions. Then " *not-p* " will stand for the denial of " p ". It will often be found convenient to write " $\bar{p}$ " for " *not-p* ".

[1] Cf. Chap. III, p. 29 above.
[2] The distinction between these three forms of propositions will be further discussed in Chapter IX.
[3] For further discussion of *not* see p. 191 below.
[4] See W. E. J., Pt. I, Chap. III. Cf. his articles on ' The Logical Calculus ' in *Mind*, 1892. I have not only adopted Mr. Johnson's terminology ; everything of importance in my treatment of compound propositions is due to his work on the subject.

The simplest of all logical conjunctions is *and*.[1] By means of *and* we combine one proposition with another. Thus '*p and q*' is a compound proposition constructed out of the two simple propositions *p* and *q*. It is important to notice that in the last sentence we have used the word " and " in two different senses. In '*p and q*' we are using " and " as a logical conjunction; its function is to combine *p* with *q* so as to construct a single proposition. In the phrase " constructed out of the two simple propositions *p* and *q* ", the word " and " expresses an enumeration of two propositions. This is the use of *and* which occurs in " Tom and Dick ". This latter use is called by Mr. Johnson the enumerative *and*. At present we shall be concerned only with the use of " and " to combine two, or more, propositions into a single proposition. This is the *conjunctive* use. A compound proposition in which the simple propositions are combined by the conjunctive *and* is called a *conjunctive* proposition, e.g. '*p and q*', '*p and q and r*'.

There are three other logical conjunctions which are of importance for the construction of compound propositions out of simple propositions, viz. *If . . . then . . ., Either . . . or . . ., Not both . . . and. . . .* Propositions combined by any of these three conjunctions are called *composite* propositions. These different modes of combination are important and have received distinctive names. They are set out in the following table in which the simple propositions to be combined are *p, q*.

TABLE I.—COMPOSITE PROPOSITIONS

Proposition	Name of Proposition
If *p*, then *q*.	Implicative.
Either *p* or *q*.	Alternative.
Not both *p* and *q*.	Disjunctive.[2]

The names of these forms are self-explanatory. An implicative proposition is a composite proposition in which one of the constituent propositions *implies* the other. The proposition *p* implies the

[1] 'The fundamental mode of logically combining propositions is represented by the conjunction " and ". . . . The relation expressed by " and " is simply the emptiest of all relations. It expresses merely the bringing of two propositions together into one system without subordination or any definable connexion other than is indicated by their being face to face in one and the same system.' (W. E. J., loc. cit.)

[2] The name " disjunctive proposition " was formerly used for propositions of the alternative form. It is clearly not applicable to this form, which asserts an *alternation*, not a *disjunction*, of propositions. Properly disjunctive propositions were not recognized by the traditional Logicians. Miss E. E. C. Jones suggested the name " alternative " (*Elements of Logic*, p. 115), and this name was adopted by J. N. Keynes in his *Formal Logic* (see Pt. II, Chap. X).

properties or characteristics. These characteristics are considered apart from the particular things which have the characteristics. In this respect a general proposition must be contrasted with a subject-predicate proposition. When we assert that *Socrates is wise*, we are asserting a characteristic, *being wise*, of a particular individual, *Socrates*. The characteristic *being wise* does not exist apart from some individual or other that has the characteristic. But we may assert the proposition. *Every one who is wise is trustworthy* without considering whether there is in fact an individual who is wise. This proposition may be most conveniently expressed in the form : *If any one is wise he is trustworthy*. A general proposition is, then, an implicative proposition. But the implicans and the implicate are not simple propositions. *Any one is wise* is not a proposition at all ; it is a form of words that enables us to show that the general proposition *All who are wise are trustworthy* asserts a relation between characteristics considered apart from the individuals that may have these characteristics. The proposition *All who are wise are trustworthy* would not usually be considered to be true unless there were individuals who were both wise and trustworthy, that is, unless *some* such proposition as *Socrates is wise* were true. Hence, relatively to general propositions, simple propositions are elementary. Combinations of simple propositions are also elementary.

We may accordingly group together all the propositions we have considered in subsections (A) and (B) as *elementary* in contrast to general propositions which are *non-elementary*. The analysis of the latter is more difficult than the analysis of elementary propositions, and must be postponed to Chapter IX. At present it is enough to point out that the distinction is important.

§ 3. THE TRADITIONAL SCHEDULE OF PROPOSITIONS

In this section we shall be concerned with the classification of propositions, due to Aristotle, which constitutes the traditional schedule. This classification is thoroughly unsatisfactory, since it is based upon an incomplete analysis.[1] Some kinds of propositions are completely ignored, others are confused. It would be an advantage if we could omit the consideration of these defects. But this is not possible. The traditional theory of the syllogism is based upon the traditional classification of propositions and cannot be understood without reference to it. We shall, therefore, give some account of it here.

We have seen that the traditional treatment of compound propositions was perfunctory. The schedule is confined to those propositions which the traditional Logicians grouped together under

---

[1] In Chapter IX we shall give reasons for thinking that this classification is absurd.

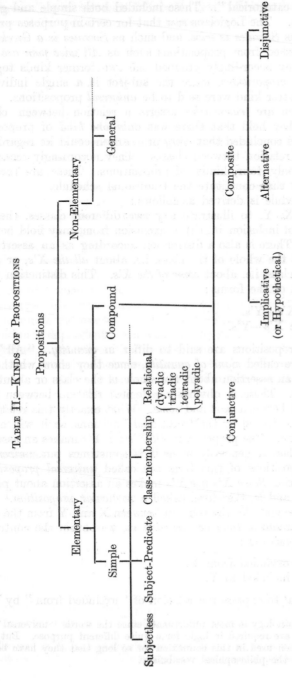

TABLE II.—KINDS OF PROPOSITIONS

This table gives the various kinds of propositions which we have distinguished. There is an infinite number of different forms of propositions, so that no Table of Kinds of Propositions can be complete.

" All X is Y ", e.g. " All wise men are trustworthy ", and so on.

The sign of quantity " some " is interpreted to mean " *some at least, it may be all* ". In ordinary speech we usually, though not always, use " some " to mean " some only ", i.e. " some but not all ", e.g. " Some men are fools ". But if " some " means " some only ", then " Some X is Y " will mean " Some X is Y but some is not₍₎". This proposition is inconsistent with the universal affirmative " All X is Y ", and is equivalent to the conjoint assertion of the particular affirmative and the particular negative propositions. Hence, the particular propositions I and O would on this interpretation of " some ", always be asserted together. Such an interpretation is inconvenient. We need some sign of quantity which would enable us to assert that " Some X is Y ", whilst leaving it an open question whether *all* are ; and to assert that " Some X is not Y " whilst leaving it an open question whether *none* are. If we want to assert both that *some are* and *some are not*, we can do so by asserting the conjunctive proposition " Some X is Y and some X is not Y ". It is desirable, therefore, to give the minimum interpretation to " some ". For example, we might say, " Some cases of cancer are curable by radium treatment ", leaving it undecided whether or not all may be so curable. We interpret " some ", then, so as to be consistent with *all* but to exclude *none*.

§ 4. DISTRIBUTION OF TERMS IN A, E, I, O PROPOSITIONS

Since in the traditional schedule the subject, and predicate, of every proposition was regarded as a class, the first distinction to be recognized was whether the reference was, in each case, to the whole, or to part of the class. If the reference is to the whole of the class, the subject, or the predicate, is said to be *distributed*. If the reference is to part of the class, the subject, or the predicate, is said to be *undistributed*.

It is clear that the *subject* of universal propositions is distributed, since a universal proposition *means* one the subject of which refers to the whole class. In saying " All scholars are pedantic ", we are clearly saying something about *every* member of the class *scholars*. So, too, in the proposition " No Spartans are poets ", we are referring to *every* member of the class *Spartans*. It is no less obvious that the *subject* of particular propositions is undistributed, since this again is what we *mean* by saying that the particular proposition is about *some* of the class. Thus " Some sinners are not penitent " refers to *some members* of the class *sinners*.

The predicate of negative propositions is distributed. In excluding *all Spartans* from the class *poets*, we necessarily exclude all members of the class *poets* from the class *Spartans*. In excluding

some sinners from the class of *those who are penitent,* we exclude
the latter from the former. The predicate of affirmative propositions is undistributed. In including *all scholars* among those who
are pedantic, we refer to *some* who are pedantic. It might be true
that *every one* who is pedantic is a scholar, but the proposition
"*All scholars are pedantic*" does not assert this, but is consistent
with the proposition 'Some who are pedantic are not scholars'.
Similarly, 'Some works of art are beautiful' refers to those members
of the class of *beautiful things* that are also works of art ; it does
not refer to *all* beautiful things, even if it were in fact the case that
they were all works of art.

We may sum up the scheme of distribution in A, E, I, O, propositions as follows :

A. The subject is *distributed,* the predicate *undistributed.*
E. The subject is *distributed,* the predicate *distributed.*
I. The subject is *undistributed,* the predicate *undistributed.*
O. The subject is *undistributed,* the predicate *distributed.*

It will be found convenient to remember the following rule :
Subjects are distributed in universal propositions.
Predicates are distributed in negative propositions.

Since the traditional Logicians assumed that every proposition
was of the same logical form, it follows that they considered that
the subject of every proposition could be regarded as either distributed or undistributed. Hence, a difficulty arose with regard
to the *singular* proposition of the form, *Socrates is wise.* It seems
obvious that it is nonsense to ask, "What is the distribution of
the subject, *Socrates,* in this proposition ?," since distribution would
seem to be applicable only to classes. However, in consistency with
their fundamental position these Logicians were bound to think
otherwise. Accordingly, they decided that the subject of singular
propositions is to be regarded as *distributed.* Mr. Joseph states
the position as follows : 'A term is said to be *distributed,* when it
is used in reference to its whole extension, or to all that it can denote.[1]
Now the subject of a singular judgement denotes one individual
only, and the judgement refers to that ; the subject of a universal
judgement is general, and may denote any number of individuals,

[1] In a note to this statement Mr. Joseph refers to the distinction he had
previously noticed ' between the relation of a generic concept to the more
specific concepts included under it and the relation of the universal to the
individual '. But he goes on to say that ' it is not always necessary to bear
this distinction in mind ', so that distribution can be applied both to singular
subjects and to the subjects of universal propositions. Hence, he reveals
his complete failure to grasp the difference in the logical form of these two
propositions. (It must be noticed that Mr. Joseph uses the word " judgement "
where I have used " proposition ".)

4

propositions (examples 2 and 3), *class-membership propositions* (example 4).

Now consider the set of propositions :

$$C\begin{cases} \text{(1) Othello loved Desdemona.} \\ \text{(2) Cassio loved Desdemona.} \\ \text{(3) Cassio loved Iago.} \\ \text{(4) Cassio hated Iago.} \end{cases}$$

These four propositions are obtained by replacing the constituents of the first proposition one at a time. The form of all is the same. Thus we see that—to quote Mr. Russell—' the form remains unchanged throughout this series, but all the constituents are altered. Thus form is not another constituent, but is the way the constituents are put together '.[1]

In discussing the different *kinds* of propositions we were, then, discussing the different *kinds of propositional forms*. We could select any examples to illustrate the form. In saying that we could " select any examples ", it is clear that what we mean is that we can vary the constituents provided that we leave the form unchanged. As logicians, we are not interested in considering whether " No Spartans are poets " is a belief entertained by anyone ; we are interested only in the *form* of the assertion. The traditional Logicians would say that " No Spartans are poets " has *the same form as* " No Eskimos are popes ", but that they *differed in matter*. The distinction between the *matter* and the *form* of a proposition is related to the distinction between *constituents* and *form*. But, as is usual with the traditional Logicians, the distinction was not clearly stated because the analysis of the proposition was not carried far enough. For example, they regarded the distinction between " All S is P " and " No S is P " as being *as fundamental* as the distinction between " All S is P " and " Some S is P ". This, however, we shall see later is a mistake.[2]

We have now to ask whether there are different *kinds of constituents*. This is the question whether there are terms *which can occur only in one way in a proposition*. The way in which the terms occur determines the form of the proposition.

The most fundamental distinction between terms is the distinction between *particular* and *universal*.[3] What precisely is the difference between these two constituents is a matter of controversy among contemporary logicians. The discussion of this problem is difficult, and cannot be entered into here. We shall state dog-

---

[1] Op. cit., p. 43.

[2] See p. 151 below. It will be remembered that the Logicians treated these general propositions (" All S is P ", etc.) as though they were *simple*.

[3] This use of the words " particular " and " universal " must be carefully distinguished from the traditional use in the A, E, I, O schedule.

matically a view that seems plausible, but it is desirable to remember that other views are possible.[1]

In the proposition " Cassio loves Desdemona ", *loves* is the relating element ; it *connects* the two subjects *Cassio* and *Desdemona*. In " Othello was jealous of Cassio because of Desdemona ", *was jealous* is the relating element. In the first example the relating element, *loves*, relates two terms ; in the second example the relating element, *was jealous*, relates three terms. Hence, the propositions are of different forms. The relating element in a proposition is the *universal* constituent. The constituents that are related are the subjects of the relation. We shall, therefore, define these two kinds of constituents as follows :

A *particular* is a term that can occur in a proposition only as a subject. (It is to be remembered that *both* the terms in a dyadic relational proposition are *subjects*).[2]

A *universal* is a term which combines the other constituents of the proposition into a unity. Universals are either predicates or relations.

It will be seen, then, that the *form* of the proposition is primarily determined by the *kind* of relating constituent, i.e. the *universal*, the function of which is to combine the constituents into the unity which is expressed as the proposition. There will be as many different kinds of simple propositions as there are different kinds of universals. We have already seen that there are different kinds of relations, determined by the number of subjects involved, viz. dyadic, triadic, etc. Mr. Russell has suggested that a predicate, e.g. a simple quality, such as *is white*, can be regarded as a *monadic relation*, that is, a relation involving only one term. There are, however, good reasons for distinguishing *predicates* from *relations*, and we shall continue to maintain the distinction between subject-predicate propositions and relational propositions.[3] A universal, then, may be either a simple quality, or a relation involving two or more terms. The relating constituent in a given proposition may be a subject in some other proposition—e.g. *loves*, *jealousy*. The logical distinction between particular and universal does not correspond to the metaphysical distinction between *particular*, regarded as substance, and *universal*, since a substance (which is sometimes called " the metaphysical subject ") is regarded as that which persists through a period of time, whereas a particular may be momentary.

---

[1] The view adopted here is that of Mr. Russell (loc. cit.). See also Chadwick, *Mind*, N.S. 141, and W. E. Johnson, *Logic*. For a contrary view see Ramsey, " Universals," *Mind*, N.S. 136.   [2] See p. 167 below.

[3] See J. A. Chadwick, loc. cit., pp. 1–3. Cf. Russell, *The Principles of Mathematics*, §§ 48, 53.

Since the traditional Logicians thought that the relating constituent of a proposition was always the *is* of predication, they neglected it in considering the number of terms. Hence their view that no proposition could contain more than two terms. This view has had an unfortunate effect upon the traditional terminology, since the word " term " is frequently used to stand for those constituents only which are not the relating constituent. In the exposition of the traditional schedule we have used " term " in this sense—and in the exposition of the traditional syllogism we shall also find it convenient to use it in the same sense. In the context, this use of the word should not lead to confusion. But, were it not for the deadweight of traditional doctrine, it would be better to avoid using the same word in two different senses.

We have now to consider those distinctions that concern *names* [1] rather than *terms, or constituents*. Of these the most important is that between *general* and *singular* names, and between *connotative* and *non-connotative* names. The latter distinction was explained in Chapter III. We must now discuss the antithesis between *general* and *singular* names.

A *general name* is a name used to refer to all the objects that possess certain characteristics, e.g. *men, centipedes, fairies*. The possession of these characteristics determines the application of the name.

A *singular name* is a name used to refer to one individual, or object, e.g. *this man, the Town, the present Prime Minister, my eldest brother, Socrates.*

Any name that can be significantly used in the plural, or with the prefix *a*, or with any numerical prefix, is general. All general names are connotative, since they stand for a set of characteristics which may, or may not, belong to something, but which, if they do belong to anything, belong to more than one object. The general name " fairies " applies to nothing, since there is nothing that possesses the characteristics connoted by " fairy ". The name " honest politician " might apply to more than one individual, even if in fact it applies to no one. But " this honest politician " *could* only apply to an individual demonstrated by " this ". Hence " honest politician " is general ; " this honest politician " is singular.

There are two kinds of singular names, viz. *proper names* and those which uniquely describe some object, e.g. *the present Prime Minister*. The latter we shall call *uniquely descriptive names*.[2] They resemble general names in being connotative, but differ from them in that general names are applicable to more than one object, if they are applicable to any.

---

[1] The traditional Logicians used " name " very widely so as to be a synonym for " word ".   [2] See W. E. J., Pt. I, Chap. VI.

Proper names are non-connotative, but they must have application. The distinction between ordinary proper names and names that are logically proper must be borne in mind. It is because ordinary proper names contain a descriptive element that the names of famous persons can be used in the figure of speech known as antonomasia. For example, " a Nero ", " a Bismarck ", " a Daniel come to judgement ". Such names are abbreviated descriptive phrases, derived from the description most commonly applied to the person so named.

We have further to distinguish between *collective* and *non-collective* names. A *collective name* is a name used to refer to a set of individuals, or objects, regarded as a unity, e.g. *army, mob, society, The Rockies*. A *non-collective name* is a name not so used. Collective names may be either singular or general ; for example, *the London Library* is a singular, *audience* is a general, collective name. A general collective name may itself be subsumed under a wider collective name, so that there may be a series of collective names of increasing generality, e.g. *patrol, company, regiment, brigade, army*. A general name which is not as such collective may be used collectively by prefixing such words as " all ", e.g. " all together ", as in " All the angles of a triangle are equal to two right angles ". What is important is to distinguish the *collective use* of " all ", which means a *totality* or a *set taken together* from the *distributive use* of " all ", which means " every ". A singular collective name may be an ordinary proper name, e.g. *The Rockies, The Dardanelles*, or a uniquely descriptive name, e.g. *The Greek alphabet, the American Navy*. These names are collective because they refer to a group considered as a unit, and are *uniquely descriptive* because they refer to that group through some characteristic which belongs only to that group and to no other.

Every name must be either connotative or non-connotative, and either general or singular ; if singular, either proper or uniquely descriptive.

§ 6. THE UNIVERSE OF DISCOURSE

Both the traditional Logicians and Mill held that every significant name must have denotation, i.e. must apply to something. It was not denied that such descriptive names as *centaur, fairy* and such names as *Aphrodite, Odin, Polonius*, applied to nothing in the real, or actual world, but it was maintained that they had application in some realm or " universe " to be distinguished from the actual universe. Hence arose the conception of a " universe of discourse ". This term was introduced into logic by de Morgan and George Boole.[1] It is thus defined by de Morgan : ' If we remember that

[1] de Morgan, *Formal Logic*, pp. 41, 55 ; Boole, *Laws of Thought*, p. 166.

in many, perhaps most propositions, the range of thought is much less extensive than the whole universe, commonly so called, we begin to find that the whole extent of a subject of discussion is, for the purpose of discussion, what I have called a *universe*, that is to say, a range of ideas which is either expressed or understood as containing the whole matter under consideration." In this sense the phrase "universe of discourse" is an unfortunate name for what would ordinarily be called the *context* within which a proposition is asserted. For example, ' Achilles sulked in his tent ' would be commonly understood with reference to the context supplied by Homer's *Iliad*. If we wished to deny this proposition, we should explicitly refer to Homer, and should express the denial in such a form as, ' Homer does not describe Achilles as sulking in his tent.' The implicit reference to a context does not involve the assumption that, although, for instance, no *actual man Achilles* acted in the way in which Homer's hero acts, yet *a man Achilles* exists in a universe of Greek epic poetry. Some logicians have, however, so interpreted " universe of discourse " as to suggest that there are several different *universes* the inhabitants of which have different modes of being, e.g. the universe of physical nature, the universe of Greek mythology, the universe of Shakespeare's plays, and so on. This assumption, as we shall see later, has been derived from a mistaken analysis of propositions. It is sufficient here to point out that a proposition asserting existence is true if, and only if, the individual described exists in the actual world. There is no other mode of existence. For example, " There is a god, Zeus " is false ; but this proposition would be ordinarily interpreted as being elliptical. When fully stated, the reference to a context would be made explicit, for example, " The Greeks believed that there was a god, Zeus." This proposition makes an assertion about the beliefs of actual men, and is true if these men actually entertained such beliefs. The supposition that there are different *universes* is rendered necessary only if it be assumed that every descriptive phrase must have application. The recognition that a description may describe, i.e. signify a set of characteristics, without describing anything, enables us to dispense with the conception of a universe of discourse in any sense other than that of a given context.[1]

[1] Cf. also Chap. V, § 4, and Chap. IX, § 5.

CHAPTER V

THE COMPOUND PROPOSITION AND THE RELATIONS BETWEEN PROPOSITIONS

'Zounds! I've never been so bethumped with words.'—*King John.*

§ 1. THE SEVEN RELATIONS BETWEEN PROPOSITIONS AND THE FIGURE OF OPPOSITION

LET p and q be any two propositions. There are seven possible logical relations that may hold between them. There are various ways of stating these relations. Perhaps the most convenient way is to consider them from the point of view of what is known with regard to the truth, or falsity, of q given the truth, or falsity, of p. It will be said that p implies q if, given that p is true, we can know that q is true. In this case q *follows from p.*[1] The relation *follows from* is one with which we are all familiar. It is used not uncommonly in ordinary conversation as when one person says to another, " But don't you see that such and such a conclusion *follows from* what you have already admitted to be true ? " Such a statement clearly asserts that you can't accept a given proposition and yet refuse to accept what follows from it. Thus, when q follows from p, we can infer q given that we know p to be true. It may also be assumed that we know what is meant when it is said that p *is incompatible with q.* One proposition is incompatible with another if they cannot be true together, but propositions may be compatible without being so related that it is possible either to infer the one from the other, or to infer from the truth or falsity of the one that the other is true or false. The relation of *bare compatibility* interests no one except a logician. The proposition *The Cornish coast is rugged* is compatible with the proposition *There are no snakes in Iceland,* and both of these with the proposition *The angle in a semicircle is a right angle.* But this bare compatibility does not interest us because *nothing else follows from it,* since knowledge of the truth or falsity of one of these propositions does not enable us to infer the truth or falsity of the others. Thus the relation of bare compatibility cannot be used as a basis of inference. Two propositions related by the relation of bare compatibility are said to be logically independent.

---

[1] See Chap. IV, p. 41, and cf. Chap. XII, § 1.

can be inferred with regard to the truth or falsity of these propositions given that one of them is true, we have the relations summed up in the following table :

Given	it can be inferred		
A true	E false	I true	O false
E true	A false	I false	O true
I true	A unknown	E false	O unknown
O true	A false	E unknown	I unknown
A false	E unknown	I unknown	O true
E false	A unknown	I true	O unknown
I false	A false	E true	O true
O false	A true	E false	I true

Singular propositions of the form *Socrates is wise* cannot properly be regarded as falling under the figure of opposition. We saw that the traditional Logicians treated such propositions as universals, i.e. as A propositions. But it is impossible to satisfy the traditional *definitions* of " contrary " and " subaltern " in finding contrary and subaltern propositions to *Socrates is wise*. Clearly the contradictory is *Socrates is not wise*. Dr. Keynes suggests as a contrary *Socrates has not a grain of sense*.[1] Certainly these two propositions cannot both be true and they might both be false, so that they are contrary in accordance with our definition, but they do not conform to the traditional form. Moreover, we must recognize that in the interpretation of these propositions *wisdom* is a matter of degree, so that these oppositions cannot be formally treated. Nor is *wisdom* a characteristic of a simple entity, *Socrates*. It is his actions, or his judgements, that are wise. It is a straining of language to say that a man who has sometimes, though rarely, failed to act wisely, is unwise. Such considerations suggest that the technicalities of the figure of opposition are unduly artificial and restricted, so that they cannot usefully be extended beyond the forms dealt with by the traditional schedule. The traditional doctrine of opposition is, indeed, restricted in two ways : (1) it is confined to the four A, E, I, O, forms, the relations being defined in terms of quantity and quality ; (2) it is interpreted so as to apply only to propositions having the same constituents, that is, the same subject-terms and the same predicate-terms, but differing in form (i.e. in quantity, or in quality, or in both). The relations as we have defined them

---

[1] *F.L.*, § 83. Those who desire a fuller treatment of the traditional, *Square of Opposition* will find it adequately treated by Dr. Keynes (*F.L.*, Pt. II, Chap. III). We shall deal with the opposition of compound propositions in a later section of this chapter.

are not so restricted. In the further discussion of these relations they will be given the wider interpretation.

Every proposition whether simple or compound has a contradictory, namely, that proposition which cannot be true if the given proposition is true, and which must be true if the given proposition is false. Thus, to contradict a proposition is the same as to deny that it is true. There are various ways in which the contradictory of a proposition may be expressed, but these will all be equivalent in the sense in which *equivalence* has been defined. It is important to notice that the assertion of p denies the assertion of *not-p*, and conversely. There is no mean between these two assertions. But the assertion of the contrary of a given proposition is not a simple denial of the original proposition, since the two propositions may both be false. That is to say, contrary propositions admit of a mean. If we can establish that *No S is P* is true, we have certainly shown that *All S is P* is false ; but *All S is P* might be false although *No S is P* were not true. This can be easily illustrated by reference to the figure of opposition, since both *Some S is P* and *Some S is not P* may be true, in which case neither *No S is P* nor *All S is P* is true. As thus stated this is, as a matter of psychological fact, self-evident. Still, it is not uncommon for mistakes to be made, which result in the substitution of the contrary for the contradictory of a given proposition. Nor is it always easy to express concisely the contradictory of a complicated proposition. So long as we keep to the canonical forms, we are not likely to make mistakes. But there would be little utility in the study of contradictory propositions, were it limited to the figure of opposition. We shall be concerned later with the contradiction of compound propositions. It may be useful here to give some examples of ordinary statements with their respective contradictories and contraries. It must be observed that, whilst the contradictories of a proposition are always equivalent, there may be several non-equivalent contraries, since contraries admit of a mean.

EXAMPLES

(1) *Original proposition :* That dress is blue.
   Contradictory : That dress is not blue.
   Contrary : That dress is green ; that dress is grey, etc.

(2) *Original proposition :* Charles I was always defeated in battle.
   Contradictory : Charles I was not always defeated in battle.
   Contraries : Charles I was never defeated in battle.
            Charles I was always overwhelmingly successful in battles, etc.

(3) *Original proposition :* Only ex-soldiers are eligible for the post.

In both propositions both terms are distributed; it will easily be seen that the propositions are equivalent.

From *Some Tories are free traders* we can infer *Some free traders are Tories*. In both propositions both terms are undistributed; it will easily be seen that the propositions are equivalent.

From *All Jingoes are militarists* we can infer *Some militarists are Jingoes*. In the given proposition the subject is distributed and the predicate undistributed. In the inferred proposition, the subject, being the predicate of the original proposition, is undistributed. Hence, the propositions are not equivalent. It will be easily seen that the original is superimplicant to its *converse*, i.e. to the proposition inferred from it by conversion.

From the proposition *Some popes are not saints* we cannot infer any proposition having *popes* for predicate and *saints* for subject, since the inferred proposition would be of the form O, hence its predicate would be distributed. But *popes* was given undistributed.

In the first two examples, the inferred proposition is equivalent to the original. In the third example, the inferred proposition is not equivalent. When an inferred proposition is subimplicant to the original proposition, the inference is said to be *depressed*, and the inferred proposition is said to be *weakened*. This is always the case when a particular proposition is inferred from a universal.[1]

We can sum up these inferences in a convenient form, using symbols. We shall use the symbol " $\equiv$ " between the two propositions when they are equivalent; and the symbol " $\dashrightarrow$ " to indicate that the inferred proposition is weakened.

SCHEMA OF CONVERSION

Original Proposition.		Converse.	
A. All S is P	$\rightarrow$	Some P is S.	I.
E. No S is P	$\equiv$	No P is S.	E.
I. Some S is P	$\equiv$	Some P is S	I.
O. Some S is P		None.	

It will be observed that in each case the converse is of the same quality as the original proposition. The converse of E and of I is called the *simple converse*; of A, the *converse per accidens*.

---

[1] We shall see later that this inference is always invalid. But we are at present dealing with the traditional doctrine.

(2) *Obversion.* To assert that *S is P* is equivalent to denying that *S is non-P.* For example, to deny that any popes are saints is equivalent to affirming that none of them are saints, or that all of them are other than saints, i.e. non-saints. Hence, it is always possible to obtain a proposition equivalent to the original by changing its quality and replacing the original predicate by its contradiction.

Obversion may be defined as a form of immediate inference in which from a given proposition, another is inferred having for its predicate the contradictory of the original predicate.

SCHEMA OF OBVERSION [1]

Original Proposition.		Obverse.	
A. All S is P.	≡	No S is non-P.	E.
E. No S is P	≡	All S is non-P.	A.
I. Some S is P	≡	Some S is not non-P.	O.
O. Some S is not P	≡	Some S is non-P.	I.

It will be observed that in each case the obverse is equivalent to the original proposition ; the quality of the proposition is changed but the quantity remains unchanged.

Conversion and Obversion are the only simple forms of immediate inference. But there is no reason why we should not convert a proposition obtained by obversion from a given proposition ; nor why we should not obvert a proposition obtained by conversion from another. Hence, there are other forms of immediate inference. Those which have interested logicians sufficiently to be given special names are the two in which the contradictory of the original predicate becomes the subject of an inferred proposition ; and in which the contradictory of the original subject becomes the new subject. These are called respectively *contraposition* and *inversion.*

* (3) *Contraposition* is a form of immediate inference in which from a given proposition another is inferred having for its subject the contradictory of the original predicate.

Since the obverse gives a proposition with the contradictory of the original predicate, contraposition is obtained by converting the

---

[1] The remaining forms of immediate inference are given in summary form. The student who does not at once see how the obverse is obtained, may find it helpful to take the significant examples given for conversion, and obvert those.

obvert of the original. In the scheme we shall omit this step, which would merely repeat the scheme of obversion.

Since nothing is said in the definition of contraposition with regard to the *predicate* of the inferred proposition, it is permissible that this should be the original subject, or its contradictory. Thus we have two contrapositives which are obverts of each other.

SCHEMA OF CONTRAPOSITION

Original Proposition.	Contrapositive.	Obverted Contrapositive.
A. All S is P	$\equiv$ No non-P is S. E.	$\equiv$ All non-P is non-S. A.
E. No S is P	$\dashrightarrow$ Some non-P is S. I.	$\dashrightarrow$ Some non-P is not non-S. O.
I. Some S is P	None.	None.
O. Some S is not P.	$\equiv$ Some non-P is S. I.	$\equiv$ Some non-P is not non-S. O.

(4) *Inversion* is a form of immediate inference in which from a given proposition another is inferred, having for its subject the contradictory of the original subject.[1]

Here again we can obtain two forms, viz. one in which the predicate is the same as the original predicate, and one in which the predicate is the contradictory of the original predicate. These will be obverts of each other.

Since all that we can do to a given proposition is to convert it or to obvert it, we must obtain the inverse of a given proposition by successively converting and obverting the derived propositions. It is required to obtain from a proposition of the form $S-P$ (where quantity and quality are not specified) a proposition of the form $non\text{-}S-non\text{-}P$, or $non\text{-}S-P$. By obversion we obtain the contradictory of the predicate term. Hence, if we can infer a proposition with S as predicate, its obvert would have non-S as predicate ; if this proposition could be converted we should have the required form. This will be possible unless the last proposition is an O proposition, which has no convert. It will be found that, starting with *All S is P*, we can obtain by successive operations of obversion and conversion (in that order) two propositions of the form *Some*

---

[1] Dr. Keynes invented the term *inversion*, although this form of immediate inference had been sometimes recognized by logicians.

non-S is non-P and *Some non-S is not P*. These are the required propositions, and are the *inverse* and the *obverted inverse* of *All S is P*. Again, starting from *No S is P*, by successive operations of conversion and obversion (in that order) we obtain two propositions of the form *Some non-S is P* and *Some non-S is not non-P*. These are the required propositions and are the *inverse* and *obverted inverse* of *No S is P*.

An inverse cannot be obtained either from the I or from the O proposition, since in both cases in attempting to obtain a proposition with *non-S* as subject we obtain an O proposition (having *non-S* for predicate), which cannot be converted.

It will be seen that the obverted inverse of A is *Some non-S is not P*. In this proposition the predicate term *P* is distributed, being the predicate of a negative proposition. This inference, therefore, breaks the rule of distribution, since *P* was given undistributed in *All S is P*. There is, therefore, as Dr. Keynes puts it, ' an apparent illicit process, which it is not quite easy either to account for or explain away '.[1] He proceeds to account for it—or rather to explain it away—by the assertion that this inference requires the implicit premiss " Some things are not P ". It is true that in this premiss P is distributed, but if inversion requires this additional premiss, it is difficult to see how it can be regarded as an *immediate* inference in the sense in which " immediate " was defined. This " apparent illicit process " " suggests rather that none of these immediate inferences are valid apart from implicit assumptions, which the traditional Logicians ignored. One such assumption, which is relevant here, is that propositions in which *S, non-S, P, non-P*, occur may all be significantly asserted, and that *S, non-S, P, non-P* exist within the universe of discourse. If this be granted, then, if *All S is P*, it follows that *non-P* cannot be *S*, so that *non-P* must be *non-S*, that is, some *non-S* is *non-P*.[2]

A surprising amount of controversy has been devoted to the question of the validity, or invalidity, of inversion, and to the problem of the distribution of the predicate in O propositions. But such controversy is futile, owing to the fact that the doctrine of distribution, and the traditional theory of immediate inference which is based upon it, rests upon erroneous assumptions as to the simplicity of the propositional forms from which they start. These propositions thus lend themselves to mistaken interpretations. We shall not, therefore, pursue this controversy here.

---

[1] *F.L.,* § 104.

[2] These assumptions will be discussed below (see § 4). The reader may be left to explain the apparent absurdity of the inference by inversion from " All great poets have failed to write a flawless epic poem " to " Some who are not great poets have not failed to write a flawless epic poem ".

By the adoption of a convenient shorthand symbolism,[1] introduced by Dr. Keynes, we can now summarize the results of these processes of immediate inference. Since the vowels, A, E, I, O, stand for the quantity and quality of the given proposition, we can insert one of these vowels between any two capital letters to signify that these terms are to be connected according to the prescribed form. Thus, *S a P* stands for *All S is P* ; *M o N* stands for *Some M is not N*, and so on, the subject always being written first. *S* and *P* will symbolize *non-S* and *non-P* respectively. Thus, *All S is non-P* is written *S a P̄*.

TABLE V.—SUMMARY OF IMMEDIATE INFERENCES

Form	A	E	I	O
Original Proposition	SaP	SeP	SiP	SoP
Converse	PiS	PeS	PiS	
Obverse	SeP̄	SaP̄	SoP̄	SiP̄
Obverted Converse	PoS̄	PaS̄	PoS̄	
Contrapositive	P̄eS	P̄is		P̄is
Obverted Contrapositive . .	P̄aS̄	P̄oS̄		P̄oS̄
Inverse	S̄iP̄	S̄iP		
Obverted Inverse	S̄oP	S̄oP̄		

A glance at the above table shows that O has no converse, and I has no contrapositive ; also that only A and E have inverses. The plain man will not need to be convinced that from the proposition *Some dogs are fox-terriers*, it is impossible to draw any conclusion concerning what is not a dog and not a fox-terrier. The process of inversion reminds us of Samuel Johnson's comment : ' Sir, a woman's preaching is like a dog's walking on his hind legs. It is not well done ; but you are surprised to find it done at all.'

---

[1] The term " shorthand symbolism " is due to Mr. W. E. Johnson. It will be further explained and discussed in Chapter VIII.

§ 3.   THE RELATIONS BETWEEN COMPOUND
PROPOSITIONS

In the figure of opposition and in the schema of immediate inferences, we were concerned only with A, E, I, O propositions. We have now to consider the relations that hold between compound propositions.[1] In Chapter IV we divided compound propositions into two forms, conjunctive and composite. If we take any two propositions, p and q, and their contradictories, $\bar{p}$ and $\bar{q}$, we can conjunctively combine them in four ways, viz. (1) p *and* q, (2) $\bar{p}$ *and* q, (3) $\bar{p}$ *and* $\bar{q}$, (4) p *and* $\bar{q}$. Any two of these conjunctive propositions are independent. In stating the four modes of combination we have assumed that the *order* in which the component simple propositions are asserted is indifferent. We can obviously say " He sent his daughter to Cambridge and he apprenticed his son to a solicitor " or " He apprenticed his son to a solicitor and he sent his daughter to Cambridge ", without affecting the sense of the compound proposition.[2]

We have now to inquire how compound propositions can be contradicted. The *conjoint affirmation* of p and q is equivalent to the denial that p and q can be disjoined. Hence the contradictory of *p and q* is *not both p and q*, i.e. a *disjunctive* composite proposition.

Now, *not both p and q* is equivalent to *either $\bar{p}$ or $\bar{q}$*. It is clear that if, *not both* of two propositions can be affirmed, *at least one* of them must be denied.

Ordinary language recognizes these equivalent propositions in the following forms : *Not both p and q* is equivalent to *either $\bar{p}$ or $\bar{q}$*. For example, *You can't both eat your cake and have it* is equivalent to *Either you can't eat your cake or you can't have your cake.*

We can, therefore, contradict *p and q* either by asserting *not both p and q*, or by asserting *either $\bar{p}$ or $\bar{q}$*, since these two composite propositions are equivalent. It will be found convenient to remember that a conjunctive proposition can be contradicted by a disjunctive, or by an alternative in which the component propositions are separately contradicted, and conversely.

As in the case of the conjunctive proposition, so in the case of the disjunctive and alternative composites, the order of the component propositions is indifferent. We conjunctively combined the components p, q, $\bar{p}$, $\bar{q}$, in four different ways. We shall now combine these components in four disjunctive and four alternative composites as follows :

---

[1] See W. E. J., Pt. I, Chap. III.
[2] The principle here exemplified is known as the " Commutative Law ", which, in this connexion, may be stated in the form : p *and* $q \equiv q$ *and* p. See further, Chap. XXIV, and cf. W. E. Johnson, loc. cit., p. 29.

(i) p or q	(ii) p or $\bar{q}$	(iii) $\bar{p}$ or q	(iv) $\bar{p}$ or $\bar{q}$
(i) Not both $\bar{p}$ and $\bar{q}$	(ii) Not both $\bar{p}$ and q	(iii) Not both p and $\bar{q}$	(iv) Not both p and q

It will be immediately obvious that these two sets are so arranged that the disjunctive written below the alternative, in each case, is its equivalent. Their corresponding *conjunctive contradictories* are : (i) $\bar{p}$ and $\bar{q}$; (ii) $\bar{p}$ and q; (iii) p and $\bar{q}$; (iv) p and q.

We have now to consider the implicative proposition of the form *If p, then q*. It is clear that the order of the implicans and the implicate is not indifferent. Thus *If p, then q* is a different proposition from *If q, then p* and is not equivalent to it. For example, *If he is not stupid, then he is lazy* is not equivalent to *If he is lazy he is not stupid* ; nor can the one proposition be inferred from the other. Unfortunately, it is possible for him to be both lazy and stupid. We may have evidence that points to the conclusion that he is one or the other, without any indication as to whether, or not, he may be both. Thus, failure to pass an extremely easy examination may lead us to conclude that he is either lazy or stupid, and we may feel satisfied that one, or other, *alone* of these alternatives would be *sufficient* to explain his failure, although *both* are *possible*.

This example illustrates three points that are of importance in considering composite propositions and their equivalences :

(1) These forms are of frequent occurrence in ordinary discussion. Sometimes we use one, sometimes another to express *the same* state of affairs ;

(2) It is not usual to interpret the " or " in an alternative proposition as expressing the *exclusion of one alternative*. That is, " or " is consistent with " perhaps both ". If " or " be interpreted exclusively, then *p or q* includes *not both p and q*. Some logicians hold that it must be so interpreted.[1] In that case we should have to use a cumbrous expression to convey the information that one or other and perhaps both of two alternatives was the case. This consideration is not in itself sufficient to rule out the exclusive interpretation of " or ". To be precise is often to be lengthy in expression, since ordinary language is ambiguous. But, as our example illustrates, the *onus probandi* lies on those who assert that the *logical* interpretation of " or " should be exclusive.[2] It cannot be maintained that the common use is exclusive. There are, however, no good logical reasons for interpreting " or " so that it includes " not both ". On the contrary, it is desirable to give the minimum inter-

[1] See Bosanquet, *Logic*, Bk. I, Chap. VIII, § 1.
[2] See Keynes, *F.L.*, § 191, and W. E. Johnson, Pt. I, Chap. III, § 6.

pretation.[1] The exclusion of alternatives can then be stated in the conjunctive affirmation of an alternative and a disjunctive proposition, e.g. *Either p or q and not both p and q.* It is not to be denied that it is sometimes clear that two alternatives exclude each other. But the exclusion is due to the nature of the alternatives, not to the form of the proposition. For example, *Either he will be first, or second* states an alternation between possibilities, not both of which can be realized. But this impossibility of realizing both is not expressed in the proposition, but is due to the incompatibility of being " first " and " second ". The " or ", then, in *p or q* will be interpreted so as to be consistent with *both p and q.*

(3) The implicative proposition cannot be simply converted, that is, the implicans and the implicate cannot be simply interchanged.

It is clear from the first consideration, viz. that different composite forms can express the same state of affairs, that these forms can be used to express equivalent propositions. These equivalent propositions can be formulated as follows :

$$\text{If } p, \text{ then } q \equiv \text{Not both } p \text{ and } \bar{q} \equiv \text{Either } \bar{p} \text{ or } q.$$

with column headings *Implicative.* *Disjunctive.* *Alternative.*

EXAMPLE :

Implicative. If he laughs, the joke is obvious.
Disjunctive. It is not the case both that he laughs and the joke is not obvious.
Alternative. Either he does not laugh, or the joke is obvious.

From the implicative proposition *If p, then q,* we can infer the proposition *If $\bar{q}$, then $\bar{p}$.* For example, from *If it rains, he stays indoors* we can infer, *If he does not stay indoors, it does not rain.* Two propositions of these forms are called *contrapositives*, since the implicans and the implicate are interchanged after they have been separately denied. The non-equivalence of *If p, then q* and *If q, then p* may be exhibited in a table by setting out the equivalent disjunctive and alternative for each of these propositions, adding the two contradictory conjunctives.

Implicative.	Disjunctive.	Alternative.	Contradictory Conjunctive.
If p, then q	Not both p and $\bar{q}$	Either $\bar{p}$ or q	Both p and $\bar{q}$
If q, then p	Not both $\bar{p}$ and q	Either p or $\bar{q}$	Both $\bar{p}$ and q

[1] Cf. the traditional interpretation of " some ". Here it was necessary to depart from the usage of common speech. The departure is *logically* justified, on the same grounds as the agreement with common speech in the interpretation of " or ", viz. that it is desirable to give the minimum interpretation to ambiguous words.

From the above considerations it should now be clear that whilst the various forms of the composite propositions are equivalent, no composite proposition is equivalent to a conjunctive. This result accords with the division, made in Chapter IV, of compound propositions into the two kinds, composite and conjunctive, and with the subsequent division of the composites into three forms.[1]

§ 4. THE DIAGRAMMATIC REPRESENTATION OF A, E, I, O
      PROPOSITIONS AND OF THE RELATIONS OF EXCLUSION
      AND INCLUSION BETWEEN ANY TWO CLASSES

We have seen that the traditional schedule may be interpreted as expressing relations of exclusion and inclusion between two classes. Since the time of the Swiss mathematician, Euler,[2] it has been customary to represent these relations diagrammatically by the coincidence, the inclusion, the overlapping, and the exclusion, of two circles. Between any two classes, X and Y, so considered, there are five possible relations, which can be represented as follows :

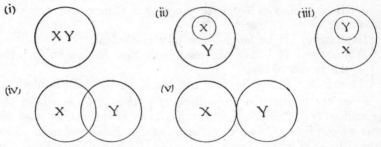

The circles are labelled X, Y, to indicate which circle is supposed to represent which class. Mr. Johnson has suggested that 'the boundary line of a closed figure may be taken as the proper analogue of the intension, while the area within that boundary is the proper analogue of the extension'.[3] Thus, the boundary of the smaller, enclosed circle in (ii) may be taken to represent the connotation, or intension, of " X ", whilst the enclosed area represents the objects, or things, to which the name " X " applies ; and so with the other figures.

Let us represent these relations by the particular example of the two connotative names " politician " and " honest ". They may be related as follows :

(1) Every politician is honest and no one else is honest. (Fig. i.)

(2) Every politician is honest and there are others who are honest. (Fig. ii.)

---

[1] Cf. W. E. Johnson, loc. cit., p. 33.   [2] Euler lived from 1707–83.
[3] Loc. cit., p. 125.

(3) Every one who is honest is a politician and some politicians are not honest. (Fig. iii.)

(4) Some politicians are honest and some politicians are not honest and some who are honest are not politicians. (Fig. iv.)

(5) No politicians are honest. (Fig. v.)

It will be observed that only one diagram, viz. Fig. v, corresponds to a single proposition of the traditional schedule. This is the E proposition, which is the only one in which both terms are distributed, i.e. in which both terms are taken in their whole extent. Since an undistributed term is indeterminate in its reference, it is clear that a proposition containing an undistributed term cannot be represented by a figure in which the relations are determinately represented. To express the relations represented by the first four figures in terms of the schedule, there is needed in each case the conjoint affirmation of two or more of the propositions of the schedule. We may say that the A, E, I, O propositions exclude, in each case, one or more of the possible relations between X and Y. Thus :

A excludes (iii), (iv), (v), and allows (i), (ii).

E excludes (i), (ii), (iii), (iv), and allows (v).

I excludes (v), and allows (i), (ii), (iii), (iv).

O excludes (i), (ii), and allows (iii), (iv), (v).

These figures, as commonly used, are extremely misleading. In this they faithfully represent the implicit assumptions of the schedule. Thus, it is assumed that " politician " and " honest " have application. We are supposed only to be able to doubt *their* mutual relations. Or, let " X " and " Y " stand respectively for " centaurs " and " four-legged ". Then, one or other of these five relations must hold ; hence, " centaur " and " four-legged " have application ; thus, for example, the characteristics for which " centaur " stands must belong to something.

We can see at this point how necessary to the traditional Logicians was the assumption of a universe of discourse.

Again, the area outside the circles, in each case, represents everything that is neither X nor Y. Hence, it is assumed that " X ", " $\bar{X}$ ", " Y ", " $\bar{Y}$ " [1] have application. For convenience, we will represent *the universe* by a rectangle within which the various circles can be drawn. It will suffice to take one example. We select Fig. (iv).

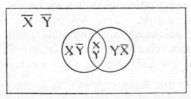

---

[1] " $\bar{X}$ " stands for "non-X " in conformity with the notation we have adopted.

In this figure the compartments are labelled with the four possible combinations : X Y, X $\overline{Y}$, $\overline{X}$ Y, $\overline{X}$ $\overline{Y}$. Now, we can substitute for the intersecting circles of Fig. (iv), any of the other figures. In each case the class $\overline{X}$ $\overline{Y}$ is represented. Hence, in every case *Some non-X is non-Y*. It would seem, therefore, that each of the A, E, I, O propositions should have an inverse, and in each case the *same* inverse. But this is absurd. We cannot, therefore, assume that there is always some area *outside* the circles, representing part of the universe. Hence, this mode of representing the four combinations does not accord with the theory upon which the immediate inferences is based. Accordingly, Dr. Keynes has elaborated a scheme of seven diagrams in which are included those cases in which there is no part of the universe outside the circles.[1] But it is scarcely worth while to follow this elaboration. The doctrine of distribution and the assumption that " X ", " $\overline{X}$ ", " Y ", " $\overline{Y}$ " always have application lead to the difficulties suggested by the misleading diagram above, so that it is advisable to discuss the assumption, rather than to attempt to rectify the diagrams.

That " X " has application is usually stated in the form *Something is X*, or *X exists*, to which is generally added, " in the appropriate universe of discourse ". We saw that in order to justify the validity of the inversion of *S a P*, we had to assume the proposition *Something is not P* or *non-P exists*. To say " S exists " is to say that S has occurrence in the universe of discourse. We saw that the notion of universes of discourse arose from the assumption that every connotative (and, therefore, every general) name has application. On this assumption the traditional schedule can be formulated as follows :

A. Every S is P and something is S.
E. Not a single S is P and something is S.
I. Some S is P and something is S.
O. Some S is not P and something is S.

These are compound propositions. Thus A, for example, will be false if nothing is S. From E it follows that something is non-P ; hence, E will be false if nothing is non-P ; and so on. But if we once assume that S, non-S, P, non-P must all exist, it seems difficult to justify the assumption that it may be the case that nothing is both non-S and non-P. Yet, without this latter assumption, every proposition, universal and particular, will have an inverse, and the *same* inverse, viz. *Some non-S is non-P*. This conclusion is absurd. It was for this reason that we rejected the attempt

---

[1] See *F.L.*, § 130. Dr. Keynes gives a thorough discussion of various diagrammatic methods and of the assumptions upon which they rest. Cf. also W. E. Johnson, *Logic*, Pt. I, Chap. IX, § 7.

to elaborate the diagrammatic scheme in such a way as to exclude this possibility.

The fundamental difficulty in the traditional interpretation lies in its failure to distinguish between propositions of the form. *This is an X* and propositions of the form *Every Y is X*. The proposition *This is an X* implies the proposition *An X exists*, or *Something is X*. But to assert that *Every Y is X* does not imply that *something is Y* or that *something is X*. This distinction is recognized by common sense. It is significant to say "Every competent statesman could solve the unemployment problem", even if one does not believe that there is some one who is a competent statesman.[1] The discussion of this distinction would take us beyond the consideration of the traditional schedule and must therefore be postponed to a later chapter.

It is possible to interpret the schedule so as to avoid the confusions we have just noted. Thus we may express it as follows:

A. Nothing is both S and non-P.
E. Nothing is both S and P.
I. Something is both S and P.
O. Something is both S and non-P.

But, as thus formulated, it is clear that A and E are of the same form; that I and O are of the same form; that these forms are different. The universal propositions deny existence; the particular propositions affirm existence. This distinction of form is not in conformity with the traditional interpretation nor with the assumptions upon which the Eulerian scheme and the immediate inferences rest. It is obvious that the existential interpretation of A as negative and of I as affirmative would render invalid the *conversion per accidens* of A. For the same reason the contraposition of I would be invalid, and the inversion of A and of E. Nor does the Eulerian scheme allow any compartment to be empty, for it rests upon the assumption that S, non-S, P, non-P all exist.

Dr. Venn [2] elaborated a diagrammatic scheme which allows a compartment to be empty. In this scheme each diagram represents an empty framework into which the information supplied by any one of the four propositions can be fitted. Given the two classes, S and P, we have

(i)

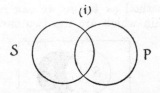

---

[1] Cf. Chap. IX, §§ 1, 3.   [2] *Symbolic Logic*, Chap. V.

Here the two circles represent two compartments which may or may not be empty. If we assert $S\,a\,P$, we deny that any S is non-P. Accordingly we block out the compartment which, if it were filled, would represent S's that were non-P. The diagram then becomes

(ii)

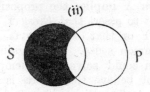

Similarly, E would be represented by

(iii)

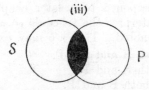

On this scheme it is less easy to represent the two particular propositions. Dr. Venn puts a bar across the compartment that is occupied. Thus I would be represented by

(iv)

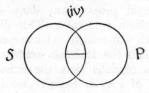

That this diagram is less satisfactory than those representing A and E is obvious. It suggests that the universal and the particular propositions cannot be satisfactorily treated by the same diagrammatic method. This is not surprising if the significance of a universal proposition is different from the significance of a particular proposition. It also brings out clearly that the distinction between A and I, or between E and O, is more fundamental than the distinction between affirmative and negative propositions in this schedule. In Chapter IX we shall see that this is the case.

By the same method as before we can represent the *universe* by a rectangle within which are the two circles. Thus,

represents that the compartment $\overline{S}\,P$ is empty, so that all P is S; and that $S\,P$, $S\,\overline{P}$, $\overline{S}\,\overline{P}$ are not empty.

It is clear that, if we admit that a compartment may be empty (i.e. that a given combination does not exist), we have not only *four* possibilities but *eight*, namely, $S\,P$, $S\,\overline{P}$, $\overline{S}\,P$, $\overline{S}\,\overline{P}$, any one of which may exist or not exist. There are accordingly *eight* independent propositions connecting any two classes S and P. These have been formulated in convenient expressions, in common use, by Dr. Christine Ladd-Franklin.[1] We give below her formulations on the left-hand side, and corresponding expressions in A, E, I, O forms on the other side.

TABLE VI.—PROPOSITIONS CONNECTING ANY TWO CLASSES S AND P AND THEIR CONTRADICTORIES

All S is P	$SaP = \overline{P}a\overline{S}$	A
Not all S is P	$SoP = \overline{P}o\overline{S}$	O
No S is P	$SeP = Pa\overline{S}$	E
Some S is P	$SiP = Po\overline{S}$	I
None but S is P	$\overline{S}a\overline{P} = PaS$	A'
Some besides S is P	$\overline{S}o\overline{P} = PoS$	O'
All but S is P	$\overline{S}e\overline{P} = \overline{P}aS$	E'
Not all but S is P	$\overline{S}i\overline{P} = \overline{P}oS$	I'

There can be little doubt that the formulations suggested by Mrs. Ladd-Franklin bring out these relations with the nearest approximation to the expressions of ordinary conversation. They also show how defective, even from this point of view, the traditional schedule is. But it may be questioned whether it is advisable thus to tinker with the traditional forms. It would be better to neglect these transformations and to develop a system in which the analysis of the propositional forms is carried further.

It must be observed that in any diagrammatic representation of propositions and of the class relations expressed in propositions, any point which falls outside any given circle represents an individual that is not identical with any individual represented by the points that fall within the circle. Thus, in the diagram

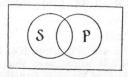

[1] Art. on "Propositions" in Baldwin, *Dictionary of Philosophy and Psychology*; also *American Journal of Psychology*, Vol. II, pp. 543–567, "On Some Characteristics of Symbolic Logic"; and *Mind*, 1890, "Some Proposed Reforms in Common Logic". Cf. also Keynes, *F.L.*, §§ 106–07; W. E. J., Pt. I, Chap. IX, § 6.

any point in the rectangle but outside the circles represents individuals that are not identical with (i.e. are other than) any individuals that are S's or are P's. Again, any point in that part of the circle S which is outside the circle P represents an individual which is other than P. In the traditional logic the latter case would be expressed by " *This S is not P* " or " *This S is excluded from P* ". There is thus considerable danger of confusing the relation of *non-identity* between individuals with the relation of *negation*. The relation of *exclusion* is, however, fundamentally different from the relation of *negation*. This being so, it may be questioned whether the diagrammatic representation of propositions has any utility, or whether it is not likely to suggest misleading ideas. On this point there is divergence of opinion among contemporary logicians. On the one hand, Mr. Bertrand Russell asserts :

'Philosophers have been slaves of space and time in the imaginative application of their logic. This is partly due to Euler's diagrams and the notion that the traditional A, E, I, O, were elementary forms of propositions and the confounding of " x is a β " with " all a's are β's ". All this led to a confusion between classes and individuals, and to the inference that individuals can interpenetrate because classes can overlap. I do not suggest explicit confusions of this sort, but only that traditional elementary logic, taught in youth, is an almost fatal barrier to clear thinking in later years, unless much time is spent in acquiring a new technique.' [1]

Mr. Johnson, on the other hand, maintains :

'Such a representation is in fact valid, although the relation of inclusion and exclusion of classes is not identical with the logical relations expressed in affirmative and negative propositions respectively ; for, there is a true analogy between the relations between classes and the relations between closed figures ; in that the relations between the relations of classes are identical with the corresponding relations between the relations of closed figures.' [2]

It seems, however, that Mr. Johnson overlooks one of the most important objections to this representation, namely, that it encourages the confusion between class-membership propositions and general propositions. On these grounds, it would seem that the diagrammatic representation of propositions is more misleading than useful.

[1] *Analysis of Matter*, p. 387.
[2] *Logic*, Pt. II, p. 87. Cf. also Pt. I, pp. 124, 147, 149. In saying that the relations are " identical " it would seem that Mr. Johnson means that the relations between classes *have the same formal properties* as the relations between closed figures. This does not, however, afford a sufficient justification for the representation. It may be noted that Mr. Johnson, in his treatment of diagrams, emphasizes the dangers of confusion, and is thus not likely to create " a fatal barrier to clear thinking ". Nevertheless the utility of the representation is not very great.

§ 5. ADDITIONAL PROPOSITIONS RECOGNIZED BY THE TRADITIONAL LOGICIANS

Even traditional Logicians found it inconvenient to confine all propositional forms within the schedule. The scholastics accordingly recognized a variety of forms under the general heading of what they called " exponible " propositions. An *exponible proposition* is one that can be analysed into two or more propositions. For example, *Few geniuses make good husbands* is analysable into *Most geniuses do not make good husbands and some do.* An exponible proposition is thus a compound proposition. The traditional limitation of the signs of quantity to *all* and *some*, combined with the ambition to include everything that any rational man might wish to assert within the fourfold schedule, led to the discussion of these forms as *irregular propositions.* On any other assumption it would seem unnecessary to discuss the prefix *few.* In ordinary speech " few " clearly stands for the combination "most are not and some are ", whilst " a few " stands for "some are but most are not ". The difference between *few* and *a few* is one of emphasis. For example, " Few great philosophers are married " asserts primarily that most great philosophers are not married whilst allowing as a secondary implication that some are. " A few popes have despised luxury " asserts primarily that some popes have despised luxury whilst allowing as a secondary implication that most have not. These words are intentionally vague ; their significance is lost if they are forced within the traditional limits. The neglect of the utility of vagueness combined with a misconception of the function of logic here led the traditional Logicians into unnecessary difficulties.

Some of their irregular propositions have received names and have thus been accorded a position in the textbooks. We shall give a list of these names, adding examples. But it would be futile to discuss their analysis in the traditional terminology.

Plurative Propositions. Most children are timid ; Several of the passengers gave way to panic ; Few mathematicians are philosophers ; A few statesmen are clear-sighted.

Exceptive Propositions. None are eligible except those who have had war service ; None but the unprejudiced were convinced. This proposition is clearly equivalent to *Only the unprejudiced were convinced* in which the distributed term is " Those who were convinced ". It can, therefore, be expressed as an A proposition, viz. *All those who were convinced were unprejudiced.* The prefix " None but " is one of those rightly included by Dr. Ladd-Franklin in her eightfold scheme of propositional forms in common use.

Indesignate Propositions. Birds of a feather flock together. The name " indesignate " is used to indicate propositions in which there is no explicit sign of quantity. The sense of the context can alone determine whether indesignate propositions should be classed as universal or as particular propositions.[1]

Propositions with Quantified Predicates. Napoleon was sometimes not successful in his military operations ; Children ought sometimes to disobey their elders.

The doctrine of the quantification of the predicate was introduced into logic by Sir W. Hamilton. It has received detailed discussion by some logicians. But there can be little doubt that the time has come when it should cease to occupy space in textbooks ;[2] we shall not, therefore, discuss the doctrine. It may, however, be noted, that a proposition of the form *All S is all P* is called a U proposition. They are of very rare occurrence in ordinary speech. Clearly *All S is all P* is an exponible proposition being equivalent to the conjoint assertion of *All S is P and All P is S*. It may be noted that the contradictory of this proposition is *Either some S is not P or some P is not S*, i.e. the alternation of the contradictories of each of the component propositions in the original conjunctive proposition.

Numerically Definite Propositions. " Half the candidates failed to pass the medical test." It is obvious that the traditional exclusion of such propositions is wholly justified.[3]

[1] The *Port Royal Logicians* distinguished two kinds of universal propositions : (1) *metaphysical* universals, e.g. " Every man is a living being " ; (2) *moral* universals, e.g. " All women love to talk ". By a moral universal they meant a generalization that was only approximately true, so that the given example is equivalent to " The majority of women love to talk ". It is thus not a universal proposition at all. (*Port Royal Logic*, Pt. II, Chap. XIII.) This curious use of the word " moral " lingers on in the popular expression " I am *morally* certain that so-and-so is the case ".

[2] See Keynes, *F.L.*, §§ 140–50.

[3] *Ibid.*, *F.L.*, § 345 ; de Morgan, *Formal Logic*, Chap. VIII.

CHAPTER VI

THE TRADITIONAL CATEGORICAL SYLLOGISM

'I hold that the invention of the form of syllogisms is one of the most beautiful which the human mind has made, and even one of the most considerable. It is a kind of *universal mathematics* whose importance is not sufficiently known.'—*Leibniz.*

§ 1. DEFINITION OF SYLLOGISM

ARISTOTLE, who first formulated the theory of the syllogism, gave the following definition : ' A syllogism is discourse (λόγος) in which, certain things being stated, something other than what is stated follows of necessity from their being so '. [1] He adds : ' I mean by the last phrase that they produce the consequence, and by this, that no further term is required from without to make the consequence necessary '. In accordance with this definition we might say that a syllogism is a form of implication in which two propositions jointly imply a third. The two premisses constitute a compound implicans and the conclusion forms the implicate. It is to be regretted that Aristotle, in working out his theory of the syllogism, interpreted his definition much more narrowly, so that he excluded all propositions not of the subject-predicate form. In this he has been followed by the traditional Logicians. It has been further assumed that the propositions must be categorical. As in this chapter we shall be concerned with the traditional doctrine, we shall define the syllogism as follows : " A categorical syllogism is a form of reasoning consisting of three propositions having between them three and only three terms, which are so related that the first two propositions jointly imply the third ".

The categorical syllogism may be illustrated by the following examples :

(1) If All credulous people are easily deceived
   and All sailors are credulous,
   then, All sailors are easily deceived.
(2) If No one who is invariably truthful is a successful politician
   and All Cabinet Ministers are successful politicians,
   then, No Cabinet Ministers are invariably truthful.

---

[1] *Anal. Priora,* 24b, 18.

to answer a question. Thus we might ask : " Is the income tax a just tax ? " Then we might reason as follows : " Well, I suppose a just tax is one which is proportioned to the ability to pay. But that is the characteristic of the income tax." Hence, we answer our question in the affirmative, because we see that the conclusion " The income tax is a just tax " follows from the two propositions which we have just admitted. The premisses are not always ' given ' in the sense that they are what we set out from ; but they are ' given ' in the sense that they are ' granted '. The premisses stated above are not in the simple logical form required by the definition of the syllogism, but it is clear that it is this form which justifies our acceptance of the conclusion " The income tax is a just tax ". Obviously it is not necessary that, in order that a man should perceive the force of his reasoning, he should be aware that he is formulating a syllogism. Our contention is that we frequently reason syllogistically but very few people know what a syllogism is. In the same way, most of us can add numbers together, but very few of us know how it is that this operation of addition can be successfully performed.[1] It is enough if it be granted that we sometimes attempt to resolve a doubt in our own minds, or to induce others to agree with us, by showing that a certain proposition that is doubtful, or is contested, follows from other propositions whose truth is not in dispute.

§ 2. FIGURE AND MOOD

Not every combination of three propositions containing between them only three terms constitutes a syllogism. For example, in the combination *All musicians are sensitive, All poets are sensitive ; All poets are musicians,* the third proposition does not follow from the first two, although it is consistent with them. In the combination, *No popes are saintly, Hildebrand was a pope ; Hildebrand was saintly,* the third proposition is inconsistent with the combination of the first two. To obtain a syllogism certain conditions must be observed. Before we attempt to determine what these conditions are, we will consider the three examples given on page 81. It will be seen that the middle term does not occupy the same position in the different examples. In the first, the middle term is subject in the major, and predicate in the minor premiss ; in the second, it is predicate in both ; in the third, it is subject in both. These syllogisms are said to be of different *figures.* The figure is determined by the position of the terms. Since, given the position of the middle term in both premisses, the position of the other term is fixed, we may define the figure of the syllogism as follows : *The*

---

[1] See p. 123, and cf. Locke, Bk. IV, Chap. XVII, § 4.

figure of the syllogism is determined by the positions of the middle term. It is customary to symbolize the terms by S for the minor, M for the middle, P for the major. If we do this we can take in at a glance the difference of the three figures. Neglecting the sign of quantity and the copula, we can symbolize the three figures as follows :

I	II	III
M — P	P — M	M — P
S — M	S — M	M — S
S — P	S — P	S — P

The shape of these three figures is different. Aristotle used the Greek word σχῆμα which means " shape " or " figure " or " form ". If we fill in the blank between the terms by " is " or " is not " and prefix signs of quantity, we shall get premisses of the forms given in the traditional schedule of propositions. In our examples (1) consisted of three A propositions ; (2) consisted of E, A, E, propositions in that order ; (3) consisted of A, A, I, propositions in that order.

The syllogism,

> If   No men are infallible
> and All priests are men,
> then No priests are infallible,

is in Figure I. But it differs in form from our first example, since the propositions are E, A, E. This difference is called a difference in *mood*. We may define " mood " as follows : *The mood of a syllogism is determined by the quantity and quality of its constituent propositions.* Comparing the last example with example (2) above, it will be seen that we can have the same mood in different figures. But not all moods, i.e. combinations of A, E, I, O propositions, are possible in all figures.

We might have obtained the conclusion " No priests are infallible " from the two premisses : " No infallible beings are men, All priests are men," which would have given us a syllogism in Figure II. We can construct a syllogism in which M is predicate in the major premiss and subject in the minor premiss. Its shape will be

$$P — M$$
$$M — S$$
$$S — P$$

This is known as the fourth figure. It is said to have been introduced into the traditional doctrine by the famous physician Galen. Most arguments expressed in Figure IV would be more naturally expressed in one of the other figures. But it is not diffi-

the definition of " syllogism " and need not be considered further.

(3) *The middle term must be distributed in one at least of the premisses.* Since it is through the middle term that the connexion between the extreme terms is secured, it is essential that the *same* part of the middle term should be related to both the extreme terms. Violation of this rule is known as the fallacy of *undistributed middle.* The importance of this rule can be illustrated by the following examples.

> If   All musicians are sensitive
> and All poets are sensitive,
> then All poets are musicians,

is an invalid argument, since it does not follow from the premisses that the sensitive people who are musicians are the same as the sensitive people who are poets, or are the same as any of those who are poets.   It may be the case, but the premisses do not justify us in concluding that it is so.

(4) *No term may be distributed in the conclusion unless it was distributed in its own premiss.* Since to distribute a term is to take it in its whole extent, a distributed term refers to every member contained under the term.[1] Then, if a term, given undistributed in its premiss, were distributed in the conclusion, it follows that the conclusion would go beyond the data.   This rule rests upon the fundamental principle that if the data refer to *some only* of a class, no conclusion referring to *every* member of the class can be deduced. Violation of this rule is known as the fallacy of *illicit major*, or of *illicit minor.*

(5) *From two negative premisses no conclusion follows.*   This rule follows from the same consideration as rule 3, viz. that both premisses must refer to the *same* part of the middle term, either by inclusion in both cases, or by inclusion in one case and exclusion in the other. If all that were given were the exclusion of both extremes from the middle, no connexion between the extremes would be established. Thus, if the premisses were : " No popes are infallible " and " No Scotchmen are popes ", no connexion between " those who are infallible " and Scotchmen could be deduced.

(6) (*a*) *If one premiss is negative, the conclusion must be negative.* (*b*) *If the conclusion is negative, one premiss must be negative.*   These rules follow from the same consideration as rule 5.

From these rules three corollaries can be deduced.

Corollaries.   (i) *From two particular premisses no conclusion follows.* There are three cases :

---

[1] It must be remembered that there is no meaning in speaking of the " distribution " of a term, unless the term be a class. See p. 49 above. (Chap. IV).

(a) *Both premisses affirmative.* Since these premisses are *ex hypothesi* particular and affirmative, no term is distributed in either premiss. Hence, the middle term cannot be distributed.

(b) *One affirmative, one negative premiss.* Since both premisses are particular and only one is negative, they distribute between them only one term (viz. the predicate of the negative premiss). But since one is negative, the conclusion must be negative by rule 6 (a). Hence, by rule 4, the major term must be distributed. Also, by rule 3, the middle term must be distributed. Thus two terms must be distributed in these premisses. But only one term is given distributed. Hence, no conclusion follows.

(c) *Both premisses negative.* This case is excluded by rule 5.

(ii) *If one premiss is particular, the conclusion must be particular.* There are again three cases.

(a) *Both premisses affirmative.* Since one is particular and both are affirmative, they distribute between them only one term. This must be the middle term (by rule 3). Hence, no other term can be distributed (by rule 4). But a conclusion with an undistributed subject must be particular.

(b) *One premiss negative, one affirmative.* Since one is particular and one negative, they can distribute between them only two terms. Of these, one must be the middle term (by rule 3) and one the major term (by rule 4) since the conclusion must be negative (by rule 6 (a)). Hence, the minor term cannot be distributed, i.e. the conclusion must be particular.

(c) The same applies to this case as to (c) under (i).

(iii) If the major premiss is particular, the minor premiss cannot be negative.

If the minor premiss were negative, the major premiss must be affirmative. But it is given as particular. It would, therefore, be particular affirmative, and neither of its terms would be distributed. But since the minor is negative, the conclusion must be negative. Hence, by rule 4, the major term must be distributed. But it has just been shown that it cannot be. Hence, the major premiss cannot be particular if the minor is negative.

The rules of the syllogism can be summed up conveniently as follows :

I. *Rules concerning quantity, i.e. distribution.*

The middle term must be distributed once at least, and no term may be distributed in the conclusion unless it was distributed in its premiss.

II. *Rules concerning quality.*

From the negative premisses no conclusion follows. If one premiss is negative, so must the conclusion be ; if the conclusion is negative, so must one premiss be. These are general rules of the

(i) The major premiss cannot be particular, if either premiss is negative. (Violation of this rule would involve illicit major.)

(ii) The minor premiss cannot be particular, if the major premiss is affirmative. (Violation of this rule would involve undistributed middle.)

(iii) The conclusion cannot be universal, if the minor premiss is affirmative. (Violation of this rule would involve illicit minor.)

Valid Moods of Figure IV.

A A I   (Bramantip)
A E E   (Camenes) A E O (weakened conclusion)
E A O   (Fesapo)
E I O   (Fresison)
I A I   (Dimaris).

§ 4. REDUCTION AND THE ANTILOGISM

Since in Aristotle's view the principle now called the *dictum de omni* is the sole principle of syllogistic reasoning, and since it applies directly only to Figure I, he regarded syllogisms expressed in the other figures as indirect moods of the first.   He, therefore, devised a method of reducing syllogisms in Figures II and III to Figure I, either by conversion of the premisses, or by *reductio ad impossible*.[1]   It is no longer supposed that the other figures are less self-evident than the first, so that reduction to Figure I has a merely historical interest. But the method of reduction can be extended so that an argument stated in a given mood or figure can be expressed in some other mood or some other figure.   Any mood can be reduced to any other provided that neither mood contains a weakened conclusion or a strengthened premiss.[2]   By this method the interrelation of the various moods can be clearly exhibited.   We have already given an example of the reduction of a syllogism in Celarent to Cesare.[3] The reduction of syllogisms provides a useful logical exercise, which the beginner in logic often finds amusing.   But the doctrine of reduction has not the importance that was formerly ascribed to it and it will be treated only very briefly here.[4]   It will be convenient

[1] Aristotle's term is ἀπαγωγὴ εἰς τὸ ἀδύνατον.   He puts the matter shortly thus : ' It is clear also that all the imperfect syllogisms are made perfect by means of the first figure.   For all are brought to a conclusion either ostensibly or *per impossibile* ' (*Anal. Priora*, 29a, 30).

[2] A premiss is said to be *strengthened* when the same conclusion could be obtained were its subimplicant substituted for it.   If we accept the modern view that universal propositions are existentially negative whilst particular propositions are existentially affirmative, it follows that syllogisms containing either a strengthened premiss or a weakened conclusion are always invalid.

[3] See p. 85.

[4] The best treatment of *Reduction* will be found in Keynes, *F.L.*, Pt. III, Chap. III.

to treat our syllogisms as arguments, that is, as syllogisms in which
the premisses are asserted to be true and, since the conclusion follows
from them, the conclusion is also asserted to be true.[1] Consequently,
it is best to take a trite example. Suppose, then, we assert,

> All Marxians are Socialists,
> No supporters of Mussolini are Socialists,
> ∴ No supporters of Mussolini are Marxians,

we have a syllogism in *Camestres*. (Figure II.)

If we transpose the premisses, i.e. reverse the major and minor
premisses, and convert the new major premiss, we have

> No Socialists are supporters of Mussolini,
> All Marxians are Socialists,
> ∴ No Marxians are supporters of Mussolini.

This is an example of *Celarent* in Figure I. Its conclusion is
the converse of our original conclusion. Hence, if it be simply
converted the original conclusion is obtained.

In this example we have shown the equivalence of the moods
Celarent and *Camestres*. It is not contended that the mood in
Figure I is superior in self-evidence to the mood in Figure II. Self-
evidence is a psychological notion, and what is self-evident to one
man will not necessarily be self-evident to another. But it is unlikely that any one who failed to see the cogency of the reasoning
in *Camestres* would be more likely to see it in the case of *Celarent*.
The traditional theory of reduction, however, is that it is a *process
of proof*. Its purpose is to show that a syllogism in a figure other
than the first is valid *because* the same (or an equivalent) conclusion
can be obtained from equivalent premisses in Figure I. A syllogism
in Figure I is supposed to be directly tested by reference to the
dictum de omni. The traditional theory does not, therefore, regard
the matter as a question of psychological self-evidence. It must
be granted that the traditional method of deducing the valid
moods of the figures only suffices to show that these moods do
not violate any of the syllogistic rules. In the case of Figure I,
the *dictum de omni* assures us that those moods which do not violate
the syllogistic rules are *valid*. So far we have not formulated any
dicta that would give us the same assurance in the case of the other
figures. The traditional doctrine of reduction results from the lack
of such dicta. Before supplying this deficiency, we shall state the
traditional theory of indirect reduction. We shall here adopt the
convenient symbolism used in Chapter V in the treatment of
immediate inferences.

[1] See Chap. XII for further discussion of the distinction between an
argument and a form of implication.

tion of a general rule to a particular case.[1] Let p stand for a proposition asserting a general rule, either affirmatively or negatively. Let q stand for a proposition asserting that a certain case falls under the rule. Then r stands for a proposition asserting the result of the application of the rule to the case.

For example :

> If All successful authors are conceited. (Rule)
> and Bernard Shaw is a successful author. (Case)
> then Bernard Shaw is conceited. (Result)

If, now, we deny that Bernard Shaw is conceited but admit the rule, we must deny that Bernard Shaw is a successful author. Then we get, *Denial of Result*, combined with *Rule*, yields *Denial of Case*. This will be a syllogism in Figure II.

If, however, we deny that Bernard Shaw is conceited but contend that he is a successful author, we must deny the rule. Then we get, *Denial of Result*, combined with *Case*, yields *Denial of Rule*. This will be a syllogism in Figure III.[2]

Generalizing from these examples we may formulate *dicta* for Figures II and III.

Dictum for Figure II. If every member of a class has (or does not have) a certain property, then any individual or individuals which do not have (or have) that property must be excluded from that class.

Dictum for Figure III. If certain individuals have (or do not have) a certain property, and these individuals are included in a certain class, then not every member of that class does not have (or has) that property.[3]

These *dicta* are self-evident in the same sense in which the *dictum de omni* is self-evident. In the case of each of these *dicta* it is probable that they would be most easily apprehended in the first instance by means of an example stated in explicit terms. But once the principle is seen to be exemplified in a particular case, it can be immediately generalized to cover other cases. Thus we may be

[1] Cf. Sigwart, *Logic*, I, p. 354, and Keynes, *F.L.*, loc. cit.

[2] The student is advised to work these out after the model given in the Antilogism on p. 95.

[3] From these dicta the special rules and valid moods may be directly deduced as follows :

Fig. II. (i) *The major premiss must be universal.* This rule excludes O, I, as major premisses. (ii) One premiss must be negative (since *have* and *have not* alternate). This rule excludes the combinations A A, I A, A I. Hence the valid moods are A E E, A O O, E A E, E I O.

Fig. III. (i) *The minor premiss must be affirmative ;* (ii) *The conclusion must be particular.* Hence, no restriction is placed upon the major premiss, but neither E nor O can be a minor premiss. Accordingly the valid combinations are A A I, I A I, A I I, O A O, E A O, E I O.

said to see the general principle in apprehending the particular
case.[1]

The fourth figure can be similarly dealt with. In this case the
equivalent triads will yield syllogisms all of which are in Figure IV.
Mr. W. E. Johnson has shown how it is possible to construct the
valid moods of this figure from the following antilogism :

' Taking any three classes, it is impossible that
    The first should be wholly included in the second
while The second is wholly excluded from the third
and   The third is partly included in the first.' [2]

The reader who is interested in pursuing this development may be
referred to Mr. Johnson's treatment.

The formulation of the dicta for the first three figures enables
us to see clearly that each figure has a special appropriateness to
a special form of reasoning. The first figure is appropriate to an
argument in which, having granted that a certain property belongs
to every member of a certain class, we recognize an individual as
belonging to that class, and hence conclude that it possesses that
property. It is not necessary that the minor term should be singular ;
it may be a subclass falling within the wider class,[3] as we saw in
the syllogism : " If no men are infallible and all popes are men,
then no popes are infallible." Aristotle called this figure the " scien-
tific figure " ($\sigma\chi\tilde{\eta}\mu\alpha$ $\dot{\varepsilon}\pi\iota\sigma\tau\eta\mu o\nu\iota\kappa\acute{o}\nu$), that is, the figure which gives
us *knowledge*, for knowledge, according to Aristotle, is always of the
essence. From this point of view the middle term is regarded as
giving the *reason why* the major belongs to the minor (or does not
belong). The syllogism is here supposed to be asserting an essential
connexion. Aristotle puts the matter thus : ' Of all figures the
most scientific is the first. Thus, it is the vehicle of the demonstrations of all the mathematical sciences, such as arithmetic, geometry, and optics, and practically of all sciences that investigate
causes : for the syllogism of the reasoned fact is either exclusively
or generally speaking and in most cases in this figure—a second
proof that this figure is most scientific ; for grasp of a reasoned
conclusion is the primary condition of knowledge. Thirdly, the
first is the only figure which enables us to pursue knowledge of the

[1] This is an example of what Mr. W. E. Johnson calls " intuitive induction ". See *Logic*, II, p. 29, and cf. p. 243 below.

[2] *Logic*, II, p. 87. Cf. Keynes, *F.L.*, §§ 266, 272. Mr. Johnson's treatment of the categorical syllogism is much the best treatment from this point
of view. It is, however, so compressed, that it can be profitably studied only
by those who have some acquaintance with the traditional doctrine.

[3] It will be remembered that the traditional Logicians did not distinguish
between these two cases.

7

procedure of reflective thinking, then fallacies of ambiguity must be taken into account. But ambiguity is not a matter of *form*. No one would be taken in by the following argument : " All bishops move only diagonally ; Winnington Ingram is a bishop ; therefore, he moves only diagonally." Yet, according to the traditional treatment, this is a *formally* correct syllogism. There is an unfortunate practice common to the writers of textbooks in logic of using obviously false premisses from which to " deduce " a conclusion that is true. Thus Welton gives the example :

> Lions are herbivorous
> Cows are lions
> ∴ Cows are herbivorous.[1]

Of this, it can only be said, *either* the premisses are intended to be significant, and in that case the conclusion does not follow : *or* the *words* used in the premisses are used merely as symbols, mere M's and S's and P's, and then the conclusion is not *true*, nor false, but is the *implied conclusion*. This consideration leads us to the distinction of validity and truth, with which we shall be concerned in a later chapter. Here it is sufficient to point out that, in so far as the syllogism is treated as a *form of implication*, ambiguity cannot arise ; in so far as it is treated as a means of establishing a true conclusion, which is *asserted* to be true, it is liable to fallacies of ambiguity which cannot be provided against by formal rules.

§ 6. THE USE OF SYMBOLS IN THE TRADITIONAL SYLLOGISM

The rapid development of the science of logic during the last thirty or forty years is undoubtedly mainly due to the systematic employment of symbols and to the consequent invention of a more and more adequate symbolism. With the precise nature of this symbolism and its importance in the development of logic, we shall be concerned in Chapters VIII—X. Here we shall only attempt to determine to what extent the traditional treatment of the syllogism has been symbolic.

What, it may be asked, constitutes a symbolic treatment of a subject ? We saw in Chapter II that all language is symbolic in the sense that, with the exception of purely demonstrative signs, it is a system of arbitrary signs used to signify certain features of a situation that have been abstracted from their context. Thus, the employment of language enables us to abbreviate our references, to indicate more or less unambiguously and precisely, and to refer to what is not sensibly presented. " The sun setting into a bank of clouds signifies a wet day to-morrow." In this sentence the words

[1] Welton and Monahan, *An Intermediate Logic*, p. 214.

written before *signifies* are a set of symbols which abbreviate and abstract from a complex situation in order to connect *it* with another situation, abbreviated and abstracted by means of the words which follow *signifies*. Suppose that we now carry the process of abbreviation further and represent the first set of words by M and the second set by P. Then we get "M signifies P". This is an abstract symbolism of a rule *generalized by means of the symbols employed*. The generality is not so obvious in the case of the verbal symbols, but apart from some degree of generalization there could be no rule.

Language has constantly to abbreviate. If we attempted to employ a phrase that would convey the same meaning as the word "civilization" conveys to the ordinary educated Englishman, the sentences in which it occurs would soon become unmanageable, so that we should be unable to apprehend the sense of what was said. Hence, it is obvious, that in attempting to make explicit the *form* of our reflective thinking, we are forced to employ symbols. Thus, Aristotle in explaining the form of the syllogism found it necessary to use literal symbols. He felt more sure of the validity of his reasoning when he said, "If R belongs to some S and P to all S, P must belong to some R",[1] than would have been the case had he used only concrete examples, such as 'motion', 'awake', 'animal'.[2] He employed symbols *to test the validity* of his reasoning by exhibiting its *form*. It is this that constitutes a symbolic treatment of the syllogism. As Boole has pointed out, 'The canonical forms of the Aristotelian syllogism are really symbolical; only the symbols are less perfect of their kind than those of mathematics. If they are employed to test the validity of an argument, they as truly supersede the exercise of reason, as does a reference to a formula of analysis.'[3] The use of symbols involves abbreviation, abstraction, emphasis upon form. This is the first essential of symbolism—*to express form*. To the extent to which the traditional treatment of the syllogism is *formal*, to that extent it is *symbolic*. Hence we shall find that the increasing generality in the treatment of logic, characteristic of modern times, is the development of the treatment begun by Aristotle.

The purpose of the Aristotelian treatment of logic is to reduce the multiform expressions of ordinary reflective thinking into one standard form of expression for the sole purpose of testing their validity. This emphasis upon form constitutes the value of the *theory* of the syllogism. The further attempt to reduce these various, and in fact irreducible, forms of expression to *one* form is the cause of the comparative sterility of Aristotelian logic. In this lies its

---

[1] *Anal. Priora*, 28*b*, 12.   [2] loc. cit., 38*b*, 1.
[3] *The Mathematical Analysis of Logic* (1847), p. 11.

main weakness. This defect is largely the result of the imperfect development of the symbols, since Aristotle, relying too much upon accidental linguistic forms, saw no necessity to symbolize the *relations* holding between the terms of the syllogism. But we cannot argue from sameness of grammatical form to sameness of logical form; hence, we cannot assume that sentences in which the *connecting verb* is the same express the same *logical relation*. Couturat has said that ' the invention of the verb *to be* is one of the conquests of the logical spirit ',[1] Mr. Russell, on the contrary, has asserted that the use of " is " to express both predication and identity ' is a disgrace to the human race '.[2] There is some truth in both these statements, as we shall see later. Here we are concerned only to point out that both lay stress upon the importance of a symbol as expressing form by reason of its abstractness. Aristotle's employment of symbols is the earliest attempt to formulate the conditions of validity in reasoning.

We conclude this chapter on the syllogism with the reflection that, absurd as are some of the traditional technicalities, and lamentable as its defective analysis is, yet the traditional syllogism is *one* important form of reasoning. Mr. Johnson has summed up admirably the value of the study of the traditional syllogism. He says : ' Syllogism is practically important because it represents the form in which persons unschooled in logical technique are continually arguing. It is theoretically important because it exhibits in their simplest guise the fundamental principles which underlie all demonstration whether deductive or inductive. It is *educationally* important because the establishment of its valid moods and the systematization and co-ordination of its rules afford an exercise of thought not inferior and in some respects superior to that afforded by elementary mathematics.' [3]

On all three counts, the traditional syllogism retains its value. But it is no longer possible to regard it as constituting the whole subject of deduction.[4]

[1] " Principles of Logic ", *Ency. Philos. Sciences*, I, p. 196.
[2] *Introd. Math. Philos.*, p. 172.
[3] W. E. J., Pt. II, p. 102.
[4] Other deductive forms will be dealt with in Chaps. VII and X. The general principles of deduction will be discussed in Chaps. XII and XXIV.

CHAPTER VII

COMPOUND ARGUMENTS AND IRREGULAR SYLLOGISMS

'I have found you an argument : but I am not obliged to find you an understanding.'—*Samuel Johnson*.

§ 1. THE MODI

IN this section we shall be concerned with a form of inference —of common occurrence in everyday life—in which from the conjunction of a composite premiss with a simple premiss a simple conclusion is inferred. We may begin by giving illustrations taken from ordinary experience in which this mode of reasoning is employed.

Example I. Two people on the seashore may both be observing a small black object bobbing up and down on the water. One says : " That must be a seal " ; the other replies : " No, I am sure it is the cork attached to a lobster-pot line." After some time has passed, they notice the object again, and the second one says : " It can't be a seal, for it has kept in the same place for a long time." The first replies : " Well, then, it must be a lobster-pot cork."

This argument can be analysed as follows :

(1) " If that object remains in the same place for some time, it cannot be a seal ;

But, it has remained in the same place for some time ;

Therefore, it cannot be a seal."

(2) " Either it is a seal or the cork of a lobster-pot line ;

But it is not a seal ;

Therefore, it is the cork of a lobster-pot line."

In (1) the first premiss is a composite premiss of the implicative form ; the second premiss is a simple proposition which affirms the implicans of the implicative premiss ; the conclusion is a simple premiss which affirms the implicate. It is obvious that this inference is valid.

In (2) the first premiss is a composite proposition of the alternative form ; the second premiss is a simple proposition in which one of the alternants is denied ; the conclusion is a simple proposition in which the other alternant is affirmed. It is obvious that this inference is valid.

Example II. " You cannot maintain that capital punishment is an effective deterrent to would-be murderers, and yet also admit that most murders are committed under circumstances which prevent

103

an adequate consideration of consequences.[1]   But you do admit the latter ; hence you must admit that capital punishment is not an effective deterrent.   Moreover, if capital punishment were an effective deterrent, there would have been an increase in the number of murders, over a period of years, in those countries which have abolished the death penalty.   But this has been shown to be not the case.   Hence, capital punishment is not an effective deterrent."

In this discussion two different sets of circumstances are said to involve the conclusion that " capital punishment is not an effective deterrent ".   The argument can be analysed as follows :

(A) Not both : capital punishment is an effective deterrent and also, most murders are committed in circumstances in which adequate consideration of consequences is prevented ;

But,   Most murders are committed in such circumstances ;

Therefore, Capital punishment is not an effective deterrent.

(B) If capital punishment were an effective deterrent, its abolition would have been followed by an increase in the number of murders ;

But,   Its abolition has not been followed by such an increase ;

Therefore, Capital punishment is not an effective deterrent.

It is obvious that the inference both in (A) and in (B) is valid.

Example III.   " If you hate your father, you will dream that you tried to murder him.   But you did dream that you tried to murder him, so that you must hate him."

Example IV.   " I knew that if I looked at the new moon through glass, I should be unlucky ; but I didn't, so I shall not be unlucky."

Example V.   " To get a good position in the Civil Service, one must either be very clever or else have influential friends.   But as he has influential friends, it follows that he is not very clever."

The last three examples are obviously invalid inferences.

We can now state formally the nature of the reasoning that is intended in arguments of these kinds.   In each case we shall add the traditional Latin name of the form.

COMPOUND MODES.

1. *Modus ponendo ponens.*[2]

If p, then q.   Implicative premiss.

p.   Simple premiss affirming implicans.

$\therefore q$.   Simple conclusion affirming implicate.

---

[1] See R. Calvert, *Capital Punishment*, p. 59.   In these examples we are not, of course, concerned to maintain that the premisses are *true*, since we are investigating the relation between premisses and conclusion.   We are, however, considering these inferences as forms of argument in which the premisses are supposed to have been *granted*.

[2] These barbarous names are derived from the Latin verbs : *ponere* = to assert ; *tollere* = to deny.   Hence, they can be interpreted as follows : (1) The mood which by affirming, affirms ; (2) The mood which by denying, denies ; (3) The mood which by denying, affirms ; (4) The mood which by affirming, denies.

2. *Modus tollendo tollens.*

If p, then q.	Implicative premiss.
not q.	Simple premiss denying implicate.
$\therefore$ not p.	Simple conclusion denying implicans.

3. *Modus tollendo ponens.*

Either p or q.	Alternative premiss.
not p.	Simple premiss denying one alternative.
$\therefore q$.	Simple conclusion affirming other alternative.

4. *Modus ponendo tollens.*

Not both p and q.	Disjunctive premiss.
q.	Simple premiss affirming one disjunct.
$\therefore$ not p.	Simple conclusion denying other disjunct.

There are two forms with an implicative premiss but only one form with an alternative premiss and only one with a disjunctive premiss. This difference is due to the fact that, as we saw in Chapter V, the order in which the simple premisses occur in the alternative and in the disjunctive proposition is indifferent, but this is not the case with the implicative premiss.[1] Hence, there are two forms according to whether the simple premiss is the affirmation of the implicans, or the denial of the implicate. If the implicans were denied, it could not be inferred that the implicate could be denied; if the implicate were affirmed, it could not be inferred that the implicans could be affirmed.[2] For, if we could treat the implicans and the implicate in the same way, it would follow that they could be simply interchanged.

The rules for these modes of inference can be stated as follows:

1. *Ponendo ponens.* From the affirmation of the implicans, the affirmation of the implicate follows.

2. *Tollendo tollens.* From the denial of the implicate, the denial of the implicans follows.

3. *Tollendo ponens.* From the denial of one alternant, the affirmation of the other alternant follows.

4. *Ponendo tollens.* From the affirmation of one disjunct, the denial of the other disjunct follows.

It will be seen that in Example III, the inference is invalid since the implicate has been affirmed. This conclusion could be drawn only if the implicate could follow *from no other premiss* than the implicans. In that case, the composite premiss could be stated in

---

[1] See Chap. V, § 3.

[2] Since the traditional name for the implicans is " antecedent ", and for the implicate " consequent ", this fallacy is known as the fallacy of *affirming the consequent.*

I. CONSTRUCTIVE DILEMMA.
 (A) *Simple*.
   If p, then q; and if r, then q,
     But either p or r,
     $\therefore q$.
 (B) *Complex*.
   If p, then q; and if r, then n,
     But either p or r,
     $\therefore$ either q or n.
II. DESTRUCTIVE DILEMMA.
 (A) *Simple*.
     If p, then q; and if p, then r,
       But either not-q or not-r,
       $\therefore$ not p.
 (B) *Complex*.
     If p, then q; and if r, then n,
       But either not-q or not-n,
       $\therefore$ either not p or not r.

It is obvious that the rules for the three modes of implicative and alternative arguments apply to the dilemma, and they need not be restated.

The dilemma is sometimes regarded as a peculiarly fallacious mode of argument. This, however, is not due to its form, but to the difficulty of finding premisses which are true and yet fulfil the conditions of the form. It is obvious that, regarded as an argument to establish the truth of the conclusion, the force of the dilemmatic situation presented in the alternative premiss depends upon the condition that the alternants must be *exhaustive*. If there is a third alternative, then we can "escape between the horns of the dilemma".

Thus, an elderly pessimist, hurrying along a slippery road to catch a train at a country station, might formulate the situation to himself in the form of the following dilemma :

"If I run and slip, then I can't get to the station in time; and If I don't run, I can't get to the station in time ;
 But either I must run and slip or I must not run ;
 Hence, I cannot get to the station in time.

Granted the truth of his premisses, he may still have overlooked the fact that the train may be late.

A dilemma is said to be *rebutted* if another dilemma is constructed which leads to a conclusion contradictory of the first. A dilemma is said to be *taken by the horns* when the alternatives are accepted, but the implications drawn from them are denied. These picturesque modes of argument have no logical significance.[1]

---

[1] Those who desire to be supplied with concrete illustrations of all these various forms and devices, are referred to Joseph, op. cit., Chap. XVI.

* § 3. POLYSYLLOGISMS

A polysyllogism is a series of syllogisms in which the conclusion of one is a premiss of the next. In such a series, the syllogism whose conclusion becomes a premiss in the next syllogism is called a *prosyllogism*; a syllogism one of whose premisses is the conclusion of a preceding syllogism is called an *episyllogism*. If the series contains more than one syllogism, then every syllogism except the first and the last, will be both an episyllogism and a prosyllogism.

The Sorites. A sorites is a polysyllogism in which only the final conclusion is stated, and which is so arranged that any two successive premisses contain a common term.

Two forms are commonly recognized :

(1) *The Aristotelian Sorites.* The minor premiss is stated first, and the term common to two successive premisses occurs first as predicate and then as subject.

$$\text{All A is B}$$
$$\text{All B is C}$$
$$\text{All C is D}$$
$$\text{All D is E}$$
$$\therefore \text{ All A is E.}$$

The special rules of the Aristotelian Sorites are : [1]

(i) Only one premiss, namely the last, can be negative. (Violation of this rule would involve two negative premisses in one of the constituent syllogisms.)

(ii) Only one premiss, namely the first, can be particular. (Violation of this rule would involve undistributed middle.)

(2) *The Goclenian Sorites.* [2] The major premiss is stated first, and the term common to the two successive premisses occurs first as subject and then as predicate.

$$\text{All D is E}$$
$$\text{All C is D}$$
$$\text{All B is C}$$
$$\text{All A is B}$$
$$\therefore \text{ All A is E.}$$

The special rules of the Goclenian Sorites.

(i) Only one premiss—namely the first—can be negative.

(ii Only one premiss—namely the last—can be particular.

---

[1] The student can easily prove these rules for himself. He may find it advisable to set out the series of syllogisms as a whole, supplying the missing conclusion in each case. There is a full discussion of the various forms in which Sorites can be stated, in Keynes, *F.L.*, §§ 325–6.

[2] So called after Goclenius, who is said to have introduced this form.

the interchange of relatum and referent gives the converse of the original relation. It is convenient to symbolize a relational proposition involving two terms by "$x \, \mathrm{R} \, y$". Here x stands for the referent, y for the relatum, R for the relation. We can sum up what we have just been saying as follows : If x and y are any two terms between which the relation R holds, in the direction $x \dashrightarrow y$, then there is some relation (call it R') which holds between y and x, in the direction $y \dashrightarrow x$. Thus R' will be the converse of R.

Classification of relations. I. Symmetrical and non-symmetrical relations. Some relations are such that if they hold between x and y, they also hold between y and x. For example, *married to, equals, different from, spouse of, cousin of, brother or sister of.* Such relations are called *symmetrical.* The interchanging of the terms does not involve any change in the relation. Thus, "This colour is different from that colour" has for its converse, "That colour is different from this colour"; "A equals B" has for its converse "B equals A"; "Tom is as tall as Jane" has for its converse "Jane is as tall as Tom".

Some relations are such that if they hold between x and y, they either never, or sometimes do not, hold between y and x. Such relations are called *non-symmetrical.* The more important set of *non-symmetrical* relations are those which are such that they *cannot* hold between y and x if they hold between x and y. These relations have been named by Mr. Russell *asymmetrical* relations. For example, *greater than, father of, wife of, precedes, older by one year than, darker than.* The converse of "This patch of colour is darker than that" is "That patch of colour is lighter than this"; the converse of "A is the wife of B" is "B is the husband of A"; the converse of "The battle of Marengo preceded the peace of Villafranca" is "The peace of Villafranca succeeded the battle of Marengo". The distinction between symmetrical and asymmetrical relations is very important. These relations may be formally defined as follows :

A relation R is symmetrical when it is such that, if $x \, \mathrm{R} \, y$, then also $y \, \mathrm{R} \, x$.

A relation R is asymmetrical when it is such that, if $x \, \mathrm{R} \, y$, then never $y \, \mathrm{R} \, x$.

There are some relations which hold between x and y, and sometimes hold between y and x, but sometimes do not. These relations are often called *non-symmetrical.* For example, *implies, friend of, benefactor of, hates.* These relations will not be further discussed here. [1]

II. Transitive and non-transitive relations. This classification is based upon the consideration of pairs of objects with reference to some given relation R.

Some relations are such that, if they hold between x and y, and

[1] For a further discussion of *Relations,* see Chap. X, § 2.

between y and z, then they hold between x and z. Such relations are called *transitive*. For example, *equals, greater than, contemporary with, richer than, matching in colour*.

Some relations are such that if they hold between x and y, and between y and z, they either never, or sometimes do not hold between x and z. In the former case they are called *intransitive relations*, in the latter case, *non-transitive*. Examples of intransitive relations are, *father of, older by one year, twin of, married to*. Examples of *non-transitive* relations are, *different from, friend of*.

These relations may be formally defined as follows :

A relation R is transitive when it is such that if x R y and y R z, then x R z.

A relation R is intransitive when it is such that if x R y and y R z, then never x R z.

A relation R is non-transitive when it is such that if x R y and y R z, then sometimes x R z, and sometimes not x R z.

On the basis of these classifications relations may be divided into four classes according as they do, or do not, possess the properties of *symmetry* and *transitiveness*. It is important to remember that these properties are independent, so that relations can be symmetrical and either transitive or intransitive ; asymmetrical and either transitive or intransitive. These will be summed up with examples as follows :

1. *Symmetrical transitive relations :* identical with ; exactly matching in colour ; exactly matching in shape ; exactly the same in age ; simultaneous with.

It will be noticed that relations of this class have the characteristics of *equality*. That is to say, transitive, symmetrical relations have the formal properties of *equality*.

2. *Symmetrical intransitive relations :* spouse of ; twin of.

3. *Asymmetrical transitive relations :* greater than ; ancestor of ; hotter than ; above ; before.

4. *Asymmetrical intransitive relations :* father of ; grandchild of.

In defining a transitive relation we said that it is such that given that the relation holds between two terms and between one of these and a third term, then that relation holds between the other term and the third term. We see, then, that transitivity is sufficient to secure a valid inference. Consider the following examples :

I.   If   A is greater than B,
     and B is greater than C,
     then A is greater than C.

II.   If   A equals B,
     and B equals C,
     then A equals C.

8

A substitute sign takes the place of what it stands for. It is merely *representative*. Such signs can only occur when there are fixed rules of manipulation, or operation, derived from the nature of their referends. Professor Stout uses the word "meaning" for what a sign signifies. In his language we can say that an expressive sign *expresses* a meaning; a suggestive sign *suggests* a meaning which it does not express; a substitute sign is a *substitute for meaning*. He thus sums up the distinction: 'A word is an instrument for thinking about the meaning it expresses; a substitute sign is a means of *not* thinking about the meaning which it symbolizes.' [1] In accordance with the distinction we made between sign and symbol, it is clear that only non-verbal symbols can be substitute signs. It might be supposed that we should never want to use symbols so as not to think about their referends. But that would be a mistake. We shall see that long and complicated trains of reasoning, such as those involved in mathematics, would be impossible without the aid afforded by a symbolism which can be manipulated in accordance with rules of operation so as to reduce intelligent thinking to a minimum.

In Chapter II we saw that language is not only ambiguous but also necessarily vague. Its usefulness, for ordinary purposes, depends upon this fact, that it is necessarily vague. It is consequently insusceptible of precise analysis. It confuses those distinctions upon which exact reasoning is based, and is often simple where the ideas expressed are complex. Since language [2] is developed under the pressure of man's practical needs, and is primarily the means of expressing the emotional side of his nature, it is clear, first, that language must be employed to express an immense variety of different experiences; secondly, that the same language-forms must sometimes be used to express what is in fact different; thirdly, that language is ill-adapted to express what is relatively abstract and logically simple. It follows that language would be hindered in its normal function were its analysis carried further than is required by the ordinary usages of everyday life. For example, we want to indicate to a thirsty man: "Here is water; drink this"; to a man overwhelmed by some tragic happening: "There is something good in life; hold on to the good bits." We are not only not concerned to know whether, or not, the word "is" expresses the same in these two cases; we should be hindered in our practical expression were we unable to use the same word. Consider, for example, the sentences "Hildebrand is a man", "All popes are men", "Some soldiers are patriotic", "Shakespeare is the author of *Hamlet*".

---

[1] loc. cit., p. 194.
[2] Throughout the rest of this chapter, we shall use "language" to mean "ordinary language", i.e. non-symbolic language.

These sentences have the same grammatical form, but, as we have already indicated, their logical analysis reveals that they express propositions that are of fundamentally different forms. The verb to be expresses indifferently *existence, predication, identity, equality*, e.g. " God is ", " Socrates is wise ", " Two and two are four ", " There were giants in those days ", " Men are fallible ".

It would seem, then, that language is misleading and that grammatical analysis is an unreliable guide to logical form. Owing to the practical function of language the ordinary languages of civilized people are well-suited to express complicated facts briefly, but are ill-adapted to express simply what is logically simple. For example, " That table-cloth is dirty " expresses briefly and clearly an extremely complicated state of affairs. Again, " That is a clock ", " One is a number " express briefly what, on analysis, is discovered to be extremely complicated. Moreover, they are of the same grammatical form. But the slightest reflection reveals that the relation of the referend of " that " to the referend of " a clock " is totally different from the relation of the referend of " one " to the referend of " a number ". To bring out this difference using ordinary language involves considerable prolixity, as the preceding sentence—which merely states the need for analysis—suggests. If we were to try to be logically precise and yet to employ ordinary language, we should soon be lost in a maze of words. This can be more briefly illustrated by a very simple example. Compare the following two expressions :

(1) " $x + y = y + x$."

(2) " If a second number be added to any given number the result is the same as if the first given number had been added to the second." [1]

Any one who understands the algebraic signs ' $+$ ' and ' $=$ ', will have no difficulty in understanding the first expression. Indeed, as thus expressed, it seems so simple that the ordinary man would regard the statement as unimportant and obvious. But the second expression is prolix. It requires a greater effort of attention to grasp what it means than was the case with the first expression. It is the *logical simplicity* of the notions involved that makes their expression in language so cumbersome. For the purposes of logic language is insufficiently analytic. Moreover, language only abstracts to the degree in which what is abstract interests the plain man. Abstraction presupposes analysis. The analysis of a complex situation involves its resolution into simple elements. An element is simple either when it is not susceptible of further analysis—in which case it will be *ultimately simple*—or when it is not necessary for the

---

[1] This formulation is taken from A. N. Whitehead, *Introduction to Mathematics*, p. 61. The whole of Chap. V in this book, from which this statement is taken, may be read with great advantage by the elementary student.

the symbols M, P, S, are illustrative symbols. They can be replaced by any terms that would make sense so as to give a particular example of a syllogism in Fig. I. An illustrative symbol is thus an arbitrarily chosen letter of the alphabet standing, not for some one definite object, but for any of a set of objects indicated by the context. We used such symbols in explaining immediate inferences ; thus *All S is P* was taken as standing for *any* universal affirmative proposition. "*S a P*" combines both illustrative and shorthand symbols, since "*a*" is shorthand for "universal affirmative proposition", whilst "S" and "P" are illustrative symbols. We saw in Chapter VI that Aristotle used such symbols in order to bring out the dependence of the validity of a syllogism upon its form.

In Chapter IV we saw that the distinction between different kinds of propositions is a distinction between different propositional forms. We pointed out that *form* is a generalized conception that it is not easy to express simply. The use of symbols enables us to exhibit form. For this reason, following the example of Aristotle, we used symbols when we were considering the syllogism, since we wanted to consider, not *popes*, *saints*, etc., nor particular men such as *Hildebrand*, etc., but only the *form of implication*. Again, in considering the relations between propositions we were concerned not with determinate examples of propositions but with their form. Thus we used p, q, r, for simple propositions, constructing compound propositions out of these, e.g. *If p, then q*. Here p, q stand for *any* simple propositions. These are, then, illustrative symbols. The verbal form "*If . . . then . . .*" expresses the form of the proposition ; it will remain unchanged whatever simple propositions we substitute for p and q. Symbols which express *form* will be called *logical constants*.[1] Some shorthand symbols are used for logical constants, e.g. $\supset$, *ent*. An arbitrary mark such as $\supset$ or $+$ is an ideographic symbol. The advantage of the ideograms is evident. They are compact so that by means of ideograms it is often possible to present at a glance a formula that would otherwise be lengthy in expression. We saw the advantage of such compactness in the case of the simple expression $x + y = y + x$. In dealing with propositions of considerable complexity some device to economize mental effort is necessary in order that we should be able to grasp complicated trains of reasoning. Any one who has reflected upon the processes of thought involved in working out a complicated mathematical theorem will admit that some economy of thought is indispensable in practice. We shall see later how the

---

[1] The expression " logical constant " is often used by symbolic logicians to mean what is symbolized, not the symbol. This seems to me to be a mistake and to lead to confusion. Hence, by " logical constant " I mean the *symbol* that *symbolizes* the form.

use of such symbols enables us to formulate precise rules of transformation which simplify the process of reasoning.   As Prof. Whitehead puts it : ' Operations of thought are like cavalry charges in a battle—they are strictly limited in number, they require fresh horses, and must only be made at decisive moments.' [1]

Logical symbolism has, then, two important functions to perform. It economizes thought, and thus makes possible the development of complicated inferences.   Secondly, by means of appropriate symbols form can be adequately revealed ; hence, generality can be attained. For this purpose two different kinds of symbols are required : shorthand symbols and illustrative symbols.   There are three important characteristics that every satisfactory logical symbolism must possess : (1) conciseness ; (2) precision ; (3) systematization.   The nature and importance of these characteristics will become clearer as we proceed.   It may be said that, while the first characteristic is rendered necessary by the limitations of human thinking, the latter two are dependent upon the nature of logic.

§ 2. ILLUSTRATIONS FROM THE SYMBOLISM OF MATHEMATICS [2]

Every one will admit that, as a matter of practical experience, it is much easier to work out a sum in addition if the Arabic notation be used instead of the clumsy Roman numerals.   Any one not convinced of this has only to make the trial with, say, three rows each representing numbers of a million odd.   Roman numerals are clumsy to write ; they cannot easily be taken in at a glance ; they represent an incomplete analysis of the notions they express. The Arabic notation, on the other hand, is concise ; hence, it can be easily comprehended ; its form represents precisely the notions to be expressed.   The notation 0, 1, 2, . . . 10, 11, . . . 100, 101 . . . 1,000, 1,001 . . . and so on, is immediately significant.   By means of ten differently shaped symbols and a system of placing them which makes their value dependent upon their positions, even very large numbers can be easily comprehended.   It will not be necessary here to explain the system, acquaintance with which may be taken for granted.   But two points are worthy of notice.   First, by means of the ten symbols, 0, 1, 2, 3, 4, 5, 6, 7, 8, 9, and the device of placing them in juxtaposition, *any* number can be symbolized.

[1] Whitehead, op. cit., p. 61.

[2] This section is inserted as the student will be familiar with the practical use of symbols in mathematics, and may thus be aided in understanding the importance of a satisfactory symbolism.   The student may be referred to A. N. Whitehead, *Science and the Modern World*, Chap. II ; *An Introduction to Mathematics* ; and to G. H. Hardy, *Pure Mathematics*.   From these writers everything of importance in this section has been derived.   See also M. Cantor, *Geschichte der Mathematik*, Vol. I.

we started with the set A, B, or with the set C, D, E. It is important to emphasize this. We are so familiar with these operations that we do not realize how difficult it must have been for primitive men to discover these characteristics. The symbolism has made the operation easy. Further, a considerable degree of abstraction is required before it is possible to grasp that we can compare not only two sets of apples with regard to their number but any set of objects with any other set. As Professor Whitehead puts it : ' During a long period, groups of fishes will have been compared to each other in respect to their multiplicity ; and groups of days to each other. But the first man who noticed the analogy between a group of seven fishes and a group of seven days made a notable advance in the history of thought. He was the first man who entertained a concept belonging to the science of pure mathematics.' [1]

Multiplication is repeated addition. We want to find, say, the number of a set of apples taken three times over. Suppose the set consists of A and B. Then we put A, B, against 1, 2 ; we repeat and put A, B, against 3, 4 ; we repeat and put A, B, against 5, 6. The result is the same as the product of 3 and 2. It is not necessary to pursue this method further. It will easily be seen that subtraction is the inverse operation to addition, and division the inverse operation to multiplication. But it is important to note that we have throughout made certain assumptions about the order in which we have taken the objects. We can now formulate these. Let us take any three numbers at random, say, 2, 5, 8. We assume that we have reached the stage at which the symbol $+$ is used for *addition*, and $\times$ for *multiplication*. Then we have :

(1) $2 + 5 = 5 + 2$.
(2) $2 \times 5 = 5 \times 2$.
(3) $2 + (5 + 8) = (2 + 5) + 8$.
(4) $2 \times (5 \times 8) = (2 \times 5) \times 8$.
(5) $(2 + 5) \times 8 = (2 \times 8) + (5 \times 8)$.

We took these numbers, 2, 5, 8, *at random*. That is to say, it did not matter what number we took. That is, we can take *any* number. But 2, 5, 8 are symbols for three different definite numbers. It will obviously be more convenient if we invent a symbolism that can stand for *any* number. The letters of the alphabet provide a convenient set of symbols ready to hand. Instead, therefore, of saying " $2 + 5 = 5 + 2$, and this will be true if we take *other* numbers than 2 and 5 ", we say " let x and y be *any* two numbers, then $x + y = y + x$ ". Here x and y stand, not for any *definite* number, but for any one of a certain set, namely, the set of numbers. We make a similar use of symbols when we say, " If M is P and S is M,

[1] *Science and the Modern World*, p. 29 (1st impression).

then S is P ", since S, M, P, stand respectively for *any* terms occurring as middle, major, and minor terms in a syllogism. The conception represented by such symbols is perfectly familiar, and it is of great importance. Such a symbol is called a *variable*. The definite objects that can be substituted for the variable, so as to make sense in a given expression, are called the *values of the variable*. The importance of this notion will be discussed in the next section. It cannot be understood apart from the notion of a function.

The importance of a good notation, i.e. of a systematic set of symbols, can be illustrated from the history of the symbols employed in the differential calculus. It will be remembered that the calculus was discovered at approximately the same time, but independently, by Newton and by Leibniz. A controversy arose as to which had the priority. Their fellow-countrymen took sides and had an unprofitable quarrel. Now, although Leibniz and Newton were concerned with the same notions, they invented different notations. The superiority of Leibniz's notation to Newton's is now admitted by every one. But at first the English mathematicians refused to adopt Leibniz's notation. They were consequently hindered in their work by having to employ a cumbersome notation which concealed the important concepts. During the following century no important mathematical discovery is to be attributed to an English mathematician, whereas on the Continent, where Leibniz's notation was used, rapid progress was made. It seems not unreasonable to suppose that the English mathematicians suffered from their use of a less satisfactory notation. It may indeed be said that an adequate symbolism is indispensable for the development of mathematics, for an adequate set of symbols both presupposes analysis of the fundamental ideas and is an aid to further analysis. By the employment of symbols used systematically expressions that appear to be of different forms can be so expressed that they are easily seen to be of the same form. For example :

(1) $x + y = 1$,
(2) $x + 2y = 2x + 3y - 1$,
(3) $4 = 2x^2 + 3x + 2$,
(4) $2 - 3x = 2x^2$,

appear to be four expressions all of different forms. If, however, they are re-expressed so that the variable symbols and the numerical symbols are all put on one side of " = " and the whole expression is equated to 0, we have :

(1) $x + y - 1 = 0$.
(2) $x + y - 1 = 0$.
(3) $2x^2 + 3x - 2 = 0$.
(4) $2x^2 + 3x - 2 = 0$.

The examples in set (C) could be regarded as having been obtained from the consideration of any number that is half some other number. Thus (1) can be expressed $4 = \frac{1}{2}(8)$; (2) can be expressed $5 = \frac{1}{2}(10)$, and so on. If we symbolize the first number by "y" we can express the number to which y is said to be equal as "half some other number". Then "some other number" can be symbolized by "x" and the expression becomes "$y = \frac{1}{2}x$". Accordingly, if we substitute for x some one definite number we know what number y is, namely, half that number. Here "x" and "y" are variables; "$= \frac{1}{2}$" is a logical constant. Now, if we think of the expression "$y = \frac{1}{2}x$" as merely symbolizing the form of the five propositions in set (C), then "x" and "y" are illustrative symbols related in the specific way expressed by the logical constant "$= \frac{1}{2}$". If, however, we regard the expression "$y = \frac{1}{2}x$" as expressing a determinate correspondence between the variables "x" and "y" such that when the value of x is given the value of y is thereby determined, then "$y = \frac{1}{2}x$" expresses a functional relation. The variable y is said to be in functional dependence upon the variable x; hence y is called the dependent variable, x is called the independent variable. This notion of functional dependence is of the greatest importance in mathematics.[1] The general notion of a function may be symbolized by "$y = f(x)$", or "$y = g(x)$", etc., where f, g, or any letter written outside the bracket signifies an undetermined, i.e. a variable, function of x. Sometimes x is called the *argument* of the function ; y is called the *value of the function*.[2] Thus in $y = f(x)$, y is the value of some undetermined function of the argument x. Familiar examples of functions are $y = x^2$, $y = 2x^2 + 3x + 1$, $y = \sin x$, $y = \log x$. It is often possible to represent a functional relation by a graph.

We have so far illustrated the notion of a variable by a functional relation between numbers. But there is no need thus to restrict the notion. It is accordingly desirable so to define *variable* and *function* as to avoid this restriction. It is to be observed that the variable represents any one of a set, or class. We may use the word "element" for a *member of a class*, which enables us to use the latter notion as widely as possible. A variable can, then, be defined as follows : *A variable is a symbol which denotes any one of a class of elements.* The notion of functional relation in its most general form is the notion of determinate correspondence in abstraction from the specific mode of such correspondence. The specifica-

---

[1] The student who is quite unfamiliar with the notion of a *functional relation* should refer to Chap. XVIII, § 2 below.

[2] It must be noticed that we speak both of substituting *values for the variables* (e.g. substituting 10 for x in $y = \frac{1}{2}x$), and of the *value* of the value of the function (e.g. 5 in the given example).

tion of the mode of correspondence is given by a rule (or a set of rules) such that the value of the dependent variable corresponding to each value of the independent variable is thereby determined. The class represented by the variable y may be called the *referents*, the class represented by the variable x may be called the *relata*, of the functional relation. A dependent variable may be determined by two independent variables. For example, the temperature of a gas is a function of its pressure and volume. It is not essential to the functional relation that y, the dependent variable, should be determined for every value of x, the independent variable ; nor that to each value of x for which y is given there should correspond one and only one value of y, for x may determine a set of values of y. It is necessary, then, to distinguish between *one-valued* and *many-valued* functions. These may be defined as follows :

A variable y is a *one-valued function* of a variable x when there is a relation of correspondence between the class represented by x and the class represented by y such that every value of x uniquely determines a value of y.

A variable y is a *many-valued function* of a variable x when there is a relation of correspondence between the class represented by x and the class represented by y such that every value of x determines a set of values of y.

It is not necessary for our purpose to discuss the different kinds of functions, but it is important to observe that these definitions do not restrict the classes represented by the variables to classes of numbers. What is most important is to be clear with regard to the use of the variable. A satisfactory definition of *the variable* presupposes the notion of *any*. It is not possible to discuss this here.[1] Frege suggested that the variable keeps *an empty place* which must be filled in by an element of the class represented by the variable in order that the expression in which the variable occurs may be completed.[2] This statement does not, however secure the condition that wherever the same letter occurs the same value shall be substituted. Thus we should not be able to distinguish between " $3x^2 + x$ " and " $3x^2 + y$ ". What is required is the notion of *any one* of a certain class defined by the function. That is to say, a variable represents *any one, but not a determinate one*, of a set of elements, the set being defined by the specific functional relation.

In the most general sense, every expression which contains two or more variables may be called a *function*. We must now consider the specific form of function called by Mr. Russell a *propositional function*. It is advisable to begin by attempting to understand what exactly Mr. Russell means by a propositional function, and then

---

[1] See Russell, *Principles of Mathematics*, Chap. VIII.

[2] Frege, *Ueber Begriff und Gegenstand*. Cf. Couturat. Op. cit., p. 148.

9

may have many different descriptions, just as the *same* man may have many different descriptions applicable to him. For example, *the number* 2 may be described by "the only even prime", "the square root of 4", "the sum of 1 and 1"; Edward VII may be described by "the successor of Queen Victoria", "the King of England in 1905", and so on. In the mathematical function $y = \log x$, y is, we have seen, *the value of the function*, and if 3 be substituted for x, then *the value of the value of the function is* ·4771 . . .

We must now consider a propositional function, e.g. "$\hat{x}$ is hurt". If we substitute a determinate value, e.g. "this boy" for "x", we get the proposition *This boy is hurt*. In this case, then, we have a proposition, not a description, for it is clear that *This boy is hurt* is either true, or false, and does not describe anything. Hence, in the case of a propositional function there is nothing analogous to the term described in the case of the mathematical function. Frege, however, supposed that there was. A brief consideration of his view may enable us to see exactly in what respect the two kinds of functions we have been discussing differ. He thought that every proposition was a description which described either *the true* or *the false*. Thus he held that "$2^2 = 4$" and "$3 > 2$" both describe *the true*, just as "2^2" describes 4.[1] Hence, the functional expression "$x^2 = 4$" would have in Frege's view only two values, namely, *the true* for one argument, viz. 2, *the false* for all other arguments, viz. 1^2, 3^2, 4^2, etc. This view certainly seems to be mistaken. It is bound up with a theory with regard to "meaning" and "denoting" that cannot be discussed here.[2] But it is worth while to notice Frege's view because, if it were correct, then propositional functions would be exactly analogous to mathematical functions. If Frege's view were correct, we could write "$y = x$ is hurt", and then y would be the dependent variable, just as in "$y = \log x$". In the case of the propositional function, "y" could have only *two* values, namely, *the true*, and *the false*. These values were called by Frege the "truth-values", namely, *truth* when the proposition obtained by substituting determinate values is *true*, falsehood when it is *false*. Thus, if in the expression "$y = x$ is hurt" we were to substitute "this boy", and if it were true *that this boy is hurt*, then "$y = x$ is hurt" would have the truth-value *truth* with the argument *this boy*; if it were not the case that this boy is hurt, then "$y = x$ is hurt" would have the truth-value *falsehood* with the argument *this boy*. According to Frege's view, then, the truth-values of "x is hurt"

[1] See Frege, *Function und Begriff*, p. 13; *Ueber Sinn und Bedeutung*, p. 32.
[2] For a discussion of Frege's theory see Russell, *Principles of Mathematics*, Appendix A. Frege held that descriptions were *proper names* for *the true* and *the false*.

would be related to " is hurt " as the values of log x are to the function *log*. But this is not the case. We conclude, therefore, that there is nothing in the propositional function standing to " x is hurt " as y stands to " log x " in the mathematical function " $y = \log x$ ". Thus the two kinds of function are not exactly analogous.

In the case of a propositional function, then, there seems to be nothing corresponding to the value of the function, since there is nothing corresponding to the term described by the mathematical, descriptive function. But there is something that may be said, in a sense, to take its place. To see this we must return to the distinction between the propositional function " $\hat{x}$ is hurt " and the undetermined value of the function " x is hurt ". It will be convenient to write " Φ " for " is hurt ", so that the two expressions become " $\Phi\hat{x}$ " and " Φx ". Φx may be said to be a variable proposition ; it is that which the function $\Phi\hat{x}$ denotes indeterminately, whereas $\Phi\hat{x}$ is that which denotes Φx indeterminately. Mr. Russell would say that Φx makes an indeterminate statement about any value of $\Phi\hat{x}$, whereas $\Phi\hat{x}$ makes a statement about an indetermination.[1] Now, the indeterminate, or variable, proposition Φx is in a sense dependent upon the variable x. It expresses *something that has the property* Φ. $\Phi\hat{x}$ expresses *the property* that something has. Hence, $\Phi\hat{x}$ corresponds in a sense to *the log*, i.e. the function ; Φx corresponds to the number of which something is the log, i.e. the indeterminate value. The variable proposition Φx is, however, really analogous to the variable description " the log of x " ; it is not analogous to the variable number y which " the log of x " describes. We cannot, then, regard the propositional function as having anything exactly corresponding to the dependent variable in the expression " $y = \log x$ ".

§ 4. ILLUSTRATIONS FROM THE SYMBOLISM OF *PRINCIPIA MATHEMATICA*

We have seen that a satisfactory symbolism must be precise, systematic and concise. The use of precise, i.e. well-defined and therefore unambiguous symbols, is an aid to the analysis of the notions which the symbols express. A concise symbolism enables us to express briefly and clearly statements that would be cumbersome and unnecessarily prolix if expressed in ordinary language. In *Principia Mathematica* Russell and Whitehead have devised a symbolism which fulfils these requirements.[2] In this section we

---

[1] See *Principia Mathematica*, Vol. I, pp. 40–1. Mr. Russell uses " ambiguous " where I have used " indeterminate ". If we were to give x a value, represented by the constant a (i.e. a value of the *argument* x), then Φa is a value of Φx, and is a value *for* $\Phi\hat{x}$.

[2] The symbolism of *Principia Mathematica* is based upon that of Peano. (See Chap. X, § 5, and cf. Chap. XXV, § 3 below.)

shall explain this symbolism so far as is required for its use in the analysis of descriptions and classes.

We have already used small latin *italic* letters to express variables occurring in propositional forms, e.g. ' x is p '. We have also used capital latin letters to express relations, e.g. R, S. We also used, in Chapter IV, the small letters p, q, r to express undetermined propositions, i.e. variable propositions. We shall now systematize this use as follows :

Variables. (i) Small latin letters taken from the end of the alphabet are used to express variable individuals : x, y, z ; (ii) the small letters p, q, r, express variable propositions.

Propositional functions. The small Greek letters, Φ, Ψ, X, are used to express variable functions involving one variable, e.g. " $\Phi(x)$ ", " $\Psi(x)$ ". It is usually found convenient to omit the brackets round the variable, and thus we write " $\Phi(x)$ " as " Φx ". Propositional functions involving two, or more, variables may be written " $\Phi(x, y)$ ", " $\Phi(x, y, z)$ ". But it is usually more convenient to express a function involving two variables by the symbols for relations, as follows : " x R y ". We are already familiar with the symbolic expression of the propositional form exhibited in any dyadic relational proposition.

Class-membership. The relation *is a*, which denotes membership of a class, is symbolized by the small Greek letter ε. This was chosen by Peano as being the first letter of the Greek word ἐστι meaning " is ". Thus ε expresses the " is " that denotes membership of a class, not the " is " expressing predication.

Variable classes. Small Greek letters, α, β, γ, are used to express a variable class. Thus, if we want to talk about any class and not about a given particular class, we use α ; if we want to talk about any *other* class, but not a given class, we use β, and so on. If we want to talk about a variable member of a class, β, we express " x is a member of the class α " by " $x \varepsilon \alpha$ ". Thus " $x \varepsilon \alpha$ " is the propositional form of class-membership propositions.

Compound Elementary Propositions. We have already distinguished four kinds of compound propositions so related that any proposition expressed in the one form could, with suitable modifications, be expressed in the other forms. We shall now symbolize these forms, using the terminology of *Principia Mathematica*. It will be remembered that each of the composite forms can be contradicted by a conjunctive proposition. We require a symbol to express negation. The symbol used is $\sim$. Thus the negation of " p " is expressed by " $\sim p$ ". Thus " $\sim p$ " may be read " *not-p* ".

Composite Propositions.

(i) " If p, then q " will be symbolized by " $p \supset q$ ".

The symbol " $\supset$ " expresses " implies ", so that " $p \supset q$ " may be read : " p implies q ".

(ii) "Either p or q" will be symbolized by "$p \vee q$".

The symbol "$\vee$" expresses "or", so that "$p \vee q$" may be read "p or q". We have hitherto used the name "alternative" to express composite propositions of this form. But the mathematical logicians use the name "disjunctive" instead of "alternative", and we shall find it convenient to adopt their terminology.[1]

Compound Propositions. The conjunctive proposition "p and q" will be symbolized by "$p \cdot q$". The dot . expresses that both propositions are asserted together.[2] Hence "$p \cdot q$" may be read : "Both p and q".

The disjunctive proposition "$p \vee q$" can be regarded as the denial of a conjunctive proposition, so that, using the symbolism just explained, we can express "either p or q" by "$\sim(\sim p \cdot \sim q)$". We do not, therefore, require an additional symbol to express "not both". We could start either with disjunction, or with conjunction, and define the one in terms of the other. Thus we can *define* the conjunctive proposition "$p \cdot q$" as the denial of the disjunctive proposition "either not-p or not-q". Expressed in this symbolism this definition is :

$$p \cdot q \cdot = \cdot \sim(\sim p \vee \sim q) \cdot Df.$$

The symbol "$\ldots = \ldots Df$" stands for "is the defined equivalent of". The symbol "$=$" must be taken in conjunction with "Df" which is written at the end of the expression on the right-hand side of "$=$". It should be noticed that in this expression *dots* are used in two ways : first, to symbolize a conjunction of propositions ; secondly, to serve the purpose of brackets, showing that a complex expression is to be treated as a *single* expression. Thus dots are used to serve the purpose of brackets in algebraic expressions. The correct use of brackets is very important. A simple illustration from elementary algebra will show this clearly.

Compare $\sqrt{a} + x$

with $\sqrt{a + x}$

The first expression means that x is to be added to the square root of a ; the second expression means that x is to be added to a and the square root of the whole is to be derived. In a logical symbolism a similar device is required. In speaking the distribution of brackets is indicated by tone of voice or by pauses. For logical purposes we require a systematic mode of indicating what is to be taken as

[1] This terminology is unfortunate since "or" expresses "one or other" without excluding the possibility of both ; hence *or* does not *disjoin* the propositions connected by means of it.

[2] The conjunction of p and q is called their *logical product*, since it is analogous to an algebraical product. Some logicians accordingly write the conjunctive proposition, given above as "pq".

a single expression. Outside brackets are indicated by a greater number of dots. This use of dots will be explained when we come to expressions in which they are so used.

We often want to say that two propositions are *equivalent* in the sense that, although they are different propositions, if the one is true, the other is, and conversely. This is the sense we gave to *equivalence*, or " coimplication "—to use Mr. Johnson's term—in Chapter VII. " Equivalence " is symbolized by " $\equiv$ ". Thus we get the expression

$$\text{"} p \equiv q \,.\, = \,.\, p \supset q \,.\, q \supset p \ \textit{Df.}$$

It should be noticed that the dot on the left-hand side of $=$ shows that the whole of what precedes it is defined by the whole of what follows the dot on the right-hand side of " $=$ " ; whereas the dot between q and q is the symbol of logical conjunction. This expression may be read : " ' p is equivalent to q ' is the defined equivalent of ' p implies q ' and ' q implies p ' ."

Non-elementary Propositions. A propositional function can be asserted to be true for all of its values, or for some of its values ; or, in the same way, it can be asserted to be false. We require, therefore, symbols to express " true for all values of the variable ", " true for some values of the variable ". These are expressed as follows :

" $\varPhi x$ is always true " is expressed by " $(x) \,.\, \varPhi x$ ".

" $\varPhi x$ is sometimes true " is expressed by " $(\exists x) \,.\, \varPhi x$ ".

Thus " (x) ", in " $(x) \,.\, \varPhi x$ ", may be read, " for all values of x ". The inverted capital in " $(\exists x) \,.\, \varPhi x$ " may be read, " There is an x such that . . ." [1] The whole expression may be read, " There is an x such that $\varPhi x$ is true ", and this expression is equivalent to : " $\varPhi x$ is sometimes true ".

To deny that $\varPhi x$ is always true is equivalent to asserting that the negation of $\varPhi x$ is sometimes true. In our symbolism this can be expressed by " $(\exists x) \sim \varPhi x$ ", which may be read : " There is an x such that ' $\sim \varPhi x$ ' is sometimes true ", or " $\sim \varPhi x$ is sometimes true ". Similarly " $\varPhi x$ is always false " can be expressed by " $\sim \varPhi x$ is always true ", i.e. by

$$(x) \,.\, \sim \varPhi x.$$

The expressions " $(x) \,.\, \varPhi x$ " and " $(\exists x) \,.\, \varPhi x$ " contain propositional functions involving apparent variables. There is no difference in meaning between " $(x) \,.\, \varPhi x$ " and " $(y) \,.\, \varPhi y$ ". In each case the small latin letter stands for an apparent variable.

Sometimes we want to say that one, and only one, value satisfies a given propositional function. This is expressed as follows :

---

[1] It will be noticed that the relation expressed by $(\exists x)$ is the *logical inverse* of the relation expressed by ε, which probably accounts for the choice of an inverted e, as being the *graphical* inverse of ε.

" $(\imath x)(\Phi x)$ ", which may be read: " the term satisfying Φx ". When we want to speak of *all the terms* which satisfy a function we use the expression " $\hat{x}(\Phi x)$ ", which may be read : " the terms satisfying Φx ", or " the x's such that Φx is true ".[1]

" The " in the singular is often used to express a description which applies to one object only, e.g. " the richest man in the world ". Such expressions are frequently used, so that it is useful to have a concise symbolic expression such as the above symbol " $(\imath x)(\Phi x)$ ". If we want to say that the term satisfying " Φx " exists, we use the symbol

$$\text{" E!}(\imath x)(\Phi x)\text{ ",}$$

which may be read : " The term satisfying Φx exists ".

Since " $(\exists x) . \Phi x$ " means " There is an x such that Φx is true ", it is convenient to write

" $(\exists c) . \Phi x$ " to express " There is an object c such that Φx is true when c is substituted for x ".

Here c expresses a constant, viz. a value of x, which satisfies " Φx ". This expression does not mean that there is *only one* object c such that Φx is true when c is substituted for x, but that there is *at least one* such object.

With the help of this expression we can define the expression " E!$(\imath x)(\Phi x)$ ", as follows :

$$\text{E!}(\imath x)(\Phi x) . = : (\exists c) : \Phi x . \equiv_x . x = c. \quad \text{Df.}$$

This whole expression is to be read :

" ' *The term satisfying Φx* ' *exists* " is the defined equivalent of " *There is an object c such that Φx is true when x is c and not otherwise* ".

With regard to the symbols used in the left-hand side expression, it should be noticed that ' $=$ ' in ' $x = c$ ' means " is identical with ". This symbol must not be confused with ' $\ldots = \ldots Df$ " which means " *is equivalent by definition* ", i.e. " *is the defined equivalent of*". It should also be noticed that the subscript x after " $\equiv$ " means "for all values of x". Thus if we wanted to say that two different propositional functions were equivalent, we could express it as follows :

$$\text{" } \Phi x . \equiv_x \Psi x \text{ ",}$$

which may be read : " Φx is equivalent, for all values of x, to Ψx ". This may also be expressed by the symbol used before, viz.

$$\text{" } (x) . \Phi x . \equiv . \Psi x \text{".}$$

Since we already have the symbol $\supset$ for " implies ", we can see that " Φx implies Ψx " will be expressed by

$$\text{" } \Phi x . \supset . \Psi x . \text{".}$$

---

[1] Thus " $\hat{x}(\Phi x)$ " expresses " the class defined by Φx ", where $\Phi \hat{x}$ would be the function and Φx an indeterminate value of the function.

If we want to say that, for all values of x, this implication holds, we can express this by

$$\text{“} \Phi x \mathbin{.} \supset_x \mathbin{.} \Psi x \text{”}$$

or by

$$\text{“} (x) \mathbin{.} \Phi x \mathbin{.} \supset \Psi x \text{”}.$$

An examination of the various symbolic expressions we have given will show how dots are used to bracket off expressions. Thus, for example, in the expression

$$E \,!(\imath x)(\Phi x) \mathbin{.} = : (\exists c) : \Phi x \mathbin{.} \equiv_x \mathbin{.} x = c. \quad \text{Df.,}$$

the two dots after $(\exists c)$ show that the *whole* of what *follows* belongs to $(\exists c)$. As another example we may contrast

$$p \vee q \mathbin{.} \supset \mathbin{.} q \vee p \qquad\qquad \text{(i)}$$
$$\text{with } p \vee q \mathbin{.} \supset \mathbin{.} q : \vee : p. \qquad\qquad \text{(ii)}$$

Here (i) means "'p or q' implies 'q or p'",
(ii) means "either 'p or q' implies q, or p is true".[1]

---

[1] The student will find a useful introduction to this subject in Prof. L. J. Russell's article on "An Elementary Symbolism for Logic" (*Mind*, Jan., 1928).

CHAPTER IX

DESCRIPTIONS, CLASSES AND GENERAL PROPOSITIONS

'Who did you pass on the road?' the King went on holding out his hand to the Messenger for some more hay.

'Nobody,' said the Messenger.

'Quite right,' said the King: 'this young lady saw him too. So of course Nobody walks slower than you.'

'I do my best,' the Messenger said in a sullen tone. 'I'm sure nobody walks much faster than I do.'

'He can't do that,' said the King, 'or else he'd have been here first.'

—*Lewis Carroll.*

§ 1. THE ANALYSIS OF DESCRIPTIONS

INSUFFICIENT analysis of propositions with consequent failure to recognize different propositional forms is the radical defect of the traditional logic. As we have seen, it was assumed that all propositions were of the subject-predicate form. Accordingly no distinction was made between propositions such as *This is yellow*, *The man in the moon is yellow*, *All lions are yellow*, *Some carnations are yellow*, which were all taken to be of the same form. This we have seen is a mistake. The first proposition is an elementary simple proposition; the others are non-elementary, but the second is of a different form from the last two. In order to ascertain what is the form of a proposition it is necessary to analyse the proposition, and thus to discover what exactly is asserted. In this section we shall consider the analysis of propositions such as *The man in the moon is yellow*, and *A careless motorist is selfish*.

We shall begin by considering four propositions:

(1) That is large.

(2) That Church is very large.

(3) A Church in Rome is very large.

(4) The Round Church in Cambridge is small.

As we saw in Chapter II, "that" is a demonstrative symbol; it indicates a referend of which the person who asserts the proposition is directly aware. The phrase "That Church" might be intended by the speaker to be a demonstrative phrase, but it contains a descriptive element. Consequently, if the description is inapplic-

139

able the phrase may fail to demonstrate ; or, as we saw, it might demonstrate although the description were rejected. Thus many phrases that appear to be merely demonstrative are elliptical since they involve a description. Hence, the proposition must be analysed into the conjoint assertion, *That is a Church and it is very large.* It would be contradicted by the assertion *That is not a Church but it is very large.* The phrases " A Church in Rome " and " The Round Church in Cambridge " are purely descriptive ; hence they are to be contrasted with " that ", which demonstrates a constituent of the proposition in whose verbal expression it occurs. Apart from a referend which it names " that " would be meaningless. Thus proposition (i) would naturally be denied by the proposition *That is not large* ; it would be absurd to say *That is not that and it is not large.* The proposition *A Church in Rome is very large* would be denied either by *There is no Church in Rome* or by *There are Churches in Rome but not a single one of them is very large.* The proposition *The Round Church in Cambridge is small* would be denied either by *The Round Church in Cambridge is not small* or by *There is no Round Church in Cambridge* or by *There is more than one Round Church in Cambridge.* We see, therefore, that these propositions are composite. Propositions (3) and (4) must be analysed as follows :

(3) There is an object which (i) is a Church in Rome, and (ii) it is very large.

(4) There is an object which (i) is a Round Church in Cambridge, and (ii) it is small, and (iii) is such that any Round Church in Cambridge is identical with it.

It must be noticed that proposition (4) involves the third assertion that there is only *one* such Church, since " the " implies uniqueness of reference. Hence, the proposition *The Round Church in England is small* is false, since there are five Round Churches in England. The proposition *The Church in Hyde Park is large* is false, since there is no Church in Hyde Park.

Phrases such as those used to express propositions (3) and (4) are called by Mr. Russell *descriptions*. He distinguishes between indefinite and definite descriptions. Phrases of the form ' *A so-and-so* ' are indefinite descriptions, e.g. ' A church ', ' A lion ', ' A unicorn ', ' A wistful smile ', ' a man '. Phrases of the form ' *the so-and-so* ' are definite descriptions, e.g. ' the Church ', ' the winner of the Schneider Cup ', ' the man in the moon ', ' the first citizen of the United States ', ' the product of 67 and 8 '. Such phrases do not express any constituent of the proposition in whose verbal expression they occur ; hence, descriptions are not *names*. Thus propositions in whose verbal expression such phrases occur must be analysed so that the description disappears. The necessity for the disappearance of the description when the proposition is analysed may be made clearer if we consider the proposition *I climbed a mountain*. For convenience we shall assume for the present purpose that "Snowdon", "Everest", "Ben Nevis", "Rough Tor" are proper names. This assumption will enable us to avoid undue prolixity. The proposition *I climbed a mountain* would be true if I climbed Everest, or if I climbed Snowdon, etc. But in asserting *I climbed a mountain*, it is not asserted that I climbed Snowdon, or that I climbed Everest, etc. This is clearly the case, since, if the proposition *I climbed a mountain* is false, then neither Snowdon, nor Ben Nevis, nor any other mountain could be concerned in the statement. Nevertheless, the proposition, though false, is *significant*. Again the proposition *I killed a unicorn* is always false, yet it is significant. It follows, therefore, that the proposition *I climbed a mountain* does not contain as a constituent a particular mountain. But there is no constituent in the world which is just *a mountain* without being any mountain in particular. Hence, "a mountain" does not name any constituent of the proposition in whose verbal expression it may occur. Thus expressions such as "a mountain", "a man", "a unicorn" stand in each case for an undetermined individual of a certain sort.

It should now be evident that the analysis we have given of propositions (3) and (4) has not been stated with sufficient precision. But before we discuss their analysis further we shall consider definite descriptions in order to see that such descriptions also are not names. It may easily be admitted that indefinite descriptions are not names, since no one is likely to suppose that "a mountain" refers to one definite object. But it may seem that "the man in the moon", "the winner of the Schneider Cup in 1929", 'the author of Waverley" are *names* for the objects which these phrases describe. That, however, is a mistake. There is no object which is a man in the moon, so it could not possibly be named. The proposition *The man in the moon is yellow* is false; the proposition *The author of Waverley is Scotch* is true. Yet these propositions are of the *same* form; hence, it must be possible to give some account of *both* phrases "The man in the moon" and "The author of *Waverley*" without bringing in some object which they name.

We shall now consider Mr. Russell's precise analysis of propositions in whose verbal expression definite descriptions occur. This whole way of looking at the matter is due to him. He first showed how it is *possible* to use phrases such as "the man in the moon", "the round square", etc., *significantly* even though there is *nothing* to which such descriptions apply, and that the analysis of propositions in whose verbal expression such descriptions occur is precisely the same whether these descriptions apply to something

or not.   Mr. Russell takes the example *Scott is the author of Waverley*.[1]
This proposition asserts an identity.   But the identity is not an
identity between two *names* applying to the same individual, but
an identity between an object *named* and an object *described*.   The
proposition asserts that the definite description " the author of
Waverley " applies to *Scott*.   (We here assume that " Scott " is a
proper name.)   Since a definite description can apply to one object
only, the proposition *Scott is the author of Waverley* is equivalent to
" one and only one man wrote *Waverley*, and that man is *Scott* ".
Thus the proposition is to be analysed into the conjoint assertion of

> (i) one man wrote *Waverley*,
> (ii) only one man wrote *Waverley*,
> (iii) that man was Scott.

The proposition will be false (i) if no one had written *Waverley*,
(ii) if more than one man had written *Waverley*, or (iii) if one man
had written *Waverley* but Scott was not that man.   Thus *Scott is
the author of Waverley*, is not, as was formerly supposed, a simple
proposition.   In the analysed proposition " the author of *Waverley* "
disappears ; thus it does not name any constituent of the proposition in whose verbal expression it occurs.   We can easily see that
" the author of *Waverley* " is not a name for Scott since, if it were,
it would be sufficient for him to have been *called* " the author of
Waverley ".   This is manifestly false.   Scott could not be the author
of *Waverley* unless he had written *Waverley* and no one else had.

Since the definite description " the author of *Waverley* " is not
a name, it is significant to ask whether the author of *Waverley* exists.
This question is equivalent to the question " Was there one and only
one man who wrote *Waverley* ? "   Thus the analysis of *The author
of Waverley exists* is :

> (i) one man wrote *Waverley*
> (ii) only one man wrote *Waverley*.

Let us now consider the analysis of the proposition *The author
of* WAVERLEY *is Scotch*.   This can now be seen to be :

> (i) one man wrote *Waverley*.
> (ii) only one man wrote *Waverley*,
> (iii) that man is Scotch.

It will be seen that (i) and (ii) in this analysis are the same as
(i) and (ii) in *The author of* WAVERLEY *exists*.   Thus to assert that
the author of *Waverley* is Scotch is to assert that the author of
Waverley exists, for ' the author of *Waverley* " *means* " one and only
one man wrote *Waverley* ".   Hence the proposition *The author of*
WAVERLEY *is Scotch* will be false unless there is one man who did in

---

[1] See *Int. to Math. Phil.*, Chap. XVI ; *Principia Mathematica*, Vol. I, p. 30,
and Pt. I (Section B) ; *Mind* (1905), pp. 479–83 ; *Mysticism and Logic*, Chap. X ;
and cf. *The Problems of Philosophy*, Chap. V.

fact write *Waverley*. It follows that to attribute any property to "the author of *Waverley* " is to assert that the author of *Waverley* exists.

The proposition *The author of* WAVERLEY *is the author of* MARMION asserts an identity and is to be analysed :

(i) one man wrote both *Waverley* and *Marmion*.

(ii) only one man wrote both *Waverley* and *Marmion*.

If we use Mr. Russell's symbolism, which was explained in the last chapter, we can state more concisely the propositions we have just analysed :

(1) *Scott is the author of Waverley*.

Using 'Φ' for 'wrote *Waverley*', we get,

$$(\exists c) : \Phi x \,.\, \equiv_x \,.\, x = c : c = \text{Scott}.$$

This may be read : " There is an object c such that Φx is always equivalent to 'x is c' and 'c is Scotch'."

(2) *The author of Waverley exists*.

Using 'Φ' as before, we get,

$$(\exists c) : \Phi x \,.\, \equiv_x \,.\, x = c.$$

This may be read : " There is an object c such that Φx is always equivalent to 'x is c'." [1]

3. *The author of Waverley is Scotch*.

Using "Φ" as before, and the additional symbol "Ψ" for " is Scotch ", we get,

$$(\exists c) : \Phi x \,.\, \equiv_x \,.\, x = c : \Psi c.$$

This may be read : " There is an object c such that 'Φx' is always equivalent to 'x is c' and 'Ψc'", or " There is an object c such that 'x has the property Φ' is always equivalent to 'x is c' and 'c has the property Ψ'." [2]

This analysis brings out very clearly *how* it is that descriptions can be used significantly even when they describe nothing. The difficulty that logicians have felt in understanding how this is possible was due to their assumption that the grammatical subject of a proposition always expressed the logical subject, and that this grammatical subject was always equivalent, for the purposes of the *analysis* of the proposition, to a *name*. Thus they took " the author of *Waverley* " to be a name which happens to apply to *Scott*, and differing from " Scott " only in what they called its " fixity of con-

---

[1] The analysis might be expressed in the form :

(1) $(\exists c) : \Phi c : x \neq c \supset_x \sim \Phi x \,.\, c = \text{Scott}.$

(2) $(\exists c) : \Phi c : x \neq c \supset_x \sim \Phi x.$

In this case (1) may be read : " There is an object c such that c wrote *Waverley* and no one other than c wrote *Waverley*, and c is Scott." It does not matter which of these expressions we use.

[2] In the alternative form of expression given in the preceding note (3) will be expressed by :

$$(\exists c) : \Phi c : x \neq c \supset_x \sim \Phi x : \Psi c.$$

notation ". Thus they failed to recognize the distinction in *form* of
the two propositions *Scott is the author of Waverley* and *Scott is Sir
Walter*,[1] or between *The author of Waverley is Scotch* and *That man
is Scotch*.

We have now to consider two different ways in which definite
descriptions may occur. We saw that if *The so-and-so* has any
property, then *the so-and-so* must exist. But *the so-and-so* may exist
and yet not have a given property. But, since, to assert that *the
so-and-so* does not have (or has) a given property implies that *the
so-and-so* exists, we must be careful to distinguish between denying
that *the so-and-so* exists and asserting that *the so-and-so* exists whilst
denying that *the so-and-so* has a given property. For example,
' The King of Utopia is kind ' implies that there is a King of Utopia ;
' The King of Utopia is not kind ' implies that there is a King of
Utopia and denies that he is kind.   Thus, using ' Φ ' for the property
of *being King of Utopia*, and Ψ for the property of *being kind*, we
can express " The King of Utopia is kind " by

$$\text{(i) } (\exists c) : \Phi x \text{ . } \equiv_x \text{ . } x = c : \Psi c.$$

We might suppose that we could express " The King of Utopia is
not kind " by

$$\text{(ii) } (\exists c) : \Phi x \text{ . } \equiv_x' \text{ . } x = c : \sim\Psi c,$$

where ' Φ ' and ' Ψ ' have the same meaning as before, so that ' $\sim\Psi$ '
means ' is not kind '. But the expression " The King of Utopia is
not kind " is ambiguous. As ordinarily used it would be taken to
mean that there is a King of Utopia and that he is not kind ; but
it might be taken to mean that there is no King of Utopia. Thus
the verbal expression is misleading. The first of these two meanings
is the one expressed by the symbolic expression (ii) above. The
comparison of (i) and (ii) shows this clearly. In both these expres-
sions there occurs ' $(\exists c) : \Phi x \text{ . } \equiv_x \text{ . } x = c$ ', and this we saw in the
last chapter is the definition of " $E!(\imath x)(\Phi x)$ ", which (using ' Φ ' as
before) expresses ' The King of Utopia ' exists. Hence, the denial
of this proposition will be expressed by $\sim[E!(\imath x)(\Phi x)]$. It is clear
that

$$\sim[E!(\imath x)(\Phi x)] = \sim[(\exists c) : \Phi x \text{ . } \equiv_x \text{ . } x = c].$$

Hence, " The King of Utopia is not kind " is expressed by

$$\text{(iii) } \sim[(\exists c) : \Phi x \text{ . } \equiv_x \text{ . } x = c : \Psi c].$$

The outside brackets show that the denial applies to the whole
of what is contained within them. When ' $(\imath x)(\Phi x)$ ' occurs as it

---

[1] If in " Scott is Sir Walter " we are using " Scott " to mean " the person
named ' Scott '," and " Sir Walter " to mean " the person *named* ' Sir Walter ',"
then " Scott " and " Sir Walter " are descriptions. If, however, we are using
" Scott " and " Sir Walter " as logically proper names, then " Scott is Sir
Walter " is the *same proposition* as " Scott is Scott ".

occurs in ' E!$(\imath x)(\Phi x)$ ', or in $[\Psi(\imath x)(\Phi x)]$, then ' $(\imath x)(\Phi x)$ ' is said to have primary occurrence ; when ' $(\imath x)(\Phi x)$ ' occurs as it occurs in $\sim[(\imath x)(\Phi x)\Psi]$, or in $\sim[$E!$(\imath x)(\Phi x)]$, then ' $(\imath x)(\Phi x)$ ' is said to have secondary occurrence.[1] It is clear that all propositions in which ' The King of Utopia ' has primary occurrence are false, since there is no king of Utopia. The denials of these propositions are true, but in them ' The King of Utopia ' has secondary occurrence.

We must now return to the consideration of propositions in whose verbal expression indefinite descriptions occur, such as, *I climbed a mountain, A unicorn is fond of cake*. To assert " A so-and-so exists " is to assert that there is an object which has the property of *being so-and-so*. Thus ' A unicorn exists ' means ' There is an object which has the property of *being a unicorn* '. This is equivalent to " There is an object c which satisfies the propositional function ' x is a unicorn ' ". This might be expressed in the form, " There is an object c such that Φx is true when c is substituted for x ". To say that " A unicorn is fond of cake " is to say that " ' x is a unicorn ' and ' x is fond of cake ' are sometimes true together ". That is, there is at least one object, c, such that the property of *being a unicorn* and the property of *being fond of cake* both belong to c. Using ' Φ ' for the property of *being a unicorn* and ' Ψ ' for the property of *being fond of cake*, we could express ' A unicorn is fond of cake ' by

' The joint assertion of Φx and Ψx is sometimes true '.

This expression shows clearly that the proposition that a so-and-so has the property Φ is not a proposition of the form Φx.

We can now state precisely the analysis of propositions (3) and (4) of the four propositions that we considered at the beginning of this chapter.

Using ' Φ ' for the property of being a *Church in Rome*, and ' Ψ ' for the property of *being very large*, the proposition expressed by " A Church in Rome is very large " can be expressed

$$(3) \quad (\exists c) : \Phi x \ . \ \Psi x : x = c.$$

Using ' Φ ' for the property of being a *round Church in Cambridge* and ' Ψ ' for the property of *being small*, the proposition expressed by " The Round Church in Cambridge is small " can be expressed

$$(4) \quad (\exists c) : \Phi x \ . \equiv_x . \ x = c : \Psi c.$$

Thus we see that (3) and (4) are propositions of different forms, although the sentences by means of which they are expressed are grammatically of the same form.

In Chapter III we distinguished two ways in which we are said to " know things ", namely, (i) by being acquainted with the thing, (ii) by knowing it through its characteristics. Obviously the

[1] See *Principia Mathematica*, pp. 68–9 ; and cf. *Mind*, 1905, pp. 489–90.

analysis of (ii) is closely related to the analysis of descriptions. Mr. Russell would call (ii) knowledge by description. Thus he says :

' I shall say an object is " known by description " when we know that it is " *the* so-and-so ", i.e. when we know that there is one object, and no more, having a certain property : and it will generally be implied that we do not have knowledge of the same object by acquaintance. We know that the man with the iron mask existed, and many propositions are known about him ; but we do not know who he was. . . . We shall say that we have " *merely* descriptive knowledge " of the so-and-so when, although we know that the so-and-so exists, and although we may possibly be acquainted with the object which is, in fact, the so-and-so, yet we do not know any proposition " *a* is the so-and-so ", where *a* is something with which we are acquainted.' [1]

In this passage Mr. Russell suggests that *knowing by description* and *knowing by description only* are to be distinguished. The former does not, as we saw in Chapter III, exclude acquaintance. These two forms of knowing can now be precisely defined. Using " S " for the knowing subject and " A " for the object known by description, we get :

(1) " *S knows A by description* " means " There is some property Φ of which it is true (i) that Φ belongs to A, and (ii) that S knows with regard to Φ that Φ belongs to one thing and to one thing only."

(2) " *S knows A by description only* " means " There is some property Φ of which it is true (i) that Φ belongs to A, and (ii) that S knows with regard to Φ that Φ belongs to one thing only, and (iii) S is not acquainted with A.

It is clear that we *can* know A by description if, and only if, we know that there is some property which does in fact belong to only one thing. Hence, we do not *know* the man in the moon by description, since there is no object A to which the description applies. We can assert propositions in whose verbal expression " the man in the moon " occurs but, unless the description has secondary occurrence, all such propositions will be false.

It must be observed that to know a proposition in which A is a constituent is not equivalent to knowing A by description.

§ 2. THE ANALYSIS OF CLASSES

In this section we shall be concerned with the use of " the " in the plural, i.e. with its use in phrases such as " the Kings of France ", " the wives of policemen ", " the people who pay super-tax ", " the Secretaries of State ", etc. That is to say we have to discuss *classes*, since these phrases are symbols which *express classes*. At the outset it is important to recognize the distinction between an individual and a class. A Chinese philosopher is reported [2] to have said that

---

[1] *Mysticism and Logic*, pp. 214–15.
[2] See Russell, *Our Knowledge of the External World*, p. 206 ; *The Monist*, 1919, p. 353.

if there is a dun cow and a bay horse, then there are three things ; for the dun cow is one thing, and the bay horse is another thing, and the two together are a third thing. Every one can see that there is some absurdity in this statement. The absurdity is due to the assumption that a collection of two things, i.e. a class with two members, is itself a thing of the same kind, or type, as its members. That every one recognizes this absurdity shows that we clearly see that an individual is of a logically different type from a class. A class is not an object of which we can be directly aware. Thus we are not acquainted with the *class men*, hence " men " is not a logically proper name for the collection of men. We must, then, ask what a class is. To answer this question we must inquire how we come to recognize a given class and how we do in fact use class-symbols, i.e. symbols (including words) which express classes.

Consider, for example, the class *the people who are learned*. There is in common use the expression " scholars " which may be regarded as a synonym for " the people who are learned ". Whether we have a single word to express a given class or whether we have to use a phrase is an accident of language. It depends mainly upon how often we want to refer to a class. Now, *the people who are learned, or scholars*, are *all the individuals who are learned*. These are a set of individuals distinguished from other sets of individuals by their possessing the property of *being learned*. There are two ways of selecting the individuals who form a class. One way is to enumerate the individuals one after the other, the order of enumeration being indifferent. For example, we might enumerate the individuals *Melchior, Balthazar, Gaspar*, and thus form the set consisting of *Melchior and Balthazar and Gaspar*. Such a set will be called an enumeration. The second way is to select a certain property which may belong to many individuals. For example, *The Magi* are a set of individuals each of whom possesses the properties of *being a wise man from the East* and *having followed the Star to Bethlehem*. *The Magi* consists of three individuals, but is not to be regarded as an enumeration of these three, *Melchior, Balthazar, Gaspar*. The set is determined by a conjunction of properties which belong to each of the individuals in the set and to no one not in the set. Such a set is a class. There is thus an important difference between an enumeration, or enumerative set, and a class, since the latter is determined by a property, or a conjunction of properties, whereas the former is selected by an enumeration. The individuals con- stituting the enumeration do however possess a common property, namely, the property of being one or other of the individuals enumer- ated. Thus in our example, the three individuals enumerated possess in common the property *of being either Melchior or Balthazar or Gaspar*, and no other set possesses this property. Hence, the connexion between an enumeration and what we have called a class is extremely intimate. It is clear that only finite classes, that is, classes consisting of a finite number of members could even theoretically be enumerated. An infinite class is not denumerable, so that such a class *must* be determined by a property, or conjunction of properties, by means of which the class is selected ; a finite class *may* be so given. The conjunction of properties which determine a class is called its intension, or connotation. The set of individuals to which the intension applies is called the extension or denotation of the conjunction of properties. The intension is said to be the defining property of the class. Regarded as an *extension* the class is many ; regarded as an *intension* the class is not many. Consequently it is often said that a class is *a many-in-one* or *a one-in-many*. But such phrases are misleading. The word " in " is metaphorical, and could not have precisely the same meaning in both phrases. The point is that a class combines an extension and an intension. Thus, as Mr. Johnson points out, it is not correct to speak of " the extension *of a class* ", but of an extension determined by a given intension. For example, the conjunction of properties *being a rectangle and having equal sides* determines the set of individuals we call the class *squares*. The conjunction of properties *being English* and *being a pope* determines the class of *English popes*. This class has (up to the present) only one member. The conjunction of properties *being Chinese and being a pope* determines the class of *Chinese popes*. This class has (up to the present) no members. Such a class is called the null-class.

There is not, then, in addition to the set of individuals and the defining property which determines these *as a class*, another individual which is *the* class. There is not, for example, in addition to the set of individuals and the property of *being human* which determines the class we call " men ", another *individual* that is *men*. When we recognize this we are able to avoid the mistake into which the Chinese philosopher fell. Since the intensional aspect is fundamental it might be supposed that we could identify the class with the defining property. This, however, would be a mistake. Two (or more) *different* defining properties may determine the same extension. But two different classes cannot have the *same* membership. Thus the class *men* is determined both by the defining property *rational animal* and by the defining property *being two-legged and featherless*. It is, as Mr. Russell points out, " this fact that a defining characteristic is never unique which makes classes useful ".[1] Defining properties which determine the same extension are said to be equivalent.

Class-symbols can be used significantly with such words as *this*,

[1] *Int. Math. Phil.*, p. 14.

some, any, every, all. Thus we can speak of " this scholar ", " some scholars ", etc. Thus the use of class-symbols in propositions involves the use of apparent variables. It is thus possible to express classes by what Mr. Russell calls propositional functions involving one variable. Looked at from this point of view we may say that, since when we speak of men we mean *every one who is human*, we can express " men " by the propositional function " x is human ". If for " x " in " x is human " we substitute the name of an individual who is human we have a sentence which expresses a true proposition. For example, the substitution of " Socrates " for " x " yields the true proposition *Socrates is human.* Thus the class *men* is equivalent to the set of individuals whose names can be substituted for ' x ' in " x is human " so as to give a sentence which expresses a true proposition. This set of individuals satisfies the propositional function " x is human ". This way of expressing classes provides a useful method for expressing the analysis of propositions in whose verbal expression class-symbols occur. But the use of propositional functions is a symbolic device ; it does not throw light upon what a class *is*. Mr. Russell has fallen into the mistake of saying that a *class* is a *symbol*. But classes are not symbols ; they are logical constructions. What this means will be explained in a later section of this chapter. Here it is sufficient to point out that what is important in the propositional function " x is human " which defines the class *men*, is not the *function* but the *meaning*. That is to say, if Φx determines the class having the property Φ, what is important is the meaning of " Φ ", and the meaning of " Φ " is a certain *property*. The set of individuals which satisfy Φx is the extension of the class *defined* by " Φ ". If Φx is formally equivalent to Ψx, then Φx and Ψx determine the *same* extension, and either Φ or Ψ could be used to define the class. It is to be noted that every property determines a class, namely, the class consisting of the individuals who possess the property. There may be no individuals which possess the property, or one individual, or more than one. A class is never identical with its members ; hence, a class with only one member is not identical with that member.

It should now be clear that the way in which a *class-symbol* refers to what is commonly called ' the denotation of the class ' is quite different from the way in which a *name* refers to the individual named. Thus, we see that the analysis of *denoting* is more complicated than was formerly supposed.

§ 3. GENERAL PROPOSITIONS AND THE TRADITIONAL SCHEDULE

In the last section we saw that we can regard assertions about all the members of a class as assertions about the values satisfying a given propositional function which determines the class. We saw also that it is not necessary to be acquainted with each member of the class since we know the class through its defining property. Thus we can assert *All men are mortal* even though we are not acquainted with every member of the class *men*. Moreover, no actual man enters into the assertion since the proposition is significant whether any given man is known or not. Thus, in order to understand *All men are mortal* it is not necessary to know what men there are. It follows that propositions of this form are fundamentally different from simple propositions. In Chapter IV we distinguished general propositions from simple propositions on the ground that the latter are elementary, the former non-elementary propositions. We can now see that the fundamental difference consists in the fact that general propositions involve apparent variables. The use of the apparent variable shows that a property, or characteristic, is being used in abstraction from the individual, or individuals, to which it may belong. We saw also that the proposition *All who are wise are trustworthy* is an implicative proposition, since it asserts that if any one is wise, he is trustworthy. " Any one " indicates a variable. We can now conveniently express this proposition in the form *If x is wise, x is trustworthy, no matter what x may be.* Thus we are again led to recognize that the traditional Logicians were guilty of serious confusion when they grouped ' singular propositions ' as a sub-class of ' universal propositions '. What is important is to distinguish singular (i.e. simple) propositions from both universal and particular (i.e. general) propositions.

Using the symbolism explained in the last chapter we can now conveniently express the traditional schedule of propositions.

Let S stand for the terms which satisfy Φx, and let P stand for the terms which satisfy Ψx. Then we have,

$$\text{' S } a \text{ P '} \quad \text{means} \quad \text{' } (x) \ \Phi x \supset \Psi x\text{.'} \quad (1)$$
$$\text{' S } e \text{ P '} \quad \text{means} \quad \text{' } (x) \ \Phi x \supset \sim\!\Psi x\text{.'} \quad (2)$$
$$\text{' S } i \text{ P '} \quad \text{means} \quad \text{' } (\exists x) : \Phi x \, . \, \Psi x\text{.'} \quad (3)$$
$$\text{' S } o \text{ P '} \quad \text{means} \quad \text{' } (\exists x) : \Phi x \, . \, \sim\!\Psi x\text{.'} \quad (4)$$

It will be remembered that to say " for all values of x, ' Φx implies Ψx ' " means the same as to say " ' Φx implies Ψx ' is always true ', or more shortly, " Φx always implies Ψx "; and to say " for some values of x, Φx and Ψx " means the same as " ' Φx and Ψx ' is sometimes true ". This latter expression means " true for *at least one* value of x " and is thus consistent with the traditional interpretation of " some ". This use of propositional functions to express the four propositions of the traditional schedule brings out very clearly the difference in form between (1) and (3), and between (2) and (4), as well as the resemblance in form between (1) and (2), and between (3) and (4).[1]

A proposition of the form " $(x) . \Phi x \supset \Psi x$ " is called a *formal implication* ; x can take any value that makes the function significant, and it is asserted that no matter what this value may be the implication holds. Those values of x which make the propositional function significant are said to constitute the *range* of the function. Those values of x which yield a true proposition are said to *satisfy* the function, just as the roots of an equation are said to satisfy the equation. It is clear that there must be values that render the function *significant* although they do not *satisfy* the function ; otherwise there would be no *false* propositions, but only meaningless collections of words. The range of x in Φx is determined by the type of Φ. If 'Φ' meant 'is a multiple of 4', then x in Φx could not take as a value *Socrates*. Since in a formal implication x can take *any* value that makes the function significant, we can see that in "All S is P" we are concerned not only with what is S, but also with what is not S, so long as we do not include any term which would render the proposition non-significant. It is for this reason that we can understand "All S is P" even though we are not able to enumerate all the objects that are S, provided that we understand what is meant by *being an S* and *being a P*. It is accordingly convenient to interpret propositions (1) and (2) as not implying the existence of S. But propositions (3) and (4) do imply existence. To say that "'Φx' is sometimes true" is to say that there are arguments (at least one) which satisfy Φx, or that arguments satisfying Φx exist. Consequently '$(\exists x) : \Phi x . \Psi x$' means that arguments satisfying *both* Φx and Ψx exist, or, as we might otherwise express it, the properties expressed by 'Φ' and by 'Ψ' *both* belong to something. This proposition is clearly existential. The only difference between (3) and (4) is that in (4) 'not-Ψx' replaces 'Ψx' ; similarly with (1) and (2). Since (1) and (2) do not imply existence, whereas (3) and (4) do imply existence, it is clear that (1) is contradicted by (4), and (2) by (3). This result is in accordance with the traditional doctrine of the square of opposition. But in accordance with our interpretation of these four propositions the universal proposition of traditional logic does not imply the particular proposition of the same quality. It follows that the conversion *per accidens* of an A proposition is fallacious, and the contraposition of E.[2] It follows also that any syllogisms in which both premises are universal but the conclusion is particular are invalid. Thus, for example, *Darapti*, *Felapton*, are not valid moods.

Since general propositions are of a different form from simple

---

[1] Cf. p. 50 above, and see Russell, *Int. Math. Phil.*, p. 161 *seq.*
[2] Cf. J. N. Keynes, *F.L.*, Pt. II, Chap. VIII.

propositions it follows that a syllogism in which both premisses are general is different in form from a syllogism in which one premiss is general and one simple. The simple proposition, e.g. *Mussolini is fallible*, will be of the form Φx. The distinction between the two forms of syllogism can be clearly exhibited by using symbols. Let the syllogisms be :

I.   If all men are mortal and all mortals are fallible, then all men are fallible ;

II.   If all men are mortal and Socrates is a man, then Socrates is mortal.

These can be symbolized as follows :

I. $(x) . \Phi x \supset \Psi x . (x) . \Psi x \supset X x : \supset . (x) . \Phi x \supset X x.$

II. $(z) . \Phi z \supset \Psi z . \Phi x : \supset \Psi x.$

If we use class symbols and $\smile$ for " is included in ", the syllogisms will be expressed by :

I. $a < \beta . \beta < \gamma : \supset . a < \gamma.$

II. $a < \beta . x \varepsilon a : \supset : x \varepsilon \beta.$

These expressions bring out clearly that the minor premiss of II is a class-membership proposition, and is accordingly to be distinguished from the minor premiss of I which is a general proposition. It is not, of course, maintained that it is essential so to express them ; what is essential is to keep clearly in mind the distinction between a simple proposition and a general proposition. The resemblance between the verbal form " All S is P " and " This X is a P " obscures the fundamental difference between the propositions which are thus expressed. The former involves an apparent variable, whereas the latter does not.

§ 4. MR. RUSSELL'S THEORY OF INCOMPLETE SYMBOLS

We have seen that since descriptions may apply to nothing, propositions in whose verbal expression they occur must be analysed in such a way that the description does not appear as the name of any constituent of the proposition. It follows that the grammatical subject of a sentence need not express the logical subject of the proposition expressed by the sentence. It is for this reason that it is important to distinguish descriptions from symbols which name some thing. Mr. Russell calls such symbols as descriptions " incomplete symbols ". He also uses the expressions " logical fictions ", " logical constructions ", and has sometimes suggested that " incomplete symbols ", " logical fictions " and " logical constructions " are synonymous. There is undoubtedly some obscurity and even contradiction in Mr. Russell's discussion of this topic, which it is worth while to attempt to clear up. The phrase " incomplete symbol " is in such frequent use nowadays that it is important to understand what it is intended to mean.

The origin of the distinction between incomplete symbols and those that are not incomplete is clearly to be found in the distinction, first made by Mr. Russell, between *acquaintance* and *knowledge by description*. It is clear that the way in which a demonstrative symbol refers to its referend is different from the way in which a descriptive symbol is used, since in the former case there *must* be a referend, and in the latter case the description may not apply to anything. In his detailed discussion of descriptions and incomplete symbols in *Principia Mathematica* Mr. Russell does not himself refer to this distinction between acquaintance and knowledge by description. He introduces the subject by referring to the " grammatical subject of a proposition ".[1] It is desirable to quote the statement in full :

' By an " incomplete " symbol we mean a symbol which is not supposed to have any meaning in isolation, but is only defined in certain contexts. In ordinary mathematics, for example, $\frac{d}{dx}$ and $\int_a^b$ are incomplete symbols: something has to be supplied before we have anything significant. Such symbols have what may be called a definition in use. . . . This distinguishes such symbols from what (in a generalized sense) we may call *proper names*. " Socrates ", for example, stands for a certain man, and therefore has a meaning by itself, without the need of any context. If we supply a context, as in " Socrates is mortal ", these words express a fact of which Socrates himself is a constituent : there is a certain object, namely Socrates, which does have the property of mortality, and this object is a constituent of the complex fact which we assert when we say " Socrates is mortal ". But in other cases, this simple analysis fails us. Suppose we say : " The round-square does not exist." It seems plain that this is a true proposition, yet we cannot regard it as denying the existence of a certain object called " the round-square ". For if there were such an object, it would exist : we cannot first assume that there is a certain object, and then proceed to deny that there is such an object. Whenever the grammatical subject of a proposition can be supposed not to exist without rendering the proposition meaningless, it is plain that the grammatical subject is not a proper name, i.e. not a name directly representing some object. Thus in all such cases, the proposition must be capable of being so analysed that what was the grammatical subject shall have disappeared. Thus when we say " the round square does not exist ", we may, as a first attempt at such analysis, substitute " it is false that there is an object x which is both round and square ". Generally, when " the so-and-so " is said not to exist, we have a proposition of the form

$$" \sim E ! (\imath x)(\Phi x), "$$
i.e. $\sim\{(\exists c) : \Phi x . \equiv_x . x = c\},$

or some equivalent. Here the grammatical subject $(\imath x)(\Phi x)$ has completely disappeared ; thus in " $\sim E ! (\imath x)(\Phi x)$ ", $(\imath x)(\Phi x)$ is an incomplete symbol.' [2]

---

[1] Strictly speaking it is only *sentences* that can have *grammatical* subjects. But Mr. Russell unfortunately frequently confuses the *sentence* with the *proposition* which is expressed by the sentence.

[2] *Principia Mathematica, Introduction*, Chap. III, p. 66. Cf. also the other references given in the footnote to p. 142.

There is no doubt that this is an unfortunate way of expressing the matter. Mr. Russell's definition of "incomplete symbol" is vague and his explanation does not fit in with his practice. We shall begin by discussing the statement that an incomplete symbol is "incomplete" because it disappears when the proposition in whose verbal expression it occurs has been analysed.

Mr. Russell uses the symbol $(\imath x)(\varPhi x)$ with two different sets of symbols. These two uses are :

(1) E!$(\imath x)(\varPhi x)$

(2) f$[(\imath x)(\varPhi x)]$ [1]

Mr. Russell evidently intends that whatever is true of $(\imath x)(\varPhi x)$ as it occurs in (1) should also be true of $(\imath x)(\varPhi x)$ as it occurs in (2). But he makes assertions about $(\imath x)(\varPhi x)$ which are true when $(\imath x)(\varPhi x)$ occurs as it occurs in (1), but which are not true of $(\imath x)(\varPhi x)$ as it occurs in (2). To make this clear we must repeat the definition which Mr. Russell gives of (1), viz. :

$$\text{E!}(\imath x)(\varPhi x) \,.\, = \,:\, (\exists c) : \varPhi x \,.\, \equiv_x \,.\, x = c. \quad Df.$$

Here both E! and $(\imath x)(\varPhi x)$ have disappeared in the analysis, so that, according to Mr. Russell's account, both E! and $(\imath x)(\varPhi x)$, or the set of symbols E!$(\imath x)(\varPhi x)$, are incomplete symbols having only a definition in use. Together they mean what is given in the right-hand expression. Now consider Mr. Russell's definition of (2). This is as follows :

$$\text{f}[(\imath x)(\varPhi x)] \,.\, = \,:\, (\exists c) : \varPhi x \,.\, \equiv_x \,.\, x = c : \text{f}c. \quad Df.$$

Now, as we pointed out above, the first part of the right-hand side expression, viz. $(\exists c) \,.\, \varPhi x \,.\, \equiv_x \,.\, x = c$, is the analysis of E!$(\imath x)(\varPhi x)$. Hence, in this case it is not true to say that $(\imath x)(\varPhi x)$ has no meaning in isolation. Nor has 'f' disappeared. Hence, the two ways in which $(\imath x)(\varPhi x)$ occur must be distinguished. It is necessary, then, to define "*incomplete symbol*" in such a way that $(\imath x)(\varPhi x)$ in E!$(\imath x)(\varPhi x)$ always will be an incomplete symbol, but $(\imath x)(\varPhi x)$ in f$(\imath x)(\varPhi x)$ need not necessarily be an incomplete symbol. Whether it is or not will depend upon the way in which it is used. Mr. Russell clearly wants so to define 'incomplete symbol' that "the author of *Waverley*" used as it is in fact used, will be an incomplete symbol. Professor G. E. Moore has suggested the following definition : [2]

---

[1] This might be read : "The term satisfying $(\varPhi x)$ has the property *f*."

[2] This definition is quoted from a letter Professor Moore wrote to me. I have made considerable use of this letter in discussing incomplete symbols. What I have said with regard to incomplete symbols and logical constructions is, in so far as it is correct, due to Professor Moore. Nothing in this section is original, except the mistakes. Professor Moore has kindly allowed me to make use of his letter. Perhaps I should not venture to put his opinions into print as I cannot hope to report them correctly, but it is not possible for me to write anything about this subject without saying what I believe myself to have learnt from him.

"S, in *this* usage, is an incomplete symbol" = " S, in *this* usage, does occur in expressions which express propositions, and, in the case of *every* such expression, S never stands for any constituent of the proposition expressed." *Df*.

Professor Moore points out that what we require to define is " S *in this usage* is an incomplete symbol " and not " S is an incomplete symbol ", since a symbol which in one usage is an incomplete symbol might, in another usage, not be one. According to this definition $(\imath x)(\varPhi x)$ in E!$(\imath x)(\varPhi x)$ will always be an incomplete symbol ; but $(\imath x)(\varPhi x)$ in f$(\imath x)(\varPhi x)$ will not be an incomplete symbol *unless* ' f ' is also an incomplete symbol.[1] It is important to observe that in this definition it is asserted that ' S ' will be an incomplete symbol *only* if, in the case of every expression expressing a proposition in which S occurs in the given usage, S never *stands for* any *constituent* of the proposition expressed. Thus the notions of ' constituent ' of a proposition and ' standing for ' are introduced into the definition in a sense such that a proposition may have complex constituents and a symbol may ' stand for ' a complex constituent.

An incomplete symbol, then, cannot stand for any *constituent* of the proposition it helps to express.[2] It will be remembered that the constituents of a proposition *make up* the proposition. In the case of every true proposition, the proposition has no constituent which is not a constituent of the corresponding fact. It is not possible to define the sense in which the constituents ' make up ' the proposition. We might say that the constituents of a proposition are what the proposition is *about*. There are, however, two quite different meanings of ' about ', which it is important to distinguish. These are : (1) the sense in which to say "I am asserting a *proposition about A* " means " I am asserting a proposition in which A is a constituent " ; (2) the sense in which to say " I am asserting *something about* A " means " I am predicating something *of* A ". The former sense cannot be defined. In the latter sense A is the logical subject of the predication. In neither sense is *Scotch* in *The author of Waverley is Scotch* about *The author of Waverley* ; but in the first sense of " about " the proposition is *about* Scotch.

We have now to inquire what Mr. Russell means by " logical

[1] Thus, for example, in the case of the proposition expressed by " The prime number between 2 and 4 is 3 ", if " 3 " is not an incomplete symbol then neither is " The prime number between 2 and 4 ". This proposition is of the form : $[f(\imath x)(\varPhi x)]$; if " f " does not disappear when the expression is analysed, then " f " is not an incomplete symbol, and it will follow that " $(\imath x)(\varPhi x)$ " is also not an incomplete symbol.

[2] Thus an incomplete symbol is neither a name nor a descriptive phrase applying to any constituent of the proposition in whose verbal expression the incomplete symbol occurs.

construction ". We shall find that " logical construction " can only be defined by means of incomplete symbol. Since Mr. Russell has not himself *defined* " logical construction ", it will be best to begin by considering what *examples* he gives of logical constructions. Thus he says, *I*, *the table*, *the wall-paper*, *classes* are logical constructions. " Wall-paper " expresses what would ordinarily be said to be a thing of a certain sort. But, Mr. Russell says :

> ' Consider, say, a wall-paper which fades in the course of years. It is an effort not to conceive of it as one " thing " whose colour is slightly different at one time from what it is at another. But what do we really *know* about it ? We know that under suitable circumstances—i.e. when we are, as is said, " in the room "—we perceive certain colours in a certain pattern : not always precisely the same colours, but sufficiently similar to feel familiar. If we can state the laws according to which the colour varies, we can state all that is empirically verifiable ; the assumption that there is a constant entity, the wall-paper, which " has " these various colours at various times, is a piece of gratuitous metaphysics. We may, if we like, *define* the wall-paper as the series of its aspects. These are collected together by the same motives as led us to regard the wall-paper as one thing, namely a combination of sensible continuity and causal connexion. More generally, a " thing " will be defined as a certain series of aspects, namely those which would commonly be said to be *of* the thing. To say that a certain aspect is an aspect *of* a certain thing will merely mean that it is one of those which, taken serially, *are* the thing.' [1]

Thus " the wall-paper " does not stand for *any* constituent of any proposition in whose verbal expression " the wall-paper " occurs. What " wall-paper " symbolizes is not what common sense would call a *single thing*, although it appears to express a single thing. It is significant to say " *is a wall-paper* " but " wall-paper " does not express any constituent of any proposition. If some one looking at a wall-paper were to say " That is a pleasant shade of blue ", it is probable that he would intend only to refer to his visual sense-datum. In that case " that " would be a demonstrative symbol standing for a particular, viz. the visual sense-datum, of which the speaker was immediately aware. But if he were to say " That wall-paper is a pleasant shade of blue ", he would be referring not only to his present visual datum, but also to the set of possible visual data which, under suitable circumstances, some one might have. In that case " that wall-paper " is not a demonstrative symbol, for it is not possible to be acquainted with *the wall-paper*. The proposition in whose verbal expression " the wall-paper " occurs is a proposition about a set of particulars, but " the wall-paper " does not *stand for* the set of particulars as a demonstrative symbol *stands for* its referend. Mr. Russell accordingly says that what " the wall-paper " stands for is a logical construction.

The proposition in whose verbal expression " wall-paper " occurs,

[1] *Our Knowledge of the External World*, pp. 106–7.

requires then to be analysed, since "wall-paper" does not stand for any constituent of the proposition. It is for this reason that Mr. Russell says that *the wall-paper* is a logical construction. If "wall-paper" is so used that it *never* stands for any constituent of a proposition in whose verbal expression it occurs, it follows that "wall-paper" is an incomplete symbol. This, then, suggests that we may define a logical construction as follows:

"Any X is a logical construction" = "X is symbolized by 'S' and 'an S' is an incomplete symbol." *Df*.[1]

Mr. Russell says that classes are logical constructions. His statement is extremely confused. He says: 'We must seek a definition [of class] on the same lines as the definition of descriptions, i.e. a definition which will assign a meaning to propositions in whose verbal or symbolic expression words or symbols apparently representing classes occur, but which will assign a meaning that altogether eliminates all mention of classes from a right analysis of such propositions. We shall then be able to say that the symbols for classes are mere conveniences, not representing "objects" called "classes", and that classes are, in fact, like descriptions, logical fictions, or (as we say) "incomplete symbols".' [2] Mr. Russell cannot mean that *classes* are incomplete symbols, but that classes are *symbolized* by incomplete symbols and are therefore logical constructions. It may, however, be doubted whether classes are logical constructions in the same sense precisely as *the wall-paper* is a logical construction, or in which *the author of Waverley* is a logical construction. But the question of different *kinds* of incomplete symbols, and hence of different *kinds* of logical constructions, is very obscure and difficult. It cannot be discussed in this book.

§ 5. EXISTENCE

The recognition that descriptions may apply to nothing throws light upon a problem that has perplexed philosophers and has led to the introduction of the doctrine that there are different universes of discourse, in the sense in which "different universes of discourse" *means* "different modes of being".[3] Mill's view, for example, that every connotative word has denotation implies this doctrine although he does not explicitly develop the consequences of it. He maintains that a significant proposition implies "the real existence of the subject, because in the case of a non-existent subject there is nothing

[1] See J. Wisdom. *Proc. Arist. Soc.*, N.S., XXIX, pp. 67–73. It seems to me probable that "logical constructions" must be defined through incomplete symbols as they occur in the verbal expression of *true* propositions, and not of *any* propositions true or false. But it is not possible to discuss this problem in detail here.

[2] *Int. Math. Phil.*, pp. 181–2.

[3] Cf. Chap. IV, § 6; Chap. V, § 4.

for the proposition to assert ". [1]   He gives as an example 'The ghost
of a murdered person haunts the couch of the murderer'. It is
here assumed that " The ghost of a murdered person " expresses
the logical subject of the proposition and is thus what the proposition is *about*. If, Mill argues, " The ghost of the murdered person "
has no denotation, then the proposition is about nothing ; but it
clearly is not a meaningless noise ; hence, it must be about something, and what could it be about except *ghosts* ?   Mr. Russell's
analysis of propositions in whose verbal expression such definite
descriptions occur reveals the nature of Mill's mistake.   It is consequently not necessary to discuss Mill's argument further.

It might still, however, be argued that, although descriptions
may describe nothing actual, i.e. nothing which has, to use Mill's
phrase, ' real existence', yet such descriptions describe something
which has some mode of *being* which is to be contrasted with *real
existence*.   This view has been clearly stated by Mr. Russell, who
at one time argued in its defence.   He has put the point as follows :

> ' If A be any term that can be counted as one, it is plain that A is something,
> and therefore that A is.   " A is not " must always be either false or meaning-
> less.   For if A were nothing, it could not be said not to be ; " A is not "
> implies that there is a term A whose being is denied, and hence that A is.
> Thus unless " A is not " be an empty sound, it must be false—whatever A
> may be, it certainly is.   Numbers, the Homeric gods, relations, chimeras
> and four-dimensional spaces all have being, for if they were not entities of a
> kind, we could make no propositions about them.   Thus being is a general
> attribute of everything, and to mention anything is to show that it is.'   He
> adds : ' *Existence*, on the contrary, is the prerogative of some only amongst
> beings.' [2]

The difficulties which this view involves, as, for instance, that
there is a round square, led Mr. Russell later to the theory of descriptions.   This theory not only shows that the view stated above
is false but also, what is more important, it shows precisely *how*
it is that such a view could be false.   The belief that whatever is
thought of must in some sense *be* is at first sight so very plausible
that it may be worth while to consider the assumptions upon which
this belief is based.   It should then be clear that to understand
the theory of descriptions is to reject this belief.

Professor Moore has formulated a possible argument in support
of this erroneous view in order, it seems, that he might bring out
more clearly the errors involved. [3]   He suggests that it might be argued :

> ' A thing cannot have a property unless it is there to have it, and, since
> unicorns . . . *do* have the property of being thought of, there certainly must

---

[1] *Logic*, Bk. I, Chap. VI, § 2, and cf. Chap. VIII, § 5.
[2] *Principles of Mathematics*, p. 449.
[3] " The Conception of Reality," *Proc. Arist. Soc.*, N.S., XVIII.   This article
is reprinted in *Philosophical Studies*, to which the references are given.

be such things. When I think of a unicorn, what I am thinking of is certainly not nothing ; if it were nothing, then, when I think of a griffin, I should also be thinking of nothing and there would be no difference between thinking of a griffin and thinking of a unicorn. But there certainly is a difference ; and what can the difference be except that in the one case what I am thinking of is a unicorn, and in the other a griffin ? And if the unicorn is what I am thinking of, then there certainly must *be* a unicorn, in spite of the fact that unicorns are unreal. In other words, though in one sense of the words there certainly *are* no unicorns—that sense namely, in which to assert that there are would be equivalent to asserting that unicorns are real—yet there *must* be some other sense in which there *are* such things ; since if there were not, we could not think of them.' [1]

This passage states clearly the kind of argument that may have led philosophers to suppose that there are non-existent objects having some mode of being different from existent objects of the same kind, or type. For example, lions exist and unicorns do not exist. But "a unicorn" means an animal of a certain sort, just as "a lion" means an animal of a certain sort. Consequently, "is a unicorn", "is a lion" are of the same logical type. We can express what is meant by the statement that these are of the same logical type by saying that anything that was a lion, or anything that was a unicorn, would be a particular, or an individual, as contrasted with a relation, or a universal. [2] Thus, if we are to admit that there must in some sense *be* a unicorn, even though we have admitted that unicorns don't exist, we are forced to conclude that there are non-existent individuals. This seems an absurd conclusion. We must therefore examine the argument that unicorns must in some sense be since I can think of a unicorn, and I can think of a griffin, and that in neither of these cases am I thinking of nothing, since what I am thinking about is different in the one case from what it is in the other. This argument rests upon the false assumption that " Unicorns are thought of " implies " Unicorns exist ", or " There are unicorns ". The assumption arises from a failure to *analyse* correctly the proposition " Unicorns are thought of ", owing to the mistaken belief that " Lions are hunted " expresses a proposition of the same form as " Unicorns are thought of " ; similarly with regard to the proposition " I am thinking of a unicorn ", and " I am hunting a lion ". We must, then, consider how these propositions are to be analysed.

The proposition expressed by " I am hunting a lion " is of the form ' $(\exists x) : x$ is a lion $. x$ is hunted by me '. Thus this proposition asserts that the property of *being a lion* and of *being hunted*

---

[1] loc. cit., p. 215.

[2] If Russell's view that lions are logical constructions is correct, then lions cannot be regarded as *particulars* in the same fundamental sense in which, for example, sense-data are so. But they are clearly particulars in some sense in which, for instance, this would exclude their being universals.

" Φ " is a property belonging to an individual (or particular) is comparatively unimportant. What is important is to see that, *whatever* the type of " Φ " may be, to assert that " There is a Φ " is to assert that Φ *belongs to something*, i.e. to assert that $(\exists x) . \Phi x$ is *true*. Mr. Russell would say that " exists " has " systematic ambiguity ". This means that there is a different sense of " exists " corresponding to each different type of " Φ ". Thus the meaning of " There are " in " There are lions " is different from the meaning of " There are " in " There are universals ", or in " There are propositional functions ". Mr. Russell insists that to say " lions exist " *means* " ' x is a lion ' is sometimes true " ; and to say " numbers exist " *means* " ' x is a number ' is sometimes true ", and so on. He asserts that this is the fundamental meaning of existence. What is fundamental is, however, the notion of *belonging* to something. It is important to observe that however many different senses " Φ's exist " or " There are Φ's " may have, corresponding to different logical types expressed by ' Φ ', *all* of them are such that the propositional function ' $(\exists x) . \Phi x$ ' cannot be true unless ' Φ ' belongs to something.

CHAPTER X

THE GENERALIZATION OF LOGIC

' Every science that has *thriven* has thriven upon its own symbols ; logic, the only science which is admitted to have made no improvements in century after century, is the only one which has *grown no symbols.*'—*Augustus de Morgan.*

§ 1. THE IDEAL OF LOGIC

EVERY logician has recognized that logic is concerned with form but only recently has it been recognized that there is a science of pure logic which is concerned with nothing but form. There is a wide divergence of opinion among those who call themselves logicians with regard to the topics properly belonging to logic and with regard to their mode of treatment. Many books purporting to be on logic have been written solely from the point of view of everyday argument, with the professed intention of showing how certain propositions important to mankind can be *proved to be true* and how the assertions of those who dispute these propositions can be *disproved.* Thus conceived, logic is regarded as the *art of thinking.* Consequently, much stress has been laid upon the fallacies incident to language and upon the *causes* of erroneous beliefs. No doubt such a study is useful but it must be distinguished from logic. Owing to the limitation of their interest to the criticism of reflective thinking as it occurs in practical problems, in scientific discovery, and in theological disputation, earlier logicians made but a slight attempt to discover the formal principles of proof. Such a discovery presupposes the attempt to analyse the various types of argument in order to detach their formal validity from any given subject-matter. The use of the significant language of everyday speech tends to conceal form and to encourage the confusion of logic with the art of disputation. The *Port Royal Logic,* for instance, affords a good example of a work belonging rather to the art of disputation than to logic.[1] It elaborates technical trivialities which do not lead towards an apprehension of the formal principles involved in correct reasoning. The *Port Royal* logicians regarded themselves as carrying on the tradition of

---

[1] The *Port Royal Logic* was first published in Paris in 1662, under the title : *La Logique ou l'Art de Penser, contenant outre les Regles communes, plusieurs observations nouvelles, propres à former le jugement.*

that " R precedes S ", " R loves S ", " All R is S " express different forms. They did not attempt to analyse these relations in order to ascertain their logical properties, but were content to take sameness of grammatical form as a guide to sameness of logical form. Thus Aristotle's successors rigidly confined deduction to the form of the subsumptive syllogism, thereby, not only wasting their time in the elaboration of technical trivialties but, what was more important, hindering the development of logic. The failure to analyse the relations involved in different types of deductive reasoning prevented logic from " growing symbols " to exhibit form.

§ 2. RELATIONS

All deduction depends upon the logical properties of relations. Hence, the concept of *relation* is of fundamental importance. It does not seem possible to define *relation* without presupposing notions no less in need of definition. All that we can do is to make some observations that will help us to grasp what exactly a relation is. Any object of which we can think possesses characteristics that enable us to distinguish it from other objects. These characteristics are of two kinds : *qualities* and *relations*. The difference between these cannot be defined since both *quality* and *relation* are indefinable.[1] By a quality we mean what is sometimes called a *simple quality*, such as would ordinarily be expressed by an adjective, e.g. *red, sweet, loud*. From the common-sense point of view we may say that if it is true that *A is red*, then A can be regarded as possessing the quality of *being red* independently of any reference to any other object.[2] By *a relation* we mean a characteristic that belongs to A considered with reference to some other object B. This statement cannot be regarded as a definition of " relation ", since the phrase " considered with reference to " repeats the concept of relation. But the statement may nevertheless be useful since it suggests that A cannot have a relation unless there is some other object *to* which it has the relation. For example, if *A has a father*, then there must be some term, of the same sort as A, which is A's father. Thus *having a father* is a relational characteristic that belongs to A. Suppose this term is X ; then the relation *father of* holds between X and A. Again, to assert *equality* of some term K is to assert that K can be considered with reference to some other term, of the same

---

[1] Mr. W. E. Johnson says : ' A *relation* is properly defined as a " *transitive adjective* ", the ordinary adjective being distinguished as *intransitive*.' (*Logic*, I, p. 204 n.) This definition rests upon a conception of relation and adjective that does not seem to me to be enlightening. Moreover, " transitive " contains the notion of *relation*. Mr. Johnson's use of " adjective " is extremely confusing.

[2] It is possible, and perhaps necessary, to regard *red* as a term in an irreducible multiple relation. But the understanding of such a view presupposes that we know what is *meant* by the statement that *red* is a non-relational quality.

sort as K in some respect, which is equal to K. If this term is L, then " K equals L " expresses a relation that holds between K and L. To assert that *D is a gift* is to assert that there are two terms such that one, say X, has the characteristic of *giving D*, and the other, say Y, has the characteristic of *receiving D*. Then " X gives D to Y " expresses a relation of *giving* that holds between X, D, and Y. To assert that £5 *is owed* is to assert that there are three other terms such that one, say A, has the characteristic of *owing*, another, say B, has the characteristic of *being owed*, and a third, say X, has the characteristic of *being that for which* something is owed. Then " A owes £5 to B for X " expresses a relation of *owing*.

All these are examples of relations that are perfectly familiar and are in common use in ordinary life. These relations differ in the number of *terms* involved. A term is anything that can have a quality or stand in a relation. Both qualities and relations are *universals*. Terms which occur as A occurs in *A is red*, or as A and B occur in *A loves B* are *particulars*, or *individuals*. These terms cannot occur as *is red* occurs in *A is red*, or as *loves* occurs in *A loves B*. Such constituents as *is red*, *loves* are universals.[1] Every proposition contains one constituent which functions as *loves* functions in *A loves B*, that is, which combines the constituents into the unity of a single proposition. The constituents thus combined need not be particulars, e.g. " Hatred is akin to love ". Nevertheless, the relating universal does not occur as *hatred* and *love* occur. We have already distinguished relations according to the number of terms involved, viz. dyadic, triadic, tetradic, pentadic, polyadic. We shall symbolize a dyadic relation *either* by $x \, R \, y$, or by $R(x, y)$; relations with more than two terms will be symbolized by $R(x, y, z)$; $R(v, x, y, z)$, and so on. We symbolize the relation in which y stands to x, when $x \, R \, y$ by $\breve{R}$, i.e. $y \, \breve{R} \, x$. We are accustomed to the converses of propositions, so that the conception of the converse of a relation presents no difficulty. The system of family relationships provides the most familiar example of relations from which we can easily derive inferences. Given any genealogical tree, say that of The *House of Hanover*, we can establish at once the precise degree of kinship in which, say, the present Duchess of York stands to George I.

The great importance of relations in deductive theory is due to the fact that they possess certain *formal*, i.e. *purely logical*, properties that lie at the basis of all inference. Relations can be classified according to their logical properties. We shall begin with some definitions that will be found useful in the statement of these properties.

Referent and Relatum. Every relation has a *sense*, i.e. the *direction* in which it goes. For example, *loves* goes *from* the *lover*

[1] Cf. Chap. IV.

may be other terms than A which stand in that relation to B. If A loves B there may be other terms than A which stand in that relation to B, and there may be other terms than B to which A stands in the same relation. We shall accordingly distinguish four kinds of relations, defined as follows :

(1) *Many-many*. The relation R may be such that if $x \, R \, y$, then there may also be $m \, R \, y$, $n \, R \, y$ . . . and also $x \, R \, b$, $x \, R \, c$ . . . For example, 1° *of latitude north of*, *subjects of Emperors*.

(2) *Many-one*. The relation R may be such that when the referent is given the relatum is determined, but there may be many referents. Such a relation is *many-one*. For example, *servant of Queen Elizabeth* ; *wife of the Sultan*.

(3) *One-many*. A one-many relation is the converse of a many-one relation, e.g. *sovereign of* is a one-many relation, *subject of* is a many-one relation.

(4) *One-one*. A relation R may be such that the selection of the referent uniquely determines the selection of the relatum, and conversely. There may be many members of the domain of R and many members of the converse domain, but the selection of a given term (either referent or relatum) determines which term must be selected to stand in the relation R (either as relatum or as referent). For example, *eldest son of a father*, *married to one spouse*. One-one relations may be regarded as a special case of one-many relations. They are of very great importance in the exact sciences. Correlations are one-one relations. It will be remembered that counting is a process of establishing a one-one relation between a set of objects and the numerals.[1]

Definite descriptions involve one-many relations, e.g. " The father of Oliver Cromwell ", " The teacher of Socrates ", " The Man in the Iron Mask ", " The author of *Waverley* ". Each of these descriptions implies that there is one, and only one, term that is referent of the relation. Thus Oliver Cromwell could have only one father, but his father might have many children. If, however, there is only one relatum, then the relation is one-one. Thus one-one relations are a special case of one-many relations, e.g. " The author of *Waverley* ", " The Man in the Iron Mask ". It should be observed that the relation of *object* to *description* is not one-one,

---

[1] These relations might be defined as follows:

(1) R is *many-many* when both the domain and the converse domain contain more than one member, and the selection of a term from either does not determine the selection of the other term.

(2) R is *many-one* when the selection of a term from the domain determines the selection of the term from the converse domain, but not conversely.

(3) R is *one-many* when the selection of a term from the converse-domain determines the selection of the term from the domain, but not conversely.

(4) R is *one-one* when both R and Ř are one-many.

since there are many correct descriptions of the same object, e.g.
" The chief speaker in Plato's dialogue *The Republic* ", " The philosopher who drank the hemlock ", " The husband of Xantippe ",
all describe *Socrates*. The relation *parent of* is not a one-many
relation since, if x is parent of y, then x may be either father or
mother of y, so that two terms stand in that relation to y. If,
however, the referents be limited to *males*, then the relation is
one-many ; if the relatum be now limited to *eldest son*, the relation
is one-one. It should be observed that mathematical functions result
from one-many relations, e.g. the cosine of x, the logarithm of y.

We have now to consider the combination of two relations.
Suppose there is a relation R such that x R y, and a relation S such
that y S z, then there is a relation between x and z compounded
out of the two relations R and S. Such a mode of combination is
called *relative multiplication* and the relation thus obtained is called
the *relative product* of R and S. We may give the following definition :
Given any two relations R and S and a term y such that x R y and
y S z ; then the relation that holds between x and z is the relative
product of R and S. Russell symbolizes the relative product of
R and S by R | S. R and S are called the factors of their relative
product. The relative product of *sister of* and *father of* is *paternal
aunt*. If the order of the factors be reversed a different relation
may be obtained. That is to say, the relative product is not as
such commutative. For example, if we reverse the order of the
factors given above, we obtain *father of*, which is the relative product of *father of* and *sister of*. The converse of a relative product
is obtained by reversing the order of the factors and then sub-
stituting their converses. That is, $(\widetilde{R | S}) = \breve{S} | \breve{R}$. For example,
the converse of the relative product of *husband of* and *daughter-
in-law*, is *father or mother of*.

Square of a relation. The relative product of R and R is the
square of R. That is, $R | R = R^2$. For example, the relative
product of *father* and *father* is *paternal grandfather*. The converse
of the square of father is *son's son*. The square of *ancestor* is *ancestor*.

Containing or being implied by. A relation R contains, or is
implied by a relation S, when it is such that if S holds, R holds.
It may be noted that a transitive relation contains its square and
that the square of a transitive aliorelative relation is asymmetrical.

So far we have been concerned only with dyadic relations. It
is possible to classify triadic, tetradic and other polyadic relations
in accordance with the definitions we have given, provided that
suitable modifications are made. We cannot, however, discuss
these definitions here. It must suffice to point out that R(a, b, c,
d . . .) will be symmetrical if the order of the terms can be changed
without altering the relation R, i.e. R(a, b, c, d . . .) $\equiv$ R(b, c, d,

of the possibility of elimination of intermediaries connected by a
transitive relation. The failure of the traditional Logicians to
apprehend the nature and importance of the logical property of
transitivity concealed from them the characteristic in virtue of
which such deduction was possible. They consequently failed to
see that the so-called *a fortiori* argument is valid in virtue of the
characteristic which renders the subsumptive syllogism valid,
although it cannot be twisted into the subsumptive form. For
the same reason they were content to rest all deduction upon Aristotle's *dictum de omni* and were thus led to their absurd limitation
of deduction to a single form.

§4. THE CONSTRUCTION OF A DEDUCTIVE SYSTEM [1]

A system consists of elements standing in certain relations. For
example, the solar system is a system consisting of certain elements,
viz. the sun, the planets and their satellites, standing in certain
relations. A social organization is a system consisting of social
classes related in a certain way. In *any* given system *the fact that*
an element stands in a given relation can be expressed by a proposition. Thus the relative positions of the earth, Jupiter, and the sun,
can be expressed by the proposition *The earth is between Jupiter and
the sun*. Given *any* system, the relation of its elements can be
expressed in a set of *related propositions*. A deductive system is a
special kind of system in which the elements are *propositions* and the
relations between the elements are *logical* relations. In this Chapter
we shall be concerned only with deductive systems. The student
will have some familiarity with the most highly developed of such
systems, deductive mathematics. But he may not have much
insight into the *nature* of the system. It has commonly been supposed that such systems are demonstrations of complex propositions
from simple axioms. These axioms were supposed to be self-evident,
that is, indubitably true. But they were thought indubitable only
because they were not doubted. Self-evidence is a relative notion.
What we are able to doubt depends upon our previous knowledge and
our mental capacity. For centuries Euclid's system of geometry was
supposed to be based upon axioms which were self-evident, or indis-
putably true, from which all his theorems followed deductively.
This belief is now known to be mistaken. The elaboration of non-
Euclidean geometries has shown that geometrical systems can be
constructed that are based upon other axioms than Euclid's and
that lead to different results. The careful examination of the nature
of these axioms and of the connexion between them and the resultant
theorems revealed the fact that Euclid's theorems do not follow

[1] The student should read Chapter XIII before reading the remainder of this
Chapter.

from his axioms, but require the assumption of further axioms not recognized by Euclid himself. Hence, we find it is important to ask what an axiom is. We cannot answer that an axiom is a proposition that is *necessarily true*, for we do not know what " necessarily true " means, nor does the use of an axiom in a deductive system depend upon its being *true*. It is probably because Euclid's axioms were regarded as descriptive of the space of our external world that they were supposed to be both self-evident and true. Now that this assumption is rejected we have further reason to doubt their self-evidence.

Self-evidence seems to combine two elements, obviousness and logical priority. Obviousness is a matter of familiarity and point of view. It is not a notion useful for logic. It might, however, be supposed that we could define axioms in terms of logical priority. Hence, axioms would be propositions logically prior to any other propositions. But logical priority is not absolute. The notion of logical priority is obscure. Its discussion has been encumbered with difficult and dubious metaphysical assumptions. We can say that in a deductive system a proposition p is logically prior to another proposition q if, and only if, p is logically simpler than q. We have now to inquire what is meant by saying that p *is logically simpler than* q. If we can assume p without assuming q but cannot assume q without assuming p, then p is logically simpler than q. But what we assume depends upon our starting-point. Hence, logical simplicity is also a relative notion. In the beginning of the construction of a system certain concepts are taken as undefined and intelligible without definition. These are called primitive concepts. Certain propositions are taken as undemonstrated. These are called primitive propositions.[1] We have to substitute for the vague notion of logical priority the notion of undefined concepts and undemonstrated propositions. But we do not say that these concepts are *indefinable*, or that these propositions are *indemonstrable*. It is as meaningless to ask whether a given concept is indefinable and a given proposition indemonstrable without specifying the system within which they are being used as it would be to ask whether the earth moves without specifying the system of reference. We must not commit the absurdity of defining a primitive proposition as a logically prior proposition. We desire *to replace* the latter notion by the former. By saying that a proposition is primitive we *mean* that it is assumed, and affords a basis for demonstration although it is not itself demonstrated. It is thus in the position of an *axiom*, or a *postulate* ; but it is not to be regarded as *axiomatic* in the old sense, i.e. as *necessarily true*.

[1] The terms " primitive concept " and " primitive proposition " are due to Peano.

established by means of the axioms.[1] In constructing an equilateral triangle on a given base Euclid assumes that the two circles used will intersect. But his system does not contain an explicit axiom to that effect, so that the demonstration fails. That it seemed satisfactory to Euclid is no doubt due to the fact that he constructed *figures* on a plane surface, which gave him the required result. But the use of figures involves an appeal to intuition ; hence the deduction is not *logical*. It gives *obviousness* but not *demonstration*. In constructing a deductive system we do not ask whether a given result will be obtained if we construct something *perceptible* ; we ask whether the proposition *follows from the axioms and definitions alone*. If the axioms are true, then the demonstrated propositions will be true. But the correctness of the demonstration is independent of the truth or falsity of the axioms. It is, indeed, *meaningless* to ask whether the axioms, or primitive propositions, are *true*. They can be so used as to lead to results that can be *interpreted* in such a manner as to make them true, or false. But apart from interpretation the question of truth does not arise.

Since the axioms are not given as true in the sense that they are supposed to be obtained by *intuition*, i.e. by appeal to the immediate apprehension of perceivable entities and their relations, the choice of the initial propositions of a deductive system is unlimited. In practice the selection of the primitive concepts and the primitive propositions is determined by the starting-point. As indicated above, the actual starting-point will not be logically primitive but will be dependent upon the acceptance of some generally recognized system. The analysis of this system will lead to the assumption that a set of elements have certain properties. In this way the primitive concepts will be obtained. Certain relations will be assumed to hold between these elements. These will yield the primitive propositions. Thus, instead of asserting " This element A will have the property Φ ", we assume the hypothesis, " If the element A has the property Φ ", and so on. Proceeding in this way we prove that such and such a set of elements have the properties required in order to demonstrate the system with which we are concerned, for example, Euclidean geometry. Different sets of primitive propositions may yield results that admit of the same interpretation. But the correctness of the demonstration is, we have seen, independent of this interpretation. Hence, we are led to regard the primitive concepts as *symbols* which are not defined but upon which we can operate by means of the primitive pro-

[1] Euclid's first Proposition is a *Problem* : To describe an equilateral triangle on a given finite straight line. The method of construction is, given the straight line AB, to describe a circle with centre A, radius AB ; and another circle with centre B, radius BA. Euclid assumes that these circles will intersect.

positions. The lack of a *determined* interpretation is compensated
for by the increased *generality* of the system. The system is purely
formal, independent of any matter of fact to which it may be applicable. Such a system provides a deductive scheme which can be
applied to various objects provided that they are capable of verifying
the primitive concepts and primitive propositions. Since the symbols
do not stand for determined objects but for *any objects having
certain formal properties*, the utmost degree of generality is attained.[1]

The selection of the primitive propositions is not purely arbitrary.
They must be both sufficient to yield the required results and mutually
consistent. A set of primitive concepts and primitive propositions
will be sufficient if it is possible to define all the concepts and to
demonstrate all the propositions that occur in the system in terms
of these initial concepts and by means of these initial propositions.
To establish the mutual consistency of the initial propositions it
is necessary to interpret the undefined concepts in order to ascertain
whether the primitive propositions will be true when so interpreted.
Such an interpretation yields an existence theorem, which asserts
that there are objects having the properties laid down in the definitions.[2] It is further desirable that the primitive propositions should
be *independent*. A primitive proposition is independent when it
cannot be logically derived from any of the other primitive propositions, or from any combination of them. To establish the
independence of the primitive propositions it is necessary to select
each in turn and to show that the remaining primitive propositions
can be combined with the contradictory of the selected proposition
so as to yield a consistent set. If it is possible to interpret the
undefined concepts in such a way that all but one of the primitive
propositions will be verified, then that proposition is independent
of the rest. The ideal is to select the fewest possible number of
primitive propositions. Such a selection satisfies an aesthetic pre-
ference for elegance and simplicity. A clear distinction between
a primitive proposition and a theorem, i.e. a proposition demonstrated by means of primitive propositions, depends upon the complete independence of the set of primitive propositions. It is possible

---

[1] Cf. Poincaré, *Science et Hypothèse*, p. 32 : ' Les mathématiciens n'étudient
pas des objets, mais des relations entre les objets ; il leur est donc indifférent de
remplacer ces objets par d'autres, pourvu que les relations ne changent pas. La
matière ne leur importe pas, la forme seule les intéresse.'

[2] Cf. Whitehead, *The Axioms of Projective Geometry*, p. 3 : ' According to the
logical " Law of Contradiction ", a set of entities cannot satisfy inconsistent
axioms. Thus the existence theorem for a set of axioms proves their consistency. Seemingly this is the only possible method of proof of consistency.
But the only rigid proofs of existence theorems are those which are deductions from the premisses of formal Logic. Thus there can be no formal proof
of the consistency of the logical premisses themselves.'

that there should be different deductive systems in which the primitive propositions of the one are theorems in the other. The characteristics of any given system will be completely determined by the logical properties of the relations given in the primitive propositions.

It is important to realize the part played by *definition* in a deductive system. From the strictly logical point of view definition is " the assignment of a short name to a lengthy complex of ideas ".[1] Such definitions are *nominal*; what is defined is a *symbol*. From this point of view definitions are symbolic conveniences. But whenever the question of interpretation arises, then the selection of the concepts to be defined is of the utmost importance, since this selection will determine the nature of the system.[2] Thus, as Professor Whitehead points out, ' if we abandon the strictly logical point of view, the definitions—though in form they remain the mere assignment of names—are at once seen to be the most important part of the subject '. To make the selection best fitted to yield a deductive system capable of important interpretations requires that insight which we call mathematical genius.

The complete generality of a deductive system is due to the fact that the primitive propositions do not determine a unique set of objects. When such deductive systems can be constructed it becomes possible to develop a part of several abstract sciences at the same time. In this way increase of generality aids the development of science.[3]

§ 5. THE SYSTEM OF PROPOSITIONS AND CLASSES

The attempt to generalize logic led to a twofold development. An attempt was made, on the one hand, to provide a calculus of reasoning; on the other, to analyse the logical relations proper to a deductive system. A calculus is an *instrument* for reasoning. Its purpose is to economize thought by providing a mechanical method of obtaining results, which can then be *interpreted* in a manner analogous to the way in which a mathematical equation can be interpreted. Such a calculus may have great value. To economize thought is not to waste time. By means of such economy important discoveries may be made that would otherwise have been beyond the reach of finite minds.[4] As a matter of historical

---

[1] Cf. Whitehead, *The Axioms of Projective Geometry*, pp. 2–3.

[2] Cf. Chap. XXII, p. 441 below.

[3] For a further discussion of different sets of primitive propositions the student may be referred to : *Transactions of the American Mathematical Society* ; E. V. Huntingdon : ' Sets of Independent Postulates for the Algebra of Logic ' (1904), and ' A set of Postulates for Real Algebra ' (1905).

[4] Any one who doubts the value of a calculus may be invited to answer the simple question : What people are not the descendants of those who are not my ancestors ? De Morgan showed by means of this example how extremely diffi-

fact recent work on the logical foundations of mathematics has grown out of the attempt to develop a logical calculus. This development has come about in this way. In order to obtain a calculus a well-defined symbolism must be used. The ambiguities of ordinary language make it unfitted for this purpose. It is necessary to use ideographic symbols which represent concepts and the relations between them *directly*. In order that conclusions should be drawn with the utmost economy of thought it is necessary to use rules of transformation of formulae analogous to those used in ordinary algebra. In this way an almost mechanical process of calculation takes the place of reasoning. Owing to the use of exact rules of transformation and to the use of ideographic symbols each of which is well defined all the premisses of the reasoning are explicitly stated. Thus the development of a calculus prepared the way for the analysis of deductive systems.

The earliest attempts to construct a logical calculus were based upon the analogy of ordinary mathematical procedure. In consequence, mathematical analogies were stressed and mathematical symbols were used to express the relations. In some respects this analogy has been unfortunate but it undoubtedly aided the earliest attempts of logicians to generalize the processes of logic owing to their familiarity with the mathematical notation. It was, however, a hindrance so far as the problem of analysis was concerned. Thus Frege in his inquiry into the foundations of arithmetic—in which he raised the question whether its basis is empirical or purely logical —was led to lay greater stress on the *differences* than on the *analogies* between ordinary mathematics and that generalization of logic which is now commonly called *mathematical logic*. A mathematical theorem is a proposition and a mathematical proof is a set of related propositions. To investigate the conditions of such proof is to analyse the logical relations in order to ascertain their properties. In this analysis subtle distinctions have to be made that are *premathematical* —to use a convenient expression of Mr. Johnson's. Accordingly Frege and Peano, to whom the inception of modern work on the foundations of mathematics is due, used ideographic symbols of a different shape from those used in ordinary algebra.[1] In this way they emphasized the aspect of logical analysis rather than the aspect of calculation.

We shall consider the calculus only in so far as it throws light upon the process of the generalization of logic. As Mr. Russell says, ' Symbolic logic considered as a calculus has undoubtedly much interest on its own account ; but in our opinion this aspect

cult it is to answer quite simple questions in the logic of relations without the help of some form of calculus.

[1] For a further discussion of Frege and Peano see Chap. XXV, § 2.

has hitherto been too much emphasized at the expense of the aspect in which symbolic logic is merely the most elementary part of mathematics, and the logical prerequisite of all the rest.' [1]

There are obvious analogies between the system of propositions and the system of classes. The most fundamental relation between propositions is *implication* ; the most fundamental relation between classes is *inclusion*. The logical properties of these two relations are the same. Accordingly, the *logical equivalence* of propositions and the *equality* of classes have the same formal properties. Hence, up to a point, a system constructed out of elements related by an undefined relation having these properties could be interpreted either as a system of propositions or as a system of classes. But there are important respects in which the parallelism breaks down. Thus, as Mr. Russell observes, ' The symbolic affinity of the propositional and the class logic is something of a snare, and we have to decide which of the two we are to make fundamental.' [2]   There can be no doubt that the propositional system is more fundamental. This can be seen by considering the distinction between an *operation* and a *relation*. An operation is a process performed upon something which yields a certain result. Thus if 3 be added to 6, the operation of *addition* is performed and yields the result 9. This result is also a number. It could replace 3, or 6, in any propositional function about *all* numbers. This might be expressed by saying that the *result of an operation* can be significantly substituted in any formula in which the elements of the operation occur. Thus, the mathematical symbols $+$, $-$, $\times$, symbolize operations. In learning the multiplication tables, or in learning to add our accounts, we are learning how to perform operations. A relation is quite unlike an operation. The connexion of two elements by a relation does not yield a result which is of the same kind as the elements related. For example, the relation between classes yields a *proposition*, not a class. A deductive system is generated by logical *relations*, not by operations.

In spite of the fact that the system of propositions is more fundamental, we shall consider the system of classes first. The reason for this procedure is to be found in the historical development of generalized logic out of the calculus. The calculus was first worked out for classes and was then *interpreted* so as to apply to propositions. Certain peculiarities in the way in which deductive systems have been developed can be more easily grasped by the elementary student if it is approached through the system of classes. The extension of a class is a familiar idea, so that the extensional interpretation of classes offers no great difficulty. But the extensional interpretation of propositions is not easily grasped by the

---

[1] *Principia Mathematica*, p. 115.   [2] *Principles of Mathematics*, p. 12.

beginner. For this reason we adopt a method of treatment not wholly satisfactory from the logical point of view.

In the system of classes we begin with the unanalysed concept of a *class*, i.e. of a set of individuals, called *members of* the class. We make the following assumptions :

(1) There is a class of all possible individuals, called the " universe ". The *universe* will be symbolized by I.

(2) There is an operation of selecting individuals which results in a class of which those individuals are members.

(3) Any class can be selected from I.

(4) Classes can be combined.

(5) Any combination of classes is a class.

At this point we pause to inquire what we already know as to the modes in which classes can be combined. It is to be observed that these modes of combination are the operations we perform upon classes. Hence, assumption (5). In our assumptions we have assumed only one mode of combination, viz. the operation of *selecting* classes. This would not suffice for the construction of a system. But there are an infinite number of modes of combination that would suffice. How, then, are we to choose which modes to assume ? The answer in practice is that we choose those modes which will yield systems capable of being so interpreted as to apply to the actual world. This is, no doubt, an accident of the logician's interest, as a thinker, in achieving knowledge of the actual world. The fact that it is possible to construct systems having no actual interpretation shows that, from the logical point of view, all that need be considered are the logical forms and relations, whether or not the system is to be interpreted. But Euclid would not have constructed his geometrical system had he not begun with spatial intuitions. Just as the logician starts from a knowledge of the modes of combination that are capable of yielding interpretable results, so the student will best understand how a system may be constructed by first considering operations that are already familiar.

We shall begin, then, with some familiar examples of selecting classes and combining them. From the universe of possible individuals we select all those that are *politicians*. From the class *politicians* we select those that are *knights*. The class resulting from these two successive operations is the class *knighted politicians*, i.e. the class of all those that are *both knights and politicians*.

We select from the universe those that are *politicians* ; we also select those that are *poets*. We combine the class *politicians* with the class *poets*. The resultant class is the class of all those that are *either politicians or poets*.

We select from the universe all individuals *except politicians*. The resultant class is the class of all those who are *not politicians*.

These familiar modes of combination involve *logical conjunctions*. These may be summed up as follows, using α, β, to stand for *any* classes :

(i) The class *without* α, i.e. not-α, symbolized by $\bar{a}$.

(ii) The class α *and* β, i.e. $\alpha\beta$.

(iii) The class α *or* β.

There are obvious analogies between these operations upon classes and the mathematical operations of *subtraction, multiplication*, and *addition*. The operation of selecting the class *without* α is analogous to subtraction. The operation yielding α *or* β is analogous to addition ; hence the resultant class is called the *logical sum* of α and β.[1] The operation yielding $\alpha\beta$ is analogous to multiplication ; hence the resultant class is called the *logical product* of α and β.

Since α, β, are to stand for *any* classes, and since one of our fundamental assumptions is that any combination of α with β yields a class, it follows that $\alpha\beta$, $\alpha + \beta$, must be classes, no matter what members α has, or β has. Suppose, for example, that α is the class *knights*, and β the class *scavengers* ; then $\alpha\beta$ is the class *knighted scavengers*. But there are no individuals that are both knights and scavengers ; hence, *knighted scavengers* is a class with no members. Such a class is said to be empty ; it is called the *null-class*. It might be objected that it is an accidental characteristic of the world up to the present that there are no knights who are scavengers ; a Gilbertian revolution might supply this class with members. It is easy, however, to find examples to which such an objection could not be made. For example, the class *squares* has no members in common with the class *circles* ; hence, their logical product, *square-circles* is an empty class ; it is the null-class. The null-class is symbolized by 0.

The class *circles* combined by *or* with knighted scavengers yields the class *circles or knighted scavengers*. This is the same as the class *circles*, since *knighted scavengers* has no members ; thus, the class consisting of every member of *circles* together with every member of *knighted scavengers* is the class circles.

The class *circles* combined by *and* with the class *squared circles* is the null-class, since the class consisting of every individual that is *both a circle and a squared circle* has no members.

These results can be expressed by giving the ordinary mathematical interpretations to the symbols $+$ and $\times$, in generalized

---

[1] But, since ' *or* ' is not to be interpreted *exclusively*, the analogy with mathematical addition is not exact. There is no inverse operation of *subtracting* β from α, since α and β may have common members. Moreover, α *or* α yields α. The proper analogue of subtraction is the selection of α *from the universe*, which leaves the class not-α. Accordingly this is sometimes symbolized by " $- \alpha$ ", but is now usually written $\bar{a}$. In Boole's system ' *or* ' is interpreted exclusively, and is thus a proper inverse of subtraction.

form, a standing for any class that is not empty, 0 for the null-class :

    (i) $a + 0 = a$.

    (ii) $a \times 0 = 0$.

That is : (i) What is either a or nothing is a.

          (ii) What is both a and nothing is nothing.

We now introduce the relation *is included in*, which at present we shall take as undefined. By its help we can give a precise definition of the logical sum and the logical product of any two classes.

The *logical product* of two classes is the class included in each and including every class including each.

The *logical sum* of two classes is the class including each and included in every class included in each.

It follows from the definition of the logical sum that the null-class is included in the class a, *whatever* a may be. That is to say, the null-class is included in every class. This result is unfamiliar, and is therefore apt to seem absurd. But it is a consequence of the fact that we are interpreting classes *extensionally*. For example, by the class *scavengers* we mean *those individuals who are scavengers* ; we do not mean what is sometimes called the *class-concept scavenger*. Since the null-class, i.e. *the class without members*, is taken extensionally, it follows that there is only *one* null-class.

The relation *is included in* is transitive and non-symmetrical, since, if a is included in β, it does not follow that there are any members of β that are not a. In other words, a and β may be coextensive, or they may not be coextensive. It will be convenient to symbolize *is included in* by $<$. Then the results we have obtained with regard to the *null-class*, i.e. the class with no members, and *the universe*, i.e. the class of all possible members of any class, can be summed up as follows :

1. $0 < a$, i.e. the null-class is included in every class.

2. $0 < 0$, i.e. the null-class is included in the null-class.

3. $a < 1$, i.e. any class is included in the universe.

4. $1 < 1$, i.e. the universe is included in the universe.

The combination of propositions can be carried out in a manner analogous to the combination of classes. We shall again begin with familiar examples of combination, and shall then consider whether it is possible to define some of these modes of combination in terms of other modes.[1]

We shall begin with the unanalysed concepts of : (i) a proposition, (ii) assertion of a proposition.

---

[1] It must be remembered that in following this mode of procedure our purpose is not to *construct* a deductive system but to exhibit the manner in which the possibility of constructing such a system might be suggested. For this reason, we begin with what is *obvious*, not with what is logically *simple*, and we then proceed to *state* formal principles without any attempt at precise proof.

We make the following assumptions:
(1) Any proposition can be asserted.[1]
(2) Propositions can be combined.
(3) Any combination of propositions is a proposition.

There is a familiar relation *not* by means of which from a given proposition p we obtain another proposition *not-p*. The proposition *not-p* will be called the contradictory of p.[2]

Three modes of combining two, or more, propositions are familiar, viz. the modes of combining by means of the logical relations *and*, *or*, *implies*. Thus, given any two propositions there is a third proposition which consists in their simultaneous assertion, i.e. the assertion of both together. This proposition is derived from combining p, q by means of *and*, which yields p *and* q. The simultaneous assertion of p and q may be meaningless in a manner analogous to the logical product of two classes which yields the null-class. Again, given two, or more, propositions there is a third proposition which consists in their alternative assertion. This proposition is derived by combining p, q by means of *or*, which yields the single proposition p *or* q. Again, given any two propositions there is a third proposition which asserts that one of these propositions implies the other. That is to say, given any proposition p, there is another proposition q, such that p *implies* q.

These modes of combination are called *functions* of the propositions so combined, and the derivation of a proposition by means of *not* is called a function of the original proposition. We can now sum up these four functions, adding appropriate names and symbols.[3]

Logical Relation.	Function.	Symbolized by :
(1) not	negation, or contradiction.	$\sim p$
(2) or	addition, or disjunction.	$p \vee q$
(3) and	multiplication, or conjunction.	$p \cdot q$
(4) implies	implication.	$p \supset q$

It is not necessary to take all the modes of combination as *undefined* modes. Given *negation*, we can define *disjunction* if we assume conjunction; conversely, we can define *conjunction* if we assume disjunction; finally, we can define *implication* if we assume conjunction, or if we assume disjunction.

(I) We begin by taking *disjunction as undefined* and define (3) and (4) in terms of negation and disjunction.

---

[1] To say " p is asserted " is equivalent to " p is true ".

[2] To deny p is equivalent to " p is false ".

[3] We use the symbolism of *Principia Mathematica*, but it is to be observed that we could use + for disjunction, × for conjunction, hence the names " addition ", " multiplication ". The *disjunctive* mode of combination is what we have called in Chapter VII the " *alternative* form ". It is much to be regretted that the name " disjunction " has been preferred by symbolic logicians.

$$(i) \quad p \cdot q \cdot = \cdot \sim(\sim p \vee \sim q) \; Df.$$

This may be read : " ' It is false that either p is false or q is false ' is the defined equivalent of ' p and q '."

$$(ii) \quad p \supset q \cdot = \cdot \sim p \vee q \cdot Df.$$

This may be read : " ' p implies q ' is the defined equivalent of ' either p is false or q is true '."

(II) Taking *conjunction as undefined*, we define (2) and (4) in terms of negation and conjunction.

$$(a) \quad p \vee q \cdot = \cdot \sim(\sim p \cdot \sim q) \; Df.$$

This may be read : " ' p or q ' is the defined equivalent of ' It is false that both p is false and q is false '."

$$(b) \quad p \supset q \cdot = \cdot \sim(p \cdot \sim q) \; Df.$$

This may be read : " ' p implies q ' is the defined equivalent of ' It is false that p is true and q is false '."

Since any proposition may be true, or may be false, there are four possibilities with regard to the truth or falsity of p and q. These possibililies are :

(1) p true. q true.
(2) p true. q false.
(3) p false. q true.
(4) p false. q false.

Any mode of combination must exclude at least one of these four possibilities. We see that

$p \cdot q$ excludes (2), (3), (4) ;
$p \vee q$ excludes (4) ;
$p \supset q$ excludes (2).

It is found to be symbolically convenient to take negation and *disjunction*, not negation and *conjunction*, as the undefined concepts. We shall later be concerned with the consequences of the definition I (ii). It should be contrasted with II (b).

The conjunction of two (or more) propositions is called their *logical product* ; the propositions thus conjoined may be called *factors* of the operation of multiplication. There may be any number of factors.

The disjunction, or alternation, of two (or more) propositions is called their *logical sum* ; the propositions thus disjoined may be called *summands* in the operation of addition. There may be any number of summands.

The logical product of the two propositions is their *simultaneous* assertion, i.e. *both are true*. This may be defined, analogously to the definition of the logical product of two classes, as follows : *The logical product* of two propositions is a proposition implying each and implied by every proposition which implies both.

The logical sum of two propositions is their *alternative* assertion, i.e. *at least one is true.* This may be defined, analogously to the definition of the logical sum of two classes, as follows : *The logical sum* of two propositions is the proposition implied by each of them and implying every proposition implied by both.

We shall now state certain formal principles which hold both with regard to the relation between classes and the relation between propositions. We shall use an undefined symbol —< which can be interpreted either as "implies", in which case the elements related will be propositions, or as "is included in", in which case the elements related will be classes. These elements will be symbolized by A, B, C, standing indifferently for classes or for propositions. When we wish to emphasize one interpretation rather than the other we shall employ a, β, γ, for the former, p, q, r, for the latter as before. We shall symbolize logical products by simple juxtaposition of the elements, i.e. "AB" stands for "Both A and B"; we shall symbolize the logical sum by +. We shall symbolize negation by a bar, i.e. "Ā" stands for "not-A". Where convenient we shall use brackets to show that two or more elements are to be taken as a single compound element, e.g. "(A + B)" shows that the logical sum of A and B is to be taken as a single element. The negation of such a compound element will be expressed by a bar drawn over the whole bracket, e.g. $\overline{(A + B)}$.

It will sometimes be found convenient to express these principles as *equalities.* Equality may be defined as follows :

$$A = B \,.\, = \,.\, (A \text{—}< B)(B \text{—}< A) \text{ Df.}$$

It should be noted that in the propositional interpretation the symbol of equality "=" is replaced by the symbol of logical equivalence "≡".[1]

Formal Principles.

1. *Principle of Identity.*
   A—<A.

2. *Principle of Commutation.*
   (i) AB—<BA.
   (ii) A + B—<B + A.

3. *Principle of Association.*
   (i) (AB)C—<A(CB).
   (ii) (A + B) + C—<A + (B + C).

It should be observed that since the definitions of addition and multiplication do not involve any determination of the order in which the elements are to be combined, these relations are symmetrical. Consequently, the above three principles are obvious. We do not attempt to prove them here.[2]

---

[1] See Chap. VIII.
[2] The student who wishes to pursue this topic further should consult Couturat, *Algebra of Logic.*

4. *Principle of Distribution.*

     (i) $A(B + C)$—$<AB + AC$.

     (ii) $AB + C$—$<(A + C)(B + C)$.

This principle connects multiplication with addition. It should be noted that (ii) does not hold for ordinary algebra, whereas (i) and the first three principles do hold.[1] Thus 4 (ii) is a distinguishing principle of a logical calculus. As an illustration of this principle we may take the three *classes, scholars, Cabinet Ministers, peers.* Then (i) is exemplified in : All scholars who are either Cabinet Ministers or peers are included in the class of those who are either scholars and Cabinet Ministers or are scholars and peers. Also (ii) is exemplified in : All those who are either both scholars and Cabinet Ministers or are peers are included in those who are either scholars or peers and are also Cabinet Ministers or peers.

5. *Principle of Tautology.*[2]

     AA—$<A$.

The class consisting of *scholars and scholars* is clearly the same as the class scholars.

6. *Principle of Simplification.*

     (i) AB—$<A$.

     (ii) A—$<A + B$.

Thus $p \cdot q : \supset p$. That is to say, the logical product of two propositions implies either of the factors taken alone. Again, $p \cdot \supset \cdot p \lor q$. That is to say, any proposition implies the logical sum of itself and any other proposition. Thus, we can always add to the implicate of a proposition any number of alternatives without affecting the validity of the implication. We can always drop one of two (or more) propositions asserted simultaneously and assert the remainder. This principle permits the simplification of an argument by dropping out a proposition that is not required for a given purpose. It is easy to see that the principle holds when the elements are classes. It will be sufficient to give an illustration of (ii). The class of *intelligent people* is included in the class of those who are *either intelligent or Socialists.*

7. *Principle of Absorption.*

     (i) $A + AB$—$<A$.

     (ii) $A(A + B)$—$<A$.

---

[1] There are non-commutative algebras for which the second principle does not hold. So long as the basis of arithmetic, and therefore of algebra, is based upon our intuitions with regard to *counting,* non-commutative algebras will seem absurd ; just as, so long as geometrical axioms are based upon our intuitions of space, non-Euclidean geometrics will seem absurd. These formal principles stand to algebra as Euclidean axioms to geometry.

[2] See W. E. J., I, p. 30. Mr. Johnson points out that the principle of Tautology (which he calls the " Reiterative Law ") indicates that the content of what is asserted is not affected by any *re*-assertion '.

For example, (i) *Those who are intelligent or are both intelligent and socialists* are included in *those who are intelligent.* (ii) *Those who are musical and also either musical or irritable* are included in *those who are musical.*

It should be observed that " A—$<$B " expresses a *proposition* whatever A, B, may stand for, since —$<$ is a relation. If A, B, be interpreted as standing for *classes,* then " —$<$ " must be interpreted as " is included in ". If A, B, be interpreted as standing for *propositions,* then " —$<$ " must be interpreted as " implies ". The remaining principles are concerned with implications between propositions relating to class inclusions, or with implications between propositions relating to implications. Hence, in both cases, the main relation is an implication relation. Accordingly we shall use $\supset$ to express these principles, distinguishing between the class interpretation and the propositional interpretation by using $<$ for " is included in ".

8. *Principle of Composition.*

    (i) $a < \beta \cdot a < \gamma : \supset a < \beta\gamma.$

       $p \supset q \cdot p \supset r : \supset p \supset qr.$

    (ii) $\beta < a \cdot \gamma < a : \supset \beta + \gamma < a.$

       $p \supset q \cdot r \supset q : \supset p \vee r \cdot \supset q.$

The two forms of this principle may be illustrated with reference to classes as follows : (i) If *pedants* are included in *scholars,* and *pedants* are included in *bores,* then *pedants* are included in the class of those who are both *scholars and bores.* (ii) If *the industrious* are included in *the competent,* and *the well-paid* are included in *the competent,* then *those who are either industrious or well-paid* are included in *the competent.*

9. *Principle of Transposition.*

    $a < \beta \cdot \supset \cdot \bar\beta < \bar{a}.$

    $p \supset q \cdot \supset \cdot \sim q \supset \sim p.$

It is easy to see that contraposition rests upon this principle. Since the implication is reciprocal this principle could be stated as an equality, viz.

    $p \supset q \cdot \equiv \cdot \sim q \supset \sim p.$

10. *Principle of Syllogism.*

    $a < \beta \cdot \beta < \gamma : \supset a < \gamma.$

    $p \supset q \cdot q \supset r : \supset p \supset r.$

This principle follows from the transitivity of the relations of inclusion and implication.

11. *Principle of Excluded Middle.*

    $p \vee \sim p.$

This may be read : ' Either p is true or p is false.' [1]

---

[1] This and the following principle should be compared with the results obtained with regard to classes, given above. (See p. 185.)

12. *Principle of Contradiction.*

$$\sim(p \cdot \sim p).$$

This may be read : " p is not both true and false."

Since " p " stands for " any true proposition " and " $\sim p$ " stands for " any false proposition ", these last two principles might be expressed as follows :

(11) Any proposition is either true or false.

(12) Not any proposition is both true and false.

Throughout the statement of these principles we have taken *negation* as undefined. If we assume the notions *true* and *false*, negation can be defined by means of multiplication and addition. We shall use " $= 1$ " to symbolize " is true ", and " $= 0$ " to symbolize " is false ".

Given any proposition p, then $\sim p$ is its negation if

$$p \cdot \sim p = 0 \; ; \; p \vee \sim p = 1.$$

That is to say, the negation of p is that proposition $\sim p$ which is so related to p that one of them must be false, and the other true. Thus p and $\sim p$ are contradictories. It should be observed that both the principle of excluded middle and the principle of contradiction are required to define " contradictory propositions ". The principle of contradiction alone does not suffice to show that p and $\sim p$ are contradictories ; they might be contraries. The above formulation of negation brings out what is involved in the denial of a proposition but it does so only because *true* and *false* have been taken as undefined notions.[1]

13. *Principle of Double Negation.*

$$\bar{\bar{A}} = A.$$

It is easy to see that this principle follows from the symmetry of the relations of multiplication and addition used to define negation. From this definition we can derive two formulae, known as *de Morgan's formulae* :

$$\text{(i)} \; \overline{(A + B)} = \bar{A} \, \bar{B},$$

i.e. the negation of a sum is the product of the negations of the summands. This holds whether the elements of the product and the sum be propositions or classes.

$$\text{(ii)} \; \overline{(AB)} = \bar{A} + \bar{B},$$

i.e. the negation of a product is the sum of the negations of the factors. This holds whether the elements of the product and the sum be propositions or classes.

[1] The principles of *identity, excluded middle,* and *contradiction* have been traditionally considered as the only fundamental logical principles. This is a complete mistake. They are neither less, nor more, important than the other principles we have stated. (See below, Chap. XXIV.)

From these formulae it is possible to derive the negations of expressions of any degree of complexity. The general rule is *For every element substitute its negation, and change sums to products and products to sums.*

Given the definitions of negation, addition, and multiplication, and the resulting principles of excluded middle and contradiction, we can derive formulae expressing an exhaustive and exclusive division of any number of elements. Since of any element we can either assert A or assert $\bar{A}$, or can assert B or can assert $\bar{B}$, and so on, it follows that, given *two elements* A, B, we can assert

$$1 = AB + A\bar{B} + \bar{A}B + \bar{A}\bar{B}.$$

That is to say : the universe contains either what is both A and B, or what is both A and not B, or what is not A but B, or what is neither A nor B. These alternatives may not all be realized, that is, any of the alternatives may represent the null-class. Collectively these alternatives are exhaustive, that is, everything in the universe must fall into one or other of these sets of alternatives.

In the statement of the formal principles we assumed that ' p ' is equivalent to ' p is true ', and that ' $\sim p$ ' is equivalent to ' p is false '. These assumptions can be expressed as follows, using 1 and 0 as before :

(i) $p \, . \equiv . \, p = 1.$ (ii) $\sim p \, . \equiv . \, p = 0.$

The formal principles stated above in terms of implication suffice for the construction of deductive systems, but they do not suffice for the *drawing of conclusions*. The transitivity of the relation of *implication* yields the principle of syllogism, but it does not yield a principle which permits the omission of the implying element.[1] To secure this there is needed the independent assertion " $p = 1$ ", or an additional principle to the effect that *the implicate* of a true proposition stating an implication can be *asserted*. Thus we have,

14. *Principle of Deduction.*

What is implied by a true proposition is true.[2]

This is called the *principle of deduction* since it is in virtue of this principle alone that we can deduce a conclusion. Without this principle implication would not yield *proofs*. It might equally well be called the *principle of assertion*, since by means of it we are enabled to *assert* a conclusion instead of merely considering the conclusion as implied by the premisses. This principle cannot

[1] See Chap. XII, § 2 ; and cf. the quotation from Russell given in the footnote to page 223.
[2] See *Principia Mathematica*, p. 94, p. 132 ; *Principles of Mathematics*, § 38 ; Couturat, *Encyclopaedia of the Philosophical Sciences*, pp. 141–2.

be formulated symbolically. It would be a mistake, for example, to suppose that the principle of deduction could be formulated by

$$p \supset q . p = 1 : \supset . q = 1,$$
or by
$$p . \supset : p \supset q . \supset q,$$

for in neither of these symbolic expressions is it shown that p can be omitted and q asserted alone.[1] Any symbolic expression will yield only *an implication*, that is *the hypothesis* that p is true, not *the assertion* that p is true. But it is the *assertion* of p that is required to enable us to draw the *conclusion* q from the implication '$p \supset q$'.

Another non-symbolic principle is required in order that in an assertion with regard to every instance of a certain set we should be able to substitute a *given* instance. This is,

15. *Principle of Substitution.*

Whatever can be asserted about *any* instance, however chosen, can be asserted about any *given* instance.[2]

The principle of deduction and the principle of substitution are involved in all demonstrative reasoning. Without these two principles it would be impossible to construct a deductive system. Once the primitive propositions have been stated it is possible by means of these principles to deduce conclusions that are more and more complicated. The development of the primitive propositions stated in *Principia Mathematica* takes place in virtue of the repeated use of these two principles. They can accordingly be seen to be of very great importance in the construction of a deductive system.[3]

The mathematical logicians have for the most part adopted the definition of implication in terms of negation and disjunction, which was stated on page 187. Certain theorems which follow from this definition have been regarded as paradoxical. These must now be considered. The definition of *implication*, which we have to consider, is:

$$p \supset q . = . \sim p \vee q . Df.$$

Since ' $\sim p$ ' means ' p is false ', and ' p ' means ' p is true ', this definition requires either p, the implying element, to be false or q, the implied element, to be true. *Whenever* this is the case the first proposition implies the second, *according to this definition of* " *implication* ". We saw that ' $p \supset q$ ' excludes only the possibility ' p *true, q false* '. Thus, for example, given the *true* proposition ' $2 + 2 = 4$ ', and the *false* proposition ' The sun is cold ', then the compound proposition " *Either* ' $2 + 2 = 4$ ' *is true or* ' *The*

---

[1] The proposition ' $p . \supset : p \supset q . \supset q$ ' is true whether p be true, or false, and whether p implies q, or not. Hence, this proposition yields only the hypothesis that p is true, so that it does not permit the independent assertion of q.

[2] See *Principia Mathematica*, * 9·12.

[3] Cf. W. E. Johnson, *Logic*, Pt. II, Chaps. I and II.

13

sun is cold' is false" is true. Consequently, the proposition "'*The sun is cold' implies '2 + 2 = 4'*'" is true, since "implies" is defined to mean "either the first (i.e. the implying) proposition is false, or the second (i.e. the implied proposition) is true", not excluding the possibility that they may both be true.

This definition of "implies" is unfamiliar, so that its consequences are apt to seem queer. It is important for the reader to become familiar with this notion. It may be made clearer if we consider the following equivalences :

$$p \supset q \quad . \equiv . \sim p \lor q \quad . \equiv . \sim (p . \sim q)^{1}$$
$$\sim p \supset q \quad . \equiv . \quad p \lor q \quad . \equiv \sim (\sim p . \sim q)$$
$$p \supset \sim q . \equiv \sim p \lor \sim q . \equiv \sim (p . q)$$
$$\sim p \supset \sim q . \equiv \quad p \lor \sim q . \equiv . \sim (\sim p . q)$$

Thus, given this definition of "implies", then, when $p \supset q$, it is not the case that p is true and q false ; also, if both p and q are true, then, again, it is not the case that p is true and q false. Accordingly, when p is false, and also when both p and q are true, then p *implies* q. These consequences of this definition of implication are analogous to the consequences that result from the introduction of the null-class into the class-system. Thus,

(i) $\sim p \supset q$ corresponds to $0 < a$

(ii) $\sim p \supset \sim q$ corresponds to $0 < 0$

(iii) $p \supset q$ corresponds to $\begin{cases} a < 1 \\ 1 < 1 \end{cases}$

From (i) we get : any false proposition implies any true proposition ; from (ii) we get : any false proposition implies any false proposition. Thus, *any false proposition implies any proposition, true or false.* From (iii) we get : any true proposition implies any true proposition ; from (i) we get : any true proposition is implied by any false proposition. Thus, *a true proposition is implied by any proposition, true or false.* These results correspond to the interpretation for classes, viz. (1) *The null-class is contained in every class* ; (2) *Any class is contained in the universe.* On the propositional interpretation the theorems italicized above are known as "paradoxes of implication". But these theorems are not paradoxical ; they are the inevitable consequences of the definition of implication in terms of negation and disjunction. It should be observed that in the case of propositions there are only two possibilities with regard to truth and falsity, i.e. $p = 1$, or $p = 0$. The elements p, q, interpreted on the analogue of the class regarded as an *extension* are limited to these two possibilities. Thus p, q, are equivalent when both are true, or when both are false. Conse-

---

[1] The first row may be read : 'p implies q' is equivalent to 'either p is false or q is true' is equivalent to 'It is not the case that p is true and q is false'.

quently, to deny that p implies q is to assert that $\sim p$ implies q.

i.e. $\sim(p \supset q) \supset (\sim p \supset q)$.

But in the case of classes, to deny that α is included in β is not to assert that α is included in $\bar{\beta}$, since α and β may overlap. Thus there are three possibilities with regard to α and β, but only two possibilities with regard to p and q. In the case of the class interpretation, therefore, these apparent paradoxes do not arise.

The fact that the consequences of the definition of implication that we have been considering should have been called " paradoxes " has undoubtedly caused some confusion. As Professor Moore has pointed out, they " appear to be paradoxical, solely because, if we use ' implies ' in any ordinary sense, they are quite certainly false ".[1] It is clear that " implies " is ordinarily used in such a sense that implication affords a basis for inference. But we have seen that, in order that q should be *inferred* from p, we must be able to omit p. But p can be omitted only if p is true, that is, only if p can be asserted. Thus, in the case of a false proposition we cannot omit the implying element. If we *know* p to be false, then we know that p implies q (in the sense defined) ; but we cannot proceed to assert p, since such a procedure would be contradictory. Hence, we cannot *infer* q, since this inference requires the assertion of p. Again, if we *know* q to be true, then we know that p implies q ; but we cannot proceed to *infer* q, since we already *knew* q to be true.[2] As Mr. Russell has admitted, ' Whenever p is false, " not-p or q " is true, but is useless for inference, which requires that p should be true. Whenever q is already known to be true, " not-p or q " is of course also known to be true, but is again useless for inference, since q is already known, and therefore does not need to be inferred.' [3] He draws a distinction between the *validity* of the inference and what he calls the " practical feasibility of the inference ". This distinction does not appear to be very happily named. What is important is to distinguish between the logical relations that may hold between propositions, in virtue of which relations deduction is possible, and the truth of the premisses without which the deduction would not be valid. False propositions imply other propositions, but they cannot be made the basis of valid inferences in which the conclusion is asserted to be *true*. There is, then, no reason to regard the consequences of the definition of implication as paradoxical. They would be paradoxical only if they were taken to be paradoxes of *inference*. But in that case they would not strictly speaking be *paradoxical*; they would be *false*.

[1] *Philosophical Studies*, p. 295.
[2] The student should have read Chapter XII before reading this section.
[3] *Introd. Math. Phil.*, p. 153.

CHAPTER XI

SYSTEM AND ORDER

' To search for " unity " and " system " at the expense of truth, is not, I take it, the proper business of philosophy, however universally it may have been the practice of philosophers.'—*G. E. Moore.*

§ 1. THE NATURE OF SYSTEM [1]

THE notion of system lies at the basis of all science and philosophy. Deductive systems, which we considered in the last chapter, are a special kind of system. The notion of " system " in general is much less precise than that of " deductive system ", for the properties of deductive systems have been carefully determined. The generating relation of a deductive system is implication. We have now to consider what modes of connexion suffice to determine a system. It is not difficult to find examples of systems exemplifying different kinds of relations, such as the solar system, the social system, the post-office system, the ecclesiastical system. These various systems are characterized by various modes of connexion ; they have in common the fact that the constituent elements are compatible and that all the elements are determined by some at least of the other elements. We shall call the constituent elements of a system the " facts " of the system, meaning by a " fact " whatever *could* be expressed in a proposition, without reference to whether the proposition is true or false. Each fact will itself consist of elements, viz., *its* constituents, but we are not here concerned with the constituents of facts but with facts as constituents of systems. The question we have to consider is under what conditions an array of facts can be regarded as a systematic array.

Facts may be conjunctively combined. Such an array would not be a systematic array. Facts may be alternatively combined. This mode of connexion would again be insufficient to determine a system. Mutual compatibility is a minimum condition without which there could be no system. But though a necessary, it is not a sufficient condition. We cannot define " mutual compatibility ". To say that the fact F_1 is mutually compatible with the fact F_2 is to say that F_1 and F_2 may both belong to the same system. But

---

[1] The beginner should read Chap. XIII, § 1, before reading this chapter.

the notion of *compatibility* is simpler than the notion of *belonging to the same system*, and cannot be defined in terms of it. It follows that any fact F_3 which is incompatible with F_1 cannot be a constituent of any system in which F_1 is a constituent. Again, any fact which requires F_3 to be in the system cannot be in the system that contains F_1. Although the constituents of a system must not be incompatible, some may be mutually independent of others. Such mutually independent facts will be conjunctive facts. But it is not possible that all the facts should be mutually independent, for in that case, conjunctive relations would suffice to determine a system.

There are, then, four conditions to which any system must conform. These may be precisely formulated as follows :

Given a system S, then

(1) If A and B are both constituent facts in S, then A and B are mutually compatible.

(2) If B is a constituent fact and B requires, or determines, C, then C is a constituent of S.

(3) If B and C are constituent facts in S, then S contains the conjoint fact BC, though neither B determines C nor conversely.

(4) If BC determines E, then E is in S, though neither B alone, nor C alone, would suffice to determine E.

A system is not necessarily inclusive ; there may be facts not included in the system but not incompatible with any fact in the system. For example, a geometrical system excludes facts with regard to colour. Thus, if A is a fact in a geometrical system, A is not incompatible with any fact with regard to a colour. If A and B are facts in a classificatory system of genera and species, then neither A nor B is incompatible with any fact containing as a constituent the relation *more valuable than*. The determination of a system does not involve the determination of everything that is possible. A given system S_1 may be wholly contained in another system S_2, and S_1 may also be wholly contained in another system S_3, although there is no system Σ that contains S_1 and S_2 and S_3.[1] Different geometries afford an example of such systems.

It is reasonable to ask whether *the world*, or *the universe*, is a system. If by " the world " we mean " everything that is the case ",[2] then it may be doubted whether the world is a system. Whether or not it is a system *could* only be determined by empirical observation of everything that is the case. But we cannot empirically observe everything that is the case ; hence, we cannot *know* that the world is a system. We may have good reason for believing that it is *not* a system, but it remains possible that it

---

[1] The assumption that there is such a system Σ is the assumption of Monism.

[2] Wittgenstein, *Tractatus Logico-philosophicus*, Prop. 1.

should be a system although we are not able to discover the mode of connexion between the constituent facts. Everything that is the case includes the facts of all known systems as well as those facts which *we* are not able to include in any system and those facts which no one knows. What we call the *real*, or *actual* world, does not include all facts that are possible. It is the assumption of scientific thinking that all that is the case in *the physical world* is included in a system. This assumption may be regarded as the fundamental postulate of science. It leads scientists to reject some facts and to include other facts in " *the system of the physical world* ". Any fact incompatible with the given facts is left out of account *in order that the constituent facts may determine a system*. The facts in the actual world must all be compatible, but there may be conjunctive facts not related by other than conjunctive relations to other facts in the actual world.

A system is said to be *coherent* if *every* fact in the system is related to every other fact in the system by relations that are not merely conjunctive. A deductive system affords a good example of a coherent system. A work of art is a coherent system. The relations that determine its coherence are peculiar to works of art, but what is meant by saying that these relations determine it *as coherent* is what is meant when it is said of *any* system that it is *coherent*. The coherence of a work of art is so easily apprehended as essential to it, that is as constituting it a work of art so that, lacking this coherence the work of art would be a failure, that the expressions we use to express coherent systems are often taken from the analogy of the arts, e.g. " the world-picture ". But not all systems are coherent systems. That is to say, " system " and " coherence " are not, as has been often supposed, coimplicant. A jig-saw puzzle is a system, but it is not a coherent system, although the picture that is cut up to make the puzzle might be coherent. Each piece of the puzzle must fit in with *some* other pieces ; hence, the position of any given piece is not indeterminate. There are no wild bits, which might or might not, fit in. But the shape of a piece in the right-hand top corner of the picture may be independent of the shapes of any pieces in the left-hand side of the picture. Thus the jig-saw puzzle, though a system, is not a coherent system. The physical world may be such a system.

It is a truism that the aim of science is the achievement of system. It is for this reason that determinism is essential to science. Determinism is a characteristic of a system every constituent of which is in determinate relations determined by some other constituent, or constituents. It does not follow that *every* constituent is determined by *every other* constituent. Where this is the case the system is completely coherent. But coherence is a matter of degree. A system may possess some degree of coherence although some of its constituent facts may be independent of *some* other facts, provided that they are determined by *other* facts in the system. Since some constituent facts in a system may be mutually independent, it follows that a system S may contain either of two contradictory facts, though it cannot contain both.[1] For example, if A and B are mutually independent, then A and not-B may both be constituents in S, and there may be another system Σ that contains both A and B. Now the actual world contains as constituent facts all facts that are actual facts. Since no system can contain both B and not-B, and since either B is actual or not-B is actual, it follows that if the world-system contains both A and not-B, it cannot contain both A and B, or if it contains A and B, it cannot contain both A and not-B. Thus the system that contains A and B (if the world contains not-B), or the system that contains A and not-B (if the world contains B) is a *possible system*, (and, therefore, a possible world), but not an *actual world*. It is for this reason that the discovery of incompatible facts is useful for science, for science is concerned not with any possible system but with *the* system (if there is one) which is *the system of the world*.

It is not logically necessary that everything that is the case, that is, all the constituent facts of the actual world, should be contained in a system; still less that they should be contained in a coherent system. But unless actual facts do constitute a system science is impossible; unless the physical world is a *coherent* system physicists will be disappointed. Whenever inference is possible the facts which constitute the basis of the inference must be in a system with the facts that are inferred; otherwise the inference is invalid. But we cannot tell what inferences are possible until we know the fact from which the inference starts. Accordingly, in order to ascertain the system of the actual world we should need to know facts the knowledge of which could not be derived from the knowledge of *possible* systems. In other words, the system of the actual world, *because it is actual*, cannot be determined by logical considerations alone. Even if the actual world were a completely coherent system, it would not follow that *knowledge* of part of the system would yield *knowledge* of the whole system, nor even that it would involve *knowledge* of precisely what *kind* of system it was. This follows from the possibility that the system Σ may contain a subsystem both in S_1 and in S_2, although some facts in S_1 were incompatible with some facts in S_2. We might know only the subsystem, call it σ, contained both in S_1 and in S_2, from which it

---

[1] We say that *two facts are contradictory* when the propositions which would express these facts are contradictory. Thus in this chapter "fact" is being used in such a sense that not all *facts* are *actual*.

follows that σ is compatible with either of two systems which as systems are not compatible with each other. Our knowledge of the system of the actual world (if we have such knowledge) may be of such a sub-system σ. There may be various other possible systems each of which includes σ, between which we could not decide as to which is actual. This would be the case if we did not know the facts compatible with σ and compatible with S_1 but not compatible with S_2. If this argument is correct, it follows that we cannot *know* that the system of the actual world is a coherent system such that given some of the constituent facts the others would thereby be determined.

We know empirically that there are facts in the actual world that are mutually independent. From this it follows that the world contains facts that are compatible with systems that are not actual and which are such that they contain facts contradictory of facts in the actual world. For example, the Newtonian law of gravitation is incompatible with the conjoint fact consisting of all the facts of the Euclidean geometrical system and of all the facts of the movements of light-waves. But there is a possible system that would include the system of Euclidean geometry and also include the facts of the movements of light-waves and also a fact contradictory to the fact of the Newtonian law of gravitation. Thus, if F be the Newtonian law, E the Euclidean system, L the movements of light-waves, then there might be a system including F, E, non-L, and another system including E, L, non-F. Similarly there might be another system including F, L, non-E. The determination of facts *other* than F, L, E, is necessary in order to ascertain which, if any, of these systems is actual. Again, consider the set of facts consisting of facts of organic development, which we may call *the fact of evolution*. Then this fact may be independent of the facts contained in the physical system. Let this system be represented by S_1; let *the fact of evolution* be in a system S_2. Then some facts will be both in S_1 and in S_2; some facts will be in S_1 but not in S_2; others will be in S_2 but not in S_1. Of these independent facts any one, or its contradictory, might be contained in a system P_1 including S_1; or in a system P_2 including S_2; or there may be a system R which includes S_1 and S_2 and also includes a set of facts independent of S_1 and independent of S_2. That is to say, a system may be enlarged by the addition of independent facts. Thus there may be many systems compatible with the sub-system containing dependent facts.

There is no good ground for supposing that the actual world is a system such that any one fact determines, or is determined by, every other fact. On the contrary, many facts are known to be actual which cannot be seen to be related to other facts, also known to be actual, as constituents in any possible system. But the world may be *a system*, since every fact may be determined by *some* other facts. In no cases, however, would there be any meaning in the assertion that the system of the actual world is a necessary system. The nature of deductive systems shows that this is so. A set of independent postulates may suffice to determine a deductive system in which all the theorems are consequences of the postulates. But these theorems might also be included in another system generated by postulates which contain all the postulates of the other system *and other* postulates, and which will therefore include other theorems as well. But the one system will not be *necessary* as contrasted with the other system, though both might be coherent systems. Thus, what is logically possible does not suffice to determine the system of the actual world ; consequently, the system of the actual world *cannot* be logically necessary, and anything that is the case might have been other than it is, so that there are an infinite number of incompatible systems. Of these possible systems, only one (if any) can be actual ; which is actual, if any, it may be impossible for us to ascertain.

§ 2. THE NATURE OF ORDER [1]

A system is an ordered system only if all its constituent elements are related by relations having certain logical properties. These logical properties *define* order. We shall begin by considering familiar examples of terms, or elements, arranged in an order. The set of whole numbers can be arranged in the order 1, 2, 3, 4, 5 . . . n, $n + 1$. . . . The set of points on a straight line exhibit order. The succession of the Kings of England is ordered. The set of words on this line exhibit spatial order and a syntactical order.

Suppose a non-defined relation symbolized by $\dashrightarrow$, of which the following assertions are true, x, y, z, being the elements :

  (i) Not ($x \dashrightarrow x$).
  (ii) Not (both $x \dashrightarrow y$ and $y \dashrightarrow x$).
  (iii) If x is other than y, then either $x \dashrightarrow y$ or $y \dashrightarrow x$.
  (iv) If $x \dashrightarrow y$ and $y \dashrightarrow z$, then $x \dashrightarrow z$.

That is, the relation $\dashrightarrow$ is aliorelative, asymmetrical, connected transitive. Since an aliorelative relation that is also transitive must be asymmetrical we can reduce the conditions to the last three. It will be seen that in each of the examples given above the elements can be related by a relation having the formal properties asserted in the three conditions. When they are so related the elements are *ordered*. For example, the Kings of England can be ordered by the

[1] See B. A. W. Russell, *Int. Math. Phil.*, Chap. IV ; *Principles of Mathematics*, Chaps. XXIV and XXV.

relation *successor of*; the points on a straight line can be ordered by the relation *to the left of*; the set of numbers can be ordered by the relation *greater than*.

A relation having these three formal properties suffices to generate an order ; the elements thus related exhibit *serial order*. It is to be observed that the series is the *serial relation* not the elements, since any given set of elements may have different orders. For example, suppose no two Kings of England were of exactly the same height, then the Kings could be arranged in the order generated by the relation *taller than* as well as in the order generated by the relation *predecessor of*, and so on. Hence, the *field* of the relation cannot be taken to be the series. The minimum number of elements required to generate an order is three. There must be one term which has to two other terms converse relations that are asymmetrical and transitive. Wherever this occurs there is order. Terms which are not in an order can be ordered by the construction of an asymmetrical transitive connected relation. Thus a series can be generated by means of the relation *between*.[1] *Between* is an asymmetrical relation *transitive by pairs*. That is to say, if *b* is between *a* and *c*, and if *c* is between *b* and *d*, then *c* is between *a* and *d*. Any triadic relation that has these formal properties is capable of ordering the elements ; it is not necessary that the elements should be spatial or temporal. Mr. Russell has shown how to order the points on a straight line by means of the relation *between*. We cannot pursue this subject here. We may, however, point out that *between* is the characteristic of an *open series*, that is a series that does not return to the starting-point. If we consider the relation *to the left of* holding between people seated at a round table, we see that we return, after a certain number of steps, to the person from whom we started. If now we have the five people A, B, C, D, E seated round the circle, we see that

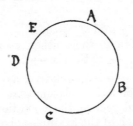

A and C are separated by B and D, and B and D are separated by C and E, etc. This relation is called the *separation of couples*.

---

[1] Cf. Russell, *Principles of Mathematics*, p. 214. ' A term *y* is between two terms *x* and *z* with reference to a transitive asymmetrical relation R when *x*R*y* and *y*R*z*. In no other case can *y* be said properly to be between *x* and *z* ; and

It has been shown by Vailati that the *separation of couples* involves a dyadic, transitive, asymmetrical relation, relative to three other fixed terms. It is easy to see that given at least four terms and the relation *between*, then we have also the relation of *separation of couples*. Thus the relation of separation of couples may be *formally* reduced to a relation having the four formal properties enumerated in the four conditions laid down for —>. By means of such reduction a closed series can be transformed into an open series.

It will be observed that a transitive dyadic relation, or any relation transitive by pairs, permits of the elimination of intermediate terms. For example, if a set of elements, a, b, c . . . are related by —>, the place of any element k is determined. If we select any pair (j, k) we can determine the place in the series of any other element f, by the combination of assertions such as $a \to c$, $c \dashrightarrow j$, $j \dashrightarrow k$. In this way we are able to base inferences upon these assertions of relation, eliminating any number of intermediate terms. Thus the possibility of *chains of deduction* is seen to depend upon the formal property of transitiveness. It will be observed that *implies* could replace —>, since it has the required property.

§ 3. SIMILARITY AND STRUCTURE

The notion of structure is one with which we all feel ourselves to be familiar, but we should probably be at a loss if we were asked what precisely we mean by it. We use such phrases as " the structure of the novel ", " the structure of a play ", and so on, meaning by " structure " the ordered connexion of the component parts. Our ordinary conception of structure is reflected in its etymological derivation. We think of a structure as an essential framework, a way in which elements are combined in an ordered manner. A house is a structure because it is not a mere heap, or agglomeration of bricks. In this sense " structure " is so used as to be hardly distinguishable from system. But when we speak of two systems *having the same structure* we are attempting to use " structure " in a sense that requires further definition. Thus we may wish to ask whether a given proposition has the same structure as the sentence by means of which it is expressed. The grammatical structure of a sentence is the syntactical arrangement of its component elements. To understand a sentence it is necessary to know both its syntax and what the separate words stand for. A dictionary-knowledge of the meaning of the words used does not, for instance, enable the beginner in Latin to construe Latin authors. He must know both

this definition gives not merely a criterion, but the very *meaning* of betweenness.' It is not possible here to do more than indicate the nature of serial order. The student who is interested in the subject should consult the chapters given in the references.

the vocabulary and the syntax.   He can then ask whether a Latin sentence and the corresponding English translation have the same structure.   Again, we may ask whether the space we perceive has the same structure as what is called physical space, or as what is called Euclidean space.

Structure is a notion of fundamental importance for science and philosophy.   Unless we have a clear conception of structure we are not likely to have a clear conception of the nature of our problems and the possibility of their solution.   It is to Mr. Russell that logicians owe the precise definition of structure.   We shall attempt to expound his explanation as simply as possible.   It must be noted first that structure does not apply to classes or collections but only to relations, or rather, to systems of relations.   There is, however, a relation that holds between classes the consideration of which is useful for the understanding of structure.   This is the relation of *similarity*.

It will be remembered that in Chapter VIII we pointed out that counting is logically a process of establishing a one-one correlation between a set of objects and the number series.   When we count we cannot take the objects in any order ; we must keep the order, *first, second, third*, etc.   It is the observance of this order that enables us to know that the last numeral required in the one-one correlation is the number of the set of objects.   Under certain conditions we can correlate the members of two sets without observing any order. If one member of the one set can be correlated with one, and only one, member of the other set, then we know that the two sets have the same number, even though we do not know what that number is.   Thus, as Mr. Russell points out, we can (assuming monogamy) establish a one-one correlation between the set of wives and the set of husbands, since (given our assumption) the relation of wife to husband is *one-one*.   We can thus know that the number of wives is the same as the number of husbands although we do not know how many married couples there are.   Two classes that can be thus correlated by a one-one relation are said to be *similar*.   The correlating relation relates each term of the one class with one and only one term of the other class.   If R is a correlating relation, then given any term in the domain of R there is one, and only one term in the converse domain of R to which the given term has R. We can now state Mr. Russell's definition of similarity, which is as follows :

' One class is said to be " similar " to another when there is a one-one relation of which the one class is the domain, while the other is the converse domain.' [1]

It is easy to see that similarity is reflexive, symmetrical, tran-

[1] *Int. Math. Phil.*, p. 16.   For the whole of this section see loc. cit., Chap. VI.

sitive. That is, if a is a class, then a is similar to a; if a is similar to the class β, then β is similar to a; if a is similar to β and a is similar to the class γ, then a is similar to γ. Similarity does not involve qualitative resemblance, which is what we usually mean when we speak of "likeness". It is a relation wholly definable in terms of one to one correspondence. By means of this notion we can define what is meant by the assertion that two systems of relations *have the same structure*.

We shall begin by considering some examples of systems of relations that have the same structure. For example, a *map* has the same structure as that of which it is a map. Suppose we have a map of England and Wales. Then the place on the map corresponding to *London* is above the place corresponding to *Brighton*, because London is north of Brighton.[1] The place on the map corresponding to *Portsmouth* is to the left of the place corresponding to *Brighton*, because Portsmouth is west of Brighton. On an accurate map the relative positions of dots representing towns correspond to the relative positions of the actual towns. The lines representing rivers correspond to the length and direction of the rivers. That is to say, the relation *north of* relates one town to another town, and corresponding to that the relation *above* relates one mark on the map to another. We often make maps to show the relations holding between a set of terms, since the spatial relations of a map are easily apprehended. Whenever we use a map we are using a special kind of correlation. We correlate each town with a dot on the map. The spatial relation on the map corresponds to the distance and direction of the towns. Call the first relation R and the second S. Then there is a one-one relation P whose domain is the field of R and whose converse domain is the field of S, such that if $x \, R \, y$, then the correlate of x has S to the correlate of y. In such a case R is said to be similar to S. Let a and b be the correlates of x and y. Then we have $x \, P \, a \, . \, a \, S \, b \, . \, b \, \breve{P} \, y$. Thus the relation R is the same as the relative product of P and S and the converse of P. That is to say,

"R is similar to S" $\equiv$ "$P \mid S \mid \breve{P}$."

The relations R and S may be what is ordinarily called very "unlike". *Relation-likeness*, or similarity, is a special kind of correlation. The members of the field of R may be of quite a different kind from the members of the field of S, so that the relations R and S may be quite different. Black dots on paper are very unlike towns, but the system of dots that constitutes the map has similarity, or relation-likeness, to the system of towns. Whatever R may be, provided that it is sufficiently simple, we can make a map of R.

[1] It is a convention of cartographers to represent *north of* by *above*, and, consequently, *south of* by *below*.

Consider, for instance, a collection of people and the dyadic relation *benefactor of*. For simplicity, we shall limit the field to six people, *a*, *b*, *c*, *d*, *e*, *f*. Suppose the relation B (benefactor of) holds as follows : *a* B *b*, *a* B *d*, *a* B *f*, *c* B *b*, *c* B *d*, *f* B *e*. We can make a map of B by taking six points and connecting with arrows the couples between which B holds. Thus we get the map,

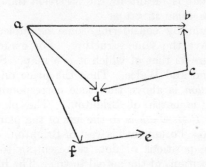

This map has the same structure as the relation B. If we add *c* B *e*, we change the structure. The generating relation of the map is *joined by an arrow*. If we changed the field but had the same map, we should have the same structure. Two relations that have the same map, or of which one could be a map for the other, have the same structure. Thus two relations which have relation-likeness, i.e. which are *similar*, have the same structure. Hence, " structure " means similarity of relations. It must not be supposed that similarity is confined to dyadic relations or to maps. It applies to relations with any number of terms, and to series. Two serial relations are similar when their terms can be correlated without involving change of order. We defined similarity by means of a one-one relation. But we can adapt the definition so as to apply to a relation in which the correlating relation is many-one. We shall not, however, pursue this topic further. Enough has been said to make the notion of structure precise.

It is not difficult to see that structure is an important notion in science. Two relations that have the same structure have the same logical properties. Thus if S and R are similar, then, if R is transitive, S is transitive, if R is aliorelative, S is aliorelative, if R is serial, S is serial, and so on. It is this identity of logical properties that makes the similarity of relations so useful. To say that the space of the external world is Euclidean is to say that the system of actual space has the same logical properties as the system of Euclidean geometry. To deny that actual space is Euclidean is to deny that they have the same logical properties. Two deductive systems that have the same structure would have identical properties. If every element in a deductive system S could be interpreted as an element in a system Σ and the generating relation of S were similar to the generating relation of Σ, then S and Σ would have identical logical properties. Since the structure is independent of the nature of the terms, and similarity is independent of the nature of the relations, it follows that two similar systems may allow of different interpretations. The development of science is due to a considerable extent to the discovery that two different systems have the same structure.

§ 4. THE METHOD OF INTERPRETATION

When we " read a map " we *interpret* the coloured markings so that they represent contour lines, isobars, rivers, mountains, etc. In the case of map-reading we know to begin with that the isobars are lines connecting places on the map correlated with places on the earth where the mean barometric pressure is equal. We know, if we look at a map of the " Chief Occupations of the World " that a green patch, for instance, can be interpreted as indicating that the correlated portion of the earth surface is an agricultural area, a red patch can be correlated with a manufacturing area, and so on. The interpretation is easy because the maker of the map knew what he wanted to represent, put in his lines and colours accordingly and then supplied a key to explain what the markings represented. We have seen that if the map is accurate it has the same structure as what it maps, and that its value depends upon its similarity.

Suppose that we found a map—or rather a sheet of paper with colours and markings which gave it the appearance of the geographical maps with which we are familiar. Suppose that we did not know how to read the map ; that the geographer had forgotten to supply a key. It is conceivable that the same coloured shapes might correspond, for a given region, both to the distribution of occupations and to the distribution of forms of government. It would depend upon our interests whether the map interpreted by the one key rather than by the other would be more important for us. In our supposed case of the map, however, it is extremely unlikely that both modes of interpretation would fit the map. But in the case of a deductive system the elements, that is, the propositions, might be taken to express different facts and yet the deductive system might be the same in spite of this difference. We saw that a deductive system can be constructed starting from undefined objects to which we assign purely logical properties. If we can find objects that can be *fitted into* the system because they are related by similar relations we are said to " interpret " the system.

The possibility of different interpretations is due to the fact that deductive systems are completely formal. The elements of a deductive system might be interpreted, for instance, as individuals, or as classes, or as sets of relations. A system of geometry is a deductive system the nature of which is determined by the initial concepts and propositions. We saw that Euclidean geometry is only one such system. It is sometimes possible to interpret a geometrical system in such a way that it can be replaced by a system initially different. Thus the two-dimensional geometries of Riemann and Lobatschewsky have been interpreted as Euclidean geometry applied respectively to a surface with a constant positive, and a constant negative curvature. It sometimes happens that a scientific theory constructed with reference to a certain set of objects is found to be a system having the same structure as a system constructed with reference to another set of objects. For example, the law of gravitation is the law of the inverse square ; the same law holds of electrical attraction. Hence problems in electrostatics can be solved by consideration of problems of gravitational attraction. Maxwell was led to his electromagnetic theory of light by consideration of the similarity of relations holding between light-waves and electric currents.[1] Thus, a set of deductive systems differently interpreted became maps, or models, or explanations of each other. The detection of such similarity of relations aids the development of science. The fact that it is possible to derive knowledge of one set of objects from knowledge of another arises from the similarity of their relations, which involves the identity of their formal properties.

It is to be observed that the method of interpretation substitutes for the initial *undefined* objects, objects that have non-formal properties. In this substitution consists the *application* of deductive systems.[2] Mr. Russell has utilized this method in constructing a philosophical theory of the external world. His explanation of the method may be quoted here.

' It frequently happens that we have a deductive mathematical system, starting from hypotheses, concerning undefined objects, and that we have reason to believe that there are objects fulfilling these hypotheses, although, initially, we are unable to point out any such objects with certainty. Usually, in such cases, although many different sets of objects are abstractly available as fulfilling the hypothesis, there is one such set which is much more important than the others. . . . The substitution of such a set for the undefined objects is " interpretation ".'[3]

---

[1] See below, Chap. XVI, p. 309.
[2] Cf. W. K. Clifford : ' Whatever can be explained by the motion of a fluid can be equally well explained either by the attraction of particles or by the strains of a solid substance ; the very same mathematical calculations result from the three distinct hypotheses ; and science, though completely independent of all three, may yet choose one of them as serving to link together different trains of physical inquiry.'   [3] *Analysis of Matter*, p. 4.

Two points in this method of interpretation require emphasis. First, the set of objects substituted for the undefined concepts are substituted *because* they have non-formal properties. It follows that such objects can only be discovered by experience of the actual world. Secondly, we have to determine what is meant by an important interpretation. The *importance* of a given set of objects is the relevance of such a set to our interests. Mr. Russell, for instance, says that an interpretation is important when ' the initial objects have been defined in terms of entities forming part of the empirical world, as opposed to the world of logical necessity '. The interpretation of a geometry which would make it a branch of pure mathematics is said to be convenient and legitimate, but it is not an important interpretation. There is no doubt that " importance " for science ultimately means " capable of verification by sensible observation ". It is in this way that deductive systems can be *applied* to the exploration of the external world. The final appeal of the scientist is experimental. The logician constructs systems which are susceptible of various interpretations; he shows that the data of experience can be fitted into various deductive systems. The experimental physicist selects that deductive system which admits of an *important* interpretation. The position is admirably summed up by Professor Eddington, who says : ' In one sense deductive theory is the enemy of experimental physics. The latter is always striving to settle by crucial tests the nature of the fundamental things ; the former strives to minimize the successes obtained by showing how wide a nature of things is compatible with all experimental results.' [1]

[1] *The Mathematical Theory of Relativity*, § 103.

14

CHAPTER XII

INFERENCE AND IMPLICATION

' It is not therefore the object of logic to determine whether conclusions be true or false ; but whether what are asserted to be conclusions are *conclusions*.'—
A. de Morgan.

§ 1. THE NATURE OF INFERENCE

INFERENCE is undoubtedly a mental process. If, therefore, our conception of logic were such as to restrict logic to the theory of propositional forms, we should no more need to consider the nature of inference than the mathematician needs to consider the psychological processes whereby a student comes to apprehend a mathematical theorem. We have, however, conceived logic more widely. We recognize that the systematic investigation of the conditions of valid thinking forms a part of logic.[1] Hence, the logician is concerned with inference.

We must begin by distinguishing inference from other mental processes that may easily be confused with it. A man walking along a familiar street recognizes more or less clearly the various objects that he sees. For instance, suppose a Londoner were walking along Oxford Street. He might see a scarlet object moving towards him and at once recognize it as a *Royal Mail* van. Such recognition is immediate. It would be naturally expressed in the judgement : " That's a mail van ". Suppose, now, that he were to put his hand in his pocket and, feeling an object against his fingers, were to think " That's a pen ". Here, again, his recognition would be immediate. That is to say, in the first case, something visually presented was *immediately interpreted as being a so-and-so ;* in the second case something tactually presented was *immediately interpreted as being a so-and-so.* Such immediate judgements are judgements of perception. We saw in Chapter I that what is visually presented to us is always less than what we correctly say we see.[2] But it does not follow from this fact that when we say " This is a pen " we are *inferring* the pen from the tactual sense-datum ; nor that we are *inferring* the table from the sense-datum, when looking at a table we judge " That's a table ". No doubt our ability

[1] Cf. Chap. XXV, § 1 below.　　　　[2] See p. 4.

to perceive that *this* is a pen and that *that* is a table is dependent
upon our past experience. But there is equally no doubt that we
are able, as a result of our past experience, *immediately to perceive*
that *this is a so-and-so*. In such immediate recognition no inference
is involved.[1] There is no passage from datum to conclusion. Recognition is not always immediate. If, on stumbling over some obstacle
in a dark room, there were an experience that would be *properly*
formulated only in some such judgement as " That *must* be the
dog", then inference is involved, however rapid the process of inferring
may have been.

Inference must also be distinguished from suggestion and recol-
lection. A certain scent may recall some occasion in the past when
that scent was perceived. A wet roof in the distance may suggest
the surface of a pond. The thought of the pond may recall a summer
holiday. In these experiences no inference need enter. There may
be nothing that could be expressed in the form : " This, *therefore*
that ". To revert to an illustration given in the first chapter. A
man lying on a rock indulged in an idle reverie in which he had
a succession of thoughts suggested partly by his sense experiences
of the moment, partly by his recollections of past events. This
random thinking was not controlled by factors within the reverie
itself. For this reason we contrasted it with the directed thinking
in which the man engaged as soon as he was confronted with a
situation that presented a problem to be solved. He then began to
connect one apprehended fact with another in a certain, definite
way. In thus connecting he was inferring.

It is no doubt difficult to distinguish precisely between those
experiences in which inference is not involved and those in which
it is. Psychologists do not agree as to where the line should be
drawn. But it is not necessary for us to discuss uncertain cases.
We are concerned only to decide as to what must be present whenever inference occurs. We may admit that a judgement is sometimes taken to be immediate, which later, can be seen to have
involved the drawing of a conclusion from a datum. It is not,
however, legitimate, to distinguish two *kinds* of inference—*psychological* inference and *logical* inference. All inference is psychological,
for inference is a mental process ; but its *validity* depends upon
conditions that are logical.

Inference, then, may be defined as a mental process in which
a thinker passes from the apprehension of something given—the
datum—to the apprehension of something related in a certain way

---

[1] See G. E. Moore, " Some Judgments of Perception ", *Philosophical Studies*,
pp. 220–1, 225–7. Cf. especially p. 226 : ' How to draw the line between judgments of this kind, which are judgments of perception, and those which are not,
I do not know.'

to the datum.   The datum may be a sense-datum, a complex perceptual situation, or a proposition.   The datum of an inference *can* always be expressed in a proposition.   Hence, we might define inference more shortly by saying that inference is the mental process in which a thinker passes from one or more propositions to some other proposition connected with the former in a certain way.   As thus defined " infer " is not equivalent to " deduce ".   These words have been used by some logicians as synonyms.   But the correct synonym of " deduce " is " formally infer ".   The word " inference " is correctly used in a sense wide enough to include not only *deduction* or *formal inference*, but also any passage from a *datum*, A, to a *conclusion*, B.   In other words, " deductive inference " is not a pleonasm, or " inductive inference " a contradiction in terms.[1]   Whether an inference is deductive or inductive depends upon the nature of the relation that holds between the given propositions and the inferred propositions.   This relation is the logical basis of the inference, so that, unless this relation holds the inference cannot be valid.   But this, though a necessary, is not a sufficient condition of inference. The possibility of inference depends both upon the logical relations holding between the propositions and upon the relation of the thinker to these propositions.   It is also to be observed that inference may be erroneous.   The thinker may believe that two propositions are so related that the one can be validly inferred from the other, and he may be mistaken in this belief.   In the next section we shall consider the conditions that are necessary in order that there may be valid inference.   But we must first discuss the nature of assertion.

It is obvious that a conclusion that is inferred is *asserted*.   Given the proposition *p*, we may infer *therefore q*.   The " therefore " marks the difference between *implication* and *inference*.   The relation of implication holds between two given propositions independently of any thinker, who may, or may not, apprehend this relation.   In order that there should be inference there must be a thinker who *asserts* the propositions.   There is clearly a difference between *asserting* a proposition and merely *considering* or *contemplating* or *assuming* it.   For example : " If *p*, then *q* " does not assert *p*, and does not assert *q* ; whereas, " *p*, therefore *q* " both asserts *p* and asserts *q*. It is not easy to determine what exactly constitutes the difference between an asserted and an unasserted proposition.   It is obvious, however, that we may use a form of words to express a proposition

[1] It may be the case that only deductive inference is *valid* inference.   This question will be discussed in Chapter XXI.   We cannot, however, even raise the question as to the validity of induction without assuming that there is such a thing as inductive inference.   It is noteworthy that Mr. Russell, who, in 1903, did not distinguish between inference and deduction, in 1927, speaks as though all inference were inductive.   Cf. *The Principles of Mathematics*, p. 11 *n.*, with *An Outline of Philosophy*, Chaps. VII and XXV.

without asserting the proposition. Thus, not every proposition that is expressed is asserted. For example, the proposition " The match will be scratched " may be the implicate of the proposition " If this heavy rain continues, the match will be scratched ". But neither of these simple propositions is asserted ; what is asserted is that the implicate is true if the implicans is true. Again, some one might say " Aristotle believed that the earth is immovable " without agreeing with Aristotle's belief, and, therefore, without *asserting* the proposition " The earth is immovable ". What the speaker *asserts* is that Aristotle believed a certain proposition. It might be supposed that a proposition that is asserted is a proposition believed to be true by the person who asserts it. But there would be a difficulty in maintaining this ; for, it cannot be held that *every* proposition that is asserted is believed by the person asserting it. He might be telling a lie, or making a joke. Thus, it does not seem correct to say that to assert a proposition is to express a proposition that is believed. Thus, belief is not the same as assertion. But a proposition that is believed is asserted when it is expressed. It may, however, be believed without being asserted and it may be asserted without being believed.[1] All that we seem able to say is that when any one asserts the proposition p, either he believes p and asserts p to be true, or he does not believe p but intends his hearers to accept p as true. The assertion of p, then, seems to be equivalent to the putting forward of p *as true*, even though the person who asserts p may not believe p. Thus, the assertion *that p* may be regarded as equivalent to the assertion *that p is true*.[2] It is, of course, obvious that " p " and " p is true " do not express the *same* proposition, since they have different constituents ; but they express *equivalent* propositions.

It seems, then, that in order that there should be inference the propositions which constitute the premisses of the inference must be taken for true. It might be objected that a proposition may be merely *supposed* in order to see what follows from it. But in this case the conclusion would not be *inferred* ; it would merely be seen to be implied by the assumed premiss. Sometimes we may say : " Let it be granted that the proposition p is true ; then q

---

[1] Cf. W. E. J., Pt. I, Chap. I, § 2. Mr. Johnson seems to regard *assertion* as equivalent to *conscious belief*, and to hold that the only alternative to asserting a proposition that is believed is merely to *utter* it, i.e. " to utter without belief ". But we have seen that a proposition may be expressed without being believed. On Mr. Johnson's view to " utter " a proposition seems to mean to use a form of words that *could* be used so as to express a proposition but which *is* so used as to express nothing.

[2] This is assumed by Frege and Russell, who use a special symbol, $\vdash$, for assertion. Thus " $\vdash . p$ " is to be read " It is asserted that p " or " p is true ". (See *Principia Mathematica*, p. 9.)

follows." Here p is *assumed* to be true, although the *assumption* that p is true may be made, as we shall see, in order to establish that p is in fact false. We conclude, then, that for the purpose of inference, the propositions must be asserted and that an asserted proposition must be taken to be equivalent to the assertion that the proposition is true.

§ 2. THE CONDITIONS OF VALID INFERENCE

In this section we shall be concerned with the conditions that are necessary in order that a deductive inference may be valid. It will be remembered that in Chapter VI we drew a distinction between the syllogism regarded as a form of implication and the syllogism regarded as a form of argument. Regarded as an *argument*, the syllogism is an inference to the truth of the conclusion from the assertion of the premisses. We marked this distinction by using " If . . . then . . . " as the sign of implication, and " therefore " as the sign of argument, i.e. as the sign of an *asserted* conclusion. In order that we should be able to pass from *If . . . then* to *therefore*, certain conditions must be fulfilled. These conditions are of two kinds, which have been clearly distinguished by Mr. Johnson. One set of conditions refers to the propositions and the relations that hold between them. These conditions are independent of the thinker and are called by Mr. Johnson the " constitutive conditions ". The other set of conditions refers to the relation of the propositions to what the thinker may happen to *know*. These relations will vary with the knowledge the thinker happens to possess. They are called by Mr. Johnson the " epistemic conditions " of inference.[1] Both sets of conditions are necessary for valid inference. This has not always been clearly seen. Mr. Russell, for instance, has expressed a view that suggests that all that is necessary for inference is that certain relations should hold between propositions. Thus he said : ' In the discussion of inference, it is common to permit the intrusion of a psychological element, and to consider our acquisition of new knowledge by its means. But it is plain that where we validly infer one proposition from another, we do so in virtue of a relation which holds between the two propositions whether we perceive it or not : the mind, in fact, is as purely receptive in inference as common sense supposes it to be in perception of sensible objects.' [2] But the possibility of *inference* is conditioned by what the thinker knows and what is true, as well as upon the logical relations between the propositions.

We shall begin with the *constitutive conditions*. In order that

[1] *Logic*, Pt. I, pp. 2–3 ; Pt. II, Chap. I, § 3.
[2] Russell, *Principles of Mathematics*, p. 33.

the proposition q may be deduced, or formally inferred from p, there must be between p and q a relation such that q is a consequence of p. This relation is usually called " implication ". What exactly is meant by " implication " and whether, or not, there is more than one relation that may hold between p and q in order that q may be deduced from p, will be discussed in a later section. Meanwhile we shall continue to use " implication " for the relation between p and q that is required for valid inference. It is to be noted that implication is a *logical* relation holding between the propositions ; it is not a relation that holds between the propositions and the thinker. It is not enough, however, that p should imply q ; it is also necessary that p should be *true*, if q is to be validly inferred from p. This is clear from the fact that in inference q *is asserted* and p must also have been *asserted*, that is, p must be *true*. Thus, as Mr. Russell puts it : ' When we say *therefore*, we state a relation which can only hold between *asserted* propositions, and which thus differs from implication. Whenever *therefore* occurs, the hypothesis [i.e the implicans] may be dropped, and the conclusion asserted by itself.' [1] That is to say, the implicative form *If p, then q* is not sufficient ; we need *If p, then q*, and p. The conditions that p must be true and that the relation of implication must hold between p and q are the constitutive conditions.

Since inference is a process in which a thinker passes from something known to something *inferred*, it is clear that we could not say we had *inferred* q if we had already *asserted* q. It is, therefore, obvious that q must not be *known* to be true, and equally obvious that q must not be *known* to be false. We must also know that p implies q. These conditions are *epistemic* ; they relate to what the thinker who is inferring *knows*. These are conditions dependent upon the relation of the thinker to the propositions involved in the process of inference. These two sets of conditions may be restated briefly as follows :

Constitutive Conditions : (1) p must be true ; (ii) p must imply q.

Epistemic Conditions : (i) p must be known to be true ; (ii) p must be known to imply q without its being known that q is true.

---

[1] loc. cit., p. 35. Cf. also *Principia Mathematica*, pp. 9–10, 94, 132. He sums up the process of inference : ' A proposition " p " is asserted, and a proposition " p implies q " is asserted, and then as a sequel the proposition " q " is asserted. The trust in inference is the belief that if the two former assertions are not in error, the final assertion is not in error. . . . The process of the inference cannot be reduced to symbols. Its sole record is the occurrence of " $\vdash q$.". . . . An inference is the dropping of a true premiss : it is the dissolution of an implication.'

This statement includes what the former statement (given on p. 195) omitted. Possibly Mr. Russell would still say that the *assertion* is *logical*. I, however, am contending that *assertion* involves the relation to a thinker.

It follows from these two sets of conditions that although p may *imply* q when q is false, yet q cannot be validly inferred from p unless it is the case both that p is true and is known to be true. It might be objected that the form of argument known as *reductio ad absurdum* is incompatible with this assertion. But such an objection would rest upon a mistake. In a *reductio ad absurdum* we assume that a proposition is true in order to show that its truth would imply a proposition to be true which is *known* to be false ; from which it would follow that the proposition assumed to be true is false. That is to say : we *know* (i) q is false ; (ii) p implies q ; we *assume* that p is true, and hence *infer* that q is true. But since the truth of q contradicts the falsity of q, and q is known to be false, we can infer that p, which implies q, is false. The implicate cannot be false if the implicans is true. In this inference the same constitutive and epistemic conditions are exhibited as in the valid inference of q from p, and p *implies* q, when both p *and* q are true.

§ 3. THE VALIDITY OF THE SYLLOGISM AS A FORM OF PROOF

In ordinary discussion the syllogism is often used (generally in an abbreviated form) as a mode of establishing that a certain proposition is true. Suppose the proposition in question is r. Then the argument takes the form : " You grant p and q ; you admit that p and q together imply r ; so you must admit that r is true." The word " proof " is sometimes applied to such a mode of establishing that a certain proposition is true. The validity of the proof depends upon the correctness of the admission that both p and q are true as well as upon the correctness of the admission that they together imply r. Now it is clear that in this case it is not permissible to use p and q to prove r unless it is the case either that p and q require no proof, or that they have been proved without the assumption of the truth of r. If r is used to prove p and then p is used to prove r, the reasoning is circular, and, therefore, fallacious. A fallacy of this kind is called *petitio principii*, or the fallacy of begging the question. For example, suppose that we attempted to prove that *Hildebrand is fallible* by deducing this proposition from the two premisses *All men are fallible* and *Hildebrand is a man*. This argument would be fallacious if the fallibility of all men had been previously established by reference to the particular case of Hildebrand among others. Owing to the circularity of the argument the conclusion would not have been *proved*. It seems, then, that whether, or not, a syllogistic argument is circular depends upon the way in which the major premiss has been obtained.

The validity and the usefulness of syllogistic inference has been a matter of dispute among logicians. But the main points that arise with regard to syllogistic inference have not always been clearly distinguished. There has been confusion owing to the fact that some of the disputants have attempted to deal simultaneously with four quite different questions. We shall begin by distinguishing these four questions. Then we shall attempt to see what bearing the discussion of these questions has upon the question whether syllogistic inference is valid. Finally, we shall briefly consider Mill's theory of the syllogism.

The four questions that must be distinguished are as follows : (1) Is the syllogism a form in which we actually do reason ? (2) Is the syllogism the only form of reasoning ? (3) Does the syllogism give us knowledge that we did not possess before ? (4) Is the major premiss of a syllogism independent of the conclusion ?

(1) That the first question should be answered in the affirmative is shown by our treatment of the syllogism as a form of argument. Undoubtedly our everyday arguments are abbreviated, but if our conclusions were challenged we should often attempt to reply to the challenge by an explicit statement of the premisses. This explicit statement will often take the form of a syllogism, or of an antilogism.

(2) When it is asked whether the syllogism is the only form of reasoning it is clear that " reasoning " must be understood as being equivalent to " deductive inference ". Certainly it is impossible to maintain that all deduction is syllogistic. Perhaps no contemporary logicians would wish to maintain that it is. Accordingly, it is not profitable to discuss the erroneous arguments that have been offered in support of an affirmative answer to this question.

(3) To ask whether the syllogism gives us knowledge that we did not possess before is to ask whether any one ever learns anything by means of syllogistic inference. This is equivalent to asking whether there is *genuine inference* in a syllogistic argument, since, unless we do learn something which we did not previously know, there is no inference. It may at once be granted that many examples of syllogisms given in textbooks on logic are so familiar that the reader does not acquire fresh information from the combination of the two premisses. For example, the reader of this book knew that Socrates is a man and that all men are mortal long before he found these propositions so put together as to constitute a syllogism in the first figure. But it would not be difficult to find examples of premisses both of which were known but which had never been combined by the thinker so as to yield a syllogism. In such a case, the thinker might apprehend a connexion between the extreme terms that he had not previously noted.[1] But it is not at all easy to see

[1] Cf. George Eliot, *Daniel Deronda*, Chap. 52 : ' I never held it my *forte* to be a severe reasoner, but I can see that if whatever is best is A, and B happens to be best, B must be A, however little you might have expected it beforehand.'

what this question has to do with the problem of the *validity* of syllogistic inference. Yet it is sometimes assumed that if this question be answered in the negative, then syllogistic inference can be seen to be invalid. Dugald Stewart, for instance, asks, ' Is it possible to conceive an understanding so framed as to perceive the truth of the major and minor propositions and yet not to perceive the force of the conclusion ? The contrary must appear evident to every person who knows what a syllogism is '.[1] There is some difficulty in seeing what exactly is meant by this question. If the writer means to assert that every one at once sees the connexion between the two premises and the conclusion, it may be doubted whether his reply is not too sweeping an affirmative. But the question as to the length of time required to apprehend the connexion between '*p and q*' and '*r*' is irrelevant to the problem at issue, for the problem is whether we *can know p* and *can know q* and *can know* '*p and q imply r*' without having previously known *r*. If we ever do see that a proposition follows from two other propositions, and we had not before *seen* that this was so, then we can gain fresh knowledge by means of a syllogistic inference. But the point at issue is not whether we thus gain fresh knowledge but whether the truth of the conclusion must be known *before* the truth of the major premiss is known. This question relates especially to the subsumptive syllogism, and leads us to the fourth question.

(4) The question whether the major premiss is independent of the conclusion cannot be answered until we know what is meant by " independent ". The major premiss can certainly be known without its being the case that the conclusion is known. That is to say, it may be *epistemically* independent. We have now to see whether it can be *constitutively* independent. In all valid inference the conclusion must be constitutively implied by the premises, so that the major premiss cannot be true unless the conclusion is true. The converse does not hold, since implication is a non-symmetrical relation. Some logicians have introduced unnecessary confusion in discussing this question by using the word " contain ". In this context " contain " is an unfortunate synonym for " imply ".[2] We have not to consider whether the premises *imply* the conclusion ; if they did not, there would be no syllogism. The question is whether the conclusion forms *part of the evidence* upon which the major premiss is based. If it does, then the reasoning is circular. This would be the case if the major premiss were a generalization enumerating a number of instances among which the minor term had been included. But not all major premises are known as the result of such an enumeration. If induction be valid, then the conclusion of a syllogism

---

[1] *Works*, ed. Hamilton, III, p. 74.
[2] Bosanquet. *The Essentials of Logic.*

may not constitute part of the evidence upon which the major premiss is based.

To sum up our discussion of these four questions. Those logicians who have supposed that no reasoning is syllogistic are mistaken, no less than those who have supposed that all reasoning is syllogistic. A valid syllogistic inference involves both constitutive and epistemic conditions. It is sometimes possible to know the major premiss without knowing the conclusion; in such cases the conclusion is epistemically independent of the major premiss. The fallacy of *petitio principii* relates to the epistemic conditions; it has no bearing upon the constitutive conditions. Consequently, since the syllogism may be epistemically valid, it cannot be regarded as circular in virtue of its form.

Mill's theory of the syllogism differs in two respects from the views we have just been considering.[1] First, whilst agreeing that "in every syllogism considered as an argument to prove the conclusion, there is a *petitio principii*", he nevertheless regarded the syllogism as a useful and valid mode of inference ; secondly, he held that the evidence for the conclusion is the same as the evidence for the major premiss, so that either could be drawn immediately from the same data. The first of these opinions results from the second, which must be examined first. There has been considerable misunderstanding of Mill's views due no doubt to the fact that his chapter on "The Functions and Value of the Syllogism" is extremely unclear in expression and contains some serious inconsistencies, some of which may be only verbal. A careful reading of the chapter suggests that Mill recognized that the problem at issue was the *epistemic* validity of the syllogism, and that its solution raises the question how we have come to know the major premiss. His answer was that the major is obtained by the summation of particular instances, not all of which need have been actually observed.[2] From the observation of certain particular instances we *infer* a conclusion that includes both those that have been observed and those that have not. Thus a universal proposition (which forms the major premiss of the first figure) is obtained by generalization

---

[1] *Logic*, Bk. II, Chap. III. It is assumed that the student will read the whole of this chapter.

[2] Mill's language is very misleading. He says : ' Now, all which man can observe are individual cases. From these all general truths must be drawn, and into these they may be again resolved ; for a general truth is but an aggregate of particular truths ; a comprehensive expression, by which an indefinite number of individual facts are affirmed or denied at once. But a general proposition is not merely a compendious form for recording and preserving in the memory a number of particular facts, all of which have been observed. Generalization is not a process of mere naming, it is also a process of inference.' (loc. cit., § 3.)

from particular cases. The generalization takes the form : " X_1, X_2, X_3, etc. is p, therefore *every* X is p ". For example, from the particular cases " Plato is mortal ", " Aristotle is mortal ", and so on, we infer the conclusion " Every man is mortal ". Taking this universal proposition Mill applied it to the case of a man then living, viz. the first Duke of Wellington, and deduced the conclusion that the Duke also is mortal. Here clearly the mortality of the Duke did not constitute part of the evidence upon which the major was based. Hence, the conclusion was epistemically valid. Mill then contended that it was not logically necessary to introduce the major in order to draw the conclusion. He argued that we could pass at once from the observation of the particular instances to the general premiss *or* to the particular case asserted in the conclusion of the syllogism. He maintained that the evidence for the conclusion " All men are mortal " is the same as the evidence for the conclusion " The Duke of Wellington is mortal ". Hence, the major premiss is not *logically necessary*. Mill did not, however, hold that the major is superfluous ; he maintained that it is psychologically useful and in complicated cases may be indispensable as a test. According to Mill the major states a generalization from the observed instances, and this generalization can be more easily remembered than the particular instances from which it is derived. The major thus provides a memory-saving device. Accordingly " the reasoning lies in the act of generalization not in interpreting the record of that act ; but the syllogistic form is an indispensable collateral security for the correctness of the generalization itself ".[1]

In reviewing Mill's theory of the syllogism Mr. Johnson sums up his argument as follows : ' Now the charge of circularity or *petitio principii* is epistemic ; and the whole of Mill's argument may therefore be summed up in the statement that the epistemic validity of syllogism and the constitutive validity of induction, both of which had been disputed by earlier logicians, stand or fall together '.[2] But Mr. Johnson appears to neglect the important part of Mill's argument which refuses to admit that the major premiss is *logically* necessary. Mill saves the validity of the syllogism only by making the inference non-syllogistic. It must also be noted that Mill is certainly mistaken in supposing that the evidence for the major and for the conclusion is *the same*. If from a set of instances of X, each of which is p, we infer that one other X is p, the probability of the truth of the inference is much greater than it would be had our conclusion been *every* X is p. Mill, it is possible, would have refused to admit this, since he maintained that a proposition obtained by induction, such as " All men are mortal ", is *certainly* true. It is, however, impossible to reconcile Mill's views on induction

[1] loc. cit., § 3.   [2] *Logic*, Pt. II, p. xix.

with what he says about the method of obtaining the major premiss of a syllogism.[1]

§ 4. IMPLICATION AND DEDUCTION

There must be some relation, or relations, in virtue of which deduction is possible. We have already pointed out that one proposition is sometimes inferred from another when it would not be possible to deduce the one from the other. That is to say, not all inference is deductive. We have now to consider what relation, or relations, that can hold between propositions would make deduction possible. This question has been very fully considered by the mathematical logicians, who desire to make explicit all the conditions of valid deduction and to carry the analysis of these conditions as far as it is possible to carry it. Mr. Russell, for instance, at the outset of his discussion says : ' Now in order that one proposition may be inferred from another, it is necessary that the two should have that relation which makes the one a consequence of the other. When a proposition q is a consequence of a proposition p, we say that p *implies* q. Thus deduction depends upon the relation of *implication*, and every deductive system must contain among its premisses as many of the properties of implication as are necessary to legitimate the ordinary procedure of deduction.' [2] It will certainly be agreed that in order that q can be deduced from p, there must be such a relation between them that q *is a consequence of* p. This relation has usually been called " implication ", so that Mr. Russell appears to be in agreement with the ordinary usage of language when he uses the expression " p *implies* q " for the relation that holds between p and q when q is a consequence of p. In the preceding chapters we have constantly used the word " implies " in this sense. We said that the premisses of a syllogism *imply* the conclusion ; that a proposition *implies* its obverse, and so on. When p implies q, then q can be deduced from p. This language is in agreement with common sense. To say that q is a consequence of p, or, to use an equivalent expression, that q "follows from " p, is to say that q *can be deduced* from p. There will be general agreement that " implication " can be properly used to express this relation. But it is not clear from this agreement whether *Mr. Russell is in fact using* the word " implies " in the sense in which " implies " means the converse of " is a consequence of ", i.e. in a sense which would express the converse of the relation " follows from ". Whether, or not, this is the case we shall have to consider.

---

[1] It is impossible to reconcile Mill's contention that the general proposition is a mere convenient abbreviation, with his view that the generalization involves inference.

[2] *Principia Mathematica*, p. 90. It is to be noted that "inferred" here means " deductively, or formally, inferred ".

property of *being mortal*", whatever X may be. Or, to use Mr.
Russell's language of propositional functions, we can say that a formal
implication is obtained when it is asserted that for every value of *x*,
the proposition ' *x* is a man ' materially implies ' *x* is mortal '. Thus
formal implication is a class of material implications ; it asserts that
in *every* case of a certain set of cases material implication holds.
" If anything has S, then that thing has M " states a formal implication.

It is the relation of *material implication* that Mr. Russell regards
as the sole relation in virtue of which deduction is possible. Thus
he says, ' The relation in virtue of which it is possible for us validly
to infer is what I call material implication.' [1] He argues, ' It would
certainly not be commonly maintained that " $2 + 2 = 4$ " can be
deduced from " Socrates is a man ", or that both are implied by
" Socrates is a triangle ". But the reluctance to admit such implications is chiefly due, I think, to preoccupation with formal implication, which is a much more familiar notion, and is really before the
mind, as a rule, even where material implication is what is explicitly
mentioned.' It is at least clear that the relation that holds between
" Socrates is a man " and " $2 + 2 = 4$ " is not the relation of *entailing*. Certainly it is true that either " Socrates is a triangle " is false
or that " $2 + 2 = 4$ " is true, since, in fact, the first of these propositions is false and the second is true. But it seems clear that it
cannot be maintained that " $2 + 2 = 4$ " *is a consequence* of
" Socrates is a triangle ". There can be no doubt that *entails* and
materially implies are quite different relations. The relation that
holds between " This is red " and " This is coloured " is totally
different from the relation that holds between " Socrates is a triangle "
and " $2 + 2 = 4$ ". If this be so, it seems unfortunate that the same
word " implies " has been used to express both relations. Mr.
Russell in defending his use of " implies " in a sense in which no one
had ever used the word says, ' Provided our use of words is consistent
it matters little how we define them.' [2] No doubt the principle of
Humpty Dumpty has something to be said for it. But the use of a
word already familiar in a certain sense to express a sense different
from its original meaning and liable to be confused with it is apt to
lead to unfortunate consequences. It is difficult not to slip back to
the original meaning, and thus to perplex oneself and others with
apparent paradoxes, and even to fall into obvious falsities. Mr.
Russell has not always been able to keep the two meanings of
" implies " distinct. He seems to have been led by the familiar
associations of the word " implies " into what Professor Moore calls
the " enormous ' howler ' " of supposing that ' " *q* can be deduced
from *p* " means the same as " *p* materially implies *q* " '. This

---

[1] *Principles of Mathematics*, § 38.   [2] *Int. Math. Phil.*, p. 146.

'howler' is the explanation of Mr. Russell's statement quoted above that "$2 + 2 = 4$" *is implied by* "Socrates is a triangle" and that "$2 + 2 = 4$" *can be deduced from* "Socrates is a man".

The distinction between *materially implies* and *entails* might be brought out in another way by introducing the notion of logical impossibility.[1] We can see that it *could* not be true that X is a right angle and yet false that X is an angle ; or that it *could* not be true that this is red and yet false that this is coloured. We do not attempt to *define* " logical impossibility ", but we say that to say that " p entails q " is to say that it *could* not be the case that p is true and q false. To say that " p materially implies q " is to say that it is *not as a matter of fact* the case that p is true and q false.   It seems plain that there is an important difference between "*could not be*" and "*is not as a matter of fact*" and that this difference is exemplified in the difference of the relation that holds between "This is red" and "This is coloured" from the relation that holds between "Socrates is a triangle" and "$2 + 2 = 4$".   Can anything be said to justify our making this distinction ?   In discussing this question it will be convenient to use shorthand symbols.   We shall symbolize "entails" by Professor Moore's symbol "*ent.*", and "materially implies" by the symbol ✱ which Professor Moore uses for Mr. Russell's symbol ⊃.

We wish to maintain that if " p *ent.* q " means " p could not be true and q false ", then there is between p and q a relation such that q *follows logically*, or *formally* from p.   No matter *what* p and q may be, if " p *ent.* q " then q can be formally deduced from p.   If " p ✱ q " means " p is not as a matter of fact true and q false ", then there is not such a relation between p and q that q can be formally deduced from p.   It may be objected that " could not be " is equivalent to " *never* as a matter of fact is ".   This means that to say " ' x is a right angle ' *ent.* ' x is an angle ' " is equivalent to saying that " ' x is a right angle ' ✱ ' x is an angle ' whatever x may be."   That is to say, we explain material implication when it holds between p and q, as equivalent to *entails* provided that " p ✱ q " is an instance of a true formal implication.   In other words, according to this explanation, " ' This is red ' *ent.* ' This is coloured ' " *means* " ' This is red ' ✱ ' This is coloured ' " *and* this is an instance of a propositional function that is always true.

This seems to be Mr. Russell's view.   To say that p could *not be false* is equivalent to saying that p *necessarily is* true.   Now, Mr. Russell says that what " necessary " *means* is that a propositional function is always true.   Thus he says, ' Propositional functions . . . are of three kinds : those which are true for all values of the argument or arguments, those which are false for all values, and those which are true for some arguments and false for others.   The first

---

[1] This is the method followed by Professor C. I. Lewis.

15

given building, say a Quakers' meeting-house. We can infer about some of them with some degree of probability that they will have characteristics usually associated with Quakers. But others than Quakers may be present. Even if we exclude these, thus assuming that only Quakers are in the building, all that we know about any one of these individuals is what is given in the defining property of *Quakerism*. But now suppose that the building is the General Post Office. Here we have persons acting in a certain way in virtue of their membership of a certain organization. The building is no longer required to select the set of individuals. We include all the individuals ordered by the Post Office organization. Again, a commercial organization, such as Selfridge's Stores, *orders* a set of individuals, whose properties are determined not merely by membership of a class but by membership of an orderly array. A law-court, a college, a school, a well-conducted household, present examples of orderly arrangement. To say that a household is " well conducted " is to say that it exhibits orderly arrangement, that the duties and privileges of its members are determined by their position in the organization. Thus an orderly arrangement is what is usually meant by a system. The system is a system because it consists of *ordered* elements. The word " system " is often used so as to restrict its application to arrangements that exhibit certain types of order. But it is better not so to restrict it, and to admit that orderliness is susceptible of degrees.

We may say more precisely that a set of elements exhibits order when, given the properties of some of the members of the set the properties of other members of the set, or at least of some of them, are thereby determined. This determination is due to the *relation* that orders the set ; it is not a property of the elements regarded as a class. For example, the individuals who are ordered by the Post Office organization may be members of various classes and of various other orders ; they may also be fathers, novelists, citizens. Thus an order is a relation that orders the members of a class, i.e. a set of elements, *in a certain way*.[1] When we know how a set of elements is ordered we have a basis for inference. The solar system provides an instance of an ordered set of elements.[2] A set of individuals subject to a code

---

[1] A crowd is disorderly when the movements of any members of it are independent of the movements of any other members. It is orderly in proportion as the members are engaged in doing the same things or are determined in their movements by the movements of other members, e.g. in a market-place where some are buyers some vendors. The difference may be formally expressed as follows : a crowd is disorderly when the movements of A, B, etc., are not in such relation to the movements of N, S, etc., as to form a basis of inference the crowd is orderly in proportion as such inference is possible.

[2] The solar system may be regarded as an *order*, since from the fact that a planet has such and such a position inferences can be drawn. Such inference

of discipline, such as an army, is an ordered set.   Order is found in all departments of life.   What is called civilization is largely dependent upon the establishment of systems of various orders which enable us to take much for granted.   Thus we can arrange our conduct with reference to the order-system of the Railways, the Post Office, the Penal Code, and so on.   Given these ordered systems we can draw inferences that relate to the behaviour of other elements of the system.   There are various types of order as well as varying degrees in which orderliness may be found.   A work of art exhibits one type of order.   It may be contrasted with the type of order exhibited in a school, a Government, a Post Office.

The introduction of order into what was disorderly may be, then, of all degrees of complication, and these complications may be of different kinds.   For the most part order is discovered by reflective thought.   It does not lie upon the surface of what is experienced. This is obvious, since any given set of individuals may be ordered in different ways.   The average man whose interests are practical easily recognizes an order in the large-scale periodic phenomena of Nature : in the recurrent change from day to night, the phases of the moon ; the ebb and flow of the tide, and, on some portions of the surface of the globe, in the return of the seasons.   No doubt the sophisticated, but comparatively uneducated, plain man of the twentieth century would assent to the statement that the phenomena of nature are ordered ; just as, in spite of the plain deliverances of his senses, he would assent to the statement that the earth goes round the sun. This readiness to admit an order that has not been apprehended is no doubt partly the result of adaptation to our mechanical civilization. Order is most *apparent* where man has been at work.   The routine of daily life in a modern community presents an order of the type that is most easily apprehended.   It shares moreover to a considerable extent in the periodicity of natural phenomena.   So long as no sudden or overwhelming disaster occurs to interrupt the routine its orderliness is accepted as *natural*, and as providing the type of order in terms of which the order of nature is to be interpreted.

The need for order in the happenings of daily life is obvious. Without some degree of orderliness our life would be a chaotic nightmare, even though it would not be *apprehended* as such.   What accounts we have of primitive peoples reveal them as struggling to impose some order on events so that they may control them.   In their *ritual uniformity*, in their *practical origin*, and in their *development in the face of different* situations, magical practices are akin to science. We are not here concerned to trace the development from primitive magic to modern science.   It is enough to point out the logical con-

are to be distinguished from those that are dependent upon the general laws of planetary motion, e.g. Newtonian law of gravitation.

lies in the appeal to what is observable. A mathematical proposition is independent of what happens to exist. The distinction between mathematics and the natural sciences is the distinction between pure science and empirical science. The opposition is between *pure* and *empirical*, not between *pure* and *applied* science. The adjective " empirical " is derived from " experience ". It is not easy to define " experience ", but the notion may be made clearer by the help of examples. A blind man cannot have an experience which consists of being aware of a red patch ; that is to say, he cannot be acquainted with the referend of " red ". Consequently, he does not know what " red " *means*. A deaf man cannot be aware of the sound of B♯ on a violin. A man paralysed from birth cannot be aware of sensations in the legs such as those experienced by normal persons in walking. Those that can see, and hear, and walk, can have such experiences ; their knowledge is empirical. If nothing in the world were red, no one could have the experience that consists in seeing a red patch. The *red patch*, the *sound of B♯ on a violin* are examples of what we have called sensible facts. They can be known only by acquaintance. The proposition " Some roses are red " must be false if there is nothing in the world that is red. It *could* only be *known* to be true if some one had seen a red rose. Facts that *could* only be known by sensible observation are empirical facts. Such empirical facts constitute the original data of the natural sciences, and consequently, they are called empirical. Mathematical propositions being independent of what exists are independent of experience. It is true that we first come to know that $2 + 2 = 4$ by observing two sets of two things and one set of four things. But it is easy to see that the truth of the proposition $2 + 2 = 4$ is independent of these sets of things and might have been known without reference to them. This is not the case with an empirical proposition. Whether the proposition " Sugar dissolves in water " is true depends upon what there actually is in the world ; it could only be *known* to be true by observation of particular pieces of sugar. This difference in the nature of a mathematical and an empirical proposition involves some difference in the method employed by the mathematician and the empirical scientist. Owing to its independence of empirical facts mathematics is a wholly deductive science ; hence it employs a method of exact demonstration. In other words, mathematics is a formal science. The empirical sciences on the other hand depend upon generalization from experience ; their conclusions are not demonstrated but are verified by sensible observation. In other words, empirical science involves induction. With the precise nature of induction we shall be concerned in the next chapter. Here it is sufficient to point out that the empirical sciences differ from mathematics both in the nature of their subject-matter and in their method. Nevertheless, both alike are *sciences* because their method has been developed solely with a view to understanding the facts with which they are concerned. The scientist seeks to order the facts so as to render them intelligible.

The sciences are, then, orderly branches of knowledge. The method of ordering the data is *scientific method*. The adjective " scientific " is, however, often used more widely than the corresponding noun " science ". It is extended to characterize all the processes of thought which terminate in conclusions that a reasonable man may accept. When we say that some one has a " scientific mind " we mean that his convictions are *reasoned* convictions ; that before he comes to a conclusion he weighs the evidence, taking into account all the relevant facts. He does not accept a conclusion simply because it is in harmony with his desires ; nor would he consider such harmony a *reason* for its rejection. This readiness to accept only what the facts warrant is a characteristic of the scientific thinker. In the narrower sense the scientific thinker is one who seeks to understand what happens simply for the sake of understanding it. To achieve such understanding he must be prepared not to accept things at their face value, to be puzzled by what is familiar and apparently obvious and yet not content to remain puzzled. The scientist, as Bacon says,[1] should be ready to seek, slow to assert, prepared to doubt yet quick to apprehend the resemblances between things, apt to distinguish their differences, and careful to arrange them in order. Doubtless no scientist exhibits these mental characteristics on all occasions. But scientific discoveries are made by those who, with reference to a given region of fact, are capable of such thinking.

§ 3. COMMON-SENSE THINKING AND SCIENTIFIC METHOD

Science has been described as organized common sense. But science differs from common sense not only in the degree of organization achieved but also in the types of order apprehended. Nevertheless, the description is not wholly inapplicable to the earliest stages of scientific inquiry. Science has grown out of common-sense knowledge, having for its origin man's need to understand his environment in order that he may control it. The disinterested desire to know is a late development. It is rare even to-day, but it is the condition without which the development of science is impossible.

A commonplace illustration will show how a practical man faced with an unexpected occurrence may attempt to explain a situation by organizing relevant facts into a coherent whole. Suppose that a man, having left his flat empty, returns in the early evening to find his front door bolted. He knows that he left no one in the flat. How, then, account for the bolted door ? That burglars have

[1] See quotation at head of chapter.

broken into the flat is the first idea likely to occur to a Londoner. The suggestion springs into his mind almost before he has had time to reflect. But then a difficulty arises to check the acceptance of this idea. How could a burglar have left the door bolted on the inside ? The flat is on the third floor of a straight-faced block, so that it is improbable that the entry should have been made through a window. Perhaps the bolt has slipped. But that idea is immediately rejected, since it is a stiff, horizontal bolt rarely used. Some one inside must have drawn the bolt. Having succeeded in forcing the door, he inspects the flat, looking for confirmation of his suspicion. There is no one in his study, but he finds the drawers of his desk open and their contents scattered. There was, he knew, no money in the desk, so he does not pause to examine the drawers, but goes at once to the dining-room to inspect the silver. He finds that two silver cups have gone and also that the table silver has disappeared. These facts are ample confirmation of his belief that he has been robbed. But there is still the puzzling fact of the door bolted on the inside. As he walks down the passage he sees a light under the kitchen door. Perhaps the burglar is still in the flat. But the kitchen is empty. On the table are the remains of a meal. The window is wide open. He remembers the parcels lift and now feels that the situation is explained. Whatever the means of entry, the exit has been by way of the parcels lift. The bolted front door was doubtless to give the burglar time to escape should the owner of the flat return too soon.

In this example a set of isolated facts are connected together in order to account for an occurrence that was felt to be in need of explanation. The idea of robbery, suggested by previous experience, was developed into a series of suppositions of the form : *If so-and-so then such-and-such*. The consequences of the supposition were tested by direct observation of a fact that had been supposed to be likely. Another fact that was observed but had not been deduced supplied an important link in the connexion of the facts. It must be noticed that the circumstance to be explained occurred within a situation familiar in its main features. Consequently, the man had no difficulty in ruling out some possible suggestions as simply irrelevant. The stages in this investigation may be summarized as follows :

1. Awareness of a familiar complex situation in which some one fact was apprehended as peculiar, i.e. as not being what might have been expected. Hence the need is felt *to account for* this fact by connecting it with a total situation in which its occurrence would not be unexpected.

2. The formation of an hypothesis which would connect the unexpected fact with other facts.

3. Deductive development of the hypothesis.

4. Testing the consequences deduced by appealing to observable facts. The successful accomplishment of this fourth stage marks the acceptance of the hypothesis as explaining the given fact. From the point of view of the ordinary Londoner it would be felt that, in the given case, no *other* supposition would so well account for all the observed facts.

With regard to such an investigation we may be said to *explain* a fact when we have shown that it is connected in an orderly manner with other facts that do not require to be explained. It is the unusual, and therefore unexpected occurrences that lead the ordinary man to ask : How has this happened ?   He undertakes the analysis of the conditions upon which a fact may be consequent only when the fact is unusual or startling.   The scientist's curiosity is not thus limited, nor in him does familiarity breed the illusion of under-standing.   This marks a departure from the plain man's point of view.   As Professor Whitehead says, ' It requires a very unusual mind to undertake the analysis of the obvious'.   Owing to this difference in their point of view the plain man is often satisfied with the answer, " Because it always happens so ", whereas the scientist recognizes that such an answer is but the beginning of an explana-tion.   Ultimately the explanation of facts is to be found in their organization into a system.   That the plain man so soon stops short in his inquiries is due to his predominantly practical interests and his consequent unwillingness to undertake a laborious analysis of the situation.   Such problems as he encounters can usually be solved to his satisfaction without going beyond the order that results from the habitual associations of one experience with another.

The four stages enumerated above are sometimes regarded as constituting what has been called *inductive method*. The word " induction " is ambiguous, and will be discussed in the next chapter. Here we are concerned only to notice the resemblance between common-sense thinking and some aspects of scientific method.   To make the comparison clearer it will be convenient to give a sim-plified illustration of scientific reasoning.   The plain man, although he has frequently experienced the resistance of the air when, for instance, he struggles to walk in the teeth of a gale, or tries to com-press with his hands a bladder filled with air, nevertheless does not usually think of the air as a body ; he does not apprehend air as having weight.   But the supposition that air has weight serves to connect a number of disconnected facts that would otherwise be puzzling because of their disconnexion.   If the plain man were asked why water *rises* in a pump, he would probably be content to answer that the water is drawn upwards by suction.   He would think of suction as a force, and would not consider that this notion of a *force* itself requires explanation.   At the beginning of the seventeenth century scientists were content to explain suction by nature's supposed abhorrence of a vacuum. But, apart from the unsatisfactoriness of regarding *abhorrence* as an explanatory notion, a difficulty arises from the observed fact that this abhorrence seems to be limited to about thirty-three feet at sea-level. Galileo [1] had already conceived that air had weight and had tried to determine its weight. Torricelli [2] thought of connecting the weight of the air with the abhorrence of a vacuum. He conceived the plan of measuring the resistance of the air by means of a column of mercury. He took a glass tube rather more than a metre in length, closed at one end and filled with mercury. This he inverted over mercury in a trough, stopping the open end with his finger. When he removed his finger the mercury fell, and remained stationary at about a level of 76 cm. This fall could be explained as due to the pressure of a column of air. This discovery not only led to the invention of the barometer but also enabled a number of hitherto unconnected facts to be connected in an orderly manner. It seemed reasonable to suppose that the pressure of the air would vary under different conditions, and would have different effects at different heights above sea-level. A committee of the Royal Society drew up a series of questions to be tested experimentally on a high mountain in Tenerife.[3] The questions were framed so as to suggest what might be expected to happen if the pressure of the atmosphere were a fact. Three of the questions will serve to illustrate the fertility of this supposition :

1. " Try the quicksilver experiment at the top, and at several other ascents of the mountain ; and at the end of the experiment at the top of the hill, lift out the tube from the restagnant quicksilver somewhat hastily, and observe if the remaining mercury be impelled with the remaining force or not. And take by instrument, with what exactness may be, the true altitude of every place where the experiment is made ; and observe at the same time, the temperature of the air, as to heat and cold, by a weather glass ; and as to moisture and dryness with a horoscope ; and note what sense the experimenters have of the air at those times respectively.

2. " Carry up bladders, some very little blown, some more, and others full blown ; and observe how they alter upon the several ascents.

3. " Observe what alterations are to be found in living creatures,

---

[1] Galileo lived 1564–1642.

[2] Torricelli invented the barometer in 1643. A good account is given of this experiment in C. D. Whetham's *Matter and Change*. See also Mach, *Science of Mechanics*, Chap. I, § viii.

[3] This account is taken from an address by Sir W. Bragg on " The Influence of Learned Societies on the Development of England ", which is published in *Craftsmanship and Science (Forum Series)*. See pp. 37–8.

carried thither, both before and after feeding ; and what the experimenters do find in themselves as to difficulty of breathing, faintness of spirit, inclination to vomit, giddiness, etc."

These examples suffice to illustrate how a supposition that is related to a set of facts to be explained may be capable of development into a series of suggestions as to what might be expected to happen under certain determinate conditions. When these conditions can be obtained, the suggestions can be tested. A supposition that in this way serves to connect facts in a regular manner is what is known as an *hypothesis*. When the consequences of the hypothesis can be tested by direct observation, further evidence is provided for accepting or rejecting the original supposition. Sometimes, as in the example of the burglary, the consequences deduced are of the kind that will either have occurred or not. All that the man had to do was to look and see. Sometimes the investigator has to arrange the conditions so as deliberately to bring about the expected result. This was the case with the scientist's problem given above. The deliberate arrangement of the conditions constitutes an *experiment*. It is to be observed that the experiments suggested above are *as experiments* very simple. They did not require the marvellously constructed and very delicate instruments by means of which physical knowledge is to-day being advanced. Doubtless they would have been performed more easily had the instruments used been more adequate, but it was not lack of suitable instruments that had prevented earlier scientists from carrying out such observations. The importance of these observations lay in the fact that they provided experiential confirmation of an hypothesis that served to connect facts that would otherwise have been unnoticed and unexplained.

There is a constant alternation between observation and hypothesis in any attempt to account for an unexpected fact. A supposition, going beyond what is immediately observed, is seen to be such that it would connect the given fact with other facts that have been and that might be expected to be observed. If observation, whether experimental or not, reveals such a fact, then the required connexion is so far established. Then another supposition may be formulated and tested by further observation. The investigation is completed only when all the circumstances that led to it have been fitted together. The hypothesis may then be regarded as established so far as the particular problem is concerned. Common sense uses in a rough and ready manner a method of alternate observation and hypothesis that has been gradually refined by scientific thinkers into an instrument more and more fitted to deal with complicated problems. There is a stage in the development of every science in which the methods of common sense can be clearly discerned. When, as the result of this method, a considerable amount of order has been introduced into our knowledge of the external world the method is developed in such a way that it is no longer recognizable as the organization of common sense, and its results are far removed from the common-sense beliefs out of which it has slowly grown. Mr. Russell has put this point very clearly. He says : ' The development of science out of common sense has not been by way of a radically new start at any moment, but rather by way of successive approximations. That is to say, where some difficulty has arisen which current common sense could not solve, a modification has been made at some point, while the rest of the common-sense view of the world has been retained. Subsequently, using this modification, another modification has been introduced elsewhere, and so on. Thus science has been an historical growth, and has assumed at each moment, a more or less vague background of theory derived from common sense.' [1]

Common-sense thinking differs from scientific thinking in two very important respects. The former is fragmentary ; it jumps from one fact to another, taking much for granted so that many intermediate links are left unexplained. The latter takes much less for granted and, in consequence, achieves a higher degree of organization. Secondly, the plain man is apt to regard the problem he is investigating as being almost completely isolated from other problems ; hence, he is unaware of the bearing of his solution upon other problems. The scientist apprehends his problem as capable of temporary isolation but as essentially connected with other problems that will have to be considered in relation to his solution of the given problem. Thus the scientist is more aware of the possible ramifications of the inquiry upon which he is at the moment concentrating. From these differences there follows the important consequence that common-sense thinking is necessarily confined to comparatively simple problems, not only because of the mainly practical interests of the plain man, but because his method of investigation does not lead him to raise the right questions. The deficiencies of common sense are most obviously revealed in the deductive development of the hypothesis. As Professor Whitehead puts it : ' Common-sense deduction probably moves by blind instinct from concrete proposition to concrete proposition, guided by some habitual association of ideas. Thus common sense fails in the presence of a wealth of material.' [2]

§ 4. THE IMPORTANCE OF RELEVANT KNOWLEDGE

An examination of the examples we have given shows that a considerable amount of previous knowledge relevant to the situation

[1] *Analysis of Matter*, pp. 193–4.
[2] *Proc. Arist. Soc.*, N.S., XVII, p. 73.

is required before a problem can even be stated. Still more knowledge is required in order that fruitful suggestions as to its solution should occur to the thinker. The primitive thinker may well have been as intelligent as a modern scientist, but he was less able to deal satisfactorily with his problems because he had less knowledge of what was *relevant* to its solution. Only by the accumulation of a large and systematized body of knowledge is it possible for science to develop. The importance and the extent of what can be taken for granted *because its connexion with the problem is already known*, is apt to be obscured by the treatment of scientific examples in a textbook of logic. Just so much as is required to provide the explicit premisses of the reasoning is given. There is too often a selection of the facts in the light of the theory of scientific method that the given example is intended to illustrate.[1] Hence, scientific method is not presented in a manner capable of suggesting the method of discovery. This is no doubt unavoidable. The only way to understand scientific method is to carry out a scientific investigation. It is for this reason that it is worth while for the beginner in logic to attempt to analyse some process of controlled thinking that he has himself gone through in order to solve some difficulty of his own. It is as impossible to obtain a grasp of scientific method from the dissection of selected examples without any practical experience in solving problems given in one's own experience, as it would be for a physiologist to understand what a living body is like if his acquaintance with bodies had been confined to the dead body on the dissecting-table. All that a textbook on method can do is to point out some of the considerations involved. Something, however, may be done to emphasize the *importance* of relevant knowledge and of the necessity for a combination of knowledge and insight. An example which brings out this point well is given by Sir William Bragg in his *Presidential Address to the British Association* (September 5, 1928). The passage must be quoted in full :

'It was in the early years of the war that a body of young scientific students from our Universities was assembled for the purpose of testing on the battlefield the value of such methods of locating enemy guns as were already known. In their mutual discussions and considerations it became clear to them that the great desideratum was a method of measuring very exactly the time of arrival of the air pulse, due to the discharge of the gun, at various stations in their own lines. If the relative positions of the stations were accurately known it would then become a matter of calculation to find the gun position. But the pulse was very feeble : how could it be registered ? Various methods were considered, and among them was one which no doubt seemed far-fetched and unlikely to be successful. A fine wire is made to carry an electric current by which it is heated. If it is chilled, for example, by a puff of cold air, the resistance to the passage of

---

[1] Limitations of space often make this procedure inevitable, but not the less regrettable.

the current increases, and this is an effect which can be measured if it is large enough. If, then, the hot wire could be made to register the arrival of the air pulse from the gun a solution of the problem was in hand. No doubt this method occurred to several members of the company ; it was certainly turned over in the mind of one of them who had had considerable experience of these fine heated wires. They had been in use about thirty years, having been employed for the measurement of temperature in many circumstances where their peculiar characteristics gave them the supremacy over thermometers of the ordinary form. But, and this was the important point, was it to be expected that the effect, though it must be there, would be big enough to see ? Could the faint impulse from a gun miles away produce an obvious chill in a hot wire ? On first thoughts it did not seem likely, and the suggestion lay in abeyance.

' But it happened that one summer morning an enemy aeroplane came over at daybreak on a patrolling expedition. The officer of whom I have spoken lay awake in his bunk listening to the discharges of the anti-aircraft guns and the more distant explosions of their shells. Every now and then a faint whistling sound seemed to be connected with the louder sounds. The wall of the hut was of felt ; it was in poor condition and there were tiny rents close to his head where he lay. The gun pulses made a feeble sound as they came through. This set the officer thinking : if the pulse was strong enough to make a sound, it might be strong enough to chill a hot wire perceptibly. So the method was proposed to the company as worth trying. It was tried, and proved to be a complete success. The sound ranging of the British Armies was based upon it, with results that have already been described and are fairly well known.'

This experience illustrates two important considerations ; first, that a considerable amount of previous knowledge and scientific training is required in order that some detail of a complicated situation may be apprehended as being *the* fact significant for the solution of the problem ; secondly, the man who has the relevant knowledge must be in those circumstances in which he can actually observe the important occurrence. Vague general knowledge of sound currents would have been insufficient to suggest the possible solution. What was required was a definite estimate of the effects of the quantities actually given. Only " a man actually on the spot " could have been in possession of these essential details.[1]

Relevant knowledge and the opportunity though essential are not always sufficient for the solution of scientific problems. There is needed also that incalculable element of scientific insight which is the mark of genius, and which cannot be reduced to rules capable of formation.

§ 5. THE FORM OF SCIENTIFIC METHOD

Starting from the point of view of common sense we have seen that the initial problem of science is to order the facts given in sensible experience. We saw in Chapter IV that by " fact " is meant *whatever is the case*. *What* is the case is always complex, for example, a thing in its relations, or with its properties. Facts are complex in the same way in which propositions are complex. When the pro-

[1] See Sir W. Bragg, loc. cit., p. 22.

position is a proposition about the external world, then the fact which the proposition expresses is an actual state of affairs, provided that the proposition is true. It is this kind of fact with which we are at present concerned, for the data of science are observable facts. We have already seen that it is not easy to draw a precise line between what we actually observe and what is inferred. It is sufficient for our purpose if we recognize the distinction between a *fact* taken as a *datum* and an *interpretation* of the fact, which may develop into an elaborate theory *about* the facts.   An illustration, given by Professor T. P. Nunn, may make this point clearer :

'The scientific traveller on a high plateau of the Andes and his native guide view in different ways the impossibility of getting their potatoes to cook. To the latter the impossibility is due to the simple fact that "the cursed pot", doubtless owing to the devil in it, "did not wish to cook potatoes"; to the former it is an interesting example of the dependence of the boiling point upon the pressure. But although the whole "situation" may be very different in the two cases, there is yet a common basis of inevitable *fact* upon which the scientist and the native (if he is intelligent enough) can see that their "animistic" or "scientific" *interpretations* are simply embroideries.' [1]

In this illustration the factual basis—' the fire, the pot, the luke-warm yet boiling water, the unsoftened potatoes '—is so interpreted both by the natives and the scientist, as to be constructed into an ordered situation. Professor Nunn emphasizes the point that the basis of fact is ' inevitable '; the pot, for instance, is apprehended *as a pot* by native guide and scientific traveller alike, however much preliminary experience may have been required in order that it should be so apprehended. The unperceivable connexions, viz. the devil's desire that the potatoes should not cook; the dependence of boiling point upon pressure—are not *inevitable* constructions; they are different modes of interpretation, their difference being due to the wide difference in the context of the experience from which they are drawn. In both cases the purpose is so to order the constituents of the factual situation that it may be understood. The first step in understanding is achieved by generalization, that is, by connecting a given fact with other facts that resemble it. But *facts* are complex; the resemblance between facts holds between some, but not all, of their constituents. Hence, facts must be analysed. The constituents of primary fact must be grouped in classes; these classes must then be ordered among themselves. In this way increasing generality is obtained. The scientist wants to make assertions about what *always* happens, not about what *sometimes* happens. The zoologist, for instance, is not concerned with this particular cow staring at this particular tree; he wants to

[1] *The Aim and Achievements of Scientific Method*, p. 46.   It is very much to be regretted that this excellent book is out of print.

16

Hence, we pass to the conclusion that *any* red patch is darker than *any* pink patch. Thus we generalize from the particular instance. The intuition is of the *form* but it relates to the material exemplified in the form.   That we do in fact apprehend general principles in this way is not likely to be denied.   To describe this method of discovering axioms as *inductive inference* involves an extension of the word "inductive " as ordinarily used, but no doubt this extension is desirable.

Aristotle's second use of the word is concerned with the enumeration of particular instances.   From the consideration of each of the members of a limited class we may pass to a generalization concerning all the members of that class.   This process has usually been known as " complete induction " or " perfect induction ".   The name is peculiarly inappropriate.   It was supposed that induction consists in generalization from particular instances, and that therefore, if *every* instance were included in the enumeration the inductive process would be perfected.   But it is difficult to see what useful purpose could be served by calling such a mode of inference " inductive ", since the reasoning is clearly syllogistic in character.   For example, from the examination of the particular cases of an ellipse, a parabola, an hyperbola we might conclude that, since no one of them cuts a straight line at more than two points, no conic section cuts a straight line at more than two points.   When explicitly stated it is seen that this reasoning is syllogistic.   It can be formulated as follows :

No circle, no ellipse, no parabola, no hyperbola cuts a straight line in more than two points ;

Every conic section is either a circle, or an ellipse, or a parabola, or an hyperbola ;

Therefore, no conic section cuts a straight line in more than two points.

It is essential that the class that is enumerated should contain only a limited number of instances.   It is not possible to enumerate a class that has an infinite number of members, nor to enumerate a class which, though not infinite, contains members that are not known by us.   In neither of these cases could we complete the summation.   This mode of inference is of very little value save as a shorthand device.   It can be symbolized as follows :

$S_1, S_2, S_3 \ldots S_n$ is P.

Every S is either S_1, or S_2, or $S_3 \ldots$ or S_n.

$\therefore$ Every S is P.

Mr. Johnson has suggested the convenient name *summary induction* for this mode of inference.   It is certainly a more appropriate name than " perfect induction ".[1]

---

[1] Mr. Johnson holds that by summary induction it is possible to establish general propositions in Euclidean geometry by means of figures.   He concludes

Generalization from a number of examined instances which are not assumed to constitute *all* the instances of the given class is now usually known by the name " Induction by Simple Enumeration ". With this mode of inference we shall be concerned in the next section. Sometimes " induction " has been understood as an exact synonym for " simple enumeration ". The great importance of simple enumeration in scientific investigation is no doubt responsible for the fact that " induction " has also been used as a synonym for " scientific method ". When so used it has been called " imperfect induction " to distinguish it from " perfect " or summary induction. This variation in terminology is unfortunate. It seems now to be generally agreed that induction essentially consists in generalization from particular instances, and that scientific method involves not only induction but also deduction. J. S. Mill defined induction as " the operation of discovering and proving general propositions ". This is undoubtedly too wide a definition. It was, however, Mill's views on the nature of *induction* and *proof* that led him so to define " induction ", rather than a desire to use the *word* in a sense different from the usual.[1] Since generalization from particular matters of fact constitutes induction, it follows that the empirical sciences are based upon induction. But it does not follow that such scientific general propositions could be established *solely* by induction, nor that any inductive proposition is capable of proof. Whether or not this is the case will be discussed in Chapter XX. Here we are concerned only to point out that, since all the sciences except mathematics are empirical, i.e. based upon particular experiences, it follows that without induction there could be no science. Whether the belief, which we all in fact share, that some scientific propositions are true is capable of logical justification cannot be profitably discussed until we have considered the method by which scientific propositions are obtained.

We may begin by considering a proposition of a type readily recognized by the plain man as scientific, e.g. *Acids are sour to the taste and turn blue litmus red*. We may contrast this with a proposition such as *I don't like this sour orange*. The latter would not be regarded as a scientific proposition because it states an isolated fact, an individual judgement of taste. The former would be regarded as scientific because it states a generalization. It could be tested and agreement

that there is ' a more interesting type of summary induction in which the conclusion applies to an infinite number of cases which are non-enumerable ' (loc. cit., p. 200). But it does not seem to me that Mr. Johnson's contention can be admitted.

[1] See *Logic*, Bk. III, Chaps. I and II. Mill *also* defines induction as ' the process by which we conclude that what is true of certain individuals of a class is true of the whole class, or that what is true at certain times will be true in similar circumstances at all times ' (Chap. II, § 1). For a further discussion of Mill's views see below, Chap. XVII, § 5.

as to its truth or falsity could be attained. If for the second proposition we were to substitute *No child likes sour oranges* we should have a scientific proposition capable of being tested by the investigation of children's tastes. In order that a proposition should be scientific it must relate to something other than the immediate experience of an individual. Our first proposition was not an assertion about a particular instance of an acid and a particular individual's experience, but an assertion about the properties of *any* acid. It was of the form : *If anything is an acid, it is sour to the taste and turns blue litmus red*. This proposition might be combined with the proposition *This is hydrochloric acid* to yield the conclusion *This is sour to the taste and turns blue litmus red*. This is a valid deductive form. But the question whether the conclusion is *true* could not be answered by a consideration of the validity of the form. If both premisses are true, then since the form is valid the conclusion is true. But the proposition asserted in the conclusion might be true even though this were not hydrochloric acid, and even if not all acids had the property of turning blue litmus red. Validity and truth are quite different. Science is concerned with propositions that are not only valid in form but are also true. We need not attempt to discuss the problem as to what is meant by a *true* proposition. We all know what it is to assert that a given proposition is true, and another given proposition is false. When we say that " *This is an acid* " *is true* we are asserting that it is the case that this is an acid. If it is the case that the sun's interior is hot, then the proposition " *The sun's interior is hot* " is true. If it is the case that tomatoes are juicy, then the proposition " *Tomatoes are juicy* " is true. If it is not the case that Socrates is alive, then " *Socrates is alive* " is false. It has sometimes been said that to say that a proposition is true is to say that there is a fact to which the proposition corresponds ; and to say that it is false is to say that there is no such fact. We need not, however, discuss what is meant by " correspondence " here, nor consider between what exactly the correspondence holds. It is enough for our purpose to accept the plain man's view that he knows what he means when he asserts that a proposition is true. What is important to observe is that unless there are general propositions about particular matters of fact, and unless some of these propositions are both true, and are believed to be true, there can be no knowledge that is rightly called scientific.

The first question we have to discuss is, then, how we are to obtain knowledge of general propositions such as *acids turn blue litmus red*. It is this type of inductive inference that must now be considered.

§ 2. SIMPLE ENUMERATION

The simplest kind of induction is that in which from the premiss *All observed S's are P's* we infer the conclusion *All S's are P's*. It is assumed that the observed S's are not all the S's there are ; hence this mode of induction is quite different from summary induction. The inference is not logically valid, for in inferring from a premiss about *some S* to a conclusion about *all S* there is an illicit distribution of S. For example, from the fact that all observed crows have been found to be black, we may infer that all crows are black. This mode of inference as we saw is known as induction by *simple enumeration*. It is the basis of generalization. Every one makes inferences by simple enumeration. Having met half a dozen Scotsmen all of whom are somewhat lacking in humour, we conclude that no Scotsman can see a joke. This precarious generalization is liable to be upset by the next Scotsman we meet ; it could not survive a reading of the works of David Hume. The appearance of a single contradictory instance disproves the conclusion.[1] It is obvious that if the number of observed instances are few in comparison with those that have not been observed, there is considerable likelihood that contradictory instances may be found among the latter. An example of simple enumeration, found in every elementary book on logic, has become famous because contradictory instances were discovered. The conclusion *all swans are white* was derived by many people from their observation of swans in Europe all of which happened to be white. On the discovery of Australia black swans were discovered.

Simple enumeration is so called because it appears to be a process simply of counting the instances and finding them all to have a certain property. It does not seem to involve analysis. For this reason Bacon and Mill attempted to reject simple enumeration from their account of scientific method. Thus Bacon says : ' the induction which proceeds by simple enumeration is childish ; its conclusions are precarious, and exposed to peril from a contradictory instance ; and generally it decides on too small a number of facts, and on those only which are at hand.'[2] Mill says : ' Popular notions are usually founded on induction by simple enumeration ; in science it carries us but a little way. We are forced to begin with it ; we must often rely on it provisionally, in the absence of means of a more searching investigation. But, for the accurate study of nature, we require a surer and a more potent instrument.'[3] Whether such a ' surer and more potent ' instrument can be found we shall have to consider later. It must be admitted that simple enumeration is a precarious mode of inference, that we constantly employ it ; and that our *belief* in the truth of propositions so inferred is out of all proportion to the *likelihood* of their truth. But it must also be admitted, as Mill saw, that without simple enumeration science would never have begun.

[1] Bacon named this mode of inference in the phrase : ' Inductio per enumerationem simplicem, ubi non reperitur instantia contradictoria.'

[2] *Novum Organum*, Bk. I, Aph. 105.   [3] *Logic*, Bk. III, Chap. III, § 2.

An inductive argument of this type can be expressed in the form :
" Such and such instances of Φ have the property Ψ ; no instances of
Φ that had not got Ψ have been found ; therefore, every Φ has Ψ."
The instances of Φ constitute a class having the properties connoted
by " Φ ". The examples so far given have all been of classes whose
members have many properties in common : *crows, swans, Scotsmen*.
The popular use of this mode of induction is always confined to such
classes. This point is worth considering. Any set of things can be
classed together. Some modes of grouping things into classes are felt
to be important ; some are felt to be trivial. For example, the class
formed of all the things in the world that are scarlet would appear to
be a class based on a trivial resemblance. Poppies, scarlet-fever rash,
doctors' gowns, covers of certain books, some tablecloths, and so on,
would constitute a class having very little in common except their
scarlet colour. But the class consisting of all books, or the class consisting of all crows, seems less artificial. Thus the property of *being
scarlet* has never been regarded as important enough for all the things
that have the property to be called by a *class-name*. We can refer
to them only as " scarlet things ". But " *swans* ", " *politicians* ",
" *Scotsmen* " are class-names. This point has been put very clearly
by Dr. Broad as follows : ' Now the mere fact that ordinary language
has taken the trouble to invent a general name like *swan* or *crow* tells
us a good deal about nature. It implies that a large number of
objects have been met with which have combined pretty constantly a
large number of properties varying only within fairly narrow limits.
It is true that you may *define* a crow or a swan or a man by a few
properties. But this very fact is symptomatic. Whatever may be
the dictionary meaning of ' man ' *we* always mean by it something with
a great many more properties than animality and rationality or two-
leggedness and featherlessness. Anything that had these properties
but differed widely in other respects from the men that we had met
would only with great hesitation be called a man. Hence the fact
that we are content with the dictionary definition is due to the fact
that so far in our experience the properties mentioned therein have
been associated with a whole bunch of other properties, and that all
these have been exemplified together with but slight variations in a
great number of instances.' [1] That is to say, such classes as *swans* and
men differ from such classes as *scarlet things* and *sour things* in the fact
that every member of the class *swan*, for instance, has several properties in common with all the other members, whereas the members
of the class *scarlet things* have few properties in common which are not

[1] *Mind*, N.S., Vol. XXIX, p. 17 : ' The Relation between Induction and
Probability.' Dr. Broad's two articles in *Mind* (Oct., 1918, January, 1920), on
this subject are of the greatest importance. Much of what I have to say about
scientific method has been learnt from him.

also possessed by things that are not scarlet.   Such classes as *swans* were called by Mill " natural kinds ".[1]   It is useful to adopt this term, although we should reject the assumptions upon which his choice of the name rested, and should, therefore, not be prepared to define a " natural kind " as he defined it.

Simple enumeration is not, then, to be regarded as a process *simply of counting* ;   it is a counting of instances *recognized as having certain properties in common*.   The inference is dependent upon recognition of *resemblances*.   An inference from resemblance is an inference from *analogy*.

§ 3.   ANALOGY

The word " analogy " has been used in various senses.[2]   We are now concerned with it in that sense in which *analogy* is to be opposed to simple *counting of instances*.   There has been considerable confusion of terminology, some logicians maintaining that analogy is a *form* of induction, some maintaining that induction is *based upon* analogy, whilst others maintain that analogy is a process of inference subsidiary to induction.   This divergence of opinion is due mainly to the ambiguity of " induction " and " analogy ".   As Mr. W. E. Johnson puts it :   ' In what sense these two terms are used is not clear, except that induction is understood to depend primarily upon the number of instances known to be characterized by a certain adjective ; [3] while the force of analogy depends upon the number of adjectives that are known to characterize a certain instance.   But it is essential to insist that neither by accumulating instances alone, nor by accumulating adjectives alone, can any inference be drawn, and that inference of this type, by whatever name it may be called, is governed by principles which underline both induction and analogy— requiring an intensional as well as an extensional link.   For example, no mere accumulation of instances S_1, S_2, S_3 ... S_n that are p could give any probability that a new instance s will be p, unless s were known to have at least one character predicable of all these instances. And conversely, no accumulation of characters p_1, p_2, ... p_m that are predicable of s could give any probability that a new character p is predicable of s, unless p were known to be predicable of at least one instance having all these characters.' [4]   That is to say, the opposition

---

[1] See Mill, *Logic*, Bk. III, Chap. XXII.

[2] For a discussion of Aristotle's treatment of analogy, see Joseph, *Introd.*, Chap. XXIV.

[3] Mr. Johnson uses the word " adjective " for " characteristic " or " property ", and not as a purely grammatical term.   His peculiar use of *adjective* is due to his view of the relation of grammar to logic—a view which seems to me to be profoundly mistaken

[4] *Logic*, Pt. III, Chap. IV, § 3.

The second example is taken from a chapter on *Analogy* from the works of the philosopher, Thomas Reid.

' We may observe a very great similitude between this earth which we inhabit, and the other planets, Saturn, Jupiter, Mars, Venus and Mercury. They all revolve round the sun, as the earth does, although at different distances, and in different periods. They borrow all their light from the sun, as the earth does. Several of them are known to revolve round their axis like the earth, and, by that means, must have a like succession of day and night. Some of them have moons, that serve to give them light in the absence of the sun, as our moon does to us. They are all in their motions, subject to the same law of gravitation, as the earth is. From all this similitude, it is not unreasonable to think, that these planets may, like our earth, be the habitation of various orders of living creatures. There is some probability in this conclusion from analogy.' [1]

It is not difficult to determine the properties which in this argument constitute the known positive analogy. Some of those properties belonging to the known negative analogy are indicated, for example, varying distances from the sun, with the connected property, increased length of orbit ; but for the most part the negative resemblances are not stated. Such a statement would be necessary to complete the argument. We are concerned, however, only to compare this argument with the use made of analogy by Francesco Sizzi. It is obvious that Reid's argument depends upon the consideration of properties that are important in the sense that one property is connected with others. Thus the property of *revolving round the sun* is connected with the property of *having some degree of warmth* ; the property of *revolving on its own axis* is connected with the property of *having alternate light and darkness*, and so on. These properties render the argument not unplausible. Further investigation would be required with regard to the properties known to be connected with the *inferred property* of *being inhabited by various orders of creatures*, such, for instance, as the possession of atmosphere, the effects of gravity at the surface of each planet, and so on. Suppose it were granted that the existence of a creature such as man is dependent upon the presence of air, then the question whether a given planet, say Mars, was surrounded with air would be an important question to decide. Assuming that the consideration of such questions is left open, it may be admitted that the analogy is suggestive, whereas Sizzi's analogy is not. Its superior suggestiveness consists in the fact that the positive analogy admits of development. This is not the case with the property *being seven in number* upon which Sizzi's argument is based.

It will be observed that Reid's conclusion is restricted to the

cited merely as an example of the way in which argument from analogy has been used. I do not suggest that the statement in the text does justice to the system of organization within which Sizzi was arguing.

[1] Reid's *Works* (Hamilton's edition, p. 236).

possibility that these planets are " the habitation of various orders of creatures ".   There would have been less plausibility in the argument had he included the determinate properties, *being such creatures as men*, who have the characteristics of *being prone to fight, sometimes sensitive to beauty, very rarely capable of creating works of art, often tolerating slum conditions*, etc.   Had he done so, he would have increased what J. M. Keynes calls the *comprehensiveness* of the conclusion, and in so doing he would have decreased the probability of its truth.

We can now make precise the characteristics upon which the strength of an analogical argument depends.   Its strength depends upon the character of the initial resemblance and upon the relative comprehensiveness of the properties which are asserted to be connected.   When one property p_1 is said to be connected with another property p_2, we can infer the one from the other.   In that case we shall say that the property p_1 *implies* the property p_2, and we shall call p_1 the *implying* property, p_2 the *implied* property.   Whenever we argue from analogy we assume that this relation holds between the property that is the basis of the analogy and the property which we infer from it.   An *implying* property is an *important* property.   Thus, in our illustration, the property of *being surrounded with air* would be an *important* property relatively to the conclusion that is inferred. The initial resemblance must be a resemblance between properties that are *important* in this sense.   The more we can increase the total known analogy the more likelihood there is that we shall increase the number of important properties that it contains ; hence, the less likelihood of our overlooking an important difference or resemblance. For this purpose it is useful to examine a number of instances having the properties which constitute the initial resemblance.   The examination of a number of such instances, which in other respects differ as much as possible, is likely to reveal those properties which are important, negatively or positively.

We have now to consider the second factor upon which the strength of an argument from analogy depends.   The more comprehensive the inferred properties are the less likely is the conclusion to be true. We saw that Reid's argument was more plausible because he was contented with inferring to a restricted property.   On the other hand, the less comprehensive the implying properties are the less likely is the conclusion to be true.   Thus Sizzi's argument was based upon the single property of resemblance in number, eked out with a fanciful arrangement into sets of planets corresponding to facial characteristics.   A metaphor expanded into an analogy has this characteristic of not being sufficiently comprehensive with regard to the implying property.   In attempting to develop an argument from analogy we must, then, seek to increase the comprehensiveness of the implying

nebula.[1] We are not here concerned with the hypothesis itself but with the fact that it was suggested to Laplace by the remarkable positive analogy which we have just described. It is not difficult to see that the analogy is suggestive. If it be contrasted with Sizzi's analogy it will be obvious that its suggestiveness is due to the fact that the resemblances noted are capable of being connected systematically in such a way as to exclude merely arbitrary likeness.

Analogy in the widest sense is not a special form of argument but an element in *all* inductive investigation. We saw that an induction by simple enumeration is possible only when the instances enumerated have common properties, and it is thus based upon analogy. There must be not only *repetition* of instances but also resemblance and variety in the instances themselves. We desire to rely not merely on number but on resemblance. As Mr. Keynes points out : ' Scientific method, indeed, is mainly devoted to discovering means of so heightening the known analogy that we may dispense as far as possible with the methods of pure induction.' [2]

[1] This hypothesis has been shown not to be tenable, but, Sir James Jeans says : ' Laplace's conception has been amazingly fruitful. It would hardly be too much to say that it has either revealed or given a valuable clue to the origin of every normal formation in the sky, with the single exception of that of the solar system which it set out to seek.' (*The Nebular Hypothesis and Modern Cosmogony : Halley Lecture*, 1922, pp. 26-7.)
    [2] op. cit., p. 241.

CHAPTER XV

CAUSALITY

'We wish to know whether knowledge of one fact throws light *of any kind* upon the likelihood of another. The theory of causality is only important because it is thought that by means of its assumptions light *can* be thrown by experience of one phenomenon upon the expectation of another.'—*J. M. Keynes.*

§ 1. UNIFORMITIES AND MULTIFORMITIES

FEW people would be seriously perplexed by the discovery that swans may be black ; the appearance of a white peacock is interesting but not alarming. We are accustomed to seeing brown hens and white hens, black horses and chestnut horses, red tulips and yellow tulips, stormy seas and calm seas. But most men acquainted with snow would be startled if a lump of snow placed in front of a fire were not to melt ; or if the pavements remained dry throughout a downpour of rain ; or if a man shot at short range through the heart were to remain standing upright and apparently unaffected. Again, a man might be surprised if on arriving one morning at a station he found that there were no porters, nor trains, nor any signs of the bustling activity usually to be seen at railway stations. His surprise would be of a very different kind from that with which he would observe pavements remaining dry in spite of the heavy rain that fell upon them, or with which he would observe the man shot through the heart yet remaining undisturbed in position. He would probably at once explain to himself the unusual state of the railway station by supposing that there had been a " lightning strike ". He knows that the working of a railway station is partly dependent upon human volitions, and he would believe that these are capable of variation. But the other occurrences would produce a feeling of nightmare. A world in which rain did not wet pavements would appear chaotic. It would appear chaotic because, since in our experience we have always found rain to wet the surface upon which it falls, we have come to expect that it will always do so. Rain that lacked this property would not *be* rain. But that a man should be caught in a shower without his umbrella surprises no one who lives in England. In other words, we believe that there are dependable regularities in the external world, although some things " just happen so ". The life of civilized man is conditioned by the

(2) A *uniformity* is a set of occurrences, or of properties, such that if any one of them recurs, the others recur.

§ 2. THE COMMON-SENSE NOTION OF CAUSE

The plain man quite well understands how to use the word " cause ". Most transitive verbs, except those that express emotional attitudes, express causation, e.g. *make, produce, influence, cure, fell, cook, raise, build, destroy.* If the plain man is asked, " What do you mean by a cause ? " he will probably reply " What makes a thing happen ". He knows that he is using the notion of cause when he says, " The child died from pneumonia ", " It was a fused wire that set the house on fire ", " The heat has expanded the railway line ", " She moved the clock so roughly that it has stopped ". He means something definite when he says, " You won't find a cure for cancer until you know its cause ". This correct *use* of the notion of causation is, however, compatible with an extremely confused conception of what exactly causation is. The discussions of philosophers have done little, if anything, to clear up these confusions. There is some justification for Mr. Russell's remark that ' the word " cause " is so inextricably bound up with misleading associations as to make its complete extrusion from the philosophical vocabulary desirable '.[1] But, whatever may be the case with philosophy, it is not possible to expel the word or the conception from science. " Cause " expresses a concept indispensable to the earlier stages of the attempt to order the facts of experience. It is by reference to this concept that the conception of uniformities may be made determinate. It is from this point of view that we have now to consider what is meant by causal connexion.

As the examples given above suggest, the primitive notion of cause assimilates causation to agency. A cause is what makes things happen. Every one knows what it is actively to produce changes in his environment. We move things about. We pinch a piece of india-rubber and its shape changes. We blow into an air-cushion and it swells. We poke the fire and a flame bursts out. We strike a golf ball and it rises. These various things that we *do* are followed by changes that we can *perceive.* Upon such experiences as these the popular notion of cause is based. Locke, who is pre-eminently the plain man among philosophers, thus defines *cause* : ' A cause is that which makes any other thing . . . begin to be, and an effect is that which had its beginning from some other thing '.[2] It is to be noted that *cause* and *effect* are here defined

---

[1] *Mysticism and Logic,* p. 180. Mr. Russell himself has recently based his philosophy of science upon the conception of " causal lines ", which, however, he does not attempt to analyse, and which perhaps cannot bear the weight of the construction he rests upon it.

[2] *Essay on the Human Understanding,* Bk. II, Chap. XXVI, § 2.

as terms in a relation of *producing*. From this point of view the effect is regarded as relatively passive ; it is *made* what it is by the cause which is regarded as an agent. Thus the notion of cause is interpreted in terms of the experience I have of being active when I exert effort to force something, or some one, to do what I want done. This analogy is revealed in such expressions as " the cause *compels* the effect ", " a *power* in the cause to produce the effect ", which have been constantly used in statements of causation. This view is known as the activity view of causation. It is undoubtedly the view of the unsophisticated person. He feels that he understands what happens when one billiard ball hits another, since he assimilates it to his own experience of pushing something. This anthropomorphic tendency is natural at the beginnings of science. The technical language of the sciences shows how deeply rooted it is : *force, work, energy, least action*, are terms assimilating what happens in nature to human experience. But with the advance of science anthropomorphic elements are gradually eliminated. It may be confidently asserted that the notion of cause as exerting compulsion, as an agent forcing something to act in some way, no longer merits serious consideration. Nevertheless the activity view dies hard. Professor T. P. Nunn has pointed out that ' the average student of physics to-day is probably still at heart an anthropomorphist. He takes his science to be a hunt after causes and not merely a search for what Lucretius, with fine inspiration, called *naturae species ratioque* ; and the causes he reads into nature almost always convey into the transactions between material bodies features of the traffic between man's mind and his environment '.[1] This persistence of the activity view hinders the analysis of the causal relation since it places the emphasis upon the *terms* instead of upon the *relation*. The result of this emphasis has been to stress unduly both the temporal priority of the cause to the effect and the distinction between cause and condition. With these two points we shall be concerned later. They are both essential to the common-sense notion, which we must first examine more carefully.

Consider the proposition *The rain wets the pavement*. This might be expressed by " The rain causes the pavement to be wet ". In asserting such a proposition the plain man would mean that on this occasion the pavement would not have been wet unless the rain had fallen on it. He would be ready to admit that on other occasions the wetness might be due to the spraying from a water-cart, or from a burst water-main. Again, " Charles I died because his head was cut off " would be taken to mean that the beheading of Charles I was that occurrence that ended his life ; that had the axe not struck

---

[1] *Anthropomorphism and Physics*, p. 5. (*British Academy. Annual Philosophical Lecture*, 1926.)

his neck with some degree of force he would not have died as and when he did die. Thus common sense seems to regard the cause as an occurrence *relevant* to the happening of the effect. Given that the cause occurs, then the effect occurs. It seems clear that the conception of causation is confined by common sense to what happens in space and time (or in time only in the case of mental events [1]) and to this only in so far as what happens is regarded as changing, that is, as altering in character. In the example, " The rain wets the pavement ", clearly it is *the falling of the rain* that is the cause, and what it causes is a change *in the character* of the pavement. It does not cause *the pavement* but the *wetness* of the pavement which was previously dry. If the pavement had not been there, there could not be a wet *pavement* ; but the pavement may be there without being *wet*. Or, to take an example given in an earlier chapter, " The air pulse chills the hot wire ". Here the effect is *a change in the temperature* of the wire. Thus the notion of causation seems to be applied to a change in the character of something. We have used " occurrence " to denote a spatio-temporal happening having determinate characters, or properties. Thus *the cause* is an occurrence related to some other occurrence, *the effect*. " Occurrence " suggests something changing. But the effect is considered to be a change in something which relatively to it continues unchanged.

The notion of cause, then, seems to arise when we observe a change occurring in something. It is obvious that common sense will pay most attention to striking changes. A change is striking when it is sensationally impressive or emotionally affecting. It is for such changes that common sense seeks causes. Further, in determining which of the various occurrences that are present is to be taken as *the* cause common sense again selects what is striking. This selection is due to the practical attitude of the plain man who wants to know not only *what has caused* a given effect but *how to produce* such an effect on another occasion. This practical attitude is reflected in the traditional problems of causation. On the one hand, the occurrence selected as *the cause* has been isolated from other occurrences which are in fact joint-factors with it ; on the other hand, the occurrence regarded as *the effect* has been left un-analysed so that different sets of factors have been regarded as the *same* effect. Hence has arisen what is known as the problem of the plurality of causes. The hackneyed illustration " Many causes may produce death " affords the best example. There are more

---

[1] Common sense certainly regards mental events as non-spatial, and somewhat waveringly applies the conception of causation to such events. It is not necessary for our purpose to discuss this application. Hence, our discussion is limited to non-mental events.

ways of killing a cat than drowning it in butter. Each of these ways would effectually kill the cat, although its state of mind and body might be very different according to what mode of killing it was actually adopted. The procedure of a coroner's court is based upon the assumption that if the total characters of the effect-occurrence, viz. *the death of the person*, be made determinate, then the precise character of the cause-occurrence can be ascertained. This assumption may be mistaken but it is at least plausible. It suggests a refinement of the common-sense notion of cause, and one, moreover, that would be quite useless to common sense. For practical purposes it is a positive advantage to know various different ways of obtaining a certain result, and it is often irrelevant for the given purpose what *other* results are also brought about. Thus, if a man desires to kill his enemy he can achieve his object by stabbing him through the heart, or by poisoning him, or by drowning him, and so on. One can obtain roast pig by burning down the house that contains the pig. The method may be wasteful, but it does not *therefore* fail of its effect. A desire to roast pigs with less expensive apparatus would suggest the elimination of certain factors from the causal occurrence, and this would involve the elimination of certain factors from the effect-occurrence.

Again, since its standpoint is practical, common sense can afford to ignore those conditions that are usually present and can therefore be taken for granted. For example, the plain man wants to light a match. He rubs it on the side of the match-box and obtains the desired result. He would say that the friction caused the flame. If, however, the operation were performed inside a jar from which the air had been exhausted, it would be found that the match did not light. He would thus find that the presence of oxygen is also necessary for the production of the effect. Since, however, air is always present when the plain man strikes a match, he takes its presence for granted and pays attention to those factors only in the total situation which he is aware of as changing. So, too, he takes for granted the prepared surface of the box and a certain amount of phosphorus on the match. If a match struck in the ordinary way fails to light, he is forced to notice some counteracting condition such as dampness of the surface. The failure of his intended action leads him to reflect upon the conditions and thus to analyse a situation that would otherwise have been taken for granted. In this way practical activity is replaced by theoretical investigation.

§ 3. DEVELOPMENT OF THE COMMON-SENSE NOTION OF CAUSE

We have seen that as practical agents we start from a complex situation within which we desire to bring about certain changes.

Provided that the desired result is achieved what *else* is achieved can be neglected. Similarly with what is *not* desired. It is what is *always* present when death is present that matters from the practical point of view. Hence ," death " stands for a set of properties abstracted from a complex set of conditions. Whenever a man is shot through the heart, *he dies*. Whenever *a man is dead*, he ceases to respond to our entreaties. The italicized words stand for complex situations which, in each case, is from the practical point of view a *single* occurrence. Such occurrences, taken as *single*, are of varying degrees of abstractness. Thus *death* is an abstraction requiring analysis. Such analysis takes us away from the standpoint of common sense. It involves looking at the whole situation retrospectively, not prospectively. The former attitude is that of the coroner's court and the scientific investigator, the latter is that of the practical agent ; the one is concerned with *knowing*, the other with *doing*. Both are concerned with uniformities, i.e. regular connexions. The practical agent, however, is content with a relation that is determinate only in the direction *from* cause *to* effect : *wherever X occurs, E occurs*. Such a relation may be many-one : given the cause, then the effect is determined, but not conversely. But the scientific investigator wants to find a relation that is equally determinate in either direction, that is, he seeks a one-one relation : *wherever X occurs, E occurs, and E does not occur unless X has occurred*. He has accordingly to analyse the conditions into their constituent factors so that he may ascertain whether any are irrelevant, and whether any, though necessary, are not sufficient to the occurrence of the result. The appearance of a plurality of causes, for example, that death may sometimes be caused by pneumonia, sometimes by drowning, etc., or that thirst may be quenched by water or by cider, arises from the neglect of certain factors in the total situation that constitutes the effect-occurrence. This should be clear from what has preceded.

The question of one-one determination belongs to the retrospective attitude ; it concerns knowledge, not action. Action takes place within a concrete situation having a one-way time direction *from* present *to* future. As an investigator the thinker is also an agent, situated within a one-way time direction. He observes an occurrence, e.g. the shooting of a man, or the dissolving of a lump of sugar in a liquid, which as a definite event does not recur. Nor could he resuscitate this particular man and try whether the same effect will occur if he is again shot in the same way. But when he says " Shooting a man through the heart causes his death " he is asserting that *whenever* a man is shot through the heart, he dies. The statement of a causal uniformity is a generalization ; consequently, it involves abstraction. Certain factors in the total situation are neglected as being irrelevant. Belief in the general causal proposition *Whenever a man is shot through the heart, he dies* is based upon the experience of particular instances in which it was judged that some factor in the immediate past was *relevant* to the effect-occurrence, viz. *his dying*. A given factor is observed to be *relevant*. This is not to say that it is observed to be *necessary*. The question of necessity does not arise for the practical agent and cannot arise for the scientific investigator until he has generalized from the particular instances so as to obtain the form *whenever X, then E*. The investigator must, then, neglect those factors which are peculiar to the happening of the particular event described as " *this* occurrence ", and which consequently determine the impossibility of *its* recurrence. In such generalization from the particular occurrence emphasis is placed upon the causal *relation* instead of upon the terms. This change of emphasis marks an advance from the point of view of common sense. It is, however, a development of, not a radical departure from, the common-sense notion. We must now attempt to trace this development.

We pinch a piece of india-rubber and its shape changes. We drop a lump of sugar into hot coffee and it dissolves. Here we have two examples of common-sense things whose characteristics change. The india-rubber left lying on the table does not change in shape. The sugar in the bowl does not dissolve. If the table is pinched, it does not change in shape. This last example suggests that the occurrence of an effect depends upon the nature of both the things that are brought into relation. The same movement of pinching will change the shape of the india-rubber but will not change the shape of the table. Thus the common-sense notion of cause seems to involve three assumptions : (1) that it is things that enter into the causal relation ; (2) that the characteristics which belong to the thing, or, as common sense would say, " the nature of the thing ", is relevant to the causal situation ; (3) that things left to themselves do not undergo changes. The attempt to see what precisely is involved in these assumptions may enable us to understand more clearly what causation is.

(1) The conception of what constitutes a *thing* is more or less vague. The philosopher Locke who inclined to the common-sense point of view as to what constitutes a thing considered that there must be some imperceivable *substratum* to which the sensibly perceptible characters of the thing belonged. He believed this substratum to be unknowable. Common sense does not, however, regard the *thing* as an unknown support of perceivable characters. The plain man feels that he knows quite well what, for instance, the *table* is. The prototype of the common-sense notion of *thing* is a solid body, just as the prototype of the common-sense notion

of *causation* is our experience of activity. A solid body has spatial boundaries; it is tangible; it resists pushing; it in some sense persists, or endures, for a longer or shorter duration; it has characteristics recognizable as belonging to it. On reflection, the plain man would admit that a gas, for example, hydrogen is a thing, that rain is a thing, that air is a thing, and so on. These are things because they *have* characteristics; they are not characteristics *of* something else. But common sense distinguishes between a *thing* and *its states*. For example, the paper covering a wall would be regarded as a thing; the changes in colour as the wall-paper fades would be regarded as *states* of the wall-paper. These states also have characteristics. For example, the state of the wall-paper has the characteristic of being a pale grey-blue. The wall-paper is a thing; it has characteristics of a different kind; for example, it has the characteristic of altering in colour under the action of sunlight. Or consider *this piece of india-rubber*. It is a thing; it has the characteristic of altering in shape when pinched. *This lump of sugar* is another thing; it has the characteristic of *dissolving in water*. These characteristics of *fading*, of *elasticity*, of *solubility* belong to the thing not to its states. We shall call such characteristics *causal characteristics*.[1] Each state of the thing has determinate characteristics, a definite shade of colour, a definite shape, and so on. Such characteristics we shall call *primary characteristics*. When a thing changes from one state to another these primary characteristics may be different. Since these states are states *of* the thing we say that *the thing* changes. But we want also to regard the thing as *persisting through* its changes. It is for this reason that we seek for a cause of change but not of persistence. What changes are the states; what does not change is the thing *of* which the states are states. The state of a thing is an occurrence. We easily recognize this in the case of water that has become frozen. We recognize the water *in a frozen state* and we see that this is an occurrence that has happened to the water. We do not so easily recognize *persisting in a state* as an occurrence. For example, if the table is in the state of continuing to be a definite shade of brown, we do not commonly think of this persisting in a definite shade as an occurrence. But if the table is knocked over we think of it as in the state of falling. There is no logical justification for thus distinguishing between these two cases. In both cases the table *has* a certain state, or is *in* a certain state, and each state has determinate, primary characteristics. Common sense usually calls such primary characteristics " simple qualities ". Although it is *things* that common sense regards as entering into the causal

---

[1] The expression 'causal characteristic' is taken from Dr. C. D. Broad (see *The Mind and its Place in Nature*, p. 432). In the discussion of this problem I am, as always, much indebted to Dr. Broad's writings.

relation, it is not *a thing* that is taken to be the cause but a certain *state* of the thing. For example, a table is not a cause, but a table *in the state of falling* may cause some one's leg to be hurt. It is, however, a state *of the table*, so that the causal relation involves reference to things.

(2) What common sense calls "the nature of the thing" is the set of characteristics that belong to it. But common sense does not clearly distinguish between the causal characteristics which belong to the thing and the primary characteristics which belong to its states. Nor is common sense at all clear with regard to the distinction between a *state* of a thing and a *characteristic*. Some of the confusions and difficulties in the common-sense conception of substance and causation are due to the failure to make these distinctions. The *thing* does not have primary characteristics; its characteristics may be called *non-primary* characteristics. A non-primary characteristic differs from a primary characteristic in not being determinate. Borrowing a useful expression from Mr. W. E. Johnson we may say that the non-primary characteristics of *the thing* are determinable.[1] A determinable is a characteristic of a certain sort exhibited in certain determinate characteristics. For example, *being coloured* is a determinable; *being a certain definite shade of red* is a determinate. Thus the primary characteristics of the states of a thing are determinates. The determinable, or non-primary characteristics of the thing are of two kinds: causal and non-causal. Examples of non-causal characteristics of a thing (e.g. *this piece of indiarubber*) would be *having some colour or other, having some shape or other*. The causal characteristics are what the chemist calls the "properties" of a chemical substance, e.g. an acid, a metal, a fat. We can now define this notion. *A causal characteristic of a thing is a characteristic mode of behaviour in relation to other things.* Thus "the nature of a thing" includes those characteristics that it exhibits in relation to other things. Thus it seems clear that the conception of *the nature of a thing* cannot be made precise without reference to causal connexions; conversely, causal connexions cannot be made precise without reference to states of things, which states have non-causal characteristics.

(3) The assumption that "things left to themselves" do not undergo change also fails of precision, since it involves the notion of "one thing". The conception of what constitutes *one thing* is vague. Whether X is to be called one thing or an aggregate of things depends, so far as common sense is concerned, mainly upon practical considerations. A lampstand and the electric-light bulb and the shade all constitute *one thing* if the lamp be used to light

[1] See W. E. J., Pt. I, Chap. XI, and cf. pp. 444–5 below.

a room.   From the point of view of purchasing the lamp, there are
at least three things.   It is easy to multiply examples to show how
vague is the conception of one thing.   Coffee and milk are two
things ; when mixed in the breakfast cup they are one thing.   Apart
from purely practical purposes common sense would probably regard
one thing as definable by reference to the occupation of a sensibly
continuous spatial boundary, either neglecting the time dimension
or including it under the notion of persistence of sensibly similar
characteristics through a period of time.   We have seen that common
sense distinguishes between a thing and its states.   When there is
considerable alteration in the primary characteristics, then common
sense would refuse to admit the persistence of the thing.   Thus
common sense requires sensible continuity of characteristics, and
assumes that there is such sensible continuity even when it has not
been continuously perceived.   Hence, it is argued, if there is a
change in the sensible characteristics manifested by a thing in a
certain state, there must be something to *make* it change.   In this
way arises the assumption that things left to themselves do not
change.   For example, given that a candle is one thing, then common
sense does not expect it to change while the candle is standing
unlighted on the table.   If the candle which was standing upright
in the candlestick is, after a few hours, bending over the candlestick, common sense assumes that something other than the candle
has caused the change, e.g. the heat of the room.   It is a causal
characteristic of the candle to become bent under certain conditions
of temperature.   These conditions are dependent upon other things,
for example, the fire, the relative positions of the fire and the candle,
etc.   From the causal point of view these conditions constitute one
situation, or set of related things, which may be regarded as a *system*.
If the candle in its stick were regarded as one system, we should
have to distinguish at least three different things, viz. candlestick,
tallow, wick.   These things are in spatio-temporal relations.   If no
change were occurring in this system, then it would be assumed
that no change would occur *unless* something outside the system,
e.g. a fire, or a lighted match, came into spatio-temporal relation
with it.   If, however, change were occurring in the candle-system
independently of anything outside it, then it would be assumed
that something was going on all the time *in* the system, whether
it were at first perceptible or not.

We see, then, that the attempt to analyse a total causal situation
involves the distinction of different factors standing in spatio-
temporal relations.   *What* occurs will be dependent upon the causal
characteristics of the things in that situation.   Thus the fire which
melts the candle merely warms the brass candlestick.   A roaring
fire in the kitchen does not melt the candle in the bedroom.   The

factors in a causal situation must be in spatio-temporal proximity.[1] But not everything in the given situation is relevant to the given causal occurrence. If it were there would be no causal uniformities since some factors in the situation do not recur. No two causal situations are exactly alike. A causal uniformity is a connexion between factors *recognizable as the same* on different occasions of their occurrence, i.e. under varying conditions and at different places and times.

The development of the common-sense notion of cause brings out several points of importance. The consideration of these will enable us to make clear certain distinctions with regard to which common sense is confused.

(1) A causal uniformity is an abstraction since it connects sets of recurrent characteristics belonging to events which do not recur.

(2) Neither the distinction between a thing and its states, nor the distinction between the qualities that a thing has and the way in which it behaves in relation to other things is clearly drawn at the level of common sense. Thus common sense would say, for example, that an orange has the qualities of being yellow, having a rough surface, being juicy, giving out an easily recognizable smell. It would thus include in the qualities of an orange characteristics that are not always perceptible when an orange is perceived and that are exhibited only when the orange is in relation to other things. It would also be admitted that an orange combined with sugar in a certain way and under suitable conditions, e.g. cooking over a fire, becomes marmalade. The perceptible change between the uncooked orange and the orange in the marmalade would be regarded by common sense as the result of a causal process, the result being partly dependent upon the original qualities of the orange. If the orange were squeezed very hard so that it were slightly flattened and the juice began to run out, the state of the orange would be said to have changed. When the orange is made into marmalade, the orange would no longer be said to exist as an orange ; it has been *made into* something else. Common sense would not attempt to determine the exact point at which the orange ceases to be an orange and becomes pulp, or becomes marmalade.

In accordance with the distinctions that we have been led to recognize the *qualities* attributed to an orange are primary characteristics of its *states* ; its modes of behaviour in relation to other things, e.g. sugar and the heat of the fire, or a person's hand squeezing it, are causal characteristics of the *orange*. Since common sense neglects the state of *persisting in a state*, and takes notice of a state only when there is change of state, this conception of *a state of a*

---

[1] In saying that there must be ' spatio-temporal proximity ', I mean that the various factors cannot be separated by a spatio-temporal gap.

thing is itself falsely conceived. Hence, common sense fails to apprehend clearly the relations between the two pairs of distinctions that we have been discussing. This misconception is due to a natural but erroneous conception of substance. *The thing* is regarded as something substantial, i.e. as a *substance*. A substance is then taken to be something persisting through a period of time and possessing simple qualities, i.e. primary characteristics. A lump of gold, or an orange, could be yellow, it is supposed, even if it existed alone in the universe, and but for a moment. That this assumption is mistaken should have been evident as soon as it was recognized that light is transmitted and requires a finite time for its transmission. Locke has stated the common-sense point of view very clearly, and has also indicated that it is mistaken, in a passage which it is worth while to quote :

> ' We are wont to consider the substances we meet with, each of them as an entire thing by itself, having all its qualities in itself and independent of other things ; overlooking for the most part, the operations of those invisible fluids they are encompassed with, and upon whose motions and operations depend the greatest part of those qualities which are taken notice of in them, and are made by us the inherent marks of distinction whereby we know and denominate them. Put a piece of gold anywhere by itself, separate from the reach and influence of all other bodies, it will immediately lose all its colour and weight, and perhaps malleableness too ; which, for aught I know would be changed into a perfect friability. . . . This is certain, things however absolute and entire they seem in themselves, are but retainers to other parts of nature for that which they are most taken notice of by us.' [1]

Here Locke lays emphasis upon the necessity of taking into account the relation of the thing to other things. This is in accordance with the importance of the distinction we have made between the thing and its states, and the consequent distinction between causal characteristics and primary characteristics. These distinctions throw light upon the distinction, so vaguely conceived by common sense, between *cause* and *condition*. Since the causal characteristics of the thing are its characteristic modes of behaviour in relation to other things, it follows that how a thing behaves depends upon what other things are in relation to it. This may be made clearer by means of an example. Let us consider a simple experiment. A bell so arranged that it can be continuously rung by clockwork is hung by silk threads inside a glass jar. The air

---

[1] *Essay concerning the Human Understanding*, Bk. IV, Chap. VI, § 11. It is not suggested that this passage represents Locke's usual view. On the contrary, Locke himself took the plain man's view, making it the basis of his discussion. But in his treatment ' Of Universal Propositions ' he was led to this valuable and, so far as his main thinking is concerned, extremely inconsistent conclusion.

in the jar is exhausted by an air-pump. As the air is withdrawn, the sound decreases, and very soon ceases to be heard, although the tongue of the bell still strikes against its sides. Given this arrangement, then, the air is a necessary condition for the propagation of sound. Now, it would commonly be said that the striking of the bell was the sufficient cause of the sound. This experiment shows that a material medium, such as air or water, is also required for the production of the sound. This material medium is then said to be a *condition*. Both the air and the striking of the bell are necessary for the production of the sound ; together they are sufficient. Reflection upon this distinction emphasizes the importance of the causal characteristics of things. In the bell experiment the medium has the causal characteristic of being able to propagate sound-waves ; the bell has the causal characteristic of vibrating in such a way when struck as to set up sound-waves in a suitable medium in spatio-temporal proximity to it. A condition is, then, whatever must be present in a given situation in order that a casual characteristic of a thing may be manifested in a state of the thing, which state will have certain determinate characteristics. This state is the effect. The cause is that state of some other thing upon which the effect is consequent. In the example of the bell, the cause may be said to be the impact of the tongue upon the sides ; the effect is the vibration of the sides which has for *its* effect the communication of sound-waves to the surrounding air. This distinction between cause and condition cannot be made perfectly precise and is misleading if pressed too far. What is important is to distinguish between a *sufficient* condition and a *necessary* condition. A condition X is a *sufficient condition* of an occurrence A provided that whenever X is present A occurs. But if A may occur when X is absent, then X, though a sufficient, is not a *necessary* condition of A. Thus a condition N is a *necessary condition* of A provided that A never occurs in the absence of N. A condition NS is a *necessary and sufficient condition* of an occurrence A provided that (i) whenever NS is present A occurs, and (ii) whenever NS is absent A does not occur. Owing to the failure of common sense to recognize these distinctions X is sometimes said to be " the cause " of A when it is a necessary but not a sufficient condition, and also when it is a sufficient but not a necessary condition. This ambiguity in the use of the word " cause " is due to the *practical* interests of common sense, which, as we saw, leads to the selection of a striking, or impressive, factor out of the set of factors that are jointly sufficient and independently necessary to the production of the effect. Hence, common sense fails to recognize that what we have to take into account is a system the parts of which are in mutual dependence. This dependence is casual dependence.

(3) It follows from what has just been said that the distinction between cause and effect cannot be made as sharply as common sense makes it.   The emphasis must be placed upon the relation, *cause* and *effect* being merely the terms in the relation, selected because they are striking, or practically important, or are easily discriminated.   This practical emphasis leads, as we saw, to the neglect of other factors that are relevant, and hence to the conception of the causal relation as being not only asymmetrical but also many-one.   But it is usually assumed that if the cause and the effect are determined with equal precision, the relation will be one-one, so that given the effect, the cause is thereby determined, given the cause, the effect is thereby determined.   Whenever the distinction between cause and effect is applicable to a causal situation, then the cause precedes the effect.   The relation is thus asymmetrical since the relation of temporal priority is asymmetrical.[1] We shall find that this distinction becomes less important as science advances.   This, however, is due to the fact that the relation of *causation* ceases to be of importance and is replaced by the relation of *functional dependence*.   With this we are not at present concerned.

(4) Common sense assumes that if in a system in which no change has been occurring, a change begins to occur, then that system must be in causal relation to something outside it which causes the change. Such causation is called *transeunt*.   Thus we are led to the distinction between a thing left to itself and a thing not so left.   We saw that this distinction is vague.   It must be replaced by the distinction between an *isolated system* and *a system in causal relations to something outside the system*.   Changes occurring in an isolated system are determined by the mutual relations of the parts.   Such determination is called *immanent causation*.   For example, the works of a watch constitute an isolated system.   Once the watch is wound up the changes occurring in it are causally determined by the mutual relations of the parts of the works.   Thus the movement of the hands over the dial is immanently caused.   If, however, the watch is put in very cold or very hot temperatures, the temperature of the surrounding medium will cause a change in the metal case which will cause a change in the working of the watch.   This would be an example of transeunt causation.   The business of a good watchmaker is to construct a watch as little subject as possible to changes

---

[1] Mr. Russell has said : ' It is customary only to give the name " effect " to an event which is later than the cause, but there is no kind of reason for this restriction. We shall do better to allow the effect to be before the cause or simultaneous with it, because nothing of any scientific importance depends upon its being after the cause.'   (*Our Knowledge of the External World*, p. 226.) There can, however, be little doubt that it is extremely inconvenient to give the *name* " cause " to that which is temporally successive to the effect.

occurring outside the watch-case. His ideal would be the construction of a completely isolated system, save for the fact that the watch must be periodically wound up by external agency. This ideal is unattainable. The distinction between systems that are causally isolated and systems that are not cannot be made absolute. The latter may always be regarded as sub-systems in a wider system. But unless there were systems that are practically isolated with regard to many changes occurring in these systems, the discovery of causal uniformities would be impossible. The determination of practically isolated systems is again a problem of determining what is relevant to the occurrence of change. The belief that some occurrences are irrelevant to the happening of other occurrences is, in fact, the belief that there are causal uniformities. These causal uniformities are the laws in accordance with which changes occur.

Our discussion of causation has shown that there is a close interrelation between causal uniformities, or, as we may call them, causal laws, and things. The attempt to determine more precisely the nature of this interrelation takes us beyond the standpoint of common sense.

§ 4. CAUSAL LAWS AND THE BEHAVIOUR OF THINGS

We have seen that the way in which a thing, for example, a lump of sugar, a candle, a poker, a living being, will behave in a given situation depends both upon the nature of the thing and upon the nature of the situation in which it is placed. This lump of sugar dissolves in water ; this piece of gold does not. The poker put into a fire will become red-hot ; when it is taken out and put in the fender it will become cold again, and will revert (approximately) to its former condition. The thing has characteristics which distinguish it from other things. Some of its characteristics are causal characteristics, i.e. modes of behaviour in relation to other things, e.g. *solubility in water* which belongs to this lump of sugar. We saw also that the thing has non-causal characteristics, e.g. *having some shape or other, having some temperature or other.* The states of the thing have determinate characteristics. These determinate characteristics of the states are *caused* by the causal characteristics and the situation in which the thing is placed. For example, the determinate characteristics of the state of the poker when it is red-hot are *being red* and *being hot.* These characteristics are caused by the causal characteristics *altering in colour* and *altering in temperature* (which belong to *the poker*, not to its states) and by the situation, viz. the fire.

So far we have considered definite examples of things, *this poker,*

18

this lump of sugar. But each of these is recognized as belonging to a class consisting of *things of a certain sort*, or as we have called them *natural kinds.* Every instance of *a kind of thing* has certain characteristics of a certain sort which makes it the *sort of thing* it is, and is what we mean by a *kind.* The way in which a thing behaves depends upon its kind. These modes of behaviour are causal laws. Wherever there are things of a certain kind in certain situations there will be certain modes of behaviour, that is certain variations in the primary characteristics of the states of the thing. These changes *recur* under suitable conditions at different times and places. Hence, the characteristic modes of behaviour of things are recurrent modes of change. Causal laws are the laws of these recurrent modes of change.

There can be no doubt that we do distinguish kinds of things by observing their modes of behaviour in the presence of other things, that is in different situations. We observe the primary characteristics of the states of a thing, and we know that that kind of thing has states having those characteristics. If the thing fails to exhibit that mode of behaviour which is characteristic of that kind of thing, we know that we were mistaken as to the kind of thing it was. For example, we may see a dish of apples which *look like* Blenheim pippins. We may take up one and bite it, only to find that it tastes of soap. We conclude (rightly) that *this thing* is a piece of soap made to look like a Blenheim pippin. It *isn't* a Blenheim pippin because it doesn't behave like one. Thus we see that the distinguishing characteristics of a kind involve modes of behaviour, i.e. causal laws. The notion of kinds of things, then, leads us to the consideration of causation and conditions. This point is important, since it shows that there are modes of change which recur in *different* situations and which take place in accordance with laws. From this it follows that there are occurrences to the happening of which much else that is also happening is irrelevant. If this were not true, there could be no causal laws and no science. The discovery of a causal law is the discovery of what is *relevant* to a given mode of behaviour. It is for this reason that the discovery of causal laws requires observation of particular situations. We do not know independently of experience that sugar dissolves in water and that gold does not, or that arsenic is poisonous. We discover these facts by observing how sugar, gold, arsenic behave in certain situations. The necessity of this appeal to experience is not, as has sometimes been supposed, an argument against there being any causal laws. It does, however, show that causal laws cannot be deduced from observed characters, " read off ", as it were, from a given situation. On the contrary, causal laws are discovered only by analysis of causal situations ; things must be brought into relation with other things, so that they can be observed in *varying* situations. By eliminating factors present in different situations we discover which factors present in those situations are nevertheless irrelevant to the result. This process of elimination has to be carried out with due precautions, for it is easy to make mistakes and to neglect precautions the need of which might be supposed to be obvious. We shall be concerned later with the various ways in which causal laws may be ascertained. Here we need only notice that we do in fact know many causal laws, and that these causal laws refer to modes of change which recur in relative isolation from what else is happening.

To say that X is the necessary and sufficient condition of the occurrence of E is, then, to say that X *alone* is relevant to the occurrence of E. It might be objected that, if we can discover what is relevant only by eliminating what is irrelevant, then we could never tell whether permanent factors in the universe, for example, the presence of the fixed stars, are relevant to a given causal situation, for example, *sugar dissolving in water*. This is true, but it is also unimportant since the statement of the given causal law does not require us to take account of the fixed stars, nor should we ever be concerned with causal situations in the absence of the fixed stars. Moreover, although the annihilation of the fixed stars might affect the result, we have not the slightest reason for supposing that this would be the case. On the other hand, we do find that the substitution of gold for sugar in the water does not yield the result *dissolving in water*. It seems, then, that experience does provide us with examples of multiformities, and with examples of causal occurrences that are independent of other causal occurrences happening contemporaneously and in the same neighbourhood. That is to say that there are relatively independent causal series. The difference between the causal set A_1, A_2, A_3 . . . and the causal set B_1, B_2, B_3 . . . depends upon the different natures of A and B. We have seen what is meant by the phrase " the nature of " in this context. It is the fact that A has a certain nature, or is a thing of a certain kind, which determines in what situations A is a causal factor.

It is important to distinguish causal laws from the particular causal propositions which exemplify them. It is the causal law that is fundamental. A particular causal proposition asserts a definite causal occurrence happening once, and once only, for example, *This shot through his heart caused this man's death*. In asserting that this man's death was *caused* by his being shot through the heart we are asserting more than the historical fact that two particular occurrences were conjoined. This is clear, since there are many occurrences happening together (simultaneously or successively) which we should not regard as being causally connected. It may be that what *more* we are asserting is simply that this is an instance of a conjunction of two occurrences of a certain sort such that the one is *always* conjoined with the other, or it may be that we are asserting that the two occurrences are related by a unique relation of causation. We shall consider in the next section what can be said in favour of either of these two views. Whatever view we adopt we must admit that there would be no significance in the assertion of causation unless we at least meant to assert that *whenever* a given occurrence happens, then some other given occurrence happens. The causal law which the example given above exemplifies can be stated precisely. Whenever there is an occurrence which is the passage of a bullet through a man's heart, there follows an occurrence which is the cessation of the beating of the heart. Thus the form of such a causal law is : Whenever an occurrence having the property Φ happens at a time t_1 to a thing of the kind K_1, then an occurrence having the property Ψ happens at a time t_2 to a thing of the kind K_2. It may be the case that (i) Φ and Ψ are properties of the same sort ; (ii) K_1 and K_2 are the same thing ; (iii) t_1 and t_2 are the same time. When (iii) is the case, there is an instance of simultaneous causality. In the examples we have given the *things* have been of different degrees of complexity, e.g. *gold*, an element, *water*, an inorganic compound, *heart*, *man*, organic compounds. The behaviour of each of these kinds is expressed by causal laws. These causal laws will differ in the degree of their abstractness, and from some points of view and with regard to certain problems the differences between the *kind* of these kinds, or sorts, of things will be very important. But it is sufficient here to notice that the *simplest* causal law is abstract.

Throughout the preceding discussion we have made many assumptions. Thus we have assumed that we can know that there are independent causal series, and that we can know particular propositions of the form *This X caused this Y*. It is not, of course, asserted that such knowledge is demonstrative. On the contrary, we have seen that causal uniformities have to be discovered by observation of what happens, and it is clear that generalizations from these observations will require justification. Whether these assumptions can be justified, and if so, *how*, are questions to be discussed later. There is, however, an assumption that we have not so far made, but that is often supposed to be made in all inductive investigation. This is the assumption that, not only are there causal uniformities but also that *everything* that happens can be exhibited as an instance of a causal uniformity. This assumption is known as the Law of Universal Causation. It is often expressed in the form that *every event has a cause*. It should be clear from what we have already said that this is a misleading expression. *Events* as such do not cause other events. It is because an event has a certain property that it causes another event having a certain property to have another property. In order to make clear this reference to *properties* we have used the word " occurrence " instead of " event ". The Law of Universal Causation might, then, be expressed as follows : Given an occurrence having the properties $\Phi_1, \Phi_2 \ldots$ then there is some other occurrence having the properties $\Psi_1, \Psi_2, \ldots$ so related to the first that the one occurrence is the cause of the other. This Law is equivalent to the assertion that there are no uncaused events. This involves a much wider assumption than the assumption that there are causal uniformities, since the latter is consistent with the admission that there may be some occurrences not causally related with *any* occurrence. That is to say, there may be causal laws although not everything that happens is an instance of a causal law. The Law of Universal Causation refers to particular occurrences, whereas causal laws arc, as we have seen, abstract. The Law of Universal Causation assumes that every occurrence can be *uniquely* described by a set of characteristics, whereas a causal law is a generalization just because it takes no notice of those characteristics which belong to a *given* situation, uniquely determining it to be *this* situation. The Law of Universal Causation can be most concisely expressed as follows : Every event uniquely described by a set of characteristics is so related to another event also uniquely described by a set of characteristics that the one is the cause of the other.

§ 5. MILL'S THEORY OF CAUSATION

Probably no logician to-day would contend that Mill's treatment of causation is satisfactory. Nevertheless, the inquiry as to what exactly Mill's theory was and in what respects it was unsatisfactory will throw light upon the conception of cause since his theory resulted from an attempt to refine the common-sense notion. It must be admitted at the outset that Mill was exceptionally inconsistent. He was a careless and inexact writer ; his verbal inconsistencies are obvious so that destructive criticism of Mill is easy. But such verbal criticism is also profitless. It is not always difficult to see what Mill's meaning was in spite of the vague and inexact way in which his views were expressed. It is desirable to attempt to state Mill's theory without laying stress upon his verbal inaccuracies. But it cannot be denied that these inaccuracies are sometimes the result of vague and confused thinking. Mill did not carry his reflections far enough, so that he seldom apprehended a problem in all its details. His occasional flashes of insight were disconnected.

But this insight enabled him often to raise the right problem and to suggest the most fruitful line of inquiry.[1]

The marks of a scientific proposition are, according to Mill, universality and certainty. He believed that it was possible by means of inductive argument to establish universal propositions with regard to the external world that were certainly true. He sought an instrument for " unravelling the complexity of nature ", and he believed he had found this instrument in the " Four Inductive Methods ", which rest upon the law of universal causation. These methods will be discussed in Chapter XVII. At present we are concerned only with Mill's statement of the law of universal causation. He says, ' We must first observe that there is a principle implicit in the very statement of what Induction is ; an assumption with regard to the course of nature and the order of the universe ; namely, that there are such things in nature as parallel cases ; that what happens once will, under a sufficient degree of similarity of circumstances, happen again, and not only again, but as often as the same circumstances recur '.[2]   So far Mill is simply pointing out what is in fact the minimum condition of science, namely, that ' there are such things in nature as parallel cases ', or, in other words, that there are uniformities.   He also emphasizes the fact that ' the course of nature is not only uniform, it is also infinitely various ' ; [3] and that ' in the contemplation of that uniformity in the course of nature which is assumed in every inference from experience, one of the first observations that present themselves is, that the uniformity in question is not properly uniformity, but uniformities '.[4]   These uniformities Mill distinguished as of two fundamentally different kinds : uniformities of coexistence and uniformities of succession. Natural kinds, symbolized by class-names, afford examples of the first kind of uniformities.   Mill thus states the point : ' When we affirm that all crows are black, or that all negroes have woolly hair, we assert a uniformity of coexistence.   We assert that the property of blackness, or of having woolly hair, invariably coexists with the properties which, in common language or in the scientific classification that we adopt, are taken to constitute the class crow, or the class negro '.[5]   These uniformities are to be sharply distinguished

---

[1] This same characteristic is apparent in Mill's ethical writings.   His *Utilitarianism* is one of the most confused and inconsistent books that have ever greatly influenced subsequent thinkers.   He makes mistakes so crude that they provide material for the easy criticism of candidates in elementary examinations in logic.   Yet, in spite of these defects, Mill's insight into the nature of the moral life is revealed in every chapter.   Had his insight been less keen he might have achieved the superficial consistency of his master Bentham.   A similar estimate may be made of his work in logic.

[2] *Logic*, Bk. III, Chap. III, § 1.   [3] *ibid.*, § 2.
[4] *ibid.*, Chap. IV, § 1.   [5] *ibid.*, Chap. XXII, § 3.

from uniformities of succession since the latter are causal uniformities and depend upon the law of universal causation. No proposition asserting a uniformity of coexistence can be certain since ' there is no general axiom standing in the same relation to the uniformities of coexistence as the law of causation does to those of succession '.[1]

Mill gives various different statements of the law of causation, but it will be sufficient to quote one : ' The Law of Causation, the recognition of which is the main pillar of inductive science, is but the familiar truth that invariability of succession is found by observation to obtain between every fact in nature and some other fact that has preceded it '.[2] He adds : ' To certain facts, certain facts always do, and, as we believe, will continue to, succeed. The invariable antecedent is termed the cause ; the invariable consequent the effect. And the universality of the law of causation consists in this, that every consequent is connected in this manner with some particular antecedent or set of antecedents. Let this fact be what it may, if it has begun to exist, it was preceded by some fact or facts with which it is invariably connected. For every event there exists some combination of objects or events, some given concurrence of circumstances, positive and negative, the occurrence of which is always followed by that phenomenon '.[3] Three points are involved in this statement of causation, namely, (i) every fact, or event, has a cause ; (ii) the same cause is always followed by the same effect ; (iii) the cause precedes the effect. Mill agrees with common sense in finding causal connexion only where there is change ; he recognizes that causal connexion is uniform, and he stresses the notion of succession. He defines cause as follows : ' The cause, then, philosophically speaking, is the sum total of the conditions positive and negative taken together ; the whole of the contingencies of every description, which, being realized, the consequent invariably follows '.[4] By ' the negative conditions ' Mill means the absence of counteracting causes, for example, the absence of a resisting medium in the case of freely falling bodies, or the absence of an emetic speedily administered in the case of a man poisoned with arsenic, and so on. Mill differs from common sense in recognizing that the distinction between cause and condition is often arbitrarily drawn, and in that case corresponds to no fundamental distinction.[5] He

---

[1] *ibid.*, § 4.   [2] Bk. III, Chap. V, § 2.

[3] *ibid.* It should be noticed that Mill uses the word " fact " where we should have used the word " occurrence ".

[4] *ibid.*, § 3.

[5] Cf. loc. cit., § 3. ' Nothing can better show the absence of any scientific ground for the distinction between the cause of a phenomenon and its conditions, than the capricious manner in which we select from among the conditions that which we choose to denominate the cause.' The whole of this paragraph is worth careful reading.

lays stress upon the *invariability* of the succession of antecedent and consequent, and he explains that he includes under the notion of invariability also *unconditionality*, for he is unwilling to admit that *all* invariable successions are causal. He insists, for example, that day is not the cause of night, although day is invariably succeeded by night. The differentia of causal from non-causal successions is to be found, he asserts, in the fact that the former are *unconditional*. He says, ' If there be any meaning which confessedly belongs to the term necessity, it is *unconditionalness*. That which is necessary, that which *must* be, means that which will be, whatever supposition we may make in regard to all other things ', and he concludes, ' Invariable sequence, therefore, is not synonymous with causation, unless the sequence, besides being invariable, is unconditional. There are sequences as uniform in past experience as any others whatever, which we do not regard as cases of causation, but as conjunctions in some sort accidental.[1] Such to an accurate thinker is that of day and night '. This consideration leads him to a second definition of cause : ' We may define, therefore, the cause of a phenomenon to be the antecedent, or the concurrence of antecedents, on which it is invariably and unconditionally consequent '.[2]

Although Mill lays such stress upon the element of *succession* in causal uniformities, he does not attempt to discuss the nature of the temporal relation itself. He is content with the assertion that whether the beginning of the effect be simultaneous with the cause or not, still ' the beginning of a phenomenon [3] is what implies a cause, and causation is the law of the succession of phenomena '. Hence, he reaches a third definition of cause : ' the assemblage of phenomena, which occurring, some other phenomenon invariably commences, or has its origin. Whether the effect coincides with, or immediately follows, the hindmost of its conditions, is immaterial. At all events it does not precede it ; and when we are in doubt between two coexistent phenomena, which is cause and which effect, we rightly deem the question solved if we can ascertain which of them preceded the other '.[4] At this point Mill seems to have abandoned the notion of *succession* as a fundamental element in causation. He does not seem ever to have definitely made up his mind whether succession or unconditionalness is the more important element. There is much in Mill's treatment that suggests that he

---

[1] It is extraordinarily difficult to see what Mill could have meant by the statement that the conjunction *day following night* was ' accidental '. This example affords a good illustration of the insufficiency of Mill's analysis of the causal relation.

[2] *ibid.*, § 6.

[3] By " phenomenon " Mill means what we have called an " occurrence ", which he also often calls a " fact ".

[4] *ibid.*, § 7.

should have substituted " uniform succession " for " unconditional and invariable sequence ", since he often implies that the importance of unconditionalness is its value as a test of uniformity. On the other hand, Mill was concerned to establish the *certainty* of causal laws ; consequently, he sought to replace the notion of necessity by that of *unconditionalness*. When, however, we try to make precise what Mill could have meant by an " unconditional sequence " we encounter difficulties. The cause is said to be the sum-total of conditions positive and negative, but the negative conditions consist in the absence of counteracting causes. If we attempt to make precise the notion of a " counteracting cause ", we find that we must take into account the *nature* of the phenomenon, or occurrence, that constitutes this counteracting cause. The notion of invariability of succession is not enough. For example, the presence of air is a " counteracting cause " which prevents a feather and a stone dropped simultaneously from the same position, from reaching the ground together. The causal characteristic of *resisting impact*, which is a property of the air, is relevant to the total situation. Thus it seems that invariable and unconditional succession cannot be what is *meant* by causal connexion. Mill obscures the problem by his loose use of language. Thus he speaks indifferently of *events, facts, objects, phenomena,* as the terms of the causal relation. He then ignores the nature of the terms and considers only one relation between them, that of succession. But, he insists, the relation is not that of *mere* succession but of invariable and unconditional succession. He failed to see, however, that the " invariability and unconditionalness " of the succession is dependent upon *the nature* of the terms so related. The terms in the relation of succession are *events*, but the causal relation does not relate bare events, but events having certain properties, or what we have called " occurrences ". That is to say, the terms of the causal relation have temporal properties, but they have also other properties in virtue of which one is the cause of another. The neglect of this important consideration accounts for Mill's failure to make clear whether succession or unconditionalness is the fundamental element in causation, or, if they are equally fundamental, what is the relation between them.

It must be admitted that a causal law is unconditional in the sense that it does not admit of exceptions. This is indeed implied in calling it a " law ", for a scientific law expresses a uniform connexion. In this sense a *cause* is an " unconditional antecedent ", since it is a term in an unconditional law of the form : *Whenever A, then B.* From the fact that A is the *unconditional* antecedent of B, it follows, then, that A is invariably connected with B. Hence, the invariability of the connexion follows from the unconditionality,

and not conversely. If it were the case that A happens always to
be followed by B, but that, under conditions that do not in fact
occur, A would not be followed by B, then A would not be the cause
of B, i.e. the succession would not be invariable. Mill does, then,
mean by " invariable " something other than " unvarying ", although
he often speaks as though these two expressions had the same
meaning.

§ 6. CAUSATION AND REGULAR SEQUENCE [1]

The problem we have now to discuss is whether causal laws
express *nothing but* regularities of sequence. If so, it would follow
that all regular sequences are causal, e.g. the sequence of day and
night. If not, the difficulty arises of finding some characteristic distinguishing regular sequences that are causal from those that are
not.

There is undoubtedly something to be said in favour of the view
that causal regularities are nothing but observed regularities of
sequence. Its best-known recent exponent is Mr. Bertrand Russell. [2]
Unfortunately his argument is so carelessly expressed that it is
difficult to extract the main points. Perhaps they may be said to
lie in the two following considerations. Starting with the admission
that causal laws are of the form ' A causes B ', e.g. ' Arsenic causes
death ', Mr. Russell argues that such laws are liable to exception,
and that, consequently, they cannot be universal and necessary.
Now a ' law ' that has exceptions would not generally be regarded
as a law. Mr. Russell, however, does not take this view, for he seems
to wish to maintain that *A causes B,* expresses a law and that it
means " A is the nearly invariable antecedent of B ". By " nearly
invariable " Mr. Russell seems to mean " almost *unvarying* ". He
argues that we cannot say that arsenic always causes death since a
man who has swallowed arsenic ' might be shot through the head
after taking the dose, and then it would not be of arsenic that he
would die.   Again, it may happen that immediately after the man's
death his body is blown to pieces by a bomb. We cannot say what
will happen after the man's death, through merely knowing that he
has died as the result of arsenic poisoning '. Accordingly, he argues,
that ' if we are to take the cause as one event and the effect as another,
both must be shortened indefinitely. We are thus left with laws
expressing the direction of change from moment to moment '. The
upshot of this argument appears to be that since a change occupies a
finite time, and since a change A that is usually followed by a change

---

[1] This section should be omitted on a first reading.
[2] See *The Analysis of Mind,* Chap. V.

B may be interrupted before the completion of the process, we cannot assert that ' A is always followed by B ', so long as we are concerned with perceptible changes. Thus causal laws are not universal. The second point concerns the difficulty of finding any *one* event which can be regarded as *the* cause of a given event. This difficulty leads Mr. Russell to deny the uniqueness of the causal relation. He argues : ' Cause, in the only sense in which it can be practically applied, means " nearly invariable antecedent ". We cannot in practice obtain an antecedent which is *quite* invariable, for this would require us to take account of the whole universe, since something not taken account of may prevent the expected effect.' The man who first swallowed arsenic, who was immediately afterwards shot through the head, and whose body was, immediately after death, blown to pieces by a bomb is said to provide an illustration of such ' prevention '. Hence Mr. Russell concludes that ' in fact we cannot find any antecedent that we know to be quite invariable ', but ' we can find many that are nearly so. For example, men leave a factory for dinner when the hooter sounds at twelve o'clock. You may say the hooter is *the* cause of their leaving. But innumerable other hooters in other factories, which also always sound at twelve o'clock, have just as good a right to be called the cause. Thus every event has many nearly invariable antecedents, and therefore many antecedents which may be called its cause '.

If Mr. Russell's view be correct, then *every* regular sequence is causal, since there is nothing more in the notion of cause than regularity of sequence. Thus night will be the cause of day and day will be the cause of night. On this view we should have to admit that the blowing of the hooters was the cause of the position of the hands of the clock when the men begin to leave the factory for dinner, and that the blowing of the hooter in a Manchester factory caused both the departure of the men from that factory and also the departure of the men from factories in Liverpool and in London, and conversely. The most surprising point with regard to Mr. Russell's argument is his belief that such an account of causation gives the only sense in which the notion can be practically applied. Presumably we apply the notion of cause when we use it for purposes of inference. It is not obvious that the hooter illustration could be used satisfactorily in practice, so that it may be doubted whether this definition of causal connexion could be recommended on the ground of its practical utility. It is unlikely, however, that the reasons Mr. Russell gives for his view are in fact the reasons that led him to it. Possibly his main reason for adopting such a paradoxical view is to be found in the extreme difficulty of pointing out *any* characteristic which suffices to distinguish regular sequences that are causal from those that are not. This difficulty may have led to the conclusion that there is no such char-

acteristic. Such an argument is by no means conclusive. Dr. Broad
has put this point very clearly.[1] He argues that if causation did
involve a unique and not further analysable relation it would be
' impossible to define it in any but tautologous terms '. In that case
it ' might be that regular sequence was not even *part* of what we mean
by causation, but was merely a sign (though by no means an infallible
one) by which the presence of this other relation is indicated '. Dr.
Broad admits that we do not seem to be directly acquainted with any
' extra factor ' in causation in the way in which, for instance, we are
directly acquainted with the unique and unanalysable relation of
inside and outside in space. Thus it remains *possible* that the main
reason for rejecting Mr. Russell's view may simply be its paradoxical
consequences. But, as Dr. Broad further argues, ' there are many
cases where we should admit regular sequence and *unhesitatingly deny*
causation ', although, he adds, ' there are perhaps no cases where we
can *unhesitatingly assert* causation in addition to regular sequence '.
It may certainly be admitted that the working scientist would
unhesitatingly deny that the blowing of a hooter in Manchester was
the cause of the departure of the London workmen.

If we ask why the hooter illustration is paradoxical we may be able
to discover the ' extra factor ' that is missing from Mr. Russell's
account. Dr. Broad says, ' the missing factor seems to be a certain
spatio-temporal continuity between the sequent events ', and he
adds, ' I am inclined to think that it is the absence of such continuity
between the blowing of the Manchester hooter and the movement of
the London workmen which makes me so certain that the former is not
a cause of the latter '. This suggestion will meet the difficulty only if
" a *certain* spatio-temporal continuity " be interpreted as involving
reference to continuity of change of character of the events happening
in Manchester, or in London. It is the absence of continuous change
of character that leads to the paradox. If what we have already said
about causal laws is correct, then it is a mistake to suppose that one
event causes another *event*. We have insisted that it is an event's
having a certain character that causes another event having a certain
character to have some other character. The missing factor must
then be found in the character of the event. Causal laws connect
changes in the characters of events, and there must be continuity in
this change of character. That this reference to character is essential
is shown by the fact that we speak of " *regular sequences* ". Events
do not recur. As we have seen, we can speak of the *same* cause on
different occasions only because the causal connexion is primarily
between the characters, and is derivatively between the events to
which these characters belong. Mr. Russell's view is, then, to be
rejected because it takes no account of the continuity of change of

[1] *The Mind and its Place in Nature*, pp. 453–6.

character that is essential to causation. We conclude that causation cannot be regarded as *equivalent to* regular sequence.

We have still to consider whether any meaning can be given to the statement that a causal connexion is a *necessary* connexion. To assert that the causal relation is a necessary relation is to assert that if it is true that A causes B, then it *could not* be the case that A happens and B does not. To assert that the causal relation is uniform but not necessary is to assert that if it is true that A causes B, then it is *not in fact* the case that A happens and B does not. The distinction between these two relations is equivalent to the distinction between *entailing* and *material implication*.[1] It is not possible to provide conclusive arguments in favour of either view. Many logicians have held that the causal relation resembles entailing.[2] Those who have held this view have by no means always seen clearly the consequences of regarding causation as equivalent to entailment, and have thus been led into holding views that are extremely unplausible. It will be granted that the causal relation holds only between terms having temporal properties, that is to say, that the field of the relation is natural entities, possibly including mental events. Now, on inspection, it seems obvious that the relation that holds between *This is a right angle* and *This is an angle* is fundamentally different from the relation that holds between *a flame* and *burning*, or the relation that holds between the occurrence consisting in *the absorption of a certain quantity of arsenic by a living organism* and the subsequent *cessation of life in that organism*. But what seems obvious on inspection is often false, so that the fact that these relations do seem very different does not justify us in asserting that there is such a fundamental difference. It does, however, suggest, that the *onus probandi* lies on those who assert that there is no such difference. On the other hand, there seems not the slightest justification for the view that, for example, the causal law *Sugar dissolves in water* must hold in all possible worlds, in the sense in which " must " means " *could* not be otherwise ".

The discussion of this question may be made clearer if we approach it from a slightly different point of view. We have insisted that the causal relation holds between events having determinate characters. What we have said is in this respect in agreement with Mr. Joseph's statement : ' the causal relation which connects *a* with *x* connects a cause of the *nature a* with an effect of the *nature x* '.[3] But Mr. Joseph's view of the causal relation makes it equivalent to the relation of entailing. Accordingly we cannot follow him with regard to what he takes to be the implications of the above statement. Mr. Joseph

[1] See Chap. XII, § 4.
[2] Cf. McTaggart, *The Nature of Existence*, Chap. XXV.
[3] *Introduction*, p. 409.

seems to hold that if it is true that A causes X, then it follows that anything that does not cause X could not be A. ' It could only act differently ', he says, ' if it *were* different ', and he adds, ' to say that the same thing acting on the same thing may yet produce a different effect, is to say that a thing need not be what it is. But this is in flat conflict with the Law of Identity. A thing to be at all, must be something, and can only be what it is. To assert a causal connexion between *a* and *x* implies that *a* acts as it does because it is what it is ; because, in fact, it is *a*. So long therefore as it is *a*, it must act thus '.[1] In drawing this conclusion Mr. Joseph at least appears to be confusing two different propositions which it is of the utmost importance to distinguish. These two propositions are : (1) A has the causal property P because it in fact has it ; (2) A must have the causal property P because nothing which had not P could be A. Whilst the first of these two propositions is a truism, the second is by no means obviously true. Professor Moore's analysis of the distinction between *material implication* and *entailment* makes it possible to state exactly what it is that the second proposition asserts. It will be remembered that to assert that one proposition entails another is to assert that the first *could* not be true and the second false ; to assert that one proposition materially implies another is to assert that the first is not *as a matter of fact* true and the second false. Now proposition (2) above is equivalent to the assertion that it is not the case that " A has the causal property P " is true whilst " anything that had not P must be other than A " is false.[2] This may be more simply expressed if we use the expression " AP " for " A has the causal property P ", and " $x\bar{P}$ " for " anything that has not P ". The proposition can then be expressed : ' It is not the case that AP is true while " $x\bar{P}$ entails *x* is other than A " is false.' As Professor Moore has shown, it very often is false that $x\bar{P}$ entails *x* is other than A, so that the compound proposition (2) is seldom true. It only is true when P is a special kind of property of A, namely an *internal property*, that is a property that necessarily belongs to A, i.e. a property such that it *could* not be that that property did not belong to A. For example, the property *being darker than yellow* is an internal property of *orange*, since anything that was *not* darker than yellow *could* not be orange. This might be expressed by saying that from the assertion that A is *not* darker than yellow *it follows* that A is *not* orange. Clearly not all properties are internal in this sense. For example, from the fact that this book is on this table it does not follow

---

[1] *Introduction*, p. 408.

[2] Inverted commas are used here for the sake of clearness in order to distinguish the subordinate propositions ; they are not used to mark the distinction between symbols and what is symbolized. Proposition (2) might be expressed in the form : From the fact that A has the causal property P *it follows* that anything that has not P *could* not be A.

that this book *could* not have been anywhere but on this table. That is to say the property *being on this table* is an external relational property of *this book*. The distinction between internal and external relational properties is admitted by common sense which certainly holds that whilst some properties are such that they could not but belong to those things to which they do belong, yet admits that there are many properties which things have which are such that these properties *might* not have belonged to the things to which they do in fact belong. The recognition that some properties are external is the recognition that there are *mere matters of fact*, i.e. things that *might* have been other than they in fact are.

It should now be clear that proposition (2) above is equivalent to the assertion that causal properties are internal. This assertion is certainly not a truism, and may even not be true ; hence, it is clearly different from proposition (1), which is a truism. It is probable that Mr. Joseph assumes the truth of proposition (2) owing to a failure to distinguish between the two following propositions :

(*a*) If A has P, then it follows that if *x* has not P, then *x* is other than A.

(*b*) It is not the case that " *A has P* " is true, and that " *if x has not P* it follows that *x is other than A* " is false.

If we use the shorthand symbols " ent." for " *entails* ", i.e. for the converse of *it follows*, and ⋆ for " materially implies ", i.e. for " it is not the case that the first proposition is true and the second false ", then we can express propositions (*a*) and (*b*) more clearly as follows :

$$(a)\ \ \mathrm{AP\ ent.}\ (x\bar{P} \star x \neq \mathrm{A}).$$
$$(b)\ \ \mathrm{AP} \star (x\bar{P}\ \mathrm{ent.}\ x \neq \mathrm{A}).$$

It is very easy to confuse these propositions, but it is extremely important to distinguish them, since (*a*) is certainly true, but (*b*) will be true if, and only if, P is an internal property of A. Mr. Joseph has either failed to distinguish these propositions or he has simply *assumed* that causal properties are internal.[1] The statement which was quoted from him suggests that he has failed to distinguish these propositions, for he seems to believe that it follows from the law of identity, viz. that A is identical with A, that A *could* not lack any of the properties which it does *in fact* possess. This is equivalent to the assertion that every property of A is an internal property. There is no reason to suppose that this assertion is true.

Although neither Mr. Joseph nor any other logician has given any

---

[1] Mr. Joseph might reply that he is concerned to assert that *the nature of A* cannot be determined apart from P, or that, in other words, to say that " things have natures " is equivalent to saying that " causes are necessary ". This, however, is the point at issue. Mr. Joseph *either* merely assumes that causal relations are necessary *or* begs the question by attempting to deduce the necessity of causation from the Law of Identity. Cf. p. 225 above.

reason for the belief that causal properties are internal, and although it may be the case that those who hold this view do so only because they have failed to distinguish between the very different propositions which we have expressed by (*a*) and (*b*), it may nevertheless be true that all causal properties are internal. To say that the causal relation is *necessary* is equivalent to saying that causal properties are internal. It does not seem possible to provide any evidence in favour of this view, so that we must conclude that it may be the case that the causal relation is not a necessary relation.

If the causal relation is not a necessary relation, then causal uniformities are equivalent to formal implications.[1] Thus (using ' A ' and ' X ' to stand respectively for ' a thing of the nature *a* ' and ' a thing of the nature *x* ') *A causes X* is equivalent to *Whenever A, then X*. This might otherwise be expressed " It is not the case that A occurs and that X does not occur ". Now, from *p ent. q* (where *p, q*, are any two propositions) there follows $p \star q$, but the converse does not hold. Similarly, if a causal uniformity expresses a necessary relation, there follows from it the matter of fact relation expressed by such a proposition as ' It is not in fact the case that A ever occurs and X does not occur '. Accordingly we might be able to assert the latter in spite of the fact that we could not assert the former. Hence, the latter relation is all that is required in order that we should be able to assert causal uniformities. But even if this should be the case it does not follow that causation is nothing but regular sequence. What is peculiar to the causal relation is not any characteristic of *necessity* distinguishing causal uniformities from regular sequences but the reference to determinate characters, or properties of events that are related by recurrent modes of change.

Contemporary philosophers tend to reject the notion of causation for one, or both, of the following reasons. In the first place the traditional Logicians have insisted that the causal relation is a *necessary* relation and that every event has a cause. Consequently it has been supposed that to deny the *necessity* of the causal relation is to reject the notion of cause, whilst to throw doubt upon the Law of Universal Causation is to render the conception of causation otiose. This we have seen not to be the case. There might well be causal uniformities even if it were in fact the case that *not every occurrence* was an instance of such a uniformity. In the second place it has been maintained that science makes no use of the notion of cause so that scientific method is not concerned with the concept of causation. Those who hold the view that science makes no use of the notion of cause have generally been more interested in the physical than in the biological and social sciences. Thus Mr. Russell says ' in advanced

---

[1] See above, p. 223. It will be remembered that formal implication is general material implication, and is of the form : $(x) . \Phi x . \supset \Psi x$.

sciences such as gravitational astronomy, the word " cause " never occurs ', and he adds, ' the reason why physics has ceased to look for causes is that, in fact, there are no such things '.[1]   It may certainly be admitted that ' in advanced sciences ' the notion of cause is replaced by the notion of functional dependence.   But it is a mistake to suppose that apart from the ' advanced sciences ' there is no scientific method.   On the contrary, the development of science from its earliest stages to its most advanced stages has been continuous.   It is the merest dogmatism to confine the " sciences " to physics and to argue that because the physicist does not employ the notion of cause, therefore " science " has no use for it.   The most superficial acquaintance with the earlier stages of a science is enough to reveal that the notion of cause is indispensable.   There is no doubt, for instance, that the word " cause " frequently occurs in the works of biologists.[2]   Those sciences that are concerned with the recurrent modes of behaviour of different *kinds* of things undoubtedly use the notion of cause in the form of causal laws.   The bio-chemist carries out careful experiments with regard to the action of chemicals upon living organisms in order to discover their modes of behaviour, that is, their causal laws. Thus, for instance, he uses such expressions as " Nitrites cause a fall in blood-pressure ", and he employs the notion of cause when he infers that an injection of amyl-nitrite will cause such a fall in blood-pressure.   He is content to leave to philosophers doubts as to the validity of the concept of cause so long as he is able to continue to use it.   Hence, it seems rash to conclude from an examination of the *words* used by physicists that ' there are no such things ' as causes.

No doubt the main reasons for the attempt on the part of philosophers to reject the notion of cause are to be found in the difficulty of stating precisely what exactly the concept involves, and in the close connexion between the traditional treatment of causation and the general problem of the validity of inductive inference.   The substitution of the notion of functional dependence for that of causal connexion does not, however, as Mr. Russell seems to suppose, throw any light upon the latter problem.   It is just as difficult to establish a necessary relation in the case of a functional correlation as in the case of a causal connexion.   The difficulties created by the traditional conception of *causation* as *necessary connexion* should not prevent us from recognizing that there are causal uniformities, although these difficulties should lead us to reject the traditional analysis of the concept of causation.   It is important not to confuse two quite different questions, namely :   (1) Do scientists employ the notion of

---

[1] *Mysticism and Logic*, p. 180.
[2] We have seen that the physicist also employs the *notion* of cause, although no doubt its analysis would be different in the case of the physical sciences from its analysis in the biological sciences.

19

conceived natural occurrences as taking place in accordance with the decrees of God. Thus everything that happened was in essential relation to the divinely ordained destiny of man. Nature thus regarded was both orderly and intelligible. It was ordered to secure an end ; it was intelligible in terms of purpose. From this point of view the correct question is " Why ? " ; the correct answer is " Because the result is *valuable* ". The appeal to value is final ; it marks the termination of purpose.

At the beginning of the scientific period stress is laid upon the difference between *Why ?* and *How ?* It is insisted that the latter is the only proper question to ask about events in nature. This is the scientific attitude, but it is of comparatively recent development. The question " Why ", i.e. " For what purpose ? " is the proper question to ask when we are concerned with personal agency, divine or human, and with the operation of motives. For example, a politician puts forward an election programme. He proposes a reduction in the income tax, or a return to the penny post. We want to know *why* he does so, what object he hopes to secure. Is it to catch votes, or is it a measure dictated by economic policy ? Our question is based upon the assumption that men act in certain ways to bring about a result they deem valuable. The answer in terms of value, ultimate or instrumental, satisfies us. But when we ask " How ? " there is no reference to purpose ; hence, value is irrelevant. It might be supposed that these two questions are so different that they would never be confused, that the one would be confined to actions, the other to the happening of natural occurrences. But it is not always easy to keep these questions distinct, confining each to its proper sphere. As we saw in considering the activity view of causation there is a tendency deeply rooted in human thinking to interpret natural occurrences in terms of man's own experience, to endow nature with purpose, and thus, finally, to attribute all that happens to the purposes of the Creator, God. The most primitive form in which this tendency is revealed is in the belief in animism. This belief is described by W. H. Hudson as ' that sense of something in nature which to the enlightened or civilized man is not there, and in the civilized man's child, if it be admitted that he has it at all, is but a faint survival of a phase of the primitive mind. And by animism I do not mean the theory of a soul in nature, but the tendency, or impulse or instinct, in which all myth originates, to *animate* all things ; the projection of ourselves into nature ; the sense and apprehension of an intelligence like our own but more powerful in all visible things '.[1] Something of this attitude is present whenever we assimilate natural occurrences to human experience. It lingers in the anthropomorphic

---

[1] *Far Away and Long Ago*, pp. 224–5.

tendency of science ; it is present to some extent in the medieval conception of nature as acting in accordance with laws that God had made. To it is due also the expression " law " for natural uniformitites.

An interpretation based upon purpose is called teleological. The appeal to value need not, however, take this explicit form. Greek thinkers also interpreted nature in accordance with their conception of value. Their criterion was not moral purpose but beauty ; their interpretation was determined by their aesthetic ideal of elegance, perfection and simplicity. This aesthetic element is present also in the familiar dicta of the Middle Ages : " Nature does nothing in vain " ; " Nature works by the simplest methods " ; " Nature seeks the shortest paths ". No doubt, we flatter ourselves, we have freed our scientific thinking from the appeal to value. Certainly our ideal is no longer conditioned by the reference to purpose ; nor do we make any explicit assumption of value. It is for this reason that the present age is an age of science ; its greatest achievements are in science ; its greatest men are scientists. Nevertheless, the decision between conflicting scientific theories is still determined by aesthetic considerations. The choice is always between different *kinds* of order. The medieval order, which placed man at the centre of the universe whose culmination is God, is replaced by an order the controlling principle of which is simplicity. Our belief in the principle of simplicity is no doubt partly due to the fact that unless natural laws are ultimately simple, there is not much likelihood of our discovering them. The evidence upon which this belief is based will be considered in a later chapter. Here it must be sufficient to point out that there are two kinds of simplicity. There is first simplicity in the formulation of the law itself ; there is secondly simplicity in the kind of elements, or entities with which the formulation is concerned. Newton's law of the inverse square is simple in both respects. Medieval order possessed only the first kind of simplicity. But even this simplicity was in the end reduced to the inscrutable purposes of God. The Greek and modern ideal is the simplicity of mathematical laws.

§ 2. THE DEVELOPMENT OF HYPOTHESIS

The mode in which a scientific hypothesis develops, and in its development is gradually freed from anthropomorphic elements, can be most easily illustrated from the science of astronomy. We shall, therefore, consider at some length the development of the Ptolemaic and Copernican hypotheses.

The problem is to account for the observed movements of the heavenly bodies, and in particular of those " wandering stars ", the

296 A MODERN INTRODUCTION TO LOGIC

these assumptions were of such a kind that there *could* be no further
evidence in support of them. They were essentially unverifiable.
They were not susceptible of development; they did not suggest
the deduction of *observable* data. Further, the supposition that the
moon was periodically swallowed by a sow is not in conformity with
what was known about the behaviour of sows. The continual
rebirth of the god Râ was a supposition not based upon known
analogies with living bodies on the earth. The Egyptian theory,
therefore, could neither be developed nor tested. But a theory is
scientific only if it admits of testing and development. The Egyptian
climate of opinion was not favourable to the production of scientific
theories.

The theory associated with Ptolemy is thoroughly scientific.[1]
It was based upon observations that were both careful and extensive ;
it was stated in the precise language of mathematics ; finally, it rested
upon *explicit* assumptions. There were three assumptions : (1) that
the earth is an immovable sphere at the centre of the universe ;
(2) that the heavens revolve round the earth and contain the sun,
the moon and the planets, whilst beyond these is the fixed sphere
containing the stars ; (3) that the revolutions are circular. Ptolemy's
problem was *to work out in detail* the paths followed by sun, moon
and planets. Ptolemy's third assumption was derived from Aristotle
and his followers. The circle was regarded as the perfect figure.
Consequently, it was assumed that the heavenly bodies must move
in circles, since their motion must be perfect. We see here how
the reference to notions of *value* seemed to afford a satisfactory
answer to the question *why* the heavenly bodies move as they seem
to move. From Aristotle also Ptolemy derived his belief that the
earth is immovable.[2] These are the assumptions that rendered
necessary the elaborate hypothesis known as the Ptolemaic system.
It was not difficult to account for the position of the stars on the
assumption that the earth is the centre of the revolving system,
since the stars were observed to be uniform. But the movements
of the planets did not conform to the circular theory. Ptolemy
explained these movements as resulting from the combination of
two motions. Each planet revolves round a circle whose centre
was on the circumference of an imaginary circle round the earth
as centre. This imaginary circle was called the " deferent " ; the
smaller circle is known as an epicycle. Hence, the path of a planet
as viewed from the earth as a fixed centre can be accounted for

---

[1] Ptolemy lived in the second century A.D. The system called by his name
was developed but not originated by him.

[2] Ptolemy supported this assumption by the argument that if the earth
moved its motion would be proportionate to its great mass, so that animals and
objects thrown into the air would be left behind. But this does not happen.

by the combination of the two motions—circle revolving round a circle. This hypothesis accounts for the backward movement of the planet at some stages of its revolution. The following simplified diagram shows the planetary motion.

Owing to the number of the planets, to their varying distances from the earth and their varying rates of movement, Ptolemy found it necessary to introduce a great number of epicycles revolving round epicycles. In developing the mathematical consequences of his system Ptolemy proved himself to be a great mathematician. He succeeded in accounting for the observed movements. It is probable that he did not think of his system as a physical fact. He says : ' I do not profess to be able to account for all the motions at the same time ; but I shall show that each by itself is well explained by its proper hypothesis '.[1] In beginning the theory of a particular part of the planet's motion he says : ' Let us imagine a circle '. Ptolemy

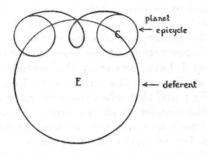

E represents the Earth. The larger circle is the deferent. The planet moves round the epicycle the centre of which, c, moves round the deferent. Hence the planet traces out the path marked by the darker curve.

was thus able to work out a satisfactory theory, whose only defect was its complexity. It is obvious that this theory is scientific. That it has now been discarded as practically useless does not mean that it was not a properly scientific theory. It is scientific because (1) it ordered the movements of the heavenly bodies in a regular manner ; (2) it did not assume the existence of anything that could not be observed ; (3) it did not require the aid of any mysterious and unintelligible activity ; (4) all the various movements were accounted for by *one* type of hypothesis. Finally, it may be observed that Ptolemy was clearly aware as to what assumptions he was making ; his theory of planetary motion was put forward as an hypothesis capable of ordering the observable data. It was superseded only when a theory *equally* scientific but mathematically

mistress of their credulity '.[1] Nevertheless, Galileo did not doubt that this rape of reason upon the senses would be ultimately justifiable in terms of sensible experience. Mathematical theory might outrun the available experiential confirmation but in the end we must ' come to the particular demonstrations, observations and experiments '.[2] He was himself so firmly convinced that ' mathematics is the language in which the Book of Nature is written ', that he did not feel the need of experiments to verify his mathematical deductions. But where it is not a question of mathematical deduction, appeal must be made to sensible fact. For example, the contemporaries of Galileo argued that the moon's surface must be uniformly bright and even, and that none of the planets had satellites. By means of his telescope Galileo was able to refute both these assertions. We saw in Chapter XIV how Sizzi tried to argue against Galileo's discovery. When one of his opponents refused to look through the telescope to test the truth of Galileo's statement, he wrote to Kepler :

> ' Oh, my dear Kepler, how I wish that we could have one hearty laugh together ! Here, at Padua, is the principal professor of philosophy whom I have repeatedly and urgently requested to look at the moon and planets through my glass, which he pertinaciously refuses to do. Why are you not here ? What shouts of laughter we should have at this glorious folly ! And to hear the professor of philosophy at Pisa, labouring before the grand duke with logical arguments, as if with magical incantations, to charm the new planets out of the sky.' [3]

The grand duke's "logical arguments" were derived from the writings of Aristotle so far as the philosophers of the seventeenth century were able to understand them. But Galileo believed that Aristotle would have agreed with him had he been able to look through a telescope. He saw that Aristotle's method was essentially empirical. ' I do believe for certain ', Galileo wrote, ' that he [Aristotle] first procured, by the help of the senses, such experiments and observations as he could, to assure him as much as was possible of the conclusion, and that he afterwards sought out the means how to demonstrate it ; for this is the usual course in demonstrative sciences '.[4] The senses provide the data of our problems and to them also we must look for the final test of our theories. But the

---

[1] *Dialogues concerning Two Great Systems of the World* (London, 1661), p. 301 (*pub.* 1632).

[2] *ibid.*, p. 31. Cf. also p. 96 : ' Our disputes are about the sensible world, and not one of paper ' ; also, *Two New Sciences*, p. 4 : ' Please observe, gentlemen, how facts which at first seem improbable will, even on scant explanation, drop the cloak which has hidden them and stand forth in naked and simple beauty.'

[3] Quoted by Sir Oliver Lodge, *Pioneers of Science*, p. 106.

[4] *Two Great Systems*, p. 37.

senses do not suffice to *order* the data they provide. Hence, the mathematical theory must first be thought out, then tested experimentally. The mathematical statement must be exact. For example, it is not enough to know that bodies fall with an accelerated motion ; the mathematical relations must be precisely determined. Thus Galileo says : ' Neither does this suffice, but it is requisite to know according to what proportion such acceleration is made ; a problem that I believe was never hitherto understood by any philosopher or mathematician, although philosophers, and particularly the Peripatetics [i.e. the Aristotelians], have writ great and entire volumes touching motion '.[1]

It is because Galileo combined mathematical theory with experimental confirmation that we can trace to him the beginning of modern science. He was a supreme experimental genius, but his experiments were controlled and directed by exact mathematical deduction.[2] For this reason he has been the main influence in determining the present scientific climate of opinion.

§ 3.   EXPERIMENTAL TESTING OF HYPOTHESIS

It is not difficult to devise ingenious and complicated hypotheses as to how things *might* have happened so long as we are not concerned carefully to observe what has *actually* happened. The ancient Egyptian explanation of lunar eclipses was ingenious but, as we saw, it did not take sufficient account of observed modes of behaviour. The explanation of the eclipse in terms of the relative positions of the earth, moon, and sun not only fitted better into the observed facts, it did not require the assumption of hypotheses that *could* not be tested by appeal to observable experience. Scientific method differs from all other modes of thinking by reason of this ultimate appeal to observable experience. Common-sense thinking relies mainly upon simple and uncritical observation combined with vague and uncriticized beliefs. Mathematics is wholly deductive, its fundamental principles are neither based upon experience nor necessarily in conformity with it. Historical writing in so far as it consists in the imaginative reconstruction of past events is almost entirely independent of experimental confirmation. A scientific theory, however, is at every stage controlled and tested by appeal to what happens, that is, by appeal to what *could* be observed. But the appeal is never to *random* observation ; it is to *directed* observation. Nothing is easier than to *mis-observe* ; to suppose that one has observed what is not there to be observed, or to fail to observe what could have been observed. There is no such thing as bare observation. A scientific ' fact ' is already an interpreted datum, often a generalization. Hence, the scientist finds it necessary to

[1] *ibid.*, p. 144.   [2] Cf. below, Chap. XVIII.

elaborate his observations, to check one observation by another and his own observations by other people's. He checks his observations in order to eliminate what has been called the *personal* factor. In other words, the scientist must *experiment*. A scientific theory that is incapable of experimental testing is valueless. Experiment is deliberate observation in the light of a definite expectation *as to what will be observed*. In this sense, all observation of facts that have been deduced from a given hypothesis is experimenting. The householder who, having formulated the hypothesis that he has been robbed, proceeds to look about him in order to discover whether, for example, his valuable silver has gone, is experimentally testing the validity of his hypothesis. He *expects* a certain result and he looks to see whether this result has taken place. Sometimes, however, the " fact " that the scientist wants to observe will not present itself unless he *makes* it happen. Then he deliberately arranges the conditions in which it will happen, if his expectations are not mistaken. It has become usual to confine the word " experiment " to such deliberate observation under conditions deliberately arranged by the observer. This restriction is the natural result of the increasing complexity and subtlety of scientific theories and the increased skill in the devising and manipulation of scientific apparatus. But from the logical point of view we must recognize that there is experiment wherever there is *deliberate* observation of *expected* results. We are apt to oppose the experimental to the non-experimental sciences. There are, indeed, good reasons for this opposition. But the point that is of importance is that experiment enables us to *obtain* the expected result. It affords a means of unravelling the complexity of nature.

Whereas we oppose the experimental to the non-experimental sciences, a medieval scientist opposed experiment, i.e. *experience* to *reasoning*. Thus Roger Bacon in the thirteenth century [1] urged the necessity of ' experimental science ', by which he meant ' knowledge based on experience '. In his *Magnum Opus*, in which he attempted to expound the correct method of discovering the truth about nature, he began his exposition by insisting upon the importance of testing the consequences of a theory by appeal to experience. He says :

' Having laid down fundamental principles of the wisdom of the Latins so far as they are found in language, mathematics and optics, I now wish to unfold the principles of experimental science, since without experience nothing can be sufficiently known. For there are two modes of acquiring knowledge, namely, by reasoning and experience. Reasoning draws a conclusion and makes us grant the conclusion, but does not make the conclusion certain, nor does it remove doubt so that the mind may rest on the

---

[1] Roger Bacon lived from 1214 to 1294.

intuition of truth, unless the mind discovers it by the path of experience ; since many have the arguments relating to what can be known, but because they lack experience they neglect the arguments, and neither avoid what is harmful, nor follow what is good. For if a man who has never seen a fire should prove by adequate reasoning that fire burns and injures things and destroys them, his mind would not be satisfied thereby, nor would he avoid fire, until he placed his hand or some combustible substance in the fire, so that he might prove by experience that which reasoning taught. But when he has actual experience of combustion his mind is made certain and rests in the full light of truth. Therefore, reasoning does not suffice, but experience does.' [1]

Reasoning, i.e. the deductive development of the hypothesis, must then be *tested* by appeal to experience. Roger Bacon no doubt overestimated the certainty of the conclusion thus tested. But he was undoubtedly right in maintaining that without such testing the theory is comparatively valueless. Moreover, if an hypothesis leads to the conclusion that under certain conditions some definite occurrence will take place ; then, if we can produce those conditions we are able to ' put questions to nature '. Thus, as Herschel says, in experimenting ' we cross-examine our witness, and by comparing one part of his evidence with the other, while he is yet before us, and reasoning upon it in his presence, are enabled to put pointed and searching questions, the answer to which may at once enable us to make up our mind '.[2] The question is *pointed* because we *expect* the answer. When Torricelli inverted the glass tube in the bowl of mercury he expected the mercury to rise ; for, that it would rise followed from his hypothesis. When Galileo dropped two cannon balls of different weights from the Tower of Pisa, he expected them to reach the ground together. When the Committee of the Royal Society planned experiments with regard to the pressure of the air to be carried out on the ascent of a mountain, they expected definite results to be observable. They also hoped that unexpected observations might provide more data for their hypotheses, for they knew fairly well what observations would be relevant. Simple observation, that is, observation without deliberate interference with the conditions, is as much under the direction of theory as is experiment, if the observation be scientific. The scientist is not a person who just observes ; he observes with a purpose, namely, the purpose of discovering relevant data. He observes in the light of a theory about the facts. This theory may be very vague ; nevertheless, it directs his observation. An erroneous theory may be the cause of mistaken observation ; hence the necessity for checks and counter-checks. The scientific thinker will be prepared for the

[1] *Magnum Opus*, trans. R. B. Burke, Vol. II, p. 583.
[2] *A Preliminary Discourse on the Study of Natural Philosophy* (ed. 1842), p. 77.

our conceptions of the truth that are at fault, though each conception seems valid and proved. There must be a truth which is greater than any of our descriptions of it. Here is an actual case where the human mind is brought face to face with its own defects. What can we do ? What do we do ? As physicists we use either hypothesis according to the range of experiences that we wish to consider. . . . We know that we cannot be seeing clearly and fully in either case, but we are perfectly content to work and wait for the complete understanding.' [1]

Jevons's second condition must, then, be interpreted as being merely cautionary. Otherwise it is likely to lead to a mistaken conception of the practical function of hypothesis. The conflict of hypotheses is an incentive to further development in order that the conflict may be overcome. It must be admitted that two incompatible theories cannot both be *true* ; but two incompatible hypotheses may both be *useful*. Their function is to guide observation by suggesting fruitful experiments. Nor is it the case that one or the other of two such hypotheses must be rejected *en bloc*. To quote Sir William Bragg again : ' The theories of one time are supplanted by those of a succeeding time, and those again yield to something more like the first. But it is no idle series of changes, of vagaries of whimsical fashion ; it is growth. The older never becomes invalid, and the new respects the old because that is the case '. The conditions of a satisfactory hypothesis are the conditions of scientific method. They cannot be isolated and tabulated for the convenience of the elementary student of logical method. Jevons's third condition can be accepted subject only to the same qualification. The consequences that are deduced must be tested by appeal to observed facts. In so far as there is conflict the hypothesis must be modified or must be held *provisionally*. Jevons undoubtedly overstates the position when he asserts : ' A single absolute conflict between fact and hypothesis, is fatal to the hypothesis ; *falsa in uno, falsa in omnibus* '. When a deduced consequence is found to be true, the hypothesis is so far verified. If a careful experiment shows that a deduced consequence is false, then, it follows logically that the hypothesis as it stands cannot be true. But it does not follow that it is entirely wrong. Sometimes the negative experiment itself affords a suggestion as to what kind of modification is required.

Two contrary hypotheses may then account equally well for all the known facts. If, however, a point arises at which it is possible to deduce a consequence from one hypothesis that would be inconsistent with the other, an opportunity arises for what is known as a crucial experiment. The theory of light again affords a well-known illustration. While both the wave theory and the cor-

---

[1] *Craftsmanship and Science*, pp. 27–8. Cf. also Whitehead, *Science and the Modern World*, p. 257 ; and see Eddington, *Nature of the Physical World*, Chap. IX.

puscular theory accounted fairly well for the optical phenomena, it
was shown that the two theories diverged with regard to the velocity
of light in different media. According to the wave theory light
should have a greater velocity *in vacuo* than in material media;
according to the corpuscular theory the contrary should be the case.
The crucial experiment consisted in determining the velocity of light
in different media. The experiment was not performed until 1850,
when Foucault by determining the velocity in both air and water
showed that the velocity of light is inversely proportional to the
refractive index of the medium. Thus the experiment was decisively in favour of the wave theory. But, as we have seen, it would
be rash to say that the other theory was definitely disproved. A
crucial experiment is *crucial* with regard only to a particular fact.
Jevons says: 'A crucial experiment must not simply confirm one
theory, but must negative another; it must decide a mind which
is in equilibrium, as Bacon says, between two equally plausible
views'.[1] This confirmation, however, is never more than partial;
the result of the experiment provides additional reason for believing
the favourable hypothesis. No experiment, nor series of experiments, can suffice to establish an hypothesis beyond the reach of
doubt. The final test is to be found only in the comprehensiveness
of the system into which a given hypothesis fits. We shall be concerned later with the problem of the verification of hypotheses and
the justification of the hypothetical method. It must be sufficient
here to point out that verification does not amount to proof. To
suppose otherwise is to commit the fallacy of the consequent.

It must further be observed that hypotheses are not used for
one purpose only. There are different *kinds* of hypotheses and the
nature of the hypothesis varies with its function. We may distinguish three main kinds—*explanatory*, *descriptive* and *analogical*.
These may again be subdivided. The simplest kind of hypotheses
fall into the first class. These hypotheses are intended *to explain*,
i.e. to account for, the occurrence of a certain fact by the inter-
polation of facts that might have been observed under suitable
conditions. Such is the hypothesis of burglary to account for the

---

[1] op. cit., p. 519. The reference is to Bacon, *Novum Organum*, Bk. II,
Aph. 36. The term "experimentum crucis" is due to Bacon. He says:
'When in search of any nature, the understanding comes to an equilibrium,
as it were, or stands uncertain as to which of two or more natures the cause of
the nature in question should be assigned, on account of the frequent and
ordinary concurrence of many natures, then these Crucial Instances [cruces
instantia, i.e. instances of the Fingerpost] show the union of one of these
natures with the nature in question to be sure and indissoluble, of the other
to be varied and separable; and thus the question is decided, and the former is
admitted as the cause, while the latter is rejected.'
Cf. also Hume, *Enquiry concerning Morals*, § 178.

trolled by hypotheses held more or less tentatively in face of the facts.   The history of the atomic theory of matter also affords many excellent examples of the way in which different kinds of hypotheses have contributed to the development of science.[1]

Unless the rôle of hypothesis be grasped the structure of scientific method cannot be understood.   It was contended by the great German chemist Ostwald that hypotheses were a hindrance to science.[2] This view cannot, however, he maintained.   Ostwald seems to have thought of hypothesis as essentially a picture, or model, or image (*Bild*) containing elements not given in the original observations but imported by the scientist and therefore not necessarily in accord with what was given.   Now it is clear that a descriptive hypothesis may well contain such elements, as in the case of the luminiferous ether, and yet the hypothesis may be of the utmost value as a guide to experiment.   Such hypotheses are psychologically valuable in the art of discovery.   The precise form which hypotheses take will vary from one individual scientist to another.   Some scientists are not content unless, like Lord Kelvin, they can devise a 'mechanical model all through'; others are content with a vaguer form such as Maxwell's hypothesis of 'displacement'; others again formulate hypotheses of more abstract kinds.   These differences relate to the art of discovery; in the perfected scientific method hypothesis remains as the 'anticipation of nature' which conditions the process of experimental inquiry.

§ 5.   NEWTON'S CONCEPTION OF SCIENTIFIC METHOD [3]

In an article in *The Times* written in February 1929 Einstein asserted : ' Advances in scientific knowledge must bring about the result that an increase in formal simplicity can only be won at the cost of an increased distance or gap between the fundamental hypotheses of the theory on the one hand, and the directly observed facts on the other.   Theory is compelled to pass more and more from the inductive to the deductive method, even though the most important demand to be made of every scientific theory will always remain that it must fit the facts '.   Einstein's statement is in accordance with Galileo's practice and with his conception of scientific method.   We have already seen that Galileo was prepared to commit ' the rape of reason upon the senses ' since he was convinced that by mathematical reasoning *alone* could the laws of nature be dis-

---

[1] See Meyerson, *Identity and Reality*, Chap. II.

[2] Ostwald says : ' Ich habe mich bemüht, ein Buch zü schreiben, in welchem keine Hypothese aufgestellt oder benutzt worden ist.' (See *Vorlesungen über Naturphilosophie*, p. 212.)

[3] This section should be omitted by a student on a first reading.

covered.[1] It would be natural to suppose that Newton should have had a like trust in reason and in the adequacy of mathematics. This, however, was not the case. Newton, great mathematician though he was, insisted upon the necessity of the appeal to sensible fact at every stage ; he was not content to trust to his mathematical deductions without feeling the necessity for experimental confirmation. There must be no gap between hypothesis and observation ; nothing must be supposed that is not *directly* derived from the phenomena, nor any hypothesis accepted without being put to the proof. Thus, for example, Newton protested against the claim made by Robert Hooke that he had discovered the law of the inverse square, since this claim was not supported by any attempt at detailed proof. It remained a mere guess. Moreover, Newton at least *appears* anxious to deny that hypothesis has any essential part to play in scientific investigation. As Whewell has pointed out : ' Newton appears to have had a horror of the term *hypothesis*, which probably arose from his acquaintance with the rash and illicit general assumptions of Descartes '.[2] His writings are full of attacks against the use of hypothesis and he angrily repudiated the suggestion that he himself made use of them. His celebrated dictum " *Hypotheses non fingo* " has perhaps been too often quoted out of its context and has been subject to some misinterpretation. It is worth while to attempt to bring together Newton's scattered remarks on the nature of scientific method in order to discover in what sense he was concerned to exclude hypotheses from scientific investigation. He makes the following definite statement with regard to scientific method :

' For the best and safest method of philosophising [3] seems to be that we should first diligently investigate the properties of things and establish them by experiments, and then later we should seek hypothesis to explain them. For hypotheses ought to be fitted merely to explain the properties of things and not attempt to predetermine them except so far as they can be an aid to experiment.' [4]

In this passage Newton seems to admit that hypotheses may be ' an aid to experiment ', and that *after* the properties have been experimentally determined it may be possible to formulate explanatory hypotheses. His views on this question seem to have

[1] See below, Chap. XVIII, § 2.

[2] *Philosophy of Discovery*, Chap. XVIII.

[3] It must be remembered that for Newton and his contemporaries " natural philosophy " means what we now call " physical science," so that "the method of philosophizing " means " scientific method ".

[4] Letter to Oldenburg. (See *Isaaci Newtoni Opera quae exstant omnia.* Ed. Horsley, 1782, IV, p. 314. All quotations except those otherwise specified are from this edition, which will henceforth be cited N. Op. I have translated those given in Latin.)

instance, that Newton himself determined the concept of refrangibility in optics. The fourth Rule shows very clearly the importance Newton attached to the initial and the verifying experiments. The *addendum* to this Rule is very significant. It runs : ' This rule we must follow, that the argument of induction may not be evaded by hypothesis.'

There thus seems to be considerable evidence in favour of the view that Newton rejected the use of hypothesis and that he himself did not follow what we have called the hypothetical method. There is, however, some danger of misinterpreting this evidence and of misunderstanding the conclusion it warrants. For the proper discussion of this question we must consider the famous passage in the " General Scholium " at the end of the *Principia*, which runs as follows :

> ' Hitherto we have explained the phaenomena of the heavens and of our sea by the power of gravity, but have not yet assigned the cause of this power. This is certain, that it must proceed from a cause that penetrates to the very centres of the sun and the planets, without suffering the least diminution of its force ; that operates not according to the quantity of the surfaces of the particles upon which it acts (as mechanical causes used to do), but according to the quantity of the solid matter which they contain, and propagates its virtue on all sides to immense distances, decreasing always in the duplicate proportion of the distances. . . . But hitherto I have not been able to discover the cause of those properties of gravity from phaenomena, and I frame no hypotheses (*hypotheses non fingo*) ; for whatever is not deduced from the phaenomena is to be called an hypothesis ; and hypotheses, whether metaphysical or physical, whether of occult qualities or mechanical, have no place in experimental philosophy. In this philosophy particular propositions are inferred from the phaenomena, and afterwards rendered general by induction. Thus it was that the impenetrability, the mobility, and the impulsive force of bodies, and the laws of motion and gravitation, were discovered. And to us it is enough that gravity does really exist, and act according to the laws which we have explained, and abundantly serves to account for all the motions of the celestial bodies, and of our sea.' [1]

From the consideration of this passage alone we should certainly not be led to interpret the statement " hypotheses non fingo " in the way in which it has often been interpreted. Newton is here clearly speaking of the *cause* of the properties of gravity, and it is with regard to the cause of gravity that he asserts that he frames no hypothesis. He rejects two classes of hypotheses, namely, (i) metaphysical hypotheses involving occult qualities, and (ii) physical hypotheses involving mechanical qualities. These are rejected on the ground that they cannot be inferred from the phenomena.[2] It

---

[1] Vol. II, pp. 313–14.

[2] Cf. the important statement in the *Opticks* where Newton says that he does not consider the principles of motion (mass, gravity, etc.) as occult qualities but ' as general laws of Nature, by which the things themselves are formed : their appearing to us by phaenomena, though their causes be not yet discovered.

is not the business of 'experimental philosophy' to introduce unobservable causes; on the contrary, its business is to infer particular propositions from the phenomena, and to generalize these by induction in accordance with Rules I and II. Whatever is not 'deduced from the phenomena' is an hypothesis and may not be entertained by the physicist. The word "deduced" here requires some explanation. Since the purpose of the initial experiments is to determine those properties which vary quantitatively, so that these variations may be expressed mathematically, it is possible to pass back from the mathematical formulation to the mode of behaviour of the properties. The element of induction comes in when the conclusion is generalized. Newton is not using "deduction" in the precise sense of "proof". Once again he is insisting upon the empirical basis of science. There is, however, *nothing in this passage* to suggest that hypotheses are inadmissible, provided that they be not put forward as demonstrations, nor that experimental investigation may not be aided by such hypotheses. The concluding paragraph of this *scholium* does indeed suggest that Newton was not unwilling to consider an hypothesis with regard to the mode of production of gravity, namely, that there was 'a most subtle spirit' to whose activity gravity, cohesion, the phenomena of electricity and light are due. But he declares 'these are things that cannot be explained in few words, nor are we furnished with that sufficiency of experiments which is required to an accurate determination and demonstration of the laws by which this electric and elastic spirit operates'. This statement brings out Newton's distinction between experimental laws, capable of demonstration, and hypothesis which we lack the knowledge to establish.

Finally, we may ask whether Newton himself appears to have been guided by hypothesis. Owing to his opposition to the notion

For these are manifest qualities, and their causes only are occult. And the *Aristotelians* gave the name of Occult qualities not to manifest qualities, but to such qualities only as they supposed to lie hid in bodies, and to be the unknown causes of manifest effects: such as would be the causes of gravity, and of Magnetik and Electrik attractions, and of fermentations, if we should suppose that these forces, or actions, arose from qualities unknown to us, and uncapable of being discovered and made manifest. Such Occult qualities put a stop to the improvement of natural philosophy, and therefore of late years have been rejected. To tell us that every species of things is endowed with an occult specific quality, by which it acts and produces manifest effects, is to tell us nothing: but to derive two or three general principles of motion from phaenomena, and afterwards to tell us how the properties and actions of all corporeal things follow from those manifest principles, would be a very great step in philosophy, though the causes of those principles were not yet discovered: and therefore, I scruple not to propose the principles of motion above mentioned, they being of very general extent, and leave their causes to be found out.' (N. Op., IV, p. 261.)

of hypothesis Newton was careful to distinguish his unverified speculations from propositions that he had demonstrated. Thus in the *Opticks* he formulated what were undoubtedly guiding hypotheses as " Queries ", excluded from the main body of the work. There can be no doubt that Newton performed his experiments in the definite expectation that such and such results would ensue. When these expectations were realized the way was open for the inference of " particular propositions " from the phenomena. An hypothesis that yielded no such definite expectation would be useless for science. An hypothesis that postulated causes lying beyond the reach of human observation must remain unverified. Consequently Newton excluded the former as mere guesses, the latter as metaphysical speculations. In this sense, and in this sense only, did Newton reject hypotheses.

CHAPTER XVII

PRINCIPLES OF CAUSAL DETERMINATION

'The first work therefore of true induction (as far as regards the discovery of Forms) is the rejection or exclusion of the several natures which are not found in some instance where the given nature is present, or are found in some instance where the given nature is absent, or are found to increase in some instance where the given nature decreases, or decrease when the given nature increases.'—*Francis Bacon.*

§ 1. THE SEARCH FOR CAUSES

THE earliest stage of scientific investigation assumes the form of a search for the causes of occurrences. No two sets of occurrences differ merely in their spatial and temporal characteristics; consequently, the first stage in any inductive investigation is the determination of certain factors as irrelevant. By the accumulation of judgements of irrelevance the problem is narrowed down to the investigation of a comparatively restricted region. We are often confronted with a problem of determining the cause of an occurrence happening in conditions with which we are fairly familiar. There are certain definite principles in accordance with which such causal investigation is carried on. The complex situation must be analysed into its constituent factors in order to determine which of them are jointly sufficient and independently necessary to the production of the given occurrence. For example, a glass into which hot water has just been poured cracks. It might be supposed that the hot water is the sufficient cause of the cracked glass. Such a supposition is in accordance with the common-sense conception of cause. The glass standing on the table is a situation into which a new factor *contact of glass with hot water* has been introduced. The introduction of this factor is followed by a change in the glass. Accordingly, this factor is regarded as the cause of the change. If now hot water poured into another glass standing beside the first does not have the same result, we conclude that pouring hot water into a glass is not a circumstance sufficient for the production of the effect. This conclusion is based upon the assumption that a factor which is present although the given effect does not occur is not the cause of that effect. The two glasses must then be examined in order to ascertain whether any difference can be found between them which would be relevant to the difference in the result. It is then found that the two glasses differ in thickness. It might also be the case that they differ in colour. Previous experience may have shown that difference in colour would not be relevant to the difference in the result. It remains to inquire whether the difference in thickness is relevant. If we knew that various substances expand when heated, we should recognize that the difference in thickness was an additional factor sufficient to account for the difference in the result. We should, then, conclude that the inner surface of the thicker glass expands before the outer surface has been heated ; that, consequently, this expansion causes the glass to crack. The thinner glass is more evenly heated, so that no crack results. Had the case of the thin glass not been observed, the first instance might have been generalized in the causal proposition : *Hot water poured into a glass breaks the glass*. The consideration of the second instance leads to the more exact statement : Hot water causes glass to expand : glass of a certain thickness will expand on the surface to which hot water is applied before the outer surface is heated ; the expansion of the inner surface of the glass causes the glass to crack.

It is important to observe that such an investigation presupposes a considerable amount of previous knowledge relevant to the situation. The importance of relevant knowledge can scarcely be over-emphasized. Any one who successfully investigates a problem with regard to the cause of an occurrence is in possession of relevant knowledge, but he does not need to ponder its relevance. He can take it for granted since his object is the discovery of a causal factor, not the examination of the method whereby it is discovered. When, however, as logicians we are considering the nature of the principles in accordance with which causes may be determined, our problem is not practical but theoretical. Accordingly we examine *a problem that has been solved*. The problem as stated in a textbook of logic has been transformed into a museum specimen. The consideration of museum specimens is useful for the student of nature who can relate the specimen to its natural habitat. In so doing he is aware that he is dealing with a specimen placed in an artificial isolation. The student of logic is in a similar position. He must study examples of scientific investigation which have to a greater or less extent been artificially isolated. His study will be fruitful only in so far as he is aware of the limitations of his inquiry. It is important, then, to remember that in this chapter we are concerned with a narrowly restricted problem, namely, to formulate precisely certain principles involved in the determination of causal factors within a limited field of research.

The analysis of a causal situation into its constituent factors may involve literal separation of the factors, i.e. physical analysis, or it may involve isolation only in thought. Those sciences in which physical analysis is possible are experimental sciences in the narrower sense of " experimental ". The rapid advance of such sciences is due to the fact that when the conditions can be varied it is possible to determine what is irrelevant. Such analysis is guided by two principles which follow directly from the nature of a cause. These principles are : (1) Nothing is the cause of an effect which is absent when the effect occurs ; (2) Nothing is the cause of a given effect which is present when the effect fails to occur. Accordingly, in seeking for the cause of an occurrence A, we shall look for cases where A is present and cases where A is absent such that many factors present in the former set of cases are present also in the second set notwithstanding the absence of A.

§ 2. AN EXAMPLE OF EXPERIMENTAL INVESTIGATION

Experiment is possible only when the field of inquiry is limited within a fairly definite range. The experimenter must have more or less detailed knowledge as to what alternatives are possible under certain conditions. It is true that sometimes unexpected results have occurred, whilst experiments performed in the confident expectation of a given result have sometimes failed to produce any observable result. Such a completely negative result may be of considerable significance, provided that the situation as a whole is well understood. This was the case with the famous Michelson-Morley experiment to detect the ether-drift.[1] But unless the details of the situation are clearly apprehended no significant questions can be asked. To experiment is to ask such questions.

We shall now examine at some length an experimental investigation carried out by the famous French scientist Louis Pasteur. His purpose was to ascertain the conditions under which certain microorganisms were generated. He sought to provide evidence in refutation of the theory of spontaneous generation. This was the theory that certain kinds of living organisms were generated from inorganic matter. Although it was recognized that in most cases organisms are produced by parents whom the offspring tend to resemble, it was believed that certain forms of life could be produced from the earth and from decaying animal and vegetable matter. There was evidence apparently in favour of this view. Worms and maggots breed on putrefying flesh ; maggots are sometimes found at the core of apples, pears, and other soft fruit, the skin of which is unpierced. After the discovery of the microscope numerous tiny organisms were discovered in rain water and in any liquid that had been exposed to the air. These tiny organisms were named " infusoria ", and the liquids in which they were generated were described as " putrescible ".

Pasteur set himself the task of showing that when all living

[1] See p. 398 n. below.

organisms are carefully excluded from contact with these liquids, no organisms appear in them, and that, consequently, there is no evidence in favour of the spontaneous generation of infusoria. He recorded his experimental investigation in a *Memoir* presented to the *Académie des Sciences* in 1862.[1] He began with an historical résumé of the position of the theory, from which the opening paragraphs are quoted below :

‘ In ancient times, and until the Middle Ages, every one believed in the occurrence of spontaneous generations. Aristotle says that animals are engendered by all dry things that become moist and all moist things that become dry.

‘ Van Helmont describes the way to bring mice into existence.

‘ Even in the seventeenth century, many authors give methods for producing frogs from the mud of marshes, or eels from river water.

‘ Such errors could not survive for long the spirit of investigation that arose in Europe in the sixteenth and seventeenth centuries.

‘ Redi . . . demonstrated that the worms in putrefying flesh were larvae from the eggs of flies. His proofs were as simple as they were decisive, for he showed that surrounding the putrefying flesh with fine gauze absolutely prevented the appearance of these larvae.’

These experiments were, as Pasteur says, very simple. Redi put gauze over the meat the smell of which came through the gauze and attracted flies. They laid eggs on the gauze ; from these eggs larvae were hatched that, had the gauze not been there, would have been hatched on the meat. Later another Italian scientist showed that the grub in fruit is hatched from eggs deposited by insects before the fruit has developed. Thus evidence was provided to account for some of the facts upon which the theory of spontaneous generation had been based, and which was now interpreted as being decisively against that theory. The discovery of the microscope, however, seemed to provide new support to the theory. As Pasteur goes on to say :

‘ But in the second part of the seventeenth and the first part of the eighteenth centuries, microscopic observations rapidly increased in number. The doctrine of spontaneous generation then reappeared. Some, unable to explain the origin of the varied organisms which the microscope showed in their infusions of animal or vegetable matter, and seeing nothing among them which resembled sexual reproduction, were obliged to assume that matter which has once lived keeps after its death, a special vital force, under the influence of which its scattered particles unite themselves afresh under certain favourable conditions with varieties of structure determined by these conditions.

---

[1] *Memoir on the organized corpuscles which exist in the atmosphere.* Extracts from this *Memoir* are given in *Cambridge Readings in the Literature of Science* by W. C. D. and M. D. Whetham. All quotations are taken from this work unless otherwise specified. My account of this investigation is drawn from this *Memoir* and from Vallery-Radot's *Life of Pasteur.* (Pasteur lived from 1823 to 1895.)

' Others on the contrary, used their imagination to extend the marvellous revelations of the microscope, and believed they saw males, females, and eggs among these Infusoria, and they consequently set themselves up as open adversaries of spontaneous generation.'

Pasteur adds : ' One must recognize that the proof in support of either of these opinions scarcely bore examination.' [1]

The problem which he had to solve was to account for the development of micro-organisms in putrescible liquids. Those who supported the hypothesis of spontaneous generation maintained that the minute organisms revealed by the microscope came spontaneously into being in any liquid, even though it had originally been quite free from any such organisms. The chief contemporary exponent of this theory, Pouchet, and his two students, Joly and Musset, in urging the theory of heterogenia or spontaneous generation asserted that ' they did not mean a creation out of nothing, but the production of a new organized being, lacking parents, and of which the primordial elements are drawn from ambient organic matter '.[2] To Pasteur this hypothesis appeared extremely unplausible. He wrote to Pouchet pointing out that no decisive evidence had been offered in favour of the theory. ' I think ', he said, ' you are wrong, not in believing in spontaneous generation (for it is difficult in such a case not to have a preconceived idea), but in affirming the existence of spontaneous generation. In experimental science it is always a mistake not to doubt when facts do not compel affirmation. . . . In my opinion, the question is whole and untouched by decisive proofs. What is there in air which provokes organization ? Are they germs ? is it a solid ? is it a gas ? is it a fluid ? is it a principle such as ozone ? All this is unknown and invites experiment '.[3] In this letter Pasteur reveals the scientific temper. It is necessary to be guided by an hypothesis ; but no hypothesis should be affirmed unless it is adequately supported by experimental evidence. He therefore set himself—as he explained in the *Memoir* setting out the fruits of his work—' to supply sure and decisive proofs, obliging non-prejudiced minds to reject all idea of the existence in the atmosphere of a more or less mysterious principle, gas, fluid, bone, etc., having the property of arousing life in infusions '.[4]

These ' sure and decisive proofs ' could, he saw clearly, only be provided by experiments so carefully conducted that all the conditions should be under control. In this way alone would it be possible to analyse out the factors that were involved. Pasteur was fully aware of the difficulty of performing decisive experiments. Writing to his father about the opposition of Pouchet and Joly, he said : ' They do not know how to experiment ; it is not an easy

---

[1] loc. cit., pp. 217–18.   [2] *Life of Pasteur*, I, p. 123.
[3] *ibid.*, p. 122.   [4] *Memoir*, p. 226.

from different places : from the laboratory cellars, from the city of Paris, from rural districts, from Alpine heights, and even from a glacier. The purer the air the less the concentration of atmospheric dusts. In every case he found that contact with purer air produced a less degree of putrescence. Thus Pasteur took the greatest care to vary as much as possible any condition that might seem relevant to the production of the effect that he was investigating. His experiments were carried on throughout a period of years and were so uniformly successful that he might well feel justified in regarding the result as conclusive. He had answered the question that he had proposed to himself, and which we have already quoted : "What is there in air which provokes organization ? " He had shown that it was not a gas, nor a fluid, nor a principle, such as " vital force ", but a germ.

What, we may ask at this point, had Pasteur actually established ? He had *not* shown that biogenesis is the only possible hypothesis to account for the existence of living organisms. But he had shown decisively that there was no evidence in favour of the spontaneous generation of micro-organisms in putrescible liquids. He had accounted for the appearance of such evidence by showing that it was due to the neglect of factors relevant to the production of the result. He had analysed out the factors involved and had shown that one factor, viz. *organized corpuscles closely resembling the germs of inferior organisms*, was *sufficient* to the production of the result, and *necessary* in all the cases investigated. Whenever this factor was present, then infusoria appeared ; whenever it was absent, the relevant conditions remaining the same, no such organisms were produced. He had destroyed the evidential basis of the theory of spontaneous generation, and had consequently shown not only that the hypothesis was unplausible but also that it was unfruitful. He had not shown, nor is it probable that he would have wished to claim that he had shown, that the synthetic production of living organisms in a laboratory is impossible. A further consequence of his investigation was that it laid the foundation of the modern science of bacteriology. In a significant statement in a report of his work, presented to the *Académie* in 1880, he said : ' What would be most desirable would be to push those studies far enough to prepare the road for a serious research into the origin of various diseases '.[1] It is well known that the result of Pasteur's work was to prepare the way for this further research. His experimental investigations led to generalizations with regard to the connexion between specific micro-organisms and specific diseases. It was the beginning of a systematic organization of a branch of knowledge.

An examination of Pasteur's investigation brings out several

---

[1] Quoted by Vallery-Radot, op. cit., I, p. 128.

points of the greatest significance with regard to experimental inquiry. It will be useful to sum these up here :

(1) The investigation must be determined by a question formulated with sufficient definiteness to guide the inquiry.

(2) The complex situation from which the investigator starts must be carefully analysed into its constituent factors.

(3) All the relevant conditions must be carefully noted and kept in mind throughout the course of the inquiry. Numerous examples could be given of erroneous results due to the neglect of some relevant factor. Previous investigators of the theory of spontaneous generation had frequently failed in this respect. For example, Needham —an English priest in the eighteenth century—claimed to have obtained infusoria in vases that had been filled with putrescible liquid, boiled, and then closed. But he had closed the vases with cork stoppers that are sufficiently porous to let micro-organisms through. A contemporary opponent, the Abbé Spallanza, repeated this experiment with greater care. He thus records the experiment : ' I used hermetically sealed vases. I kept them for an hour in boiling water, and after having opened them and examined their contents within a reasonable time I found not the slightest trace of animalculae, though I had examined with the microscope the infusoria from nineteen different vases.' [1]

(4) Relevant factors must be varied one at a time. This condition was observed by Pasteur when he prepared flasks differing only in the circumstance that dust could pass through the neck of one, but not of the other. [2]

(5) Those circumstances which are supposed to be irrelevant must be varied as much as possible in order to test whether they are in fact irrelevant. In accordance with this requirement Pasteur substituted a mineral filter (asbestos) for cotton.

(6) The utmost possible care must be taken not to *introduce* unnoticed factors that may be relevant to the result. Failure to observe condition (2) frequently leads to violation of this rule of experimental inquiry.

These rules state the conditions that must be observed in order that experiments may be performed in such a manner as to be decisive in scientific investigation. They may be summed up in the formula : Analysis of the given situation and control of the conditions so that every relevant factor can be varied one at

---

[1] Quoted by Vallery-Radot, I, p. 119.

[2] There was difference in one *relevant* circumstance. That this was an assumption must be granted. The flasks differed in their spatial position, in the time at which they were filled, and so on. But these factors were judged to be irrelevant. Under what conditions we are justified in making these judgements of irrelevance we shall discuss later.

of a single factor A from that situation is accompanied by the with-drawal of X, then A is causally connected with X ; and conversely, if in a complex situation X does not occur, and if A alone is intro-duced into that situation and X occurs, then A is causally connected with X.

IV. If in a complex situation containing both A and X, the factor X varies in some manner whenever A varies in some manner, then A is causally connected with X.

It is clear that the first special principle directs investigation in accordance with the fundamental principle that nothing that is absent when the effect occurs can be the cause of that effect. A well-known experiment of Newton's affords a good example. He wanted to ascertain whether all substances, notwithstanding their chemical constitution, are equally affected by gravitation. He had, then, to observe a situation in which one factor only was varied in each instance. The motion of a pendulum is conditioned by the resistance of the air, or other medium in which it swings. Newton accordingly made pendulums, the oscillations of which were to be compared, of ' equal boxes of wood, hanging by equal threads, and filled with different substances, so that the total weights should be equal and the centres of oscillation at the same distance from the points of suspension. Hence, the resistance of the air became approximately a matter of indifference ; for the outward size and shape of the pendulums being the same, the absolute force of resist-ance would be the same, so long as the pendulum vibrated with equal velocity ; and the weights being equal the resistance would diminish the velocity equally. Hence, if any inequality were ob-served in the vibrations of the two pendulums, it must arise from the only circumstance which was different, namely the chemical nature of the matter within the boxes. No inequality being observed, the chemical nature of substances can have no appreciable influence upon the force of gravitation '.[1] It is clear that in this experiment only one factor was varied ; the variation of this factor was not accompanied by any difference in the result, hence the given factor was not causally connected with the result. Newton's decision to vary this factor was due to the natural expectation that this factor might be causally connected with the given effect. In showing that it was not, Newton was reasoning in accordance with the first principle.

It is important to observe that this principle requires agreement in all the relevant factors but one, and is thus concerned with in-stances in which there is a *single difference*, throughout the instances of the causal occurrence and *no difference* in the effect. It is easy to confuse this principle with the principle called by Mill the principle

---

[1] Jevons, *Principles of Science*, p. 443.

of *agreement*, which we shall discuss in the next section. It is also easy to fall into the mistake of supposing that since what is not present when an effect occurs cannot be the cause, then what is present must be the cause. But a factor may be present and yet may not be the cause. Failure to recognize this fact has been the cause of hasty generalizations that are as ill-founded as many of the generalizations derived from simple enumeration. Thus the following pseudo-principle has often been assumed : If two occurrences constantly accompany each other they are probably causally connected. It may be admitted that constant conjunction may *suggest* a causal connexion, but no conclusion can be safely drawn until instances are found, or devised, which provide variation in one of the factors. The fallacy which such hasty generalization exemplifies is known as the fallacy of *post hoc ergo propter hoc*. Popular superstitions illustrate this fallacy, for example, that passing under a ladder brings ill-luck ; that looking at the new moon through glass is unlucky ; that if thirteen people sit together at a meal one of them will die within a short time ; that a journey taken on a Friday is unlucky, and so on. It is unlikely that *nothing* but the constant conjunction of the two occurrences enters into the reasoning. In the case of the last two superstitions it is probable that the origin can be traced to the Last Supper. But such superstitions linger on mainly because reliance is placed upon this pseudo-principle. Instances where the two occurrences are conjoined are noted ; instances where the conjunction fails are ignored. Everyone knows how hard it is to take heed of instances contrary to our prejudices ; we are prone to fail to *observe* negative instances. Darwin, who was aware of this danger, formed the habit of paying attention to instances unfavourable to his hypotheses. He says : ' I had also, during many years followed a golden rule, namely, that whenever a published fact, a new observation or thought came across me, which was opposed to my general results, to make a memorandum of it without fail and at once ; for I had found by experience that such facts and thoughts were far more apt to escape from the memory than favourable ones '.[1]

The second principle leads us to select sets of instances so related that one group contains in every set a certain fact A, and the second group, which is *in pari materia*, is such that no instance contains the factor A but every instance contains some of the other factors contained in the first group. The former group constitutes the set of *positive instances*, the latter the set of *negative instances*. If the positive instances are accompanied by X, and the negative instances are not, then, in accordance with the principle we can draw the conclusion that A is probably causally connected with X. This

[1] *Life and Letters*, ed. by F. Darwin, 1887, Vol. I, p. 87.

of scientific method, therefore, culminated in the formulation of four methods which he sometimes called the ' direct inductive methods ', sometimes the ' methods of experimental inquiry '. These " methods " resemble in some respects the four principles stated in the preceding section but, as we shall see later, Mill's conception of their function was different from ours. The " methods " as Mill stated them, have played an important part in the development of inductive logic during the period that has elapsed since the publication of his *System of Logic*. They have played a part—out of all proportion to their importance—in university examinations in elementary logic.[1] They have been both hotly espoused and derisively criticized. The student would be well advised to read Mill's own exposition of these methods.[2] The following discussion will make no attempt to make a reading of Mill's own statement superfluous.

Exponents of Mill's logical theory seem often to forget the motive that led him to write his *Logic*. Mill was primarily interested in the social sciences ; he was anxious to discover whether those methods which had been so signally successful in the natural sciences could be applied with equal success to the study of men in society. He accordingly set himself the task of carrying out a critical examination of the procedure which he believed to have been followed by scientists. There is but slight evidence for the not uncommon belief that Mill believed himself to be instructing the scientist how to perform his job. He studied the history of science and accounts of scientific investigation ; he prosecuted a *post-mortem* examination, and formulated the results in his celebrated " methods ". Mill was by no means the first logician to attempt to formulate methods of causal determination. The ' methods ' now called by Mill's name were indicated by Hume ; [3] something resembling them was stated fairly clearly by Bacon ; [4] whilst Herschel [5] formulated ' methods ' which are often taken to be equivalent to Mill's. But Mill did not only give a more elaborate and definite statement of the methods than those of his predecessors ; he approached the problem from a different point of view, since he sought to discover " methods of *proof* ". His exposition is not free from serious defects. His actual statements abound in absurdities. Nothing, however, would be gained by commenting upon any of these absurdities except those for the

---

[1] Cf. N. R. Campbell, *Physics : The Elements*, p. 89. ' These rules are termed by Mill the Canons of Induction, and there are few of us sufficiently fortunate as to have escaped encounter with them in the examination room.'

[2] See Bk. III, Chap. VIII. The student should also consult Mill's ninth chapter, in which he gives examples of the use of the methods. In the analysis of these examples many of the deficiencies of his exposition of the methods are corrected.

[3] *A Treatise of Human Nature*, Bk. I, Pt. III, § xv.

[4] *Novum Organum*.   [5] *Natural Philosophy.*

avoidance of which some care is necessary. One anomaly, which scarcely amounts to an absurdity, may be mentioned at the outset. Mill's chapter is entitled " *Four* Methods of Experimental Inquiry ". Yet he gives *five* methods—a point which exponents and critics alike seem to have overlooked. The inclusion of a fifth method would appear to have been an oversight due to his not having clearly decided what exactly a " method " was. We shall see the importance of this point later on. The fifth method, given in his exposition but excluded from the title of his chapter, would appear to be the one he gives *fourth* and calls the " Method of Residues ", not, as might have been expected, the one given fifth, nor, as is often supposed, the one given third and called the " Joint Method ". Certainly the " Method of Residues " is in no sense an *inductive* method, even in the sense in which Mill usually understood this phrase.

It is desirable to state Mill's " methods " in his own words. In explaining these " methods " Mill used letters to symbolize the factors in what we have called a causal situation, and which Mill would call the phenomenon under investigation.[1] These factors are called *antecedents* if they are factors in the cause-complex ; *consequents* if they are factors in the effect-complex ; the former are symbolized by capital letters, the latter by the corresponding small letters. As the use of symbols brings out clearly the assumptions upon which the analysis rests, a consideration of Mill's symbolism will enable us more easily to recognize the difficulties of his exposition. Mill begins by laying down two rules of experimental inquiry, which, indeed, follow from the fundamental principles that nothing which is absent when an occurrence happens can be the cause of that occurrence, and that nothing which is present when an occurrence fails to happen can be the cause of that occurrence. These rules are : (1) Compare different instances in which the phenomenon under investigation occurs ; (2) Compare instances in which the phenomenon occurs with instances in other respects similar in which it does not occur. From these two fundamental rules Mill's four " methods " are derived. Each " method " is formulated hypothetically in what Mill calls a " canon ".

STATEMENT OF MILL'S FOUR METHODS

1. *The Method of Agreement.*

Canon : ' If two or more instances of the phenomenon under investigation have only one circumstance in common, the circumstance in which alone all the instances agree is the cause (or effect) of the given phenomenon.'

---

[1] Mill uses " phenomenon " to include both what we have called an " occurrence " and what we should call a " property " or a set of properties.

that would have to be fulfilled in order that Mill's symbolism should adequately represent the procedure. These conditions are : (1) the total situation must be capable of being regarded as causally disconnected from other situations ; (2) the cause-factors must be in one-one correspondence with the factors in the effect-complex ; (3) one factor must be capable of being withdrawn (or added) without alteration of any other factor ; (4) there must be one, and only one, factor present in the one instance but absent from the other instance.
     The first condition is a condition of there being any causal uniformities. It is a matter of experience that there are such uniformities in apparent causal disconnexion from other occurrences. This disconnexion, however, may be only apparent. Factors either assumed to be irrelevant or totally unnoticed may be present. These factors should be represented by the symbolism. The second condition is certainly not usually fulfilled. It is indeed difficult to give any precise statement of what would constitute such a one-one correspondence between the two sets of factors. In giving *examples* Mill habitually ignored this condition. Hence, the first respect in which the symbolism must be emended is by the substitution of a *single* letter for the effect-occurrence. The third condition may be approximately realized but the fourth is realizable only if by " factor " we understand " *relevant* factor ".
     It is necessary, then, to substitute for $a\,b\,c$ the single letter E, and to add symbols representing the factors which, though present, are either unnoticed or are judged to be irrelevant. Since not all these factors would remain unaltered, their variation must be symbolized. The " method " may then be represented as follows :

$$A\,B\,C\,(x_1,\ x_2,\ x_3'\ldots) \rightarrow E\,(y_1,\ y_2\ldots)$$
$$B\,C\,(x_1',\ x_2',\ x_3''\ldots) \rightarrow E\,(y_1',\ y_2'\ldots)$$
$$A\underline{\qquad}E$$

The x's and y's in brackets symbolize factors only some of which will have remained unaltered ; the dots symbolize unnoticed factors, whilst the brackets indicate that whatever is contained within them is judged to be irrelevant. Similar modifications of Mill's symbolization must be made with regard to the other " methods " if the symbolism is to be in the least adequate. An attempt to symbolize the Joint Method along these lines may make clearer the nature of this " method " which Mill tried with singular lack of success to formulate in his third canon. His defective formulation of this canon results from the defects in his formulation of the canon of the " method of agreement ", for he regarded his third " method " as being a double application of the " method of agreement ". Hence the Joint Method is intended to apply to cases in which a set of instances agreeing *in the presence* of a given factor are to be compared with a set of instances agreeing *in the absence* of the same factor. Both in the first and third canons Mill states that the instances must agree ' in one circumstance only '. This is absurd even apart from the fact that no such instances could be found. Constant conjunction may be a sign of causal connexion when such conjunction occurs in situations having a good deal in common. But that this consideration represents only a part of what Mill had in mind when he formulated the " method of agreement " is shown by his statement that ' the method of agreement stands on the ground that whatever can be eliminated is not connected with the phenomenon by any law '.[1] This statement certainly suggests that the " method of agreement " should have been so formulated as to require a *single difference*, not a *single agreement*. Mill seems to have fallen into the mistake that we noticed on page 329. The condition that there must be a single *agreement* is too obviously absurd to require discussion, but it must be noticed that this absurdity is repeated in a more aggravated form in the third canon which requires the negative instances to have ' nothing in common ' except the absence of the factor in which the positive instances agree.[2] In spite of the canon, however, even Mill realized that the two sets of instances must be drawn from the same field of inquiry, and that the greater the resemblance between them in all the respects save one, the more plausible was the conclusion derived from them.[3] The negative instances must be such that they contain factors occurring in the positive instances, although these factors are not sufficient to produce the result. In this way the negative instances afford a means of *testing by exclusions*. Following the symbolism suggested for the " method " of difference, Mill's Joint Method could be symbolized as follows :

Positive Instances.

H B J A Y C K	$(x_1, x_2 \ldots)$	$\rightarrow$ E $(y_1, y_2 \ldots)$
H B A L C N	$(x_1', x_2 \ldots)$	$\rightarrow$ E $(y_1, y_2'' \ldots)$
H A R L Y K N P	$(x_1, x_2'' \ldots)$	$\rightarrow$ E $(y_1', y_2' \ldots)$
H J B Y N P	$(x_1'', x_2''' \ldots)$	$\rightarrow$ E $(y_1', y_2' \ldots)$
H Y L N O M P	$(x_1', x_2'' \ldots)$	$\rightarrow$ E $(y_1'', y_2''' \ldots)$
H A K P J O	$(x_1'' x_2''' \ldots)$	$\rightarrow$ E $(y_1''', y_2' \ldots)$

H——E

[1] loc. cit., § 3.

[2] Jevons' symbolization of the Joint Method is instructive since it precisely corresponds to Mill's formulation of the canon. He gives for the positive instances ABC, ADE, AFG, AHK, and for the negative instances PQ, RS, TV, XY. The absurdity of this procedure requires no comment. (See *Elementary Lessons in Logic*, Ch. XXVIII.)

[3] See *Logic*, Bk. III, Chap. IX, § 4. Mill's *example* here violates the condition that there should be ' nothing in common save the absence of that circumstance ', although in commenting upon the example he makes the *false* statement that there is agreement only in the one circumstance.

22

these factors cannot be relevant.   Such determination occurs at an
early stage of the investigation.   Proceeding in accordance with
the rule derived from Principle II, the investigator may be led to
suppose that there is some causal connexion since the omission of
a given factor from a set of circumstances having much in common
with instances in which the factor was present is followed by a
change in another factor.   Rule III is applicable only when an
investigator is dealing with a situation with regard to which he
has already formulated a definite hypothesis that two factors are
causally related.   It is further necessary that in this case he should
have such control of the situation that he can omit, or introduce into
it, a single factor.   By reasoning in accordance with Principle IV
the investigator may again be led to formulate an hypothesis concerning the causal relation of two definite factors.   The experimental
application of Rule IV will enable him to test such an hypothesis.
It seems clear, then, that the special principles and the rules derived
from them are relevant to different stages of a scientific investigation.

   We must now consider the relation of Mill's Four Methods to
the four special principles.   The Method of Difference clearly corresponds to Principle III and the Method of Concomitant Variations
to Principle IV, whilst the Joint Method resembles Principle II,
although the resemblance is far from exact owing to Mill's absurd
formulation of this Method.   The Method of Agreement, however,
does not correspond at all to Principle I, owing to Mill's failure to
see that what is required is a single *difference* and not a single *agreement*.   This Method, indeed, corresponds rather to Principle II than
to Principle I, since Principle II corresponds to some extent to the
Joint Method, and this Method is, as we have seen, a double application of the Method of Agreement.   Since Mill's Methods do correspond, although not exactly, to the four special Principles, and since,
as we have seen, these principles are relevant to different stages of
a causal investigation, it follows that Mill's Methods also are relevant
at different stages.   Mill, however, failed to see that this was the
case.   On the contrary, he believed his Methods to be *alternative*
modes of procedure each more or less complete in itself.   This
mistake was due to his failure to recognize that the Methods were
in fact not *methods* but *principles*.   That Mill was not at all clear
as to what he meant by a "method" is indicated by the fact that
he sometimes asserts that the Four Methods 'reduce' to two,
namely, the Method of Agreement and the Method of Difference.
He clearly intended to base these two Methods on the two fundamental principles of causal connexion, that *Nothing that is absent
when an effect occurs can be the cause of that effect*, and that, *Nothing
that is present when the effect fails to occur can be the cause of that
effect*.   These two principles are independent of each other ; the

four derivative special principles are independent of each other, but each or all conjointly may determine a given causal investigation. Mill, confusing " method " with principle, believed that there were four independent *methods*. It is clear, however, that neither of the two fundamental principles nor any of the four derivative special principles is *alone* sufficient to constitute a complete mode of procedure, that is, a *method*.

Mill's confusions do not end here. In his anxiety to provide models to which inductive arguments should conform he was led to suppose that his methods were identical with *rules* regulating scientific investigation, or, as he expressed it, ' contrivances for unravelling the web '. Thus he tried so to formulate his methods that they should be at the same time both canons, or rules regulating discovery, and methods.

Finally, Mill believed that his Methods were the only instruments of *proof*. We saw in Chapter XIV that Mill was aware that all empirical knowledge ultimately rests upon simple enumeration, that is, on pure induction combined with analogy. Thus he defines *induction* as ' the process by which we conclude that what is true of certain individuals of a class is true of the whole class, or that what is true at certain times will be true in similar circumstances at all times '.[1] But he did not himself recognize that such a definition of induction reduces it to simple enumeration. On the contrary, he sought, as we saw, to discover ' a surer and more potent instrument '. This instrument was, he believed, provided by the four Methods.

Much of the difficulty in Mill's conception of scientific method is due to the fact that he believed both of two mutually inconsistent propositions. He believed both that all our knowledge is derived in the last resort from simple enumeration, i.e. generalization from particular instances, and also that propositions thus derived were capable of being known to be certainly true.[2] Accordingly, he believed that general empirical propositions could be *proved*. He conceived proof to be strictly inductive. It must be remembered that Mill regarded deduction as consisting in the *interpretation* of inductions, the rules of the syllogism being rules for the process of interpretation. Although he admitted that induction must sometimes be combined with deduction owing to the complexity of the phenomena under investigation, he refused to admit that *every* scientific investigation must combine both deductive and inductive reasoning. Thus he says : ' If discoveries are ever made by observation and experiment, without Deduction, the four methods are methods of discovery : but even if they were not methods of discovery, it would not be the less true that they are the sole methods

---

[1] op. cit., Bk. III, Chap. II, § 1.   [2] Cf. Chap. XV, § 5 above.

of Proof ; and in that character, even the results of deduction are amenable to them.   The great generalizations which begin as Hypotheses must end by being proved, and are in reality proved, by the Four Methods '.[1]   In this statement can be found the explanation of Mill's attitude to what he calls the Hypothetical Method.   He refused to admit that hypothesis has an indispensable part to play in scientific method.   He accorded to hypothesis a subsidiary function in the process of discovery ;   he saw that a scientific theory would sometimes have been incapable of being established unless it had first appeared in the guise of an hypothesis.   But he believed that this state of affairs was exceptional, and he wholly misconceived the relation of his methods to hypotheses.   This misconception was due to his belief that scientific method is a process of establishing laws that can be known to be certainly true.   Mill saw that to *prove* an hypothesis it is necessary to show not only that the given hypothesis is consistent with the facts but also that *no* other hypothesis is consistent with them.   He believed that if the Method of Difference could be used to establish the negative instance, then the hypothesis could be so proved.   He gives as an example Newton's law of gravitation, and asserts that it was shown that no other hypothesis could accord with the facts, and that in consequence the ' hypothesis became an inductive truth '.[2]   It is unfortunate for Mill's theory that Einstein has succeeded Newton.   Mill's conception of the nature of a scientific theory was dependent upon his belief that the work of the scientist was to discover ' proved laws of nature '.   Hence, he concluded : ' It appears, then, to be a condition of the most genuinely scientific hypothesis that it be not destined always to remain an hypothesis, but be of such a nature as to be either proved, or disproved, by comparison with observed facts '.   With the aid of the law of universal causation and with the unrecognized assumption that the constituents of natural phenomena are finite in number and have the formal properties of the letters of the alphabet, Mill was able to see in the Method of Difference a ' complete method ' of establishing true and universal empirical propositions.   It was because the Method of Agree-

---

[1] op. cit., Bk. III, Chap. IX, § 6.

[2] *ibid.*, Chap. XIV, § 4.   It is in his controversy with Whewell with regard to the nature and function of the Methods that Mill showed most clearly his conception of the nature of Induction.   Thus in criticizing Whewell he says : ' If after assuming an hypothesis and carefully collating it with facts, nothing is brought to light inconsistent with it, that is, if experience does not *dis*prove it, he is content ; at least until a simpler hypothesis, equally consistent with experience, presents itself.   If this be Induction, doubtless there is no necessity for the Four Methods.   But to suppose that it is so appears to me a radical misconception of the nature of the evidence of physical truths.'   (Bk. III, Chap. IX, § 6.)

ment could not be relied upon to give certainty, owing to the possibility of a plurality of causes, that Mill regarded it as the least valuable of the Methods. Accordingly this Method must be reinforced by the addition of negative instances. This means that the Method of Agreement must be used twice over, or, in other words, we must substitute for it the Joint Method. Mill saw clearly that the superior value of the Joint Method consists in the fact that the negative instances enable us to eliminate possible causes. If this elimination is carried far enough only *one* possible cause will remain. It is this consideration that accounts for Mill's insistence that the negative instances must agree *only* in the absence of the supposed cause.[1] By this means Mill supposed that the danger of a plurality of causes would be avoided. But the most that this method could establish would be that *in a certain situation*, X is a necessary condition of E ; it could not suffice to show that in other situations, E would not be present unless X were. Mill also failed to observe that this result is secured only by the *combination* of two Methods which were intended to be complete and independent.

Neither the principle of the Method of Agreement nor the principle of the Joint Method is such that reasoning in accordance with it yields a certain conclusion. Nor does the Method of Difference, which is undoubtedly the most cogent of the Methods, avoid the difficulty of a plurality of causes. It is true that if in a situation A B C $\rightarrow$ X, the withdrawal of A is followed by the withdrawal of X, then it can be asserted that in *this* situation A is the cause of X. There may, however, be another situation D B C $\rightarrow$ X, such that the withdrawal of D is followed by the withdrawal of X, and in that case D is the cause of X. The possibility of a plurality of causes can be avoided only by increasing the negative analogy.[2] Just as Mill failed to grasp the importance of hypothesis in inductive investigation, so he failed to grasp the logical nature of analogy. This failure is responsible for the incompleteness of his analysis of scientific method, which hindered him from realizing that *none* of his methods were either complete or cogent.

[1] ' In the joint method, it is supposed not only that the instances in which *a* is, agree only in containing A, but also that the instances in which *a* is not, agree only in not containing A. Now, if this be so, A must be not only the cause of *a*, but the only possible cause ; for if there were another, as, for example, B, then in the instances in which *a* is not, B must have been absent as well as A, and it would not be true that these instances agree *only* in not containing A.' (Bk. III, Chap. X, § 2.)

[2] The assumption that the plurality of causes is only *apparent* is the assumption that a given occurrence E is caused by one and only one set of conditions which are both jointly sufficient and independently necessary for its occurrence, so that, if E appears to be caused on one occasion by C_1, and on another occasion by C_2, there must be a factor, or set of factors, common to C_1 and C_2. It is doubtful whether this assumption can be justified.

CHAPTER XVIII

DEDUCTIVE CAUSAL DETERMINATION AND FUNCTIONAL ANALYSIS

'There is a tradition of opposition between adherents of induction and of deduction. In my view it would be just as sensible for the two ends of a worm to quarrel.'—*A. N. Whitehead.*

§ 1. THE ANALYSIS OF COMPLEX EFFECTS

THE modes of causal determination discussed in the last chapter are appropriate to the investigation of the cause of an effect regarded as a single factor, e.g. the cracking of a glass, the appearance of micro-organisms in a liquid. Although such effects may be further analysable into constituent factors, for the purpose of the given investigation such analysis is not required. What was sought was an occurrence X so related to the given occurrence A that whenever X occurred, A occurred. We have now to consider the case of effects recognized as resulting from the combination of two, or more causes. The *combination of causes* must be distinguished from the *plurality of causes*. The latter, as we saw, means that the *same effect* is on one occasion the effect of X_1, on another occasion the effect of X_2, and so on. When two causes are combined neither alone could be properly said to be *the* cause of the given effect, since both are necessary for its occurrence. The effect is thus complex. Such effects may be of two kinds. Two causes X, Y, may combine in producing an effect similar in kind to the effect that X alone, or that Y alone, would have produced. For example, the combined effect of placing a cardboard box and some chocolates on a scale pan is similar in kind to the effect that would result from placing the cardboard box there alone. The combined effect of hitting a billiard ball simultaneously with two other balls is similar in kind to the effect that would have been produced by hitting it with one of them only. Such complex effects are said to be *homogeneous*. Mill, who described such cases under the name "homogeneous intermixture of effects", spoke of the "composition of causes". Mechanical phenomena provide the most striking examples, e.g. the theorem of the addition of velocities employed in classical mechanics. Thus a man walking along a train that is travelling at the rate of 60 miles an hour traverses a distance compounded of his own velocity and that of the train. In the second class of cases the combined effect is not similar in kind to the effect of the two causes acting separately. For example, the combination of the gas *chlorine* and the metal *sodium* is common salt, or sodium chloride. Such an effect was called by Mill " heteropathic ". Chemical compounds afford the most obvious examples.

Mill distinguished sharply between the methods required for dealing with combined effects and for dealing with simple effects. The latter he assumed to be capable of treatment by induction alone ; for the former he believed it necessary to appeal to deduction to ' unravel ' their complexity. But he misconceived the part played by inductive and deductive reasoning and assumed an absolute distinction between simple and compound effects that is not in fact tenable. The distinction between homogeneous and heteropathic effects which is of importance is that the former can be deduced from knowledge of the separate effects whereas the latter cannot. No knowledge of the properties of oxygen *alone* nor of the properties of hydrogen *alone* would enable us to deduce that their combination *under certain conditions* would result in a chemical compound having the properties known as *water*. It is for this reason that such properties are often called *emergent*. But the possibility of the deduction in the one case and its impossibility in the other may be merely the result of our ignorance. That Mill himself is not clear is shown by the fact that he speaks of oxygen and hydrogen as *the cause* of water. But oxygen and hydrogen may be mixed in a vessel and the resultant compound will have the properties both of oxygen and of hydrogen. In order that water may be produced the compound must somehow or other be fired. The fact that the compound chemical substance *pure water* can be analysed without residue into the two elements *oxygen* and *hydrogen* does not justify our saying that these two elements are *the cause* of water in any sense in which the word " cause " is commonly used. Mill himself recognized that the relation between water and its chemical components, H_2O, is different from the relation between, say, *being shot through the heart* and *dying*, since the former is a reciprocal relation, so that, as Mill expresses it, the effect and its cause are ' mutually convertible into each other '.[1]

We have now to consider the investigation of a complex situation the analysis of which has already been carried so far that we know that certain factors in the causal-occurrence determine certain factors in the effect-occurrence. Given that in such a situation we discover a residual factor in the effect-occurrence we seek for its cause ; if the residual factor be in the causal-occurrence we seek for its effect. A " residual factor " is a factor not yet taken into account

[1] *Logic*, Bk. III, Chap. X, § 4.

in a situation that is fairly well understood. Herschel expressed very clearly this mode of procedure, and its importance in scientific discovery :

'Complicated phenomena, in which several causes concurring, opposing, or quite independent of each other, operate at once, so as to produce a compound effect, may be simplified by subducting the effect of all the known causes, as well as the nature of the case permits, either by deductive reasoning or by appeal to experience, and thus leaving as it were a *residual phenomenon* to be explained. It is by this process, in fact, that science, in its present advanced state, is chiefly promoted. Most of the phenomena which nature presents are very complicated ; and when the effects of all known causes are estimated with exactness, and subducted, the residual facts are constantly appearing in the form of phenomena altogether new, and leading to the most important conclusions.' [1]

The most famous, and the simplest, example of this mode of causal determination is afforded by the discovery of the planet Neptune as the cause of an unexplained residual factor in the orbit of Uranus. The planet *Uranus* had been discovered by Herschel in 1781. It was subsequently found that *Uranus* had in fact been observed before but had been mistaken for a star. By reference to these earlier observations it was possible to determine its orbit although its period of revolution is eighty-four years. But the calculated orbit did not agree with the observed positions. It must be noted that the orbit of a planet is determined by the other bodies in the solar system. Newton had shown how, given these bodies and their positions and motions at any time, to deduce by mathematical calculation their positions and motions at any other time. When thus calculated the orbit of *Uranus* could not be accounted for by the known factors. Thus, to quote Sir Robert Ball, ' it was perfectly obvious that there must be some other influence at work besides that which could be attributed to the planets already known '. He adds : ' Astronomers could only recognize one solution of such a difficulty '. There must be some other planet. It was clear that such a planet was not visible to the naked eye, but it might be visible through a high-powered telescope. The difficulty was to know in what region of the heavens it was to be sought.[2] The French astronomer, Le Verrier, after many trials ' ascertained that, by assuming a certain size, shape, and position for the unknown planet's orbit, and a certain value for the mass of the hypothetical body, it would be possible to account for the observed disturbances of Uranus '. He was thus able to assign the region of the heavens

---

[1] *Natural Philosophy*, § 158.
[2] It is worth remarking that the error in the orbit of Uranus never exceeded 2′, a distance imperceptible to the ordinary eye, so that were the two stars side by side in the sky, one at the true position, one at the calculated position, these two stars would appear as one.

towards which the telescope should be directed. This being done, the planet was discovered, and subsequently named Neptune.[1]

An analysis of this discovery brings out several points of methodological importance. Representing the orbit of Uranus as the complex effect a, b, c, d, e, then the effect of the known bodies in the solar system, sun, planets, satellites, can be represented by a, b, c, d, leaving e as an unexplained residual effect. Since $a\,b\,c\,d\,e$ is a function of the known causes and some unknown cause it is possible to determine the unknown cause by subtracting the known causal factors. It is clear that such a procedure is essentially deductive ; it involves no generalization of instances but is wholly a mathematical calculation once the hypothesis, *The discrepancy is due to an unknown planet*, has been formulated. There is no justification for Mill's inclusion of such a process of deductive reasoning among his " Inductive Methods ". The so-called " Method of Residues " is a process of conjecturing a cause from the examination of a situation containing a single unexplained residual phenomenon. As stated by Mill this method involves an application of the principle of difference *from* effect *to* cause. Thus, given that the effect A is known to be accounted for by X, and that X has its full effect in A, then, if A occurs in conjunction with B, it follows from the principle of difference that something other than X is the cause of B.

It must not be supposed that this method is confined to the region of mathematical calculation. It is exemplified in the discovery of the cause of any residual phenomenon. For example, ' Arago, having suspended a magnetic needle by a silk thread, and set it in vibration, observed that it came much sooner to rest when suspended over a plate of copper, than when no such plate was beneath it '. This effect might have been due to the resistance of the air and the nature of the thread ; but ' the effect of these causes being exactly known by the observation made in the absence of the copper, and being thus allowed for and subducted, a *residual* phenomenon appeared in the fact that a retarding influence was exerted by the copper itself '.[2] This discovery is given by Herschel as an example of the method of residues. It is obvious in this case that the induction consists in an application of the principle of difference. There seems, indeed, no justification for distinguishing the " method of residues " from the procedure of the hypothetical

---

[1] The quotations are from Sir Robert Ball's *Great Astronomers* (section on *Le Verrier*). The English astronomer, Adams, also calculated the position of Neptune but no telescopic search was made for it by English astronomers until after it had been detected by Dr. Galle of Berlin, who was directed by Le Verrier's computation. A full account of this remarkable discovery cannot be given here. It has been related very fully in many popular works on astronomy.

[2] Herschel : *Natural Philosophy*.

method. The element of hypothesis is *less obvious* in such cases than in the case of an experimental investigation such as that of Pasteur discussed in the previous chapter but it is none the less present. The difference between these two cases is wholly due to the fact that the investigation of residual phenomena cannot take place until the situation as a whole has been very thoroughly analysed. Mill's formulation of the canon of the " Method of Residues " bring this out very clearly : ' Subduct from any phenomenon such part as is known by previous inductions to be the effect of certain antecedents, and the residue of the phenomenon is the effect of the remaining antecedents '. It is here assumed that the remaining antecedents are known. In the case of the discovery of Neptune the " remaining antecedent " was conjectured to be of such a kind as was familiar to astronomers ; in the case of Arago's experiment the " remaining antecedent " was an observed factor.

The discovery of the compound effect of causes acting conjointly is not fundamentally different. If it be known that a cardboard box weighs 3 oz. and a quantity of chocolate inside the box weighs 1 lb., then the compound effect of these two quantities is 1 lb. 3 oz. Conversely, given that the total weight is 1 lb. 3 oz. and it is known that the box weighs 3 oz., then the weight of the chocolate can be deduced by subtraction. Mill, however, distinguishes these two processes, confining the latter to the " Method of Residues ", the former to a special method which he calls " the Deductive Method ". He says, ' The problem of the Deductive Method is to find the law of an effect from the laws of the different tendencies of which it is the joint result '.[1] He divides the method into three steps : (1) ascertaining the laws of the several causes ; (2) computing their conjoint effect ; (3) verifying the computation by appeal to experience. It is clear that the discovery of the orbit of Uranus might have followed this method had the causes in operation all been known. Since, however, the orbit had been calculated from observations, the second step was accomplished before *all* the causes had been ascertained. Consequently, there was required a preliminary step, viz. conjecturing an unknown cause. An example often given to illustrate Mill's Deductive Method brings out very clearly its relation to the Method of Residues, viz. *the parallelogram of forces*. This may be stated as follows :

Given a force X capable of carrying a particle P, from A to C, and a force Y capable of carrying P from A to B ; the problem is to compute the conjoint effect of X and Y upon P. It is clear that the effect is a compound homogeneous effect, and that, consequently, *provided no other forces intervene*, the final result will be the same

[1] op. cit., Bk III, Chap. XI, § 1.

whether X and Y operate in succession or simultaneously. The solution is simple. It is given in the diagram, and the reasoning can be left to the reader's intelligence.

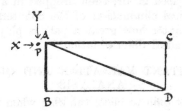

It is to be observed that, *given the conjoint effect AD and the effect of Y*, viz. AB, then the cause of the residual effect, viz. the difference between AD and AB, can be deduced, viz. AC, as the effect of the unknown X; *given the separate effects AB, AC*, then the conjoint effect AD can be deduced. In both cases the logical process is deductive. The former case is an example of precisely the same kind as the example of the discovery of Neptune; they differ only in complexity. If the forces X, Y, are equal and opposite in direction, then their simultaneous operation upon P would result in P's being in equilibrium. In such a case X is said to be counteracted by Y. Counteraction, however, is only a mode of combination having for its resultant in this case the maintenance of equilibrium. In dealing with the combination of causes it is important to take account of all the circumstances. For instance, if a tank be fitted with two taps, it might be supposed that the effect of turning on both at once would be equivalent to the sum of their separate effects. This would not be the case if both taps were supplied from the same source, so that when both were on the water flowed more slowly through the pipes. Mill rightly insisted that what he called the "laws of the separate causes" must be expressed as "tendencies", since any law is liable to be counteracted. The notion of counteraction is a survival of the activity view of causation. X *counteracts* Y when Y is what we wanted or expected to produce; every causal law has its full effect whether in isolation or in combination with other causal laws.[1] Causal laws are statements of uniformities; there are no exceptions to such uniformities but a mistake in the statement of the uniformity may lead to the disappointment of our expectations.

The separate tendencies of combined causes can sometimes only be distinguished in thought. For instance, the motion of a cannon ball can be analysed into the conjoint effect of a tendency to travel in a straight line in the direction of its discharge and a tendency

[1] Cf. Mill, Chap. X, § 5.

by applying it more precisely and systematically in accordance with the principle of convergence to simplicity with diminution of extent. By this means common-sense analysis is replaced by functional analysis.

The simplest examples of functional analysis can be expressed in conformity with Mill's canon of the Method of Concomitant Variations.[1] A rough and ready application of the canon might have been made in Pasteur's experimental investigation discussed in the last chapter. The purer the air he admitted into the sterilized liquids the fewer the micro-organisms found in the liquids. But it is clear that the variation was not capable of precise expression. It would be necessary, first, that the exact quantity of dust per cubic foot of the atmosphere in each place should have been determined ; secondly, that there should have been an exact correlation between the quantity of dust introduced into the liquids and the number of micro-organisms developed in the liquids. It is unlikely that these conditions should be fulfilled. Nor was this necessary for the purpose of Pasteur's investigation ; he sought a *cause*, not a *functional correlation*. In the more precise use of the method the notion of functional dependence replaces the notion of causal connexion. It is this notion that we must now examine.

X is said to be a function of Y when variation in X is correlated with variation in Y according to a rule. That is to say X and Y are variables that can assume different values. X is said to be the independent variable, since change in X determines change in Y ; the latter is consequently called the dependent variable. For example, the length of the circumference of a circle is a function of its radius ; the expansion of mercury is a function of its temperature ; the density of a gas is a function of its volume and pressure. In the last example there are two independent variables, the volume and the temperature, whose values must be determined in order that the value of the dependent variable, the density, may be determined. The income tax a man has to pay is a function of the amount of his income. It is not, however, a continuous function since it is subject to jumps. Nevertheless the amount of tax payable is correlated according to a rule with the amount of income. This notion of functional dependence is, then, one with which we are perfectly familiar. But we cannot use it precisely until the values for the variables are precisely determined and can be stated in terms of a repeatable unit. We must be able to replace such qualitative conceptions as *heavy, hotter*, by exactly determined units which enable us to say *how much weight, how much heat*, and so on. We must be able to express the relations between ice, water, steam in statements involving no reference to the qualitative properties of these

[1] op. cit., Chap. VIII.

different substances. The qualitative uniformity *Heavy bodies fall to the ground* is defective for the purposes of science in two respects : it is expressed in terms of the vague notion *heaviness*, and the connexion between *heaviness* and *falling to the ground* is left unexplained. This emphasis on qualitative aspects led to the belief that heavy bodies *naturally* fall, light bodies *naturally* rise, so that heavy bodies were believed to fall faster than lighter ones. This belief was explained on the assumption that the natural place of a stone, for instance, was the earth ; hence, a stone held in the hand will, when released, fall downwards to its natural place, the more rapidly in proportion to its weight. Every one now knows that this belief is mistaken. It has some empirical evidence in its favour since a body A that is bulky and lighter in weight than B will offer less resistance to the air and in consequence will fall more slowly than B. Thus, for instance, if a piece of notepaper and a penny be dropped from the same height the penny will reach the ground first. If, however, Aristotle and his supporters had attempted to determine *how* fast bodies fall they would have discovered their mistake.

It is worth while to consider a little more fully what was involved in the advance from the qualitative uniformity to the functional statement which expresses the law of freely falling bodies.[1] Galileo began by discovering a contradiction in the Aristotelian theory. If two bodies differing in weight be taken then, if bodies fall in proportion to their weight, it can be shown that the heavier body will fall more slowly than the lighter. That is to say, the theory is self-contradictory. The heavier body may be considered as made up of several bodies A_1, A_2, A_3, A_4, of which $A_1 A_2 A_3$ are together equal in weight to the lighter body B. Since A_1, A_2, A_3 are equal in weight to B they will fall at the same rate as B, but A_4 will fall more slowly. Hence the body composed of $A_1 A_2 A_3 A_4$ will fall more slowly than B, since A_4 will retard the motion. This is a contradiction.[2] Accordingly Galileo resorted to experiment. Every

---

[1] Cf. Chap. XVI, p. 303 above.

[2] Galileo's own statement of his reasoning is so admirably clear and affords such an excellent example of method that it is worth quoting in full:

'*Salv.* [i.e. Galileo]. It is possible to prove clearly, by means of a short and conclusive argument, that a heavier body does not move more rapidly than a lighter one provided that both bodies are of the same material and in short such as those mentioned by Aristotle. But tell me, Simplicio, whether you admit that each falling body acquires a definite speed fixed by nature, a velocity which cannot be increased or diminished except by the use of force or resistance.

Simp. [i.e. the *Aristotelian*]. There can be no doubt but that one and the same body moving in a single medium has a fixed velocity determined by nature and which cannot be increased except by the addition of momentum [impeto] or diminished except by some resistance which retards it.

Salv. If then we take two bodies whose natural speeds are different, it is

23

analysis. By means of such analysis we are enabled to employ the notion of functional correspondence between two or more factors. We are thus able to state their exact relationship. When a variation in X determines an exact variation in Y, there is a functional dependence of Y upon X. Thus we saw that the rate of fall of a freely falling body is an exact function of the time it has been falling from rest. In other words its acceleration is constant. Given a value of the variable time we can determine precisely a corresponding value of the variable velocity. This functional correspondence replaces, we saw, the less precise notion of a causal connexion. The notion of functional dependence is of the highest importance in mathematics. Upon its use depends to a very considerable extent the rapid advance of the physical sciences. It may be said that every scientific problem involves an attempt to determine the relationship between variables. A variable, it will be remembered, represents any one of a set of values. The precise statement of a functional relation between variables presupposes that the values for the variables have been measured in terms of some unit of measurement. The physical sciences are largely concerned with measurement, so that these sciences can employ the method of functional analysis. Consequently, physical laws are exact and invariable.

We have now to inquire whether this extremely fruitful method of functional analysis can be employed in dealing with occurrences that are usually but not always connected. In the biological and social sciences we are concerned with factors whose correlation is not perfect. For example, there is not a constant relation between a man's height and his weight, or between his income and the rent he pays for his house ; there is not a constant relation between the intelligence and the age of children ; there is not a constant relation between the month of the year and the rainfall in that month in a given place, say London. Usually, the taller a person is the more he weighs ; but there are stout, short people and tall, slender people. A very rich man is likely to have a larger house and to pay more rent for it than a comparatively poor man, but the variation in size of income will not exactly correspond to variation in size and rent of the house occupied. Again, a house in County Donegal will probably be of a lower rent than a house of approximately equal size and convenience in Sussex, and a house in the village of Midhurst than in the town of Brighton. In using the expression " will probably be ", we are suggesting that there is some correlation between the locality of a house and its rent but that the correlation is not exact. A great many factors contribute to determine the rent of a given house. Now, the economist may want to determine the relation between density of population and urban rent. In studying this problem he will not be able to set to work in the manner of the physicist. He will not be able to isolate the relevant from the irrelevant factors ; nor even to ascertain precisely what factors are irrelevant. He cannot physically remove a factor and then observe what happens. The physicist, however, can to a very considerable extent exclude those factors with the effect of which he is not at the moment concerned. Thus he is able to perform controlled and repeatable experiments, as Galileo did in the case of his falling balls. The economist has to deal with a complicated situation. He will recognize the relevance of such factors as respectability of the district, facilities of transport, amount of open spaces in the neighbourhood, elevation of the ground, the number of people desiring to live in the district. He must, therefore, obtain records of different urban districts with different densities of population in order to determine whether there is any degree of correlation between these two factors. The methods that have been devised for dealing with such problems are the statistical methods.[1] By means of these methods it is possible to deal with complex situations that are capable of division into distinct factors between which uniform connexions cannot be directly ascertained, and with the variations between characteristics whose correlation is not perfect.

Occurrences which at first sight would appear to be disconnected may be found to have some degree of relationship, whilst others that might have been expected to vary together may be found to be but slightly dependent upon each other. Thus, for example, we may wish to ascertain whether there is any apparent degree of correspondence between the number of marriages in a society and the output of the harvest. Such an investigation must deal with these two items over a series of years. The collection of the statistical data in such problems is often extremely laborious. Further, it is necessary to devise methods by means of which these items can be correlated.

We must now very briefly consider the nature of the quantitative investigation of the data required for methods of correlation. It will be sufficient to consider an extremely simple example. Suppose a parent receives a school report on his daughter's work during her first term at the school, in which marks are assigned for the terminal examinations. If she has 65 per cent. for *History*, how is he to tell whether that mark is a *good* mark, or not ? He will need to know its relation to marks gained by other girls in the same class.

[1] Statistical methods play such an important part in the investigations of the social sciences that it is not desirable wholly to omit them in a discussion of scientific method. But it is not possible to discuss these methods in detail in such a book as this. I shall attempt only to indicate the logical nature of statistical methods and to illustrate their use. The student should refer to some of the many excellent manuals on statistical methods given in the bibliography.

If he is told that 65 per cent. is an average mark, he will probably be satisfied ; he will feel that he knows his daughter's ability with regard to the rest of her class. The conception of an average is familiar. Thus we speak of the average rainfall of a district. We say that the climate of a country is its average weather. We speak of the average number of passengers, carried *per diem* on the Metropolitan Railway. We have now to consider what exactly an average is, and what is its use in statistical investigation. It will be best to begin with an example.

Take the following set of marks gained by ten children in a school test : 66, 44, 55, 20, 36, 52, 51, 62, 22, 30. The average is determined by adding all the marks and dividing the sum by the number of separate scores. The average mark is, then, 43·8. This average is known as the *mean*. There are other forms of average, which we shall consider in a moment. It should be noticed that in this case no number in the set coincides with the average mark. This is usually the case. Whether or not there is a number which is the average number is unimportant. An average is a single number representing a whole set of numbers. What it represents is the *central tendency* of the set. If the marks had been 71, 42, 36, 58, 41, 50, 57, 12, 18, 53 the average mark would again be 43·8. But the two sets of marks differ with regard to the number of marks above and below the average. Also the difference between the highest and lowest mark gained is greater in the second case than in the first. The low marks pull down the average. This metaphor is instructive. Suppose we had a ruler, and weights representing the number of scores in a given interval placed appropriately on the ruler (e.g. the three scores between 50 and 59 placed at the 50 mark as weight 3), then the balancing point of the ruler would be at the mean. The lowest mark would be furthest from the fulcrum on the one side, the highest mark would be furthest from the fulcrum on the other side. The further a weight of the same size is placed from the fulcrum, the more it tips up the balance. This illustration may show how it is that a low mark pulls down the average, and a high mark pulls it up. Smaller variations near the central tendency have less effect in determining the mean. We can describe the difference in the distribution of the marks in the two sets by stating the deviation of each mark from the average. These deviations are called " errors ", that is " wanderings away from " the average.

Another form of average is the *median*. This is the middle number of a series of numbers arranged in order of magnitude. If the series has an even number of members, then the number midway between the two nearest the middle is the median. This can be illustrated from the two sets of marks already given. We shall rearrange them in order of magnitude, naming the first set A, the second set B, for convenience of reference.

  (A) 66, 62, 55, 52, 51, 44, 36, 30, 22, 20.
  (B) 71, 58, 57, 53, 50, 42, 41, 36, 18, 12.

  In (A) the median is midway between 51 and 44. It is, therefore, 47·5.
  In (B) the median is midway between 50 and 42. It is, therefore, 46.

  The median in (B) is nearer the average than the median in (A), owing to the fact that in (B) there are five marks below, and five above the average ; whereas in (A) there are four below and six above.

  If we want to determine whether, say 62, is a high mark, or a low mark, we need to know how many in the set are above 62, and how many below it. The mark taken in isolation has very little significance. For example, in some universities the pass-mark for the final examination is 60 per cent., in others it is $33\frac{1}{3}$ per cent. A comparison of the mark sheets, giving only totals, of the two university examinations might suggest that one set of students were much better than the other set, unless this difference of standard were taken into account. In statistical investigation it is essential to classify the data at the outset in order that the numerical results should be significant. Neglect of this precaution is no doubt responsible for the popular belief that " you can prove anything by statistics ", which—as is often the case with popular fallacies—is counterbalanced by the belief that " figures never lie ".

  The first step in classifying the data is to ascertain what is called the *frequency distribution*, that is the frequency of the occurrence of a given item. For this purpose we must divide the items into classes. For example, in the illustration of the marks, we can classify the marks in tens, putting together all those between 10 and 19, 20 and 29, and so on. These divisions are called *class intervals*. The frequency distribution can be conveniently exhibited in a frequency table (see p. 360).

  The table is constructed by making a separate row for each class interval. A cross is put for each mark falling in a given class interval. The number in the third column is the frequency of occurrence in the given class interval. Comparing series A with series B we can see at a glance that the members of A deviate less from the central tendency than the members of B. In a case as simple as our illustration it would never be necessary to prepare a frequency table. But when we are dealing with hundreds of items, not arranged in any order, such a table is a great help. But it is not necessary for our purpose to consider complicated examples.

Series A			Series B		
Mark	Tabulation	Frequency	Mark	Tabulation	Frequency
0– 9			0– 9		
10–19			10–19	× ×	2
20–29	× ×	2	20–29		
30–39	× ×	2	30–39	×	1
40–49	×	1	40–49	× ×	2
50–59	× × ×	3	50–59	× × × ×	4
60–69	× ×	2	60–69		
70–79			70–79	×	1
80–89			80–89		
90–99			90–99		

The difference between the maximum and minimum mark gained is called *the range* of the series. Thus the range of (A) is 46 ; the range of (B) is 59. The range is a measure of variability. The items in (B) are said to *scatter* more than the items in (A), that is to say, there are greater deviations from the mean.

If, now, we consider the class frequency, we see that in both series the greatest frequency occurs in the class interval 50–59. The mid-point of the class interval with the greatest frequency is called the *mode*. This is another form of average, that is, a measure of central tendency. The mode represents that mark which is most likely to occur. It must not be confused with the mean, which is what we usually understand by an average. This point can be well illustrated by cricket scores. Suppose a cricketer who often makes 0, makes, once he has " got his eye in ", say, 70, or 80, or even a century, then his most likely score will be 0, but his average may be 20, or 30. If the deviations are small, so that small deviations are as likely to occur as large deviations, then the mode, the mean, and the median, tend to coincide.[1]

Since the range depends only upon the two extreme members, it is not a very satisfactory measure of variability. Hence, it is usual to calculate what is called the *mean deviation*. If we arrange the members of series (A) about the central tendency, we can obtain the deviation of any member by subtracting it from the mean, if it is less, and by subtracting the mean from it, if it is greater. These deviations will be represented by + and − signs. Thus we get :

[1] See W. P. and E. M. Elderton : *Primer of Statistics*, pp. 21 and 45.

—23·8; —21·8; —13·8; —7·8; +·2; +7·2; +8·2; +11·2; +18·2; +22·2.

The mean deviation will, then, be 13·44. This is simply the average of the deviations, neglecting the sign. In the same way we can calculate the mean deviation of series (B). It is 14. Statisticians generally use what is called the *standard deviation*. This is the square root of the sum of the squared deviations divided by the number of items. Hence, it differs from the mean deviation in that the deviations are squared before being summed, and after the division of the sum by the number of items the square root is extracted. The standard deviation is symbolized by σ. It can be expressed in the formula,

$$\sigma = \sqrt{\frac{\Sigma d^2}{n}},$$

where d represents deviations from the mean, and Σ means " the sum of " ; n represents the number of items. The standard deviation is generally used. If the deviation is large it shows that the members of the series are scattered.

We can now sum up the three forms of average : The mean is the ordinary average. It is usually easily calculated.

The median is the middle of the series when the series has been arranged in order. Hence, it is such that there are as many items above as below it. It is important not to suppose that the median is the middle of the range. This will be the case only when the frequency distribution is symmetrical.

The mode is the most likely case.

It is important to remember that every average is a measure of central tendency, and thus represents a point on a scale. Thus a frequency distribution can be graphically represented by a curve obtained by plotting the frequencies of the class intervals on the class scale. This is undoubtedly the simplest method of dealing with large numbers of cases. But it cannot be pursued here.[1]

We have now to consider the relation between measured variables. If the economist wishes to determine whether there is a relation between urban rent and density of population, he must first obtain statistics relating to these variables. He must then ascertain whether increase of the values of one variable is accompanied by increase, or decrease, of the other variable. From the examples given at the beginning of the section, we may see that *correlation* means degree of functional relationship. If the correlation between two variables is perfect, then there is between them a relation of

[1] For further discussion of statistical methods see the books given in the bibliography.

functional correspondence. It is usual to confine the word " correlation " to imperfect correspondence. Thus the correlation between
the velocity of a falling body and the time being perfect is called
a relation of functional correspondence. This relation is *positive* ;
the longer the body has been falling, the faster it is falling. The
relation between the gravitative attraction of two bodies and the
distance between their centres is perfect and negative. The degree
of correlation is expressed by a number varying from + 1 to − 1.
Thus a perfect positive correlation would be expressed by + 1 ; a
perfect negative correlation would be expressed by − 1. These are
functional relations. Hence, we may say that degree of correlation
varies from + ·99 to − ·99. This number is called the *coefficient
of correlation*. It is important to remember that this coefficient is
a pure number ; it does not represent a *per cent*. A correlation of
+ ·5 is called " five tenths " or " fifty ". It is *not* fifty *per cent*.
It represents a degree of correlation half-way between a perfect
correlation, or functional relationship, and an *entire absence* of correlation. An entire absence of correlation is not, for instance, a
negative correlation ; it simply is *absence* of correlation. For example, there is a negative correlation between pressure and volume
of a gas at constant temperature ; there is entire absence of correlation between the size of a man's head and the size of his income.
There is, perhaps, a slight positive correlation between the size of
a man's *earned* income and his ability in some direction.

A high degree, positive or negative, of correlation suggests a
causal, or a functional relation. For example, if there were a high
degree of positive correlation between the number of breakages
made by Lyons' waitresses and the amount of their fatigue, it
would seem not unlikely that fatigue is a factor in causing the
breakages.

In order that correlation coefficients should be obtained, i.e. that
the correlation of variables should be measured, it is essential to
find a quantitative unit *in terms of which* the variables can be
measured. In the case of what are called vital statistics, viz. those
relating to births, deaths, marriages, etc., the unit is easy to discover.
But statistical methods are being increasingly used to deal with
characteristics that cannot easily be apprehended as quantitative
variables. The statistics of the results of mental tests are based
upon the assumption that *intelligence, memory, rapidity of thinking*,
can be measured in quantitative terms. The initial work of ascertaining the quantitative units suitable for measuring the variables
requires the greatest insight and skill. Until it has been adequately
accomplished it is unlikely that experimental psychology will make
considerable advance in presenting interpretable results. It is,
again, of fundamental importance in statistical work to determine

precisely the field within which the measurements are supposed to hold. Unless this is carefully done the interpretation of the results, which is the most difficult part of statistical investigation, is likely to be misleading and even completely valueless. For example, recently two London newspapers undertook to investigate the question whether religious belief was on the decline. A questionnaire was printed in each of the papers which the readers were invited to answer. A statistical summary of the answers received was published, and upon this some dubious reasoning with regard to the decline of religious belief has been based. The difficulties in the way of reaching a reliable inference from such results should be obvious. Even if it were granted that the questions were so framed as to permit of precise and enlightening answers, no attempt seems to have been made to check the results or to determine the field of the investigation. It is not unreasonable to suppose that only a certain type of reader would answer the questionnaire, so that generalizations with regard to *all* the readers are extremely unreliable. Results thus obtained are not capable of precise interpretation owing to this failure precisely to delimit the field of the investigation. The only way to prevent such mistakes is to describe carefully what exactly the statistical investigation is intended to accomplish. The exact nature of the questions asked should be stated ; the field over which the investigation has been carried out should be precisely delimited. Only when this has been accomplished is it possible to draw reliable inferences and to interpret the results fruitfully. This preliminary work is often very difficult, involving complicated and technical methods. Consequently, there is a not unnatural tendency to overestimate the importance and the reliability of the statistical results thus obtained. As Professor Whitehead has pointed out, ' there is no more common error than to assume that, because prolonged and accurate mathematical calculations have been made, the application of the result to some fact of nature is absolutely certain '.[1] The *statement* of the correlations is not itself an inductive procedure ; inductive inference enters only when there is generalization from the observed correlations to unobserved instances. Mr. J. M. Keynes has pointed out the necessity of distinguishing between these two parts of the theory of statistics. He says : ' The first function of the theory is purely *descriptive*. It devises numerical and diagrammatic methods by which certain salient characteristics of large groups of phenomena can be briefly described ; and it provides formulae by the aid of which we can measure or summarize the variations in some particular character which we have observed over a long series of events or instances. The second function of

[1] *Introduction to Mathematics,* p. 27.

the theory is *inductive*. It seeks to extend its description of certain characteristics of observed events to the corresponding characteristics of other events which have not been observed. This part of the subject may be called the Theory of Statistical Inference '.[1] The development of the second part is difficult and is bound up with the theory of probability. This cannot be discussed here. All that we are concerned to point out is that the statement of a statistical frequency cannot be regarded as an inductive generalization. The way in which generalizations may be derived from statistical frequencies is by means of probability frequencies. This raises difficult problems the discussion of which would involve a greater amount of mathematics than can be introduced in such a book as this.

§ 4. PROBABILITY

It may be assumed that every one has a rough conception of the meaning of " probability ". We oppose it on the one hand to *certainty*, on the other to *impossibility*. Thus, for example, we say that it will probably rain to-day, or that A will probably fail to pass his examination, and so on. But as thus used, probability is not a clear conception, it merely indicates lack of entire conviction that something will, or will not, happen. In mathematics probability can be exactly defined. The theory of probability has been worked out in an elaborate manner. In so far, however, as the theory is logically exact, it is a branch of mathematics, and is thus no more suitable for discussion in an introductory book on logic than is the theory of complex numbers. But it may be worth while to indicate what is meant by the calculation of probabilities.

If in ordinary discussion we say " The occurrence E will probably happen ", we mean that there are stronger reasons for supposing that it will happen than for supposing that it will not. We recognize that an occurrence may be more, or less, probable. There are all degrees of probability between the certainty that E will not happen and the certainty that it will. If we want to state exactly *how* probable its occurrence is, we must count the number of reasons favourable to the production of E, and the number of reasons that are unfavourable and can therefore be offered against the occurrence of E. To count the reasons for and against means to analyse the situation so as to determine what factors are favourable and what are not favourable. It is natural to represent the probability of the occurrence of E as the ratio of the favourable factors to the unfavourable together with the favourable factors. Thus certainty will be represented by 1, impossibility by 0. If the favourable factors are represented by r and the unfavourable factors by r', then the probability

[1] *A Treatise on Probability*, p. 327.

will be represented by $\dfrac{r}{r + r'}$. The odds *in favour* of its happening

is then represented by $\dfrac{r}{r'}$; the odds *against* by $\dfrac{r'}{r}$.

Since E will either happen or not happen, the sum of the probability of its happening and the probability of its not happening must be 1. That is $1 = E + E'$ (where E' expresses " not-E "). Consequently, if p represents the probability that E will happen, then $1 - p$ represents the probability that E will not happen.

The principles involved in the calculation of probabilities may be made clear by means of very simple examples. We select the familiar problem of throwing dice, since the factors involved are simple and can be easily counted.

(i) What is the probability that, if one die be thrown, *six* will turn up ?

It is clear that there are six ways in which a die may fall, and that it must fall in one or other of these six ways. Of these, one is favourable, five are not. Hence the required probability is $\frac{1}{6}$.

(ii) What is the probability that, if one die be thrown, *six* will not turn up ?

The required probability is clearly $\frac{5}{6}$.

(iii) What is the probability that, if two dice are thrown together, both will turn up *six* ?

Since each die has six faces, and since each of these faces may turn up with any one of the six faces of the other die, there are clearly thirty-six possible combinations. Only one of these combinations is favourable. Hence the required probability is $\frac{1}{36}$.

The probability of getting *six* with one die is clearly not dependent upon the probability of getting *six* with the other. Such events are called *independent*. The probability that both will happen is the conjunction of their separate probabilities, viz. $(\frac{1}{6} \times \frac{1}{6}) = \frac{1}{36}$. Thus we obtain the rule for calculating the conjoint probability of two, or more, independent events, as follows : *Multiply their separate probabilities*.

(iv) What is the probability that of two dice thrown together neither will turn up *six* ?

These are clearly independent events. The probability of getting not *six* is in each case $\frac{5}{6}$. Hence, the required probability is $(\frac{5}{6} \times \frac{5}{6}) = \frac{25}{36}$.

(v) What is the probability that of two dice thrown together only one will turn up *six* ?

Here it is indifferent whether *six* turns up with the first die, or with the second die. Using subscript numbers to distinguish one die from the other, we can represent the case in which *six* turns up by s_1, or by s_2, and the case in which *six* does not turn up by σ_1,

A consideration of these formulae will show that (1) the larger m is the nearer the fraction is to unity, hence the higher the probability that E will happen; (2) the larger m' is, or the larger v is, the lower the probability that E will happen.

The formula $\dfrac{m+1}{m+2}$ is known as *Laplace's Rule of Succession*.[1] Its validity depends upon the assumption that the possible alternatives are *equally likely*. This assumption is justified only under very artificial conditions, and only when the possible alternatives are of the same form.[2] Failure to recognize this has led to absurd results. For example, if the happening or not happening of an occurrence, with regard to the conditions of which *nothing* is known, be assumed to be equally likely, then the probability of its occurrence would always be $\frac{1}{2}$, since in such a case m would be equal to 0.[3] Given certain assumptions, however, and with due precautions the formula may be applied to special cases.[4]

§ 5. MEASUREMENT

Quantitative analysis presupposes measurement. ' The scope of a discussion on quantity ', says Professor Whitehead, ' may be defined by the question, How is measurement possible ? '[5] No attempt can be made here to discuss this question adequately. All that we can do is to indicate the nature of measurement and to point out the main conditions that render it possible.[6] Every one has some vague conception of what is meant by measurement. We all find it necessary on certain occasions to make more or less accurate measurements. The cook, for instance, measures out the quantity of flour required for a certain cake ; the tailor measures off a certain quantity of cloth, and takes his client's " measurements " in order to make a coat that fits him. In all such cases a certain property of an object is correlated with a number selected in a certain way. The cook says that the *weight* of the flour is 1 lb., the tailor says that the *length* of the cloth is 4 yards, and so on. Weight and length are quantities. To determine the required quantity of

---

[1] See Venn: *The Logic of Chance*, Chap. VIII.
[2] See p. 409 below.
[3] These absurdities were pointed out by C. S. Peirce. (See *Chance, Love, and Logic*, Pt. I, Sect. 4.) These formulae have been criticized in detail by Dr. C. D. Broad and by Mr. J. M. Keynes.
[4] Students who desire a fuller treatment of the elementary rules for calculating probability may be referred to C. Smith, *A Treatise on Algebra*, Chap. XXX ; or to Welton, *Manual of Logic*, Bk. V, Chap. VI.
[5] *The Principle of Relativity*, p. 40.
[6] For a fuller discussion of measurement see N. R. Campbell, *Physics : The Elements*, Pt. II ; *What is Science ?* Chaps. VI–VII ; A. D. Ritchie, *Scientific Method*, Chap. V.

cloth the tailor uses a measuring-tape, or measuring-rod ; to determine the required quantity of flour the cook uses a pair of kitchen scales. In both cases the making of the measurement involves the physical manipulation of objects, the use of a measuring appliance, and a direct judgement of comparison. Each of these points will require further consideration, but before discussing them we must notice a familiar and important characteristic of the operation of measurement. Suppose we want to stick a piece of baize on the top of a card-table. In order to get the right quantity of baize (viz. a certain area) we do not need to take the table to the shop. We measure the top of the table and find its length to be a yard each way. We then ask for a yard of baize (assuming that the width of the baize is not less than a yard). The shopman measures off a yard of baize against a scale mark on the counter, or on a measuring-rod. If we find that the baize measures a yard in width also, we conclude that the baize will fit the table. If we could assume that these operations of measuring have been correctly performed, then we could know that the baize would fit the top of the table although we have not placed it on the table. Upon this characteristic depends the usefulness of measurement for practical purposes.

A consideration of these examples will show that measurement involves the abstraction of certain properties of objects, and that it depends upon certain conventions which are so familiar that we are apt not to recognize their conventional character. The possibility of getting the right quantity of baize to fit the top of the table, although the table is at home and the baize is in a shop, depends upon the fact that one-one correlations have been established : (i) between our measuring-tape and the top of the table ; (ii) between the shopman's measuring-rod and the baize ; (iii) between *our* tape and *his* rod, so that we both mean the same by " one yard ". Now, it is clear that (i) and (ii) are possible only in so far as we can directly compare the measuring-tape, or rod, and the top of the table, or the baize, with respect to a certain property, and can immediately judge that there is a match between them. In assuming (iii) we are assuming that, were the tape and the rod laid alongside each other, they would match in the same way as the rod matched the baize, and the tape matched the top of the table. We can assume (iii) only because we have adopted a conventional system which enables us to refer in a perfectly definite way to a standard measuring appliance. We have seen that in measuring the length of the table we were making first of all a judgement of comparison which could be expressed by, " This yard measure matches the length of the table ". We must, then, first consider this relation of *matching*.

24

ment. This is what we do with a yard stick, for we subdivide it into inches, tenths of inches, and so on. But however small we make these subdivisions we cannot obtain an exact coincidence, in spite of the fact that the measured object may appear to coincide with two marks of the scale. The fact that there are incommensurable lengths, e.g. the sides and diagonal of a square, shows that there may not be an exact numerical ratio between any two lengths. Thus all measurement is only an approximation, though we can increase the degree of approximation as much as we please. The scale is a standard of straightness and a standard of rigidity. It is easy to see that if we measure with a tape we must not stretch the tape on one occasion, and let it lie slackly on another. For this reason the standard measure of length is made of the most rigid material that we can find.[1]

It should now be clear that measurement involves the manipulation of bodies ; hence it is experimental, and the rules of measurement are experimental laws. If we could not find bodies which we judge to be constant with respect to length we could not perform the ordinary processes of measurement. We have now to see that measurement involves the addition of bodies. It is for this reason that measurement is expressed by numbers, for the number series has the property that any two, or more, numbers can be replaced by another number which will be equal to the combination of these numbers. Thus measurement is made in accordance with the laws of arithmetic. Since matching in length is a transitive, symmetrical relation which can be expressed by a number, lengths can be added. Scales are a device for the addition of lengths. As we saw, the addition will be of ratios, but owing to our convention that the unit equals one, these can be expressed by numbers. Now the characteristic of the (finite) number series is that the addition of a number to any other number increases the number. We find here the characteristic in virtue of which some properties of bodies are measurable. This may be stated precisely as follows : A property of a body is measurable if the combination of bodies having that property increases that property, just as a number is increased by the addition of other numbers. It is in virtue of this fact that measured objects can be arranged in an order. Hence, there enters into measurement a transitive, asymmetrical relation which suffices to order the measured objects in a series. This is clearly the case with length. We have now to see that the same holds with regard to weight.

The weight of a body means the force with which it tends to

---

[1] It is not possible here to go into the question of the meaning of " rigidity ", nor its precise relation to " length ". For a discussion of this problem see A. S. Eddington, *Space, Time and Gravitation*, " Prologue ".

fall. This is called "absolute weight". It varies at different places on the earth, becoming smaller the nearer the place is to the equator. But we know experimentally that all bodies are affected in this way in the same proportion. Consequently, two bodies having the same weight at any place on the earth have the same weight at any other point. Thus we replace absolute weight by what is called relative weight. The relative weight of a body expresses how many times its absolute weight is greater or smaller than the absolute weight of a standard body, called the unit of weight. This standard unit is arbitrarily chosen, and is a lump of platinum-iridium, kept at Paris. It is called the *kilogramme*. The scientific standard is a thousandth part of this weight, called a *gramme*. The weight of a body is measured by placing it in the pan of an equal-arm balance and by adding known weights to the other pan until equilibrium is obtained. The judgement that the pans are in equilibrium is made by observing the coincidence of a pointer with a line on the scale. Thus measurement of weight is reduced to measurement of length, and is again seen to be ultimately dependent upon an immediate judgement that two visual sense-data coincide.

The fundamental rules for measurement must now be shortly stated. They are : (1) Two bodies matching a third with respect to the given property (length, weight) match each other ; (2) The addition of objects having the given property increases that property in accordance with the laws of arithmetic ; (3) The addition of equals yields equals. That these rules hold with regard to some of the properties of bodies is an experimental fact. It might have been the case that the addition of weights in the pan of the balance would not increase the weight. Had that been the case measurement would have been impossible. The only two properties of bodies that fulfil the second rule directly are length and weight. Hence, the measurement of these properties is the fundamental process. This can be easily seen if we consider the property of density. Density is *weight divided by volume*. If we add one pint of water to two pints we increase the weight, and mass, of the water ; but we do not increase its density. Hence, density is not directly measurable. But since weight divided by volume yields a number, and since these numbers can be arranged in an order which represents increase of density, density can be indirectly measured. This may be summed up in the statement that density is proportional to weight per unit volume.

The importance of measurement lies in the fact that by means of it *precise* relations can be stated between bodies possessing measurable properties. Thus measurement enables mathematical analysis to be applied to the behaviour of natural bodies. By measurement

affairs 'the smallest causes may produce the greatest effects, and the real application of scientific method is out of the question'. But this premiss does not justify the conclusion that history cannot be treated scientifically, but only that historical knowledge does not take the form of abstract generalizations about repeatable events. History is the record of what *has happened*. The primary aim of the historian is to ascertain what exactly did happen. The fundamental distinction between history and the natural sciences is due to the difference in the nature of their primary data. The data of the latter are obtained by observation; the chemist, for example, *observes* the changing colour of the litmus paper when it is dropped into acid ; the astronomer *observes* the shadow passing over the face of the moon ; the doctor *observes* the quickened pulse of his patient. The historian, however, cannot observe what has happened. His data are records—monuments, oral tradition, documents—from which he has to construct his primary fact. This point has been well put by Langlois : 'The facts of the past are only known to us by the traces of them which have been preserved. These traces, it is true, are directly observed by the historian, but after that, he has nothing more to observe ; what remains is the work of reasoning, in which he endeavours to infer, with the greatest possible exactness, the facts from the traces. The document is his starting-point, the fact his goal'.[2] Our knowledge of historical fact is thus indirect. History is not an observational science ; it is not concerned with what is happening here and now, nor can it abstract from spatio-temporal relations as physics may do. This essential reference to time is the distinguishing characteristic of historical knowledge ; those sciences are *historical* which cannot omit the time-direction. Consequently astronomy, geology, biology are to some extent historical sciences; wherever the concept of evolution is applicable there is an historical element. The distinction between the exact and the inexact sciences corresponds to the distinction between those sciences which can and those which cannot omit the time-direction. It is perhaps hardly necessary to labour the point that much biological knowledge falls into the latter category.[3] We shall be concerned in a later section with the historical sciences commonly known as the "sciences of society".

This conception of historical fact gives a wider interpretation

---

[1] *Principles of Science*, p. 761.

[2] Langlois and Seignobos, *An Introduction to the Study of History* (trans. York Powell), p. 64. In writing this chapter I have made considerable use of this book ; it is by far the best short account of historical methodology available to the English reader.

[3] If this be so, it would seem to follow that the methods of the physical sciences are not always appropriate to the solution of biological problems, (See J. H. Woodger, *Biological Principles*, Chap. VI.)

to the word "history" than has been customary. The earliest historians, for example, Thucydides, understood history to be the narration of *memorable* occurrences. But these facts are *historical facts* not because they are memorable but because they are known only through the records of them, although it is true that they would not have been recorded had they not been memorable. Hence, it is not difficult to see how it is that the word "history" has various meanings. What is of interest to the student of method is that what makes a fact *historical* is the way in which it is known ; this, in turn, depends upon its being a fact about a *datable* occurrence. That is to say, an historical fact is localized at a given time in a given country ; it must be reconstructed from the document with the aid of the historian's imagination and in the light of his knowledge as to what is likely to have happened. Hence, the method of history is essentially deductive, the primary fact itself being elicited only as the result of a deductive investigation.

Just as science (in the ordinary acceptation of the word) has grown out of common-sense knowledge, so history has grown out of tradition. There is no sudden break. But just as science in its developed form is something more than organized common sense, so history is something more than tradition that has become conscious of itself, and therefore critical. To quote Langlois again : 'History, in order to constitute itself a science, must elaborate the raw material of facts. It must condense them into manageable form by means of descriptive formulae, qualitative and quantitative. It must search for those connexions between facts which form the ultimate conclusions of every science '.[1] The ordered description of these connexions constitutes explanation in history. In so far as history is mainly concerned with human actions and thoughts the historian can utilize the results of psychological investigation in ordering his facts. The concept of motive must often replace the concept of cause. The method of the historian has much in common with the method of the criminal detective whilst both alike share the aim of the scientist—to discover an order appropriate to the primary facts. Finally, the historian, no more than the scientist, can free himself from his climate of thought. Consequently, as Goethe has pointed out, ' History must from time to time be rewritten, not because many new facts have been discovered, but because new aspects come into view, because the participant in the progress of an age is led to standpoints from which the past can be regarded and judged in a novel manner '. This process of elaboration depends upon the choice of concepts suitable to the correlation of the facts. As in physics, so in history, this choice is determined partly by the nature of the previous relevant knowledge, partly by

[1] op. cit., p. 264.

the prevailing climate of thought. Here, as in other fields of theoretical construction, analogy plays a dominant part. Analogy is indispensable in providing descriptive concepts but such concepts are likely to be more misleading than useful unless their analogical origin be kept clearly in mind. Thus, for instance, it is useful to speak of the " decline and fall " of a State, of the " dawn of the Middle Ages ", of " the will of the people ", provided that such concepts be regarded as merely descriptive and as standing in need of constant testing by reference to the primary facts which they are intended to correlate.

§ 2.　THE SEARCH FOR PRIMARY FACT

It is the distinguishing characteristic of historical knowledge that its primary facts are not observed but inferred. What is directly observed are written documents or archaeological remains. Using the word document to cover manuscripts, monuments and other visible remains of the past, we may accept the dictum of Langlois and Seignobos : ' No documents, no history '. It follows that there must always be immense gaps in our knowledge of the past. Some lucky find, as in the case of Tutankhamen's tomb, may suddenly provide us with unexpected data. But, in the nature of the case, such discoveries are rare. The first stage of historical inquiry is the search for documents. The historian has to ascertain whether there are any documents and then to collect and classify those that he can find. This stage of investigation has received the name *heuristic*. A classified collection of documents constitutes an annotated and indexed catalogue.[1] The work of making such a catalogue is often laborious in the extreme ; it may require the co-operation of many people extending over a considerable period of time. Yet it is only the first stage, a preliminary to the ascertainment of fact. It is not sufficient to be in possession of the document; it is further necessary to *understand* it and to evaluate it as a record of fact. Let us consider the more difficult case of written documents. Suppose, for instance, that the document is written in Egyptian hieroglyphic. It will be useless unless the hieroglyphics can be deciphered and understood.[2] Suppose that the document is written in a language that is understood, then, before it can be accepted as a record of fact various questions must be satisfactorily answered. In other words, the document must be subjected to critical examination. This critical examination falls into two parts usually distinguished

---

[1] The *Harleian* collection of MS. in the British Museum affords a good example.

[2] The way in which Champollion succeeded in deciphering Egyptian hieroglyphic affords an instructive example of method. A simple account of his discovery is given by F. H. Breasted, *Ancient Times*, Sections 12 and 68.

as *External Criticism* and *Internal Criticism*. The former is concerned
with the caligraphy, the language, the form and the source of the
document ; the latter with the conditions under which it was written
and particularly with the nature and circumstances of the author,
or the alleged author, should the document not happen to be anony-
mous. In every stage of this process, the historian is forced to go
beyond what is immediately presented to him and to infer the most
likely conclusion from what he directly observes.

It is not possible here to do more than consider very briefly
the nature and difficulties of external criticism. In the case of
ancient documents it seldom happens that the original manuscript
has been preserved. The historian's text is a copy of a copy of a
copy, and so on. Often these copies have been made by scribes
who understood not at all, or at best but imperfectly, what they
were copying. It is not, therefore, surprising that these manuscripts are often unintelligible or inaccurate. Our printed books
to-day often contain misprints in spite of careful revision by author
and printer's reader. Small wonder, then, that manuscripts, copied
and recopied, are full of errors. It is not difficult to see that the
correction of these errors and the preparation of a ' sound text '
requires the highest development of critical scholarship.[1] The ability
to suggest a satisfactory emendation of a corrupt text is rare. An
example will show most clearly the nature of critical emendation.
In the text of Seneca's Letters [2] there occurred a reading which
did not make sense ; the classical scholar Madvig suggested an
emendation which was at once accepted as obviously correct. It
must be remembered that ancient manuscripts were written entirely
in capitals, the words were not separated and the sentences were
not punctuated. The reader may form some conception of the nature
of textual emendation if he examines the following passage given
in a form approximating to that of the original text : ' PHILOSOPHI
AUNDEDICTASITAPPARETIPSOENIMNOMINEFATETURQUI
DAMETSAPIENTIAMITAQUIDAMFINIERUNTUTDICERENTD
IVINORUMETHUMANORUMSAPIENTIAM . . .' The transcrip-
tion of this passage [3] as originally made in separated words ran :
" Philosophia unde dicta sit, apparet ; ipso enim nomine fatetur.
Quidam et sapientiam ita quidam finierunt, ut dicerent divinorum et
humanorum sapientiam ". This does not make sense. It would be

---

[1] It is not possible here to do more than indicate the nature of these difficulties. A full discussion will be found in the work of Langlois and Seignobos to
which reference has already been made.

[2] See Langlois and Seignobos, op. cit., p. 78 *et seq.*

[3] The student would find it a good exercise to attempt : (i) to split this
passage into its constituent words ; (ii) to state explicitly the principles which
guided the division. He should then compare his result with Madvig's emendation.

possible to suppose that some words had been omitted in transcription, for instance, between *ita* and *quidam*. Madvig, however, starting again from the unseparated script, considered whether sense might not be obtained by dividing the words differently. He was thus led to suggest the emendation : '. . . . ipso enim nomine fatetur quid amet. Sapientiam ita. . . .' Such conjectural emendations are the fruit of a long training in classical scholarship, of a knowledge of palaeography, and of a fine sense of the niceties of the language.

It often happens that the original document has been lost and that there are several copies differing from each other. It would not be safe to conclude that the most frequent reading is the correct one, for several copies may have been made from the same copy which contained a mistaken reading. Hence, it is necessary to determine the relation in which the various copies stand to each other. It is reasonable to assume that ' all the copies which contain the same mistakes in the same passages must have been either copied from each other or all derived from a copy containing those mistakes. It is inconceivable that several copyists, independently reproducing an original free from errors, should all introduce exactly the same errors ; identity of errors attests community of origin '.[1] It follows that numerous copies of a document the original of which has been preserved are valueless. Only independent copies of the original, or copies taken directly from a first copy now lost, are of use in the collation of texts. By the method of comparison of errors it is possible to draw up a table (*stemma codicum*) showing the relative importance of the preserved copies. Such textual criticism is laborious and calls for the highest gifts of scholarship and imagination. Yet its results are purely negative ; the purpose of such criticism is merely to avoid possible sources of error. It is clear that ' the text of a document which has been restored at the cost of infinite pains is not worth more than that of a document whose original has been preserved ; on the contrary, it is worth less. If the autograph manuscript of the *Aeneid* had not been destroyed, centuries of collation and conjecture would have been saved, and the text of the *Aeneid* would have been better than it is '.[2]

When, by means of such textual criticism, a satisfactory text has been established, it is necessary to ascertain the date and the authorship. If it is not possible to determine the authorship, it is at least necessary to ascertain the circumstances under which it was

[1] *ibid.*, p. 81. Such errors are of two kinds : accidental errors and fraudulent alterations. The former are due to mistakes in copying or in writing from dictation ; they tend to take regular forms such as the transposition of letters or of words, the repetition or omission of words, incorrect divisions between words, substitution of wrong words due to confusions of sense ; the latter can be corrected only by inferences from sources other than the text in question.

[2] *ibid.*, p. 84.

written. A document purporting to record a set of occurrences is valueless if it can be shown to have been written by some one who could not have had first-hand knowledge of those occurrences. Suppose, for instance, that a document is asserted to have been written in the thirteenth century. It may be shown to be a forgery if a copy of the document is in handwriting belonging to eleventh-century style. Or again, the document may appear to belong to the eleventh century, but on examination it may be found to contain words and phrases not in use until two centuries later. Many forgeries have been detected in this way.[1] Official documents often contain characteristic formulae, which provide a test of the genuineness of the document. To quote Langlois and Seignobos : ' If a document which purports to be a Merovingian charter does not exhibit the ordinary formulae of genuine Merovingian charters it must be spurious '. By such tests as these the authenticity of a document may be decided. The problem is more difficult, though not essentially different in principle, when the document is the work of several authors. By careful criticism it has now been established that the Pentateuch, originally attributed to the sole authorship of Moses, is composed of various documents written by different authors at widely different times. For example, part of it is attributed to Ezra, who lived in the fifth century B.C.[2]

Given that the question of authorship has been satisfactorily settled, it still remains to determine the circumstances under which the document was written. Had the author (or authors) an opportunity of witnessing the events that he professes to record at first hand ? Had he any motive for falsifying his record ? Had he the ability to set down accurately what he observed ? The English historian Froude provides a striking example of a writer who was constitutionally incapable of accuracy. With no desire to falsify he nevertheless habitually misstated the facts. His is an extreme case, but any one who has compared the records of eye-witnesses of the same occurrence must have been struck by the divergence in detail, a divergence that is often important and misleading. This difficulty is increased when the document contains not only a record of what the author believed himself to have observed but also an interpretation of the observed occurrences. Here, as always, the temptation is to bend the facts to suit some preconceived ideas. This source of error is not confined to the original writer of the document ;

---

[1] There have been cases in which a will has been shown to have been forged, since it has been proved that the document was typed on a typewriter of a later date than the death of the testator.

[2] See J. E. Carpenter: *The Composition of the Hexateuch* (1902) ; W. E. Addis : *Documents of the Hexateuch* ; Kuenen : *The Hexateuch* (1886). It is now commonly admitted that the Pentateuch must be considered in relation to the *Book of Joshua*, hence the name " Hexateuch ".

from the field of anthropological and ethnological inquiry. We shall then consider the nature and utility of what has been called 'the comparative method'.

(i) THE USE OF HYPOTHESIS IN THE SOCIAL SCIENCES

'If', said the late W. H. R. Rivers, 'the analysis of culture is to be the primary task of the anthropologist, it is evident that the logical methods of the science will attain a complexity far exceeding those hitherto in vogue. I believe that the only logical process which will in general be found possible will be the formulation of hypothetical working schemes into which the facts can be fitted, and that the test of such schemes will be the capacity to fit in with themselves, or, as we generally express it, " explain new facts as they come to our knowledge ". This is the method of other sciences which deal with conditions as complex as those of human society '.[1] In thus laying down the conditions of logical method in anthropological investigation, Rivers was formulating the general method of scientific inquiry. An examination of the primary data suggests an hypothetical construction *into which* the facts will fit ; the appropriateness of the construction is to be tested by its comprehensiveness both with regard to what is already known and to facts subsequently discovered.

The problem is to account for the diffusion of similar cultures throughout widely separated portions of the earth. Two hypotheses have been offered in explanation of this fact : (1) The hypothesis of independent origin, i.e. spontaneous origination. On this view it is supposed that ' the similarities between the beliefs and customs of different peoples are due to the uniformity of the constitution of the human mind, so that given similar conditions of climate and conditions of life, the same modes of thought and behaviour would come into existence independently, which are in no way due to the influence of one people upon another '.[2] (2) The hypothesis of transmission of cultures. On this view it is supposed that an ancient culture, originating, say, in Egypt, has been transmitted by migration of peoples to distant parts of the earth. The first hypothesis, which was long maintained, had in its favour the fact that an element in the culture was the prevalence of megalithic monuments, which, owing to their immense size, could not have been transported from Egypt to, say, the Torres Straits Settlements, without the employment of skilled navigators. But in the Torres Straits only the rudest sea crafts are used to-day. The second hypothesis had in its favour

[1] *Psychology and Ethnology*, p. 138. The materials for this example are taken mainly from the writings of W. H. R. Rivers collected in the two posthumously published volumes : *Psychology and Ethnology* (henceforth cited as *P.E.*) and *Psychology and Politics* (cited as *P.P.*).

[2] *P.P.*, p. 112.

the fact that the megalithic monuments were similar in important details whenever they appeared ; it was argued that the first hypothesis could not satisfactorily account for this similarity.   Moreover, the distribution of megalithic monuments followed regular lines and was not universal.   How, therefore, account for this irregular distribution on the hypothesis of the uniform constitution of the human mind ?   It must be noted that there is associated with megalithic culture the practice of mummification.   Professor Elliot Smith showed that there was similarity in sixteen points of detail between the method of mummification used in the Torres Straits Settlements and in Egypt in the XXth Dynasty.   This correspondence was too exact to be due to chance.   Moreover, the method of mummification was not appropriate to the climate of the Torres Straits.   It must, therefore, have been introduced by an alien people.

The next point for the supporters of the second hypothesis to explain was the mode in which megalithic monuments could have been conveyed.   This point was satisfactorily settled when Rivers showed that useful arts may disappear.[1]   He was able to show this in detail in the case of the canoe, and also with regard to pottery and the use of the bow and arrow.   Such loss of a useful art might be due to : (i) temporary lack of raw material which would lead to the loss of the necessary skill ; (ii) the death of the skilled tribesmen (e.g. in an epidemic), or of the men who were familiar with the necessary rites, without which no native would venture to use a canoe.   Thus, to quote Rivers, ' It is not enough to be able to make a canoe, but you must also know the appropriate rites which will make it safe to use it for profane purposes without danger from ghostly or other supernatural agencies '.[2]   Thus the chief difficulty in the way of the transmission hypothesis was removed.   It was later suggested by Elliot Smith and Rivers that there was a connexion between megalithic art and the cult of the sun, and that this cult had passed from Egypt to Oceania.   If this were so, there should be evidence in the handwork crafts of the Malay Archipelago.   Such evidence was lacking until Professor Perry, carrying out explorations in the East Indian Archipelago, found monuments resembling dolmens.   He was able to suggest a reason for migrations from Egypt to the East Indies, viz. the presence of pearls, in search of which ancient peoples were known to wander far over the face of the globe.[3]   We may, then, conclude, that the transmission

[1] See *P.E.*, p. 190 *seq.*   [2] *P.E.*, p. 204.
[3] It is interesting to notice that Professor Perry was led to this suggestion by comparison of an economic map with Elliot Smith's map of megalithic distribution.   The correspondence of pearl areas with those in which megalithic remains had been found was close enough to suggest that the connexion was not accidental.

25

the statement of a peculiar method to be called " The Comparative Method ". It is well to bear in mind Professor Carveth Read's warning : ' every empirical science rests upon a comparison of cases ; the mere making of comparisons is not the comparative method '.

CHAPTER XX

THE NATURE OF SCIENTIFIC THEORIES

'I have no doubt whatever that our ultimate aim must be to describe the sensible in terms of the sensible.'—*J. H. Poynting.*

§ 1. EXPLANATION AT THE LEVEL OF COMMON-SENSE THINKING

THE demand for an explanation of a situation or fact is a demand that it be made intelligible. Scientific method is the means whereby intelligibility is achieved so that throughout our discussion of method we have been concerned with the conditions involved in explanation. But we have so far considered these conditions only from the point of view of the *discovery* of the type of order appropriate to what is observed. We have now to consider the use of these discoveries to *explain* the facts. To explain is to offer an answer to a definite question. The satisfactoriness of the answer will be partly dependent upon the knowledge possessed by the questioner. In seeking an explanation he is seeking to discover a connexion between what is to be explained and something that he already understands. What is familiar is usually taken to be understood, so that in its simplest form the answer to the question consists in pointing out a connexion between the fact to be explained and something that is familiar. When, for instance, the plain man asks an expert to explain some fact, the expert will probably reply by drawing an analogy between some familiar set of facts and the facts to be explained. Such explanations by analogy are very common in popular expositions of science. For example, Professor Andrade explains the way in which light is analysed by the spectroscope by the following analogy : ' The way to analyse a light, as it is called, is to use an instrument which separates out the different colours and sorts each into a different place. To get a rough illustration of what is meant suppose the tickets to different parts of a theatre were printed in different colours. . . . Outside the theatre we have a mixed crowd passing in, corresponding to the beam of mixed light, but inside the various colours are sorted out, and we know by the position in which people sit down what colour their tickets were. A sorting-out instrument for light is called a spectroscope, or, if it is suitable for photographic recording, a spectrograph.

The light which enters is spread out into a band, in which each wave length has its own position, and even a colour-blind man could tell the colours present in the light by the places in which light appears.' [1] The utility of such explanations clearly depends upon the accuracy of the analogy. If it arouses erroneous associations it will be misleading. Many popular explanations of the principle of relativity are marred by such defects. [2]

Illustrative analogies have been extremely useful to the expert himself in enabling him to apprehend a set of facts as constituting a system he can understand. For instance, the theory of the atomic structure of matter makes intelligible such facts as the contraction and expansion of gases and solids. Thus Professor Poynting says : ' I have no doubt that the atomic hypothesis was first imagined to escape the necessity of taking the expansion and contraction of solid and liquid matter as simple, inexplicable, ultimate facts. Were matter continuous, they would have to be so taken. But imagine that matter consists of separated atoms, and contraction is merely a drawing together of the members of the group, expansion is merely a separating out. We have explained them by likening them to what we observe every day in a crowd of men or a flock of birds.' The explanation here consists in likening the movements of atoms to the movements of people in a crowd, who may be pressed more or less closely together. The movement within a crowd *being familiar* is intelligible. [3] The discovery of likeness is the beginning of explanation. It is the isolated, irreducible, ultimate fact that is unintelligible. We seek connexions. Hence, the mere statement that such and such is always the case may be accepted as an explanation. [4] For example, a new young voter may ask why a given politician has devoted most of his election speeches to decrying his opponents. She may be satisfied with the reply that politicians always behave like that. In so far as this answer appears satisfactory it is because it relates the given fact to the general fact of the characteristics

---

[1] *The Atom*, p. 56. (*Benn's Sixpenny Library.*)

[2] e.g. B. Russell, *The A B C of Relativity* : ' Every one knows that if you are on an escalator you reach the top sooner if you walk up than if you stand still. But if the escalator moved with the velocity of light (which it does not do even in New York) you would reach the top at exactly the same moment whether you walked up or stood still ' (p. 36). This illustration is misleading, since a material object such as an escalator could not move with the velocity of light. The illustration arouses misleading associations.

[3] The scientist's use of *models* is an extension of such explanation by analogy. It is a step towards abstract, formal description. Cf. p. 310 above, and p. 399 below.

[4] Such a reply is called by Dr. Venn ' that scandal to the budding science of the nursery ', but, he adds, ' even this statement is a help. The answer does not merely repeat the observed phenomenon ; it to a certain extent generalizes what to the child seemed new to experience '. (*Empirical Logic*, p. 499.)

possessed by politicians. The fact is no longer isolated and, as such, unintelligible ; it is now recognized as an instance of a uniform connexion. If the questioner were to pursue her inquiries demanding *why* politicians so behave, she would be answered if it were pointed out that the effect of such behaviour is to decrease the hearer's confidence in the speaker's opponents and thus to secure votes for himself. Such an explanation takes the form of a reference to purpose. If the questioner understands the nature of this purpose and is familiar with the mental characteristics of the electorate, the explanation will be complete. We are so familiar with purposive action that an explanation in terms of purpose is always acceptable, whilst the appeal to the value implicit in the purpose is recognized as final. It was for this reason that the medieval conception of teleological order had such explanatory power that it tended to check further inquiry.[1] From this point of view explanation answers the question *why* and finds its natural termination in the statement of purpose. Where we are not seeking purpose, explanation takes the form of exhibiting connexions and terminates in the widest co-ordination of facts possible at the given stage of knowledge.

We may say, then, that the occurrence of X is explained when it is shown that whenever A occurs, X occurs, and that A has occurred. Such explanation consists in showing that X is an instance of a uniform connexion. It is the *uniformity* of the connexion that is important. If linen dipped into oil sometimes became semi-transparent, sometimes remained opaque, we could not explain the transparent appearance by reference to the immersion in oil. Since common sense is familiar with the notion of causal uniformities, and since common-sense thinking moves mainly upon the level of causal determination, explanation that takes this form will be acceptable. To explain the causal uniformity itself, we look for a wider uniformity of which the given uniformity is an instance. Thus the rise of water in a pump is explained by showing that it is an instance of the laws of atmospheric pressure. The less general is thus explained by being deduced from the more general. The wider, i.e. the more comprehensive, the generalization, the greater is its explanatory power. From the point of view of explanation it is usual to distinguish uniformities, or laws, into three kinds : (i) ultimate laws ; (ii) derivative laws, i.e. laws which are instances of more general laws, from which they can be deduced ; (iii) empirical laws, i.e. uniformities that have not been shown to be instances of more general laws. Such empirical laws remained unrelated general facts.

[1] Cf. Chap. XIII above.

§ 2. THE AIM OF SCIENCE

Before we can decide whether a scientific theory is explanatory we must attempt to ascertain the aim of science. If explanation be the object the scientist sets out to achieve, what form does this explanation take ? If he does not seek explanation, what is his aim ? Just as common sense has but a vague idea as to what science is, so it misconceives the aim of the scientist. For the plain man, who is essentially practical, the importance of science can be summed up in Bacon's aphorism ' Knowledge is power '. Accordingly the purpose of science is often taken to be to gain control over the forces of nature. Hence, millionaires not infrequently endow research fellowships in science. But, as every student of science knows, the practical control of nature is a by-product of scientific inquiry. The aim of the scientist is simply to understand ; he seeks to render the sensible facts that constitute his primary datum intelligible. Accordingly, if by " explanation " be meant the attainment of such understanding, then every scientific theory is explanatory. Scientists, however, are fond of asserting that science does not *explain* but *describe*. They are apt to elucidate this remark by the statement that explanation answers the question *why*, science answers the question *how*. This is to assume that explanation necessarily takes the form of exhibiting purpose. If this were so, science certainly could not explain. But explanation that consists in assigning purpose and a well-constructed scientific theory have in common that they satisfy the questioner.[1] An explanation that assigns a purpose is intellectually satisfying just in so far as there is reference to a value taken as ultimate. In this case no further questions can be asked. In the case of explanation that takes the causal form there is no determinate limit. It is always possible to ask another question *of the same kind* about the explanatory answer. Consequently, as science develops, the form of the question changes. Causal explanation is confined to the early stages of a science ; it is satisfactory only at the level of organized common-sense knowledge. There is then good reason for distinguishing between common-sense explanation, whether purposive or causal, and the explanation afforded by a scientific theory. The latter takes the form of constructive description.[2]

Those scientists who have been most anxious to insist that science *merely* describes have been mainly interested in the chemical and

---

[1] It is perhaps this common element of intellectual satisfaction that accounts for the frequent use of expressions such as " this phenomenon is *explained* by so-and-so " even by those scientists who most hotly repudiate the suggestion that science explains.

[2] I am aware that it may seem contradictory to speak of a *constructive* description, but I do not know otherwise how to distinguish the view that seems to me to be correct from the view that science " *merely* describes ".

physical sciences. This descriptive view of science seems to have originated in a reaction against the view that science gives us knowledge of a more ultimate reality than is given in our sensible experience of the external world. There is no point in pursuing this question. Scientists resemble the plain man in using the words "reality" and "real" so vaguely and unclearly as to empty them of all significance. We are concerned only with the bearing of this descriptive view upon the procedure of the scientist in constructing theories. It will be remembered that Galileo praised those men whose sprightliness of judgement enabled them to prefer the dictates of their reason to the evidence of their senses, whilst he at the same time condemned the Aristotelian professors for refusing to test his discoveries by using their eyes. There is here an apparent contradiction the consideration of which is suggestive. The contradiction is only apparent since Galileo's insistence upon reason was in the interests of a mathematical construction which led back to the sensible facts. Galileo's trust in his mathematical deductions was, however, so great that he was apt to regard experimental confirmation as necessary only to convince stupid objectors. Chemistry has developed rapidly as a science in consequence of its use of imperceptible entities. There is, then, the curious situation that the experimental sciences are advancing rapidly as a result of constructing imperceptible, hypothetical entities the relations between which enable the scientist to connect sensible facts. Thus the primary datum is to be rendered intelligible by means of mathematical deductions concerning entities that are not observed. Unquestionably this procedure has been of the greatest value for the advancement of science. It has, however, had the drawback of suggesting an opposition between the "scientific reality"—the world of imperceptibles, and the "sensible reality"—the world given in our sensible experience. Accordingly scientists such as Mach, Ostwald, and Karl Pearson have insisted that the *only* real world is the sensible world, and that scientific theories are merely descriptions of the sensible world. The suggestion of this view is often attributed to the great German physicist, Kirchhoff, from whom Karl Pearson quotes the famous definition of mechanics :—' Mechanics is the science of motion ; we define as its object the complete *description* in the *simplest* possible manner of such motions as occur in nature '.[1] In any ordinary meaning of the word "description", Kirchhoff's definition of mechanics would be absurd. A *complete* description of natural motions is impossible, and if it were not impossible it would be useless, for the aim of science is, we have insisted, to make the primary data intelligible by exhibiting their mode of connexion. Without abstraction this would be impossible, but a complete des-

[1] *The Grammar of Science,* p. 115.

We have not space to follow Kepler's discoveries here. It is sufficient to point out that Kepler's first law led him to the discovery of the second. He did not, however, see that the third law is connected with the other two. He regarded it as an independent numerical relation. The great importance of Kepler's laws is that they made possible the discovery of Newton's law of gravitation.[1] From the point of view from which we are concerned with these discoveries the importance of Newton's law of the inverse square can be summed up in the statement that it succeeded in formulating a single rule that would account completely for the planetary motions. From this law Kepler's laws can be deduced. Further, it could be shown that ellipses are not the only possible orbits; they may, under other circumstances, be parabolas or hyperbolas. Thus the motions of comets could be brought within the same descriptive scheme. This scheme is in fact a constructive synthesis. All the facts included in Ptolemy's mathematical description, in Copernicus' heliocentric scheme and in Kepler's three laws were fitted into the Newtonian system. But they were not merely fitted in; they could be deduced from it, and, theoretically, could have been deduced *before* they had been observed.

It is not difficult to see that Newton's theory is a constructive description. It is possible here only to enumerate some of the facts that are connected in the Newtonian system in a way that renders their connexion *intelligible*. In accordance with it the orbit of a comet can be deduced, given that we know an instantaneous position of the comet and its velocity relative to the sun. The

---

[1] This development may be briefly summarized here. Kepler's Laws are : (1) The orbit of a planet around the sun is an ellipse with the sun at a focus ; (2) The straight line joining the planet to the sun sweeps out equal areas in equal times, i.e. planetary motions are in conformity with the law of areas ; (3) The square of the time required by any planet to describe its orbit is proportional to the cube of the major axis of the ellipse described. The second law suggests that there is a force at all times directed along the line joining the sun and the planet. This force must be directed towards the sun since the orbit is a closed curve. Newton, by considering the first and third laws together, was able to determine the precise numerical law of the sun's attraction. Since the elliptical motion is referred to the sun, it was not unreasonable to suppose that a similar attraction existed between the moon and the earth. In a like manner Newton was able to show that the weight of, for example, a cricket ball, is due to the attraction of the earth. He further showed that every particle of matter in the earth attracts every particle of matter in the ball. Thus the phenomenon of weight is accounted for on the supposition that *every* particle of matter attracts *every other* particle of matter. Hence, Newton was led to formulate his law of universal attraction as follows : ' Every particle of matter attracts every other particle with a force varying directly as the product of their masses and inversely as the square of the distance that separates them.' It is not necessary for our purpose, nor have we space, to refer to Newton's laws of motion, or to show their connexion with his theory.

precession of the equinoxes is shown to be a consequence of the earth's radially unsymmetrical shape and the law of the inverse square. Such apparently independent, disconnected facts as the phenomenon of the tides, planetary motions, the precession of the equinoxes, the phenomenon of weight, the motions of cyclones, are all seen to be consequences of the law of universal attraction. Such deductive power is the mark of a constructive description. It matters little whether we use the word " explanatory " of such a theory. What is important is that by its comprehensiveness, by its fruitfulness in leading to new discoveries, in suggesting fresh experiments and in connecting what was hitherto disconnected it achieves the aim of science in making the multiplicity of sensible fact intelligible. Such a theory may be said to *explain* the sensible facts that constitute its data since it is not only based upon them but leads deductively back to them. Further, as we have seen, it leads on to other sensible facts, which were not known and thus did not form part of the original data.

The mark of a constructive description is its simplicity and its consequent lack of unverified assumptions. *All* the facts must be deducible from it. A single discrepancy between the theory and a sensible fact is liable to lead to its rejection. This point deserves consideration. It can be illustrated by a simple example. It will be remembered that an irregularity was observed in the orbit of Uranus as calculated in accordance with Newton's theory. This irregularity constituted a discrepant fact that must be accounted for. There were two ways of avoiding the discrepancy. The first was to reject the theory (viz. Newton's law) with which the fact is discrepant. The second was to introduce an *ad hoc* hypothesis which would account for the regularity in such a way as to remove the discrepancy. The Newtonian theory was so well attested, it had led to such great triumphs that it was then unthinkable that it should be abandoned. It is well known that the second alternative was adopted. But—and this is the point with which we are now concerned—the hypothesis that these disturbances were due to another planet was an *ad hoc* hypothesis. An *ad hoc* hypothesis is an hypothesis introduced in order to explain a single fact that will not fit in. It is not one suggested by the development of the theory itself. If we can appeal to an *ad hoc* hypothesis whenever there is a discrepancy between theory and fact, then we can explain everything and foretell nothing. An *ad hoc* hypothesis necessarily explains the given discrepant fact, since it has been introduced solely for that purpose. But its explanatory power is limited ; it is usually confined to the single fact for which it was invoked. In the case of the *Neptune-hypothesis* this objection did not hold, since Neptune was subsequently *observed*. Thus the hypothesis was con-

CHAPTER XXI

THE PROBLEM OF INDUCTION

'We do seem to have hit on the general ground-plan of the material world, however inadequate may be our knowledge of the details. And that ground-plan, suggested to us even by a superficial observation of nature, has shown itself to be capable of statement in a more and more rigid and exacting form as we have investigated nature more and more carefully.'—*C. D. Broad.*

§ 1. THE FAITH OF THE SCIENTIST

SINCE the aim of the scientist is so to co-ordinate the facts of sensible experience that he may be able to understand them, it follows that he believes that these facts are susceptible of such co-ordination, however difficult its discovery may be. The scientist, then, believes that careful search conducted along the right lines will reveal an order in nature that is intelligible. He admits that this order is not apparent ; that he constantly finds a multiformity where he was expecting a uniformity. He sees what appears to be the *same* cause producing *different* effects, and what appears to be the *same* effect being produced by *different* causes. But he maintains that this is only an appearance, and that, if he looks more closely, he will find, in the first case, partial difference in the alleged cause, and in the second case, partial difference in the alleged effect. It is not only that he refuses to use the *words* " cause and effect " unless this be so ; he believes that one occurrence is so related to another that the occurring of the one justifies him in expecting the other to occur. If this be a correct account of the scientist's attitude, we may agree with Professor Whitehead that ' there can be no living science unless there is a widespread instinctive conviction in the existence of an *Order of Things*, and in particular, of an *Order of Nature* '.[1] If the scientist were to believe that everything happened chaotically, that natural occurrences were not susceptible of any type of order which he would be capable of discovering, he would feel powerless in the face of Nature, and would have no motive to research. That there are *discoverable* uniformities in Nature is a belief essential to the work of the scientist. This is borne out by the fact that science does not begin until men have discovered, or believe themselves

[1] *Science and the Modern World*, p. 5.

to have discovered, what in Chapter XV we called the 'minor uniformities of nature'. Professor Whitehead goes so far as to say that 'the incredible labours of the scientists would be without hope' were it not for 'the inexpugnable belief that every detailed occurrence can be correlated with its antecedents in a perfectly definite manner exemplifying general principles'.[1] This is, perhaps, an overstatement. The scientist is quite ready to leave out of account a number of details which do not fit into his scheme. Thus the physicist ignores the qualitative aspects of experience, such as colour, warmth, sound ; the physiologist is ready to ignore mind. But it is true that the scientist seeks so to correlate one occurrence with another that their connexion shall be intelligible. This desire to understand what happens leads to the procedure which we described in Chapter XVIII, whereby for qualitative variety the scientist substitutes quantitative variation. The purpose of this substitution is to exhibit what happens as exemplifying general principles, that is to say, as obeying laws. Thus the faith of the scientist can be summed up in the statement : *What happens happens in accordance with laws, and these laws are such that we can discover them.*

It is important to observe that both these articles of faith are necessary to science. It is not sufficient that nature should be ordered ; it is further necessary that this order should be *discoverable by us*. Science, indeed, is nothing but the search for an order that is not apparent.[2] But if nature exhibited a type of order of unimaginable complexity, finite minds could not discover it. Accordingly, the second article of the faith of the scientist demands that certain conditions must be fulfilled. This point has been so well put by Dr. Broad that his statement of it may be quoted in full :

'The intelligibility of the existent world does imply that it and every part of it obeys the laws of logic : but it requires more than this. Nature might obey the laws of logic ; but, unless at least two further conditions were fulfilled, it would still be an unintelligible chaos to the scientific investigator. The first condition is that changes shall be subject to general laws, such as the laws of motion, gravitation, etc. This is in no way implied by the fact that nature obeys the laws of logic. But this is not enough. Nature might obey the laws of logic, and every change in the existent might be subject to general laws, and yet nature might be utterly unintelligible. The laws might be too numerous or too complex for us to unravel ; they might be such that it was practically impossible for us to isolate any one phenomenon from all the rest even to a first degree of approximation ; or again, our situation in nature might be so unfortunate that our sensations came to us in such an order that they failed to reveal the laws which really are present in nature. The scientist who assumes that nature is and will always remain intelligible must therefore assume that nature obeys other laws in addition to those of logic ; that these are of such a kind that we shall be able to disentangle them

---

[1] loc. cit., p. 17.   [2] Cf. Chap. XIII, § 1 above.

26

that the great discoverers are those who have viewed the facts in the light of a guiding hypothesis.[1] No doubt a preconceived idea as to what the facts *must* be may hinder the investigator in ascertaining what the facts *are*. But to come to the facts with no preconceived idea is to prosecute a directionless inquiry. The successful investigator works under the direction of a guiding idea but does not force the facts to fit into it. To belittle the part played by hypothesis in scientific inquiry is to make the stupid mistake of forgetting that " the facts " do not simply present themselves and that the order which the scientist seeks is not apparent. An empirical logic which depreciates the value of hypotheses would pay but scant consideration to the importance of regulative principles. We shall, however, make the assumption—which the history of science would appear abundantly to justify—that regulative principles (or, as Professor Russell calls them, ' demands ') are an essential element in scientific method.

It is perhaps impossible to enumerate all the demands, or regulative principles, that have guided scientific thinking. We shall consider only two groups, namely, demands for identity, persistence and continuity, and the demand for simplicity.

There seems to be a deep-rooted tendency in the human mind to seek what is identical, in the sense of something that persists through change. Consequently, the desire for explanation seems to be satisfied only by the discovery that what appears to be new and different was there all the time. Hence the search for an *underlying* identity, a persistent stuff, a substance that is conserved in spite of qualitative changes and in terms of which these changes can be explained. Identity, as applied to objects, involves discreteness. *This* remains identical and is thereby distinguishable from *that*. The influence of this demand can be seen in the history of atomic theories of matter and in the abortive theory of phlogiston.[2] The biological theory of Mendelism may afford another example. It is because they satisfy this demand that principles of conservation are so plausible. The quantitative persistence represented by the concept of energy has not infrequently been regarded as persistence of stuff through change. *What* is conserved is differently conceived at different stages of scientific thought ; so long as something remains identical it does not seem to matter much what it is. To the influence of this demand may perhaps be attributed the scientific ideal of mathematical description. The relations between occurrences can be expressed in mathematical terms only when they can be measured. But measurement is possible only when what is measured can be reduced to qualitative homogeneity with only quantitative differences.

---

[1] Cf. Chap. XVI, § 2 above.
[2] See Meyerson : *Identity and Reality*, Chaps. IV-VI.

It then becomes natural to suppose that these quantitative differences are differences in the quantity of the same stuff. Hence, the popularity of substance theories in science. Such theories as those we have mentioned not only go beyond anything that is observable ; they are not even *suggested* by what is observed. The demand for continuity is closely bound up with the demand for persistence and identity. There must be no sudden breaks, no *arbitrary* discontinuities. The appearance of such discontinuities presents a problem ; the discovery that, in spite of appearances, something identical is conserved is felt to be an acceptable solution.

The demand for simplicity in so far as it is a demand for simplicity of stuff takes the form of the demand for identity. But the demand for simplicity takes another form in which it appears as the fundamental regulative principle. We have already spoken of this *principle of simplicity* as guiding thinkers to the choice of an order.[1] From the point of view from which we are now concerned with this principle it might better be named the *principle of unity*, since it expresses the regulative ideal of what Max Planck has called ' the unity of the world picture '.[2] A completely coherent constructive description would realize this ideal if, and only if, it were completely comprehensive. This is the ideal that has inspired those thinkers who have hoped ultimately to "reduce" all the sciences to physics ; their work is controlled by the principle of unity. Planck has pointed out that this ideal is attainable only by the elimination of the anthropomorphic element from science. Each of the sciences has grown out of the study of a particular range of sense-perceptions. The physical sciences are obviously associated with special senses, heat, light, sound. But in their development they have been so completely freed from their original associations that ' the physical definitions of sound, colour, and temperature are to-day in no way associated with immediate perceptions due to the special senses, but sound and colour are defined respectively by the frequency and wave-length of oscillations, and temperature is measured theoretically on an absolute temperature scale corresponding to the second law of thermodynamics, or, in the kinetic theory of gases, as the kinetic energy of molecular motion. . . . It is in no way described as a feeling of warmth '.[3] In this way unity, with the simplification that results from unity, is achieved throughout the domain of the physical sciences. This development cannot be discussed here. Its importance is summed up by Planck in the statement : ' we may say briefly that the feature of the whole

[1] See Chap. XVI, § 1 above.
[2] *A Survey of Physics*, Chap. I. Cf. also Max Born, *Einstein's Theory of Relativity*, Introduction, especially pp. 2–3.
[3] Planck, op. cit., p. 5.

enumeration and the method of hypothesis. In using hypotheses to establish inductive conclusions deductive reasoning is employed. Mr. Russell has asserted that ' in the final form of a perfected science, it would seem that everything ought to be deductive '.[1] Even were this the case, which seems unlikely, the ' final form of a perfected science ' could not be reached without the aid of inductive inference. Unless this inductive inference can be assumed to be valid, the ' perfected science ' would reduce to a deductive system which might, or might not, have application to the existent world. Thus Dr. Broad appears to be right in saying that ' whilst the inductions of all advanced sciences make great use of deduction, they can never be reduced without residue to that process '.[2] It follows, then, that the validity of scientific method rests upon the validity of induction.

Induction by simple enumeration is of the form : *All observed S's have been P, therefore all S's are P*. Since the observed S's are supposed *not* to be all the S's there are, this inference proceeds from a premiss with regard to *some S's* to a conclusion with regard to *all S's*. It is consequently formally invalid. A formal fallacy is also involved in the inference that a given hypothesis is true because all the consequences deduced from it have been verified. In this case the inference is of the form : *If H, then c_1 . . . c_n ; but c_1 . . . c_n ; therefore H* (H stands for the hypothesis, c_1 . . . c_n for the consequences). This inference clearly commits the fallacy of affirming the consequent (or implicate). Induction is thus not a formally valid mode of inference. The *most* we can say is that since c_1 . . . c_n do occur, and since these are consequences of H, it is at least probable that H is true. The plain man is likely to assent to this statement with certain reservations. He recognizes that conclusions derived from simple enumeration are precarious, and he knows that some hypotheses have been rejected even though they led to verified consequences.[3] Hence, on reflection, he is likely to admit that conclusions derived from simple enumeration or from the use of hypotheses cannot be more than probable however strong may be his belief in them. With regard to *some* inductive conclusions he will continue to feel certainty because in inferring them he makes assumptions that do not enter explicitly into the reasoning.

[1] *Our Knowledge of the Eternal World*, p. 36.

[2] *Mind*, Oct., 1918, p. 389. The two articles " On the Relation between Induction and Probability " (from the first of which this quotation is taken) contain by far the clearest and shortest account of the problem of induction. The more advanced student should refer to Dr. Broad's paper on " Principles of Problematic Induction " in *Proc. Arist. Soc.*, N.S., XXVIII. To these three articles I owe most of what I have to say with regard to the special problem of scientific method.

[3] See Chap. XVI above.

We shall see later the importance of this distinction between those inductive conclusions which we regard as certain and those which we admit to be only probable.

If an inductive conclusion be stated in terms of probability no logical fallacy is involved, since it is not invalid to pass from the premiss *All observed S's are P* to the conclusion *That all S's are P's is (more or less) probable*.[1] This argument will require as a premiss some proposition concerning probability. Since probability is a relation holding between propositions, assertions of probability are logical principles which are independent of matters of fact. But modern logicians have shown that it is not possible to state any principles of probability which would enable us to assign any finite probability to an inductive conclusion unless certain assumptions are made with regard to the constitution of the existent world.[2] This contention cannot be established here, but it may be possible to indicate the *sort* of difficulty that arises when an attempt is made to say *what* degree of probability attaches to a given inductive conclusion. For this purpose we may consider conclusions derived from simple enumeration, taking uncomplicated cases.

Given the premiss *All observed S's are P* we may wish to conclude either (1) *The next S to be observed will be P*, or (2) *All S's whatever will be P*.[3] It has been usual to express the probability of the conclusion in case (1) by the fraction $\frac{m+1}{m+2}$, where m stands for the number of S's that have been observed to be P. This fraction has been reached on the assumption that *being P* and *being not P* are equally likely alternatives. But it is easy to see that this assumption is not usually justified. If we are evaluating the probability that a penny thrown up in the air will fall down with *heads* up, then the probability can be represented by $\frac{1}{2}$, for it is assumed that *only* two alternatives are possible since the penny will not remain balanced on its edge. The alternatives (a) *It is heads*, (b) *It is tails*, are of the same form and are equally likely. But the alternatives (a) *S is P*, (b) *S is not P*, are not of the same form, since there may be an infinite number of ways in which S is not P. Hence, in such cases, it is impossible to evaluate the fraction $\frac{m+1}{m+2}$.

In case (2) a further difficulty arises, since, if m represents the observed, and n the total number of observed and unobserved instances

---

[1] In this conclusion the subject is not *All S's* but *All S's are P*, hence there is no illicit distribution. (See Dr. Broad's article, p. 391.)

[2] See J. M. Keynes, *Treatise on Probability*; C. D. Broad, loc. cit.; J. Nicod, *Geometry and Induction*.

[3] Cf. C. D. Broad, *Proc. Arist. Soc.*, N.S., XXVIII, § 1.

of S, the probability fraction would be $\dfrac{m+1}{n+1}$, and if n is not known, the fraction cannot be evaluated. Moreover, in the case of all inductions with regard to natural kinds, or with regard to occurrences in nature, the number of unobserved cases will be immensely greater than the number of observed cases. It is clear that the greater the amount by which n exceeds m the smaller the fraction will be, hence the less the probability. Even, therefore, if we assume that the alternatives are equally likely we shall not be able to obtain a conclusion having more than a very low degree of probability. The assumption that the alternatives *are* equally likely is an assumption with regard to the constitution of the existent world, namely, that we are situated in a region of nature that is not exceptional. Granted this assumption we may get a low degree of probability that a *given number* of the observed S's will be P, but we cannot get more than a low degree of probability.

This may be made clearer by taking as an example the inductive conclusion *All crows are black*. The probability of this conclusion can be represented, as before, by $\dfrac{m+1}{n+1}$. The number of unobserved crows must greatly exceed the number of observed crows, so that the fraction must be very small since n includes both the observed and the unobserved instances. Moreover, the same crow may have been observed more than once, in which case m will be assumed to be greater than it in fact is.   Nor is it true that any crow is as likely to be observed as *any other*, owing to the fact that the observations are confined to certain regions of space, and that crows not yet born cannot be observed. Thus it does not seem plausible to maintain that the selection of instances can be regarded as a *fair* selection, that is a selection of typical instances, taken at random. But, as Dr. Broad has shown, ' when we know that a " fair selection " has not been observed the probability of a general law must fall below and can never rise above the value $\dfrac{m+1}{n+1}$ which it reaches if the observed selection be a fair one.' [1] Nor is the case better if we are concerned with occurrences instead of with substances such as crows. Hence, we must admit that the principles of probability alone cannot enable us to reach inductive conclusions that have any considerable degree of probability.

It is then necessary to inquire what must be assumed with regard to the constitution of the existent world if inductive generalizations are to have any considerable degree of probability. The problem of induction may be reduced to the following statement :

[1] loc. cit., p. 396.

We observe m instances having in common the properties $\Phi_1 \ldots \Phi_s$ and Ψ. We desire to conclude that everything which possesses the selection of properties $\Phi_1 \ldots \Phi_s$ possesses also the property Ψ. There are also a set of properties $f_1 \ldots f_r$ such that each of these properties belong to some, but none to all, of the m instances. The Φ properties with Ψ constitute the positive analogy ; the f properties constitute the negative analogy. In both cases the *total* analogy may be assumed to exceed the *known* analogy. It is clear that not all the Φ properties can be relevant to the generalization, since all the m instances agree in having been observed, and occurring within certain limits of space and time, whereas the generalization *Everything which has* $\Phi_1 \ldots \Phi_s$ *has* Ψ refers to *unobserved* instances occurring at different places and times from the m observed instances. Thus we must *know* that certain properties in the known positive analogy are irrelevant. But the only properties *known* to be irrelevant are properties in the known negative analogy. By increasing the known negative analogy we can increase the number of properties known to be irrelevant. It is for this reason that variation of conditions is so important in scientific investigation. We saw in Chapter XIV that generalizations concerning instances of a natural kind are more plausible than generalizations concerning a class the members of which have few properties in common. This greater plausibility arises from the fact that we tacitly assume that there are sets of properties connected in a certain way, namely, in such a way that anything which possesses this set of properties is an instance of what we have called a natural kind.[1] According to this assumption, if $\Phi_1 \ldots \Phi_{s-l}$ are properties defining a natural kind, and if every observed instance of this kind has the property Ψ, then there is at least some probability that *every* instance defined by $\Phi_1 \ldots \Phi_{s-l}$ has Ψ. But if *any* property can be connected with any *other* property, there are an infinite number of ways in which sets of properties may arise. In this case *every* generalization of the form *Whatever has Φ has Ψ* might be false. If, then, this greater plausibility may be taken as an indication of the greater probability that generalizations concerning natural kinds are true, we require some limitation of the way in which sets of properties may occur.

Now experience undoubtedly *suggests* to us that the immense variety of perceptible objects can be regarded as dependent upon the mode of arrangement of a comparatively small number of qualitatively different factors. We saw in Chapter XVII that the scientist attempts to express the perceptible difference between *raw meat*, perceived at a given time, and a *cinder*, perceived at a later time, by differences in the arrangement of electrons and protons. A piece of meat is *a thing* having states which possess recognizable

[1] See p. 248 above.

primary characteristics. These primary characteristics vary within certain limits under certain conditions, these conditions being determined by the presence of other things in the neighbourhood. Thus the scientist distinguishes between a chemical element, e.g. carbon, a chemical compound, e.g. sugar, and a natural kind, e.g. a cow. A natural kind consists of instances of chemical compounds arranged in a certain way. A chemical compound consists of instances of chemical elements arranged in a certain way. The scientist assumes that the properties of a chemical compound depend upon the elements (of which it is chemically composed) being arranged in a certain way; he assumes that the properties of a natural kind are likewise dependent upon the chemical compounds into which it can be chemically analysed. In saying that the properties " depend upon " the compounds, or the elements, the scientist means that these compounds, or these elements, suffice to *generate* the properties of natural kinds and of chemical compounds respectively. Working upon this assumption, scientists have in fact discovered that the properties of natural kinds can be regarded as connected with the properties of chemical compounds, and that the properties of the latter can be regarded as connected with the properties of chemical elements. That is to say, the advance of science suggests that the immense variety of perceptible objects is generated by the combination of a comparatively small number of perceptibly different objects. It is clear that if this suggestion could be justified we should have reason to suppose that some generalizations with regard to nature are true.

Mr. J. M. Keynes has stated clearly what exactly is the assumption which the procedure of the scientist suggests. He calls it the *Principle of Limited Independent Variety*. He points out that inductive generalizations can be justified on the assumption ' that the objects in the field, over which our generalizations extend, do not have an infinite number of independent qualities ; that, in other words, their characteristics, however numerous, cohere together in groups of invariable connexion, which are finite in number '.[1] He points out that such a limitation of independent variety ' does not limit the number of entities which are only *numerically* distinct '. The principle may be more precisely formulated as the assumption ' that the amount of variety in the universe is limited in such a way that there is no one object so complex that its qualities fall into an infinite number of independent groups (i.e. groups which might exist independently as well as in conjunction) ; or rather, that none of the objects about which we generalize are as complex as this ; or at least that, though some objects may be infinitely complex, we sometimes have a finite probability that an object

[1] *A Treatise on Probability*, p. 256.

about which we seek to generalize is not infinitely complex '.[1] Mr. Keynes suggests that a further assumption is required, which he calls the *Principle of Atomic Uniformity*. This is the assumption that natural occurrences can be regarded as compounded of small changes taking place in accordance with mathematical laws. ' The system of the material universe ', Mr. Keynes says, ' must consist, if this kind of assumption is warranted, of bodies which we may term (without any implication as to their size being conveyed thereby) *legal atoms*, such that each of them exercises its own separate, independent, and invariable effect, a change of total state being compounded of a number of separate changes each of which is solely due to a separate portion of the preceding state '.[2] This assumption is to the effect that the laws of organic combinations are not different in kind from the laws which express less complex modes of combination. This principle exactly expresses the assumption made in scientific investigation that proceeds in accordance with the principle of convergence to simplicity with diminution of extent. *Unless* such atomic uniformity is assumed, the principle of convergence to simplicity could not be usefully employed in the manner explained in Chapter XVII.

These two principles of the limitation of independent variety and of atomic uniformity express assumptions with regard to the constitution of the existent world. They are not logically necessary, nor are they in any sense self-evident. The working scientist, especially if he happens to be unphilosophically minded, may regard these principles as too obvious to need discussion. But, as we have seen, obviousness is no guarantee of truth. We have, therefore, to inquire what justification we have for assuming these principles. It is clear that they work in practice, since it is in accordance with these principles that the body of knowledge that we call " science " has been built up. Mr. Keynes asserts that inductive inference *can* be practically useful only ' if the universe does in fact present those peculiar characteristics of atomism and limited variety which appear more and more clearly as the ultimate result to which material science is tending '.[3] The problem remains whether we have any justification for making these assumptions. It should be observed that they amount to the assumption that nature is fundamentally finite. This assumption Mr. Keynes calls the *inductive hypothesis*. It cannot be known to be *certainly* true. If, however, it ever had a finite probability, then it can certainly be admitted that experi-

---

[1] *ibid.*, p. 258. This might be expressed more simply in the form : There are sets of a finite number of properties which are such that no one member of the set ever occurs without the other members of the set. (See C. D. Broad, *Proc. Arist. Soc.*, N.S., XXVIII, § 6·5.)

[2] *op. cit.*, p. 249.   [3] *ibid.*, p. 427.

ence has increased this probability, since our interpretation of what happens is based upon the assumption of its truth. If the principles of atomic uniformity and of the limitation of independent variety do apply to the constitution of the existent world, then we should expect to find repetition and regularity in it. This is what we do find. The more we seek such regularity, the more we find it, even in regions where at first sight the search for such regularity appears most unpromising. It is clear that to suppose that this argument affords a proof of the inductive hypothesis would involve a fallacy of affirming the consequent. But, if the inductive hypothesis has *some* degree of probability, then inductive conclusions reached in accordance with it would *strengthen* the initial probability. Mr. Keynes has shown that such a procedure is not circular.[1] It follows, that the one fundamental assumption that must be made if scientific method is to yield conclusions having some degree of probability is that there is a finite probability that the constitution of the existent world conforms to the principles of atomic uniformity and the limitation of independent variety. This is equivalent to the assertion that there is a finite probability that the system of nature is not infinitely complex. This assertion may be false, but if it is false, then there is no logical ground for believing that *any* generalization with regard to the existent world is more likely to be true than to be false. Accordingly, science as a system of *knowledge* rests upon this assumption.

§ 4. HUME'S PROBLEM AND ITS CRITICS

The special problem which we discussed in the last section was raised in its clearest form by Hume. He distinguished sharply between propositions with regard to matters of fact and propositions with regard to abstract concepts such as those of mathematics. We saw in the last section that the certainty that we feel with regard to these two kinds of propositions is very different. The distinction drawn by Hume may be stated in modern terminology with sufficient accuracy as follows. Propositions concerning matters of fact may be denied without contradiction. Thus, Hume says, the proposition ' *That the sun will not rise to-morrow* is no less intelligible than the affirmation *that it will rise*. We should in vain, therefore, attempt to demonstrate its falsehood '.[2] Such propositions must

---

[1] op. cit., p. 260. The procedure is not circular, granted the assumption that the Inductive Hypothesis started with a finite probability, since the confirmation is derived from evidence relative to a less far-reaching assumption.

[2] *Inquiry concerning Human Understanding*, § 21. Hume considered that ' all reasonings concerning matters of fact seem to be founded on the relation of *Cause and Effect*'. Consequently his treatment of the problem seems to be confined to the problem of causation. This, however, is accidental. The problem with which he was really concerned was the problem of the validity of inference from past to future generalizations.

be distinguished from those which are not assertions with regard
to existent objects, such as, to quote Hume's examples,
*That the square of the hypothenuse is equal to the square of the
two sides*, or *That three times five is equal to the half of thirty*,
since these propositions are true no matter what the constitution
of the existent world may be. Hume says that the denial of
such propositions ' involves a contradiction '. We may accept this
statement if we interpret it, in accordance with modern views of
deductive systems, as meaning that these propositions *follow
from* the initial concepts and the axioms, or primitive propositions,
which determine a given abstract system. To assert that they are
true is to assert that they are validly deduced. But to assert that
propositions concerning matters of fact are true is to assert that
they express facts with regard to *what exists*. Such propositions
cannot be *deduced* from initial concepts and axioms with regard
to the relations of such concepts. Hence, the denial of such propositions cannot be *demonstrated* to be false ; hence, *either* of two
contradictory propositions with regard to matters of fact *might* be
true. The question therefore arises as to what justification we have
for believing that general propositions with regard to matters of
fact are true. Consequently, Hume asks, ' What is the nature of
that evidence which assures us of any real existence and matter
of fact, beyond the present testimony of our senses, or the records
of our memory ? '.

Hume's answer to his own question was that there is no evidence
capable of giving us such assurance, and that ' if we believe that
fire warms, or water refreshes, 'tis only because it costs us too much
pains to think otherwise '.[1] He did not deny that we have such
beliefs ; he even asserted, with some measure of inconsistency, that
such beliefs were useful. It is, therefore, no answer to Hume to
assert that we all do in fact believe that the sun will rise to-morrow,
that water quenches thirst, and that arsenic is poisonous. The
question for which he sought an answer was by what *right* we hold
such beliefs, what is their logical justification. He did not deny
that inductive methods may lead to true conclusions, but he
maintained that it had not been *shown* that they could do so.[2]
This, it will be observed, is the special problem of inductive
method.

Philosophers since Hume have attempted to avoid the scepticism
implicit in Hume's answer. They have sought to show that some
principle of causal determination, sufficient to warrant inferences going

[1] *A Treatise of Human Nature*, Bk. I, Pt. IV, § 7.
[2] Cf. J. M. Keynes, op. cit., p. 272. ' Hume showed, not that inductive
methods were false, but that their validity had never been established and that
all possible lines of proof seemed equally unpromising.'

beyond ' the present testimony of our senses, or the records of our memory ', is a necessary precondition of our thinking, or is itself deducible from some such principle, as, for example, the Law of Identity.   The first answer may be attributed to Kant, the second to Mr. Joseph.   Kant's ' answer to Hume ' need not be considered here for the very good reason that it evades the difficulty and solves Hume's problem only by denying that there is a problem to solve. We may, however, consider briefly those answers to Hume which take the form of asserting that the principle of the Uniformity of Nature and the Law of Universal Causation are sufficient to give us that assurance of which Hume was in search.

It is not easy to ascertain what exactly logicians have understood to be meant by the " Uniformity of Nature ".   It must be so interpreted as to be compatible with what Mill calls ' the infinite variety of Nature '.   To deny that there is variety in Nature would not only be inconsistent with observable facts but also with the procedure of science, since, unless there are multiformities there is nothing for the scientist to discover.   Mr. Joseph takes ' the Uniformity of Nature ' to be equivalent to ' the unbroken reign of law '.[1]   No doubt this is the correct interpretation.   In this case the principle will not do the work required of it.   As Mr. Bertrand Russell has pointed out, what is required ' is not the reign of law, but the reign of *simple* laws '.[2]   Whatever the constitution of the existent world may be, it would be *theoretically* possible to exhibit natural occurrences as exemplifying laws, provided that these laws may be of any degree of complexity.   However " the Uniformity of Nature " be interpreted it would not enable us to see how there can be laws of nature simple enough for us to discover.   Thus such a principle would not be sufficient to justify the inductive inferences which we do all of us make and in the truth of which we believe. What we want is not a principle which merely asserts that there are natural laws but one which justifies the assertion that some generalizations with regard to some given region of facts are more likely to be true than to be false.   It is sometimes supposed that all that is required is to supplement the principle of the Uniformity of Nature by the Law of Universal Causation.   For the purpose of the present discussion this Law may be expressed in the form : Given any occurrence uniquely described by " Y ", there is some other occurrence capable of being uniquely described by " X ", which is so related to Y that the occurrence of X justifies us in inferring the occurrence of Y.   This Law, or Principle, cannot be regarded as self-evident.   We saw in Chapter XV that Mr. Joseph considers that to deny the necessity of the causal relation is equivalent to denying the Law of Identity, but we saw reason to reject this

[1] *Introduction*, p. 402.   [2] *Analysis of Matter*, p. 232.

view. If the connexion between X and Y could be *seen* to be necessary, no problem would arise. To the question with what *right* do we assume the Law of Universal Causation, it is no answer to reply, as Mr. Joseph does, that 'to deny it is to resolve the universe into items that have no intelligible connexion',[1] since the point at issue is whether they *have* such an intelligible connexion.

The empiricist logician, Mill, no less than the rationalist logician, Mr. Joseph, assumes that the Law of Universal Causation provides us with a sufficient answer to Hume's problem. It is true that Mill does not regard this Law either as self-evident or as a principle that we *must* accept. He denies that there is any 'principle, which, antecedently, to any verification by experience, we are compelled by the constitution of our thinking faculty to assume as true'.[2] On the contrary he maintains that the Law of Universal Causation is itself an induction from experience and 'by no means one of the earliest which any of us can have made'.[3] He argues that experience led us to make generalizations from experience, which assumed the causal form, and that ultimately we were led to the generalization that every event has a cause. Thus he says : 'The truth is that this great generalization is itself founded on prior generalizations. The obscurer laws of nature were discovered by means of it, but the more obvious ones must have been understood and assented to as general truths before it was ever heard of'.[4] For our purpose it is not necessary to inquire as to what extent this argument is circular. Mill's point is that experience suggests that there are causal uniformities, and that the discovery of the least apparent uniformities rests upon the assumption that every occurrence can be exhibited as an instance of a causal uniformity. The discovery of these later generalizations is then taken to afford increasing evidence for the truth of the Law of Universal Causation so that it may finally be regarded as proved. He pointed out that there is no paradox in supposing that the Law of Causation is assumed in all inductive investigation and yet is itself an instance of induction *provided that* his theory of syllogistic inference be accepted.[5] This may be granted.

It is worth observing that both Joseph and Mill regard scientific method as essentially consisting in the elimination of possible alternative causes until only one possible cause is left. Then, by using the Law of Universal Causation in the fashion of a major premiss, it is concluded that the uneliminated alternative is the cause. In

---

[1] *Introduction*, p. 424.   [2] *Logic*, Bk. III, Chap. III, § 1.
[3] *ibid.*, Chap. XXI, § 2.   [4] loc. cit.
[5] See Chap. XII, § 3 above. See *Logic*, Bk. III, Chap. XXI, § 4. For a hostile criticism of Mill's view, see Joseph, op. cit., pp. 421, 443.

27

thus exhibiting scientific method as essentially based upon elimination the real difficulty is evaded. Either induction is reduced to deduction, in which case its validity is purely formal, so that it becomes difficult to see how generalizations concerning matters of fact are possible ; or deduction is reduced to induction, in which case it still remains that the Law of Universal Causation must be proved. The first alternative is that taken by Mr. Joseph and other rationalist logicians ; the second alternative is that taken by Mill. There seems no doubt that for Mill the solution of Hume's problem should have been especially urgent, since, in his view, *all* reasoning is based upon induction and ultimately upon induction by simple enumeration. That Mill failed to appreciate the problem is due to the fact that he tacitly *assumed* that every natural occurrence is ultimately analysable into a limited number of elements, and that, in consequence, the variety of nature is due to the various modes of combination of these elements. This assumption when precisely stated is equivalent to the principle of the limitation of independent variety and the principle of atomic uniformity. Thus Mill tacitly assumed what Mr. Keynes calls ' the inductive hypothesis '. He did not, however, recognize that he was making an assumption, and accordingly he supposed that inductive method required no assumptions that could not be proved It is no doubt for this reason that Mill believed that induction could yield certainty. But without this unrecognized assumption Mill's use of the Law of Universal Causation would not have enabled him to validate inductive procedure. The important criticism to be urged against Mill is not so much that he failed to provide an answer to Hume's question, but that he scarcely appeared to be aware that there is any question to be answered. As this objection may be made against all the critics of Hume, there is no point in pursuing Mill's theory further. It would be more profitable to ask whether *granted* that we are justified in assuming the Law of Universal Causation, we are provided with a solution of Hume's problem. This we have seen not to be the case.

We have seen also that the interpretation of the Uniformity of Nature as equivalent to the unbroken reign of Law is also useless for inductive method. Mr. Keynes interprets the principle of uniformity as equivalent to a generalized judgement of the irrelevance of *mere* differences of time and place. This interpretation makes the principle of uniformity equally useless, since no two things or occurrences differ *merely* with respect to time and place. These spatio-temporal differences are connected with their being in the neighbourhood of different sets of occurrences or things, and we require to make judgements of irrelevance with respect to *these* differences. To justify scientific method it is necessary that we should be able to justify the assumption of the inductive hypothesis, which can alone permit us to conclude that the laws of nature are simple enough for us to discover them, so that we may regard nature as ultimately intelligible.   Meanwhile the scientist continues to assume that the laws of nature are ultimately simple, and it is in fact the case that in the more advanced sciences many simple laws have been discovered whilst many laws that appeared complex and disconnected from other laws have been shown to be capable of reduction to simpler and more comprehensive laws.   Nevertheless, as Mr. Russell has pointed out, ' it would be fallacious to argue inductively from the state of the advanced sciences to the future state of the others, for it may well be that the advanced sciences are advanced simply because, hitherto, their subject-matter has obeyed simple and ascertainable laws, while the subject-matter of other sciences has not done so '.[1]   With this consideration we are brought again to the demand for simplicity, which is thus seen to be not unconnected with the assumptions that are required to justify our attaching any considerable degree of probability to generalizations with regard to the existent world.

[1] *Mysticism and Logic*, p. 205.

pentameters, having a fixed rime scheme of one or other of two forms."

Any one of these statements might enable B to understand what " sonnet " means. The second is an inadequate description of " sonnet ". It might serve the purpose but it could not be called a *definition*. We are frequently content with a description, more or less adequate, of the meaning of a word. Thus we might describe a bass viol as " an instrument very like a 'cello but much larger ". Any one who knew what " 'cello " means would understand this description and would probably be able to apply " bass viol " correctly.[1] Only the third answer gives a definition of " sonnet ". In this statement two expressions are used, so related that the one is equivalent to the other. Definition always involves two expressions : the expression (which may be a single word) to be defined and the defining expression (which must contain more than one word). The former is called the *definiendum*, the latter the *definiens*.

We have now to consider the first answer. This explains the meaning of " sonnet " by giving *examples* of sonnets. If B knows these poems he is likely to understand what " sonnet " means. Some logicians recognize a kind of definition of which this first answer would be an example, viz. so-called *extensive definition*, or *definition by examples*. It may, however, be doubted whether the giving of typical examples can be rightly regarded as a process of defining.[2] B must be acquainted with the examples given if he is to understand " sonnet " by means of them. He would then know more or less how to apply the word " sonnet " but it seems doubtful whether he would know what " sonnet " expresses. Definition is only one of the means through which we come to understand words. We must be careful not to use " definition " so widely that it comes to stand for any process enabling us to learn the application of words. These processes are so different that to call them by the same name leads to confusion. We saw in Chapter II that we understand a demonstrative symbol through being acquainted with its referend. The process of pointing (whether metaphorically or other-

---

[1] See Chap. II, § 2, above.

[2] Dr. Keynes gives a more subtle account of *extensive definition*. (See *F.L.*, § 22.) He suggests that a chemist might be able ' from the full denotation of metal to make a selection of a limited number of metals which would be precisely typical of the whole class ; that is to say, his selected list would possess in common only such properties as are common to the whole class '. He points out that the chemist would take metals ' as different from one another as possible, such as aluminium, antimony, copper, gold, iron, mercury, sodium, zinc '. These selected metals define the class *metal* by example. It seems to me extremely doubtful whether this process has anything in common with what would ordinarily be called definition. It is certainly not, as Keynes calls it, a *primitive* type of definition ; it could be achieved only by someone able to select such typical metals.

wise) to the referend is not a process of defining since the referend
is not another expression equivalent to the defined expression; it
is what the expression (in this case the demonstrative symbol)
expresses. In other words, to learn the application of a word is
not equivalent to learning its definition. We must, then, refuse
to admit *extensive definition*. Thus we cannot agree with Mr. Johnson that proper names can be defined. He recognizes a form of
definition which consists in 'the act of indicating, presenting, or
introducing the object to which the name is to apply', to which
he gives the name *ostensive definition*. This is open even more
strongly to the objections urged against extensive definition. The
latter at least involves the selection of typical examples of a class
having characteristics through which the class might be distinguished
from other classes; in the case of proper names, however, and of
words such as " *red* "—which Mr. Johnson also regards as ostensively
definable—the names simply demonstrate. That is their sole function. To regard them as definable is to confuse *understanding a
symbol* with *defining it*.

The same mistake occurs with regard to what Mr. Johnson calls
biverbal definition. An example would be " *tapferkeit* means *courage* ",
or " *valour* means *courage* ". This is translation of one word by
another. It is undoubtedly a useful process; but it is not definition.
It is perhaps because he has included such forms that Mr. Johnson
has been led to the extraordinary view that definition is *nothing
but substitution* of verbal phrases. Thus he says: ' our problem
is how to define a given verbal phrase; and the answer is to substitute for it another verbal phrase. This is the complete and
quite universal account of the *procedure* of definition, which justifies
our restriction of the topic to biverbal definition; its obvious *purpose* is fulfilled if the substituted phrase is understood '.[1] But in
defining we do not *substitute* one expression (or verbal phrase) for
another. We use *two* expressions related as we have explained.
It is true that since the expressions are equivalent it is permissible
to substitute one for the other on any occasion of its use. But the
definition is not a *statement* that the one *can* be substituted for the
other, although from the fact that it is a definition it follows that
such substitution is possible. It is extremely misleading to suggest
that definition is merely substitution.

We conclude, then, that to define an expression (verbal or otherwise) we must use *two* expressions, the defining expression and the
expression to be defined; that these expressions must be asserted
to be equivalent; that, finally, the defining expression must contain
more words (or symbols) than the defined expression. That the
last condition is required for what is ordinarily meant by " definition "

[1] W. E. J., Pt. I, p. 104.

to which has occasioned considerable controversy. Do we define *expressions* or *what the expressions stand for* ? Many logicians hold that it is the latter that is defined. This, however, is a mistake. Mill stated the correct view when he said ' All definitions are of names, and of names only '.[1] The contrary view is mainly based upon two considerations both of which are important but which do not involve the conclusion that definitions are not of words. The first is the close connexion between words and what they express. This has made it difficult to determine what it is that is defined. The second is the belief that language consists of arbitrary verbal symbols so that, if definition is of words, then all definition is arbitrary. We shall discuss the second point first. It is true that there is an arbitrary element in language in so far as there is no essential connexion between a word and what it expresses, except in the case of onomatopoeic words. The existence of different languages shows this. "Moon" is not a more suitable symbol than "luna" to express what both "moon" and "luna" stand for. What is meant by saying that the expression of *moon* by "moon" is arbitrary would perhaps be more properly expressed by saying that it is *conventional*. The question how a given word has come to be used to express what it expresses is an historical question. It usually admits of no answer, except in the case of consciously devised terminology, such as "oxygen", "volt", "vitamin", "hoover". To give an etymological derivation of a word merely pushes the question back a stage further. Had all words been onomatopoeic it is unlikely that the question whether definition is of words or of what they express would ever have arisen. Fortunately, they are not.

The conventional element in language does not render the definition of words arbitrary. However a particular word (or sound) may have originally come to be associated with what it expresses, its meaning now depends upon its use. It follows that the definition of words is concerned with the way in which they are used. It is sometimes maintained, especially by those who hold that all definition is arbitrary, that definitions are not true or false, but merely correct or incorrect. This is a mistake. A definition is true if the defining expression is equivalent to the correct usage of the *definiendum*. It is not always easy to determine what is the correct usage of a word. The simplest case is provided by technical terms used by specialists who have taken the trouble explicitly to define them. At the other extreme are the everyday words that we all use more or less correctly, but which few of us could define. For the purposes of ordinary discussion we generally use words with regard to which we know fairly well what is their correct usage. What is called a

---

[1] *Logic*, Bk. I, Chap. VIII, § 5. Mill uses ' name ' where I have used ' word ' or ' symbol ' or ' expression '.

verbal dispute is a dispute about a matter of fact, namely, as to how a word is used by those who use it correctly. It is assumed that there is a correct and an incorrect use. Since the function of words is to *communicate* thought, they would fail of their purpose if their meanings were not fixed. It may be doubted whether any serious disputes are purely verbal.[1] When A and B use the same words with different meanings they generally have different conceptions with regard to the facts which they use the words to express. With regard to such topics as religion, art, and politics, which we all believe ourselves competent to discuss, what appear to be verbal disputes may arise. Suppose, for example, that A asserts that Epstein's *Night* is a work of art and B asserts that it is not. It is unlikely that their dispute concerns the meaning of the words " a work of art ". It probably arises from the fact that they have different conceptions of the nature of art. If it were purely verbal it could be properly terminated by the agreement " Oh ! well, what *you* call a work of art is not what *I* call ' a work of art '." Such disputes do not usually end thus. Something more is felt to be at stake than an arbitrary difference in the use of words.

Definitions may, indeed, be arbitrary. In discussing a topic a speaker (or writer) may assert, " I am going to use ' X ' to mean so-and-so ". For example, he may say, " What I call ' safeguarding duties ' are usually called ' protective duties '." His assertion will be true if he so uses the word ; if not, it will be false. Most definitions, however, are not arbitrary.

It is because definitions are not arbitrary that they are useful. Consider, for example, the two words ' star ' and ' planet '. The word ' star ' was used to stand for shining spots visible at night in the sky. Astronomers were led to distinguish these shining spots into two different sets, calling one set ' stars ', the other set ' wandering stars '. Later the descriptive adjective " wandering " was seen to be a more important designation than ' stars ', so that they were called " planets " (' wanderers '). Those who now use ' star ' correctly do not use it to express what are called ' planets '. The recognition of a distinguishing set of characteristics led to the use of a new word. We see then the importance of the first consideration mentioned above, viz. the close connexion between words and what they express. The usage of " planet " is determined by the characteristics which people want to talk about. Hence, it does not seem absurd to suppose that in defining " planet " we are defining *what are called planets*. Nevertheless, this supposition is mistaken. We define *the word*, but there is a word to define only because we want to talk about what it expresses.

[1] Cf. Locke : *An Essay Concerning Human Understanding*, Bk. IV, Chap. VIII.

as a technical term to be left undefined and by means of which he defines those predicables that are to be contrasted with it. It is important not to confuse *the essence of A*, in Aristotle's technical sense, with *what A essentially is*. The latter is what Aristotle calls, in the passage quoted above, a " peculiarity " of A. That part of the " peculiarity " of A that is not essence Aristotle calls by his new technical term " property ". A *property* is to be contrasted with *the definition*, for a definition of A expresses the *essence* of A, and property is not essence. Finally, those characteristics of A which are not part of its " peculiarity " (or which are not *what A essentially is*) Aristotle calls by his technical term " accidents ". An example may make these distinctions clearer. Given the subject *circle*, we may assert the following propositions : (1) A circle is a plane curve every point of which is equidistant from a given point ; (2) a circle is a plane curve ; (3) a circle is such that the angle in the segment subtending a diameter is a right angle ; (4) a circle may have a diameter of four inches. The first proposition asserts the *essence* ; it is a definition of *circle*. A *plane curve* is the genus of circle ; it is the sort, or kind, of geometrical figure that a circle is. The third proposition asserts what Aristotle calls a " property ", which is now usually called by the Latin name *proprium*.[1] The fourth proposition asserts a characteristic which a circle may have, but which not all circles have. This is an *accident*.

Aristotle gives the following definitions of these four predicables :

1. ' A " definition " is a phrase signifying a thing's essence.'

2. ' A " property " is a predicate which does not indicate the essence of a thing, but yet belongs to that thing alone, and is predicated convertibly of it.'

3. ' A " genus " is what is predicated in the category of essence of a number of things exhibiting differences in kind.'

4. ' An " accident " is something which may possibly belong or not belong to any one and the self-same thing.'[2]

The most difficult to understand of these distinctions is that between *definition* and *property*. Aristotle distinguishes two elements in the definition, the genus and the *differentia*. The nature of this distinction can only be understood if it be borne in mind that the subject defined, which Aristotle constantly calls ' a thing ', is a *species*, that is, ' things of a certain sort ', or ' a kind '. A species is expressed by what we have called a ' class-name '. Two or more species may have characteristics in common which make it possible to regard them as together constituting a kind. Such a kind is a

---

[1] We shall henceforth write ' proprium ' for ' property ', in Aristotle's sense in order to avoid confusion with the wider use of ' property ' as a synonym for ' characteristic ', which is now common.

[2] *Topica*, Bk. I, Chap. 5, 102a.

genus.[1] One species of a genus is *differentiated* from another species by a characteristic difference. This characteristic is what Aristotle meant by a 'differentia ', as the word " differentiated " which has passed into common speech suggests. Thus a differentia seems to be what we have elsewhere called the *defining property* of a class. But Aristotle did not regard a species, or a genus, as *a class* in the sense of a collection of members. He insists that the parts of a definition are *one*, and it is for this reason that the definition expresses the *essence*.[2] This conception of the genus as a unity capable of being comprehended in the single formula that constitutes or is expressed by the definition is in accordance with Aristotle's belief that things have fixed, unalterable essences. The search for a definition was the search to determine this essence, and thus to apprehend in one notion the characteristics that belong to *the thing as such*. The essence is something given; it is primary and underivable. The proprium is what is derivable from the essence. Like the essence the proprium is essential to the subject and convertible with it. Yet it is not part of the essence. The connexion between them seems to be that the proprium is *what follows from* the essence. Whilst the essence is given, or assumed, propria are demonstrated. This distinction between essence as given and propria as demonstrated is the basis of Aristotle's theory of scientific knowledge.[3] It would be difficult to apply this distinction to moral concepts, or to biological concepts, although there is a sense in which it can be applied to the concepts of geometry. What follows by demonstration from the definition of circle are propria of the circle. Aristotle himself gives the example, 'it is a property of man to be capable of learning grammar; for if A be a man, then he is capable of learning grammar, and if he be capable of learning grammar he is a man '.[4] But he does not show *how* this property could be demonstrated to follow from the essence of man. Nor is it the case even with mathematical definitions that propria can be demonstrated from them *alone*. Moreover, the distinction between propria and definition would appear to be relative, depending upon what definition is selected. This admission would be in accordance with modern views of mathematics. But Aristotle did not regard the distinction as relative, since essence is fixed and

---

[1] Aristotle's definition of ' genus ' is very unsatisfactory and seems to be circular. His statements with regard to ' differentia ' are disconnected and unclear. In one place he says : ' A thing's differentia never signifies its essence, but rather some quality, as do " walking " and " biped ".' (122*b*, 17.)

[2] Cf. Aristotle, *Met. Z.*, XII.

[3] See *Post. Anal.*, Bk. II, *passim*, especially Chaps. 4–9. Cf. also 90*b*, 30 : ' definition is of essential nature or being of something, and all demonstrations evidently posit and assume the essential nature.'

[4] *Topica*, 102*a*, 20.

adopted the latter alternative he would not need to take account of the differences between any of the vehicles that were not trams. Or again, he might decide that the most important difference between vehicles was that between slow-moving and fast-moving. In that case he might confine horse-vehicles to certain routes, leaving trams and motors free to use any routes. Or he might recognize that bulk and weight were important factors in the rate of movement so that heavily laden lorries and pantechnicons would be classed with horse-vehicles.

This rough example will enable us to see the utility of arranging classes in a certain order. *What* order is selected will depend upon the purpose for which the classification is undertaken. If the Chancellor of the Exchequer were to classify vehicles from the point of view of imposing taxes, he would adopt a different principle of arrangement from that adopted by the Minister of Transport. Thus he might consider whether vehicles were run for public or private purposes ; what style of vehicle was being used, distinguishing motor-cars according to their initial cost, horse-power, and so on. He would thus obtain a different arrangement of classes of vehicles suited to his different purpose. Vehicles are susceptible of any order that the practical man or the logician may impose upon them. The logician is interested in the principles that any satisfactory classification must exhibit. These principles can be most easily apprehended by considering a completed classification from the reverse point of view. Instead of beginning with a set of classes that have to be grouped under wider classes we may start with the widest class and consider how this class can be successively distinguished into smaller classes. This process of splitting a class into its constituent sub-classes is known as *logical division*. Thus, to revert to our example, the Minister of Transport may begin his investigation by considering the class *vehicles* and asking how *vehicles* can be differentiated into different *kinds of vehicles*. In this way he may obtain the following division :

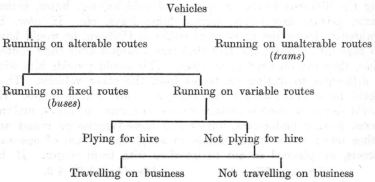

Vehicles

Running on alterable routes

Running on unalterable routes (*trams*)

Running on fixed routes (*buses*)

Running on variable routes

Plying for hire

Not plying for hire

Travelling on business

Not travelling on business

He could then see at a glance that regulations proposing alterations of routes must be confined to those vehicles included in the classes on the left-hand side ; that the group included in the class *running on variable routes* could be the most easily interfered with by means of street regulations.

It is clear that to achieve such an ordered arrangement of classes it is first necessary to have a considerable knowledge of the characteristics of each class. Nor are the obvious characteristics always the most important for the purpose of classification. For example, the landlady who undertakes to arrange a student's books is almost certain to be guided by such characteristics as *size, style of binding, colour,* etc. A classification of books based upon such characteristics would be thoroughly unscientific, and would never occur to any one acquainted with the nature of books from the inside. The old botanical division into *trees, shrubs, herbs,* though suggested by obvious characteristics, has been found not to be based upon important differences. A definition of a species, *per genus et differentiam* suggests the basis upon which the division should proceed. The basis of division (i.e. the differentiating characteristic) is often called by the Latin name "*fundamentum divisionis* ". The principles regulating a logical division are usually summed up in the following rules :

1. There must be only one *fundamentum divisionis* at each step.
2. The division must be exhaustive.
3. The successive steps of the division (if there be more than one) must proceed by gradual stages.

From Rule 1 there follows the corollary that the classes must be mutually exclusive. Violation of this rule results in the fallacy of *cross-division,* or overlapping classes. For example, if *vehicles* were divided into *public vehicles, private vehicles, motor-cars* and *lorries,* there would be more than one basis of division, with the result that the classes would overlap.

Rule 2 secures that no class be omitted, so that the sum of the sub-classes shall equal the whole class divided or classified.

Rule 3 secures that each stage of the subdivision should be in accordance with the original *fundamentum divisionis.* If, for example, in dividing *vehicles* we had further divided *vehicles running on variable routes plying for hire* into *those driven by owner* and *those not driven by owner,* we should have introduced a characteristic that had no relevance to the purpose of the ordered arrangement.

An examination of our example will show that at each stage the division was into two and only two classes distinguished by possessing or not possessing the same differentia. Such a division is called *division by dichotomy.* It possesses the advantages that the division is always formally valid since it proceeds on the prin-

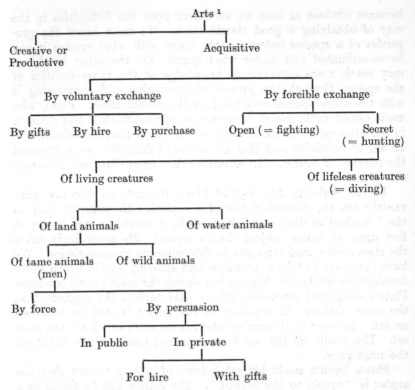

and the last, is a genus to those that succeed it and a species to those that precede it. The class from which the division starts is called a *summum genus*, or *highest class* ; the classes with which the division ends are called *infimae species*, or *lowest species*. Any intermediate genus which is subdivided is called the *proximum genus* of its constituent species. These names are not of great importance. What is of importance is to recognize that the distinction between genus and species is relative.[2]

We have treated classification and division as fundamentally the same process approached from opposite ends, the one proceeding from the unordered classes to an orderly arrangement, the other proceeding from a given class to the analysis of its constituent sub-classes. From the logical point of view this is unquestionably correct. But no scientific classification achieves the ideal of logical division. Natural species are not demarcated one from another in a way analogous to the division of classes in the examples we have

---

[1] " Art " is here used in the sense of " a capacity to do something ".

[2] Aristotle would not, of course, have admitted that the distinction is relative.

given. It is by no means always possible to discover specific characteristics differentiating one set of individuals from another set. One species is connected with another by intermediate links. Thus, as Professor Goodrich says : ' It is the universal experience of naturalists engaged in the classification of quite modern closely allied " species ", that the great difficulty of the work is due to the fact that it is usually scarcely possible to find any character at all sufficiently conspicuous and constant to distinguish them from each other. . . . What we commonly call a species is, then, an assemblage of closely allied and interbreeding races differing from each other by small factorial differences, and representing as a whole its present phase of evolution '.[1] This being the case, it follows that a biological classification cannot strictly conform to the rule that classes should not overlap. Nor can it secure an exhaustive division, since there are many gaps in the series of living organisms, some of which may perhaps be filled in by fossil animals but many of which could be at best conjectured. But although the *mode* of classification has been profoundly affected by the thoroughgoing acceptance of the principle of continuity of descent, the aim of classification remains unaffected, namely, so to arrange classes that their relations may be exhibited in accordance with the principles of hierarchical order.

§ 4. DEFINITION AND ANALYSIS

In the first section we came to the conclusion that definition is always of symbols, verbal or otherwise. We saw also that there is an important connexion between the defined symbol and the properties of that which the symbol expresses. We have now to consider what exactly is the relation between the analytic definition of a symbol and the analysis of a concept. The discussion of this relation is difficult owing to the fact that the analysis of a concept must be *expressed* in words, or other symbols, so that it is extremely easy to confuse the symbols with what they express. By *concepts* we mean abstracta, or universal notions, such as *causality, substance, space, time, fatherhood, number*. We *use* such concepts and in using them we know more or less vaguely what they mean. But we do not know their precise meanings, which involve their relations to other concepts. The analysis of concepts consists in determining precisely what are the properties present in objects which fall under these concepts. This analysis is sometimes extremely difficult ; it is never possible until after we have used the concepts correctly.

---

[1] *Living Organisms : An Account of their Origin and Evolution*, 1924. It may be observed here that in *botany* the name " species " is reserved for the lowest natural kind ; the one next above this, which includes it, is called a *genus* ; then comes the *family* ; finally the *order*.

undefined terms. In the case of expressions in common use this choice is never conscious ; it results from the development of language under the stress of practical needs. In the case of deductive systems the choice is determined by considerations of logical, i.e. deductive power, simplicity and elegance. Which expressions the mathematician takes as undefined will be largely determined by his climate of opinion and by the development of the subject by his predecessors. The choice of the initial concepts will determine the form of the system.[1]

The dependence of an analytic definition upon previously defined symbols is illustrated by the definition of " second cousins " given in the first section.[2] This definition presupposed that " first cousins " was already defined. The definition of " first cousins " presupposed that " parent of " had been defined. If we desired to define " parent of " we might do so in terms of " begetting ". The familiarity of the concept *parent of* makes such a definition seem artificial. The undefined symbols are less *familiar* than those which they help to define. But to be familiar with a concept and to know its analysis are quite different ; similarly to be familiar with a symbol and to know how to analyse it are quite different. The purpose of an analytic definition is not to *explain* the meaning of a symbol which we already understand, but to give an analysis of it in terms of more primitive symbols.

As another example of analytic definition we may take the *Frege-Russell* definition of " cardinal number ", which, Mr. Russell says, ' Marks a notable advance '. This definition is given in words by Russell in his *Introduction to Mathematical Philosophy*. It is convenient to consider it in this form.

" *A number is anything which is the number of some class.*" This presupposes the definition :

" *The number of a class is the class of all those classes that are similar to it.*"

This presupposes the definition :

" *One class is similar to another when there is a one-one relation of which the one class is the domain, while the other is the converse domain.*"

This presupposes the definitions of : " domain of a relation ", " converse domain ", " one-one relation ". These need not be given here.[3] We have said enough to show that the analytic definition of a symbol in terms of previously defined symbols, and ultimately in terms of a very few initial undefined symbols, will give important information if the initial undefined symbols *express concepts* which are of importance in the analysis of *other* concepts.

---

[1] See above, Chap. X, § 5.
[2] In Chap. IX we gave various examples of analytic definition, e.g. " $E!(\imath x)(\Phi x)$ ". See p. 137.   [3] See above, Chap. X, § 2.

CHAPTER XXIII

ABSTRACTION AND GENERALIZATION

'The paradox is now fully established that the utmost abstractions are the true weapon with which to control our thought of concrete fact.'—*A. N. Whitehead.*

§ 1. THE ABSTRACTNESS OF SCIENCE

THOUGHT as such involves abstraction. To think about a given situation is to view it in at least partial disconnexion from other situations with which it is in fact connected. Moreover, within the given situation itself some only of its characteristics will be attended to, namely those that are apparently relevant to the problem that is the occasion of the thinking. A comparison of the process of idle reverie with Mrs. Nickleby's discourse, and of both with thinking controlled with regard to a determinate problem, brings out the element of abstraction involved in all thinking. Each of these processes involves abstraction but as we pass from the first to the third we can discern a progressive increase in abstractness required by the increasing selectiveness of thought. Thinking involves both analytic and synthetic selection. There is analysis in so far as a character is separated from that with which it is in fact conjoined; there is synthesis in so far as there is a combination of characters that are in fact disjoined. The thinker is at any given moment in a situation that is concrete in the quite precise sense that no *communicable description* can be adequate to it in all its details. Whatever can be communicated is abstract. 'To be abstract', says Professor Whitehead, 'is to transcend particular concrete occasions of actual happenings.' [1] The particular concrete occasion is transcended because what is abstract has relevance to other occasions than the given occasion. For example, a man seated on a rock watches a sea-gull a few feet away from him. He is situated within a particular concrete occasion—to use Professor Whitehead's phrase. In being sensibly aware of the colour, or of the shape, of the sea-gull, or of its sharp cry as it waits for more crumbs to be thrown to it, he is seeing an

---

[1] *Science and the Modern World*, p. 221. I am conscious of owing more to Professor Whitehead in this chapter than usual. But it is probable that I have not always understood him.

absolutely specific shade of white and an absolutely specific shade of grey ; he is seeing an absolutely specific shape, and hearing an absolutely specific sound. There are no names for such absolutely specific properties. Again, the reader of this book can be sensibly aware of the blue colour of its cover ; what he is aware of is an absolutely specific shade of blue. But he will unhesitatingly and correctly use the name " blue " to describe the colour of other surfaces which are obviously not exactly similar in colour. Thus *blue* is not an absolutely specific characteristic ; nor is *white*, nor any other colour for which we have a name.[1] But the same person may be sensibly aware of the same absolutely specific shade of colour in two different situations. Thus the man watching the sea-gull may notice a second sea-gull, and it is possible that he should be sensibly aware of the *same* specific shade of whiteness in the throat of each of them, although he cannot name this shade. The particular occasion, then, is irrelevant to what is meant by the " absolutely specific shade of white ", since it can be within more than one particular occasion. It is in this sense that *the absolutely specific shade of white* is abstract. Similarly, the absolutely specific shade of grey, the absolutely specific sound of the sea-gull's cry, the absolutely specific shape of the particular bird from the position in which the man is seeing it, are abstract. He need not be aware of them as abstract, but since he can be aware of the same absolutely specific characteristic of colour, or of shape, or of sound, as present on different occasions, it follows that these absolutely specific characteristics are abstract. Similarly less specific characteristics, for example, *coloured* as contrasted with *red*, are abstract. A characteristic, then, is to be contrasted with any given particular occasions to which it may be relevant although these particular occasions are not relevant to its being what it is. The point that we are concerned to emphasize is that characteristics (which include qualities and relations) are abstract in the quite precise sense that they are what they are independently of the particular occasions in which they may be present. It is this irrelevance of the particular occasion to the characteristic that makes it possible for any simple characteristic to be predicated of more than one thing.

These considerations bring out clearly the fundamental distinction between the relation of *blue* to *coloured* and the relation of *blue* to *this blue sense-datum*. The absolutely specific shade of blue, which we see if we look at the cover of this book, is determinate, but it is not particular. The sense-datum is a particular ; it cannot recur, although the same absolutely specific shade of blue may recur.

---

[1] Cf. E. M. Whetnall : ' Symbol-Situations,' *Proc. Arist. Soc.*, N.S., XXIX, pp. 214–16, and G. E. Moore : *Proc. Arist. Soc., Supplementary Volume III*, p. 102.

Thus to be particular and to be determinate are quite different. This difference has sometimes been obscured by the common habit of speaking of a specific shade of blue as *an instance* of a less specific shade, and also of the sense-datum as *an instance* of the most specific shade of blue that characterizes the sense-datum. This double use of " instance of " is unfortunate. The confusion is further encouraged by the failure to recognize that the relation of the members of a class to the members of a sub-class is quite different from the relation of a less specific to a more specific characteristic. For this reason Mr. Johnson's expressions " determinable " and " determinate " are convenient. If we adopt this phraseology we shall say that characteristics may be more, or less, determinate, whereas classes may be wider, or narrower. A set of objects is to be regarded as a class when each of them possesses a certain more or less determinate characteristic or set of characteristics. The number of objects contained in the set is in no way dependent upon the nature of the determinate characteristic which constitutes this set a class.[1]

It follows from what we have been saying that classing and classification involve abstraction. *Crow, bird, table, heather*, etc., are what they are independently of any particular which is a crow, or is a table, and so on. It is for this reason that it is impossible to *deduce* from the defining characteristics of " crow ", the number of crows that have been, and are, and will be. Thus in classing a presented object as a *crow* disconnexion from the particular occasion and apprehension of relevance to other occasions are involved. In the classification of *crow* there is involved relations with other classes. The ordered relations of classes that constitutes classification involves propositions such as *Crows are birds*. This is a general proposition. We have seen that such a proposition expresses a relation between characters. Hence generality involves abstraction. Consequently, science takes notice of particular occasions only in order to verify general propositions. In so far as history is concerned with given particular occasions it is not science. History involves abstraction, for whatever can be communicated is abstract. But the historian who is concerned with what *has happened* may be said in a sense to avoid this inevitable abstraction by a description which accumulates details so as to be relevant to one given occasion only. Thus history is the least abstract form of knowledge. A science in the classificatory stage involves, as we have seen, abstractions that are expressible in general propositions. The constituents of such propositions may be said to be *material* constituents in that the characters related are given in sensible experience. When there is complete abstraction from all material constituents the proposition is completely formal.

[1] See W. E. J., Pt. I, Chap. XI; and cf. p. 147 and p. 267 above.

It is formal because its significance is entirely independent of any reference to what is given in experience.

As the abstraction becomes more complete, thereby achieving greater disconnexion from any given set of particular occasions, the method of science passes from classification to causal investigation, and from causal investigation to measurement. The most complete abstraction is achieved in mathematics which involves complete disconnexion from *any* particular occasions. It follows that no reference to the actual world is involved in any mathematical proposition. The consequences of this complete disconnexion from what is actual in determining the nature of mathematics will be discussed in the last section of this chapter. Here it is sufficient to point out that the fundamental distinction between mathematics, on the one hand, and all other sciences, on the other hand, is due to the fact that only in mathematics is abstraction complete. The sciences in which classification plays an important part are at the other extreme ; they have achieved the least complete abstractions. That this should be the case results from the nature of the subject-matter of the social and biological sciences. A science that has reference to historical processes, to growth and decay, to living organisms, cannot be completely disconnected from the particular occasions in which these processes are exemplified. It follows that in these sciences there must be departments to which specifically mathematical conceptions are inappropriate.

§ 2. THE METHOD OF EXTENSIVE ABSTRACTION

In Chapter XVIII we saw that the scientist in attempting to make intelligible the changes involved in the total occurrence *raw meat being burnt to a cinder* was forced to split up this occurrence into smaller and smaller pieces and smaller and smaller durations of time and to connect its qualitative changes with variations in spatio-temporal arrangement. We pointed out that this procedure is in accordance with what Professor Whitehead has called the principle of convergence to simplicity with diminution of extent. We have now to consider in more detail what this principle is and how it can be applied so as to exhibit the connexion between the abstractions with which science ends and the sensible facts with which it begins. This problem is of great importance in the discussion of scientific method. The difficulty is to see how the exact conceptions yielded by mathematical abstractions can be applied to the perceptible objects of the sensible world. That their connexion requires to be exhibited in detail follows from the fact that what we are sensibly aware of always has *some* volume, however small, and *some* duration, however brief, whereas the application of mathematics to explain the connexions of sensible occurrences involves the use of *points*, which have no size, and of *moments*, which have no durations.   Moreover, the construction with which the scientist ends (which we sometimes call the physicist's world) has a neatness and orderliness that is quite unlike the untidy and multiform world of common sense.   Yet, since science grows out of, and returns to, the world of common sense, there must be a precise connexion between the ' neat, trim, tidy, exact world which is the goal of science ' [1] and the untidy fragmentary world of common sense.   Professor Whitehead has shown in detail that the principle of convergence to simplicity provides a method of effecting this connexion.   He calls it the method of extensive abstraction.   A detailed exposition of this method would necessitate proceeding further in mathematical logic than is possible in an elementary book.   But we may be able to indicate roughly the nature of the method and to suggest its importance for science.

We must keep firmly in mind what precisely is the nature of the problem which the method of extensive abstraction is required to solve.   The problem is to exhibit mathematical concepts, e.g. points, instants, particles, momentary configurations, etc., as logical functions of what is given in sense.   We have seen that in the progressive diminution of extent which is to yield relations of the logical simplicity required by the scientist, we finally reach points and moments. Let us, at present, confine ourselves to the problem of points.   The plain man, apart from his ability to quote Euclid's definition of a point without understanding it, probably takes a point to be the limit of a line, or of an area.   He is familiar with the notion of distance in its everyday use.   He is aware, for instance, that the table and the door are at different sensible distances from the fireplace.   But if he were asked what precisely is the distance of the table from the fireplace, he might recognize that the answer depends upon whether he is to take *any* part of the table or the *mid-point* of the table ; similarly with the fireplace.   If he were to *measure* the distance, he would take the distance between two given *points*. This point would be a small area in contact with a foot rule.   It would clearly only be an approximate measurement.   Thus the notion of sensible distances is vague, but the smaller the objects taken, the less inaccurate will be the notion of the distance between them.   But however small the objects may be, they will always have some size.   The plain man, who knows that points have no magnitude, rests content with the view that a point is a limit, viz. the limit of a line that is said to end at the point.   But we are never sensibly aware of the point.   If we divide a line into smaller and smaller lines, each line will have a length, however small it may be ; it will still be *part* of the line.   Any line can be split up into a

---

[1] See Whitehead : *Proc. Arist. Soc.*, N.S., XVII, p. 61.

finite number of smaller lines. But as the plain man would admit, there are an infinite number of points in a line. A point cannot be thought of as an infinitesimal line ; it is something of a different kind, and is not a *part* of the line in the same sense in which the smaller lines into which it is divided are *parts* of the line.

We must now consider the relation *whole-to-part*. This is a temporal or a spatial relation. It is directly apprehended. Thus we can see that the space between the first and the last line of print on this page is a part of the whole page. The time taken to read one paragraph is a part of the time taken to read that paragraph and the next, provided that the two paragraphs are read continuously. Or a day in a person's life is a part of the whole period of time during which he lives. Thus there is no difficulty in apprehending what is meant by the relation *whole-to-part*. We have now to consider the logical properties of this relation. Let us consider a line AB divided into parts at C, D, E.

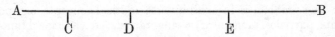

The parts AC, CD, DE, EB together make up the whole of AB. Also AC is a part of AD, AD is a part of AE, AE is a part of AB. It is clear that this relation of whole-to-part is transitive and asymmetrical. We may observe that if A is a part of X implies that X is not a part of A (i.e. that the relation is asymmetrical), then A is said to be a " proper part " of X. In this sense of " part " A cannot be a part of itself.

Now we saw that a point, e.g. on AB, is not a part of AB in the sense in which AC is a part. But it is possible to define a point in terms of the *whole-to-part* relation considered as holding between volumes. For this purpose let us take a set of volumes one of which is enclosed by all the other members of the set. Professor Whitehead uses the illustration of a nest of Chinese boxes. Suppose, for instance, that these boxes are spherical. Then we have a set of concentric spheres. On opening the set of boxes we find that each box is smaller than the one before it and larger than the one after it. We soon reach the *smallest* box, and this box is a volume. However small the smallest box may be, it is still a *volume*, viz. a sphere. Nevertheless, the consideration of these concentric spheres will help us to reach a clearer conception of a point. We shall say that a larger sphere *encloses* a smaller sphere. This relation of *enclosure* is a *whole-to-part* relation. It is (i) transitive, (ii) asymmetrical. Now suppose that the set of spheres contains, as we progress further and further to its smaller end, a sphere as small as we please. Then we have a third property of the *enclosure* relation, viz. (iii) its domain includes its converse domain. If we symbolize *encloses* by E, and the spheres by a, b, c, etc., respectively, then these three properties can be formally expressed as follows: (i) aEb and bEc always imply aEc; (ii) aEb always implies $not(bEa)$; (iii) aEb always implies that there is a c such that bEc.

In our illustration the set of volumes were spheres; they might equally well have been cubes; or alternate spheres and cubes, so that a sphere encloses a cube which encloses a sphere which encloses a cube, and so on. The logical relations would be exactly the same in these two cases as in the first case. Hence, we shall find it convenient not to specify the volumes as spheres, and shall accordingly speak of any such a set of volumes as a set of *enclosure-volumes*. Now, a set of enclosure-volumes related by a relation of *enclosure* having the three properties laid down above is such that (1) of any two of its members one encloses the other, and (2) there is no member which is enclosed by all the others, and (3) there is no member not a member of the set which is enclosed by every member of the set. As we progress down this set of enclosure-volumes we approximate to a volume as small as we please. That is to say, we converge to an ideal simplicity to any degree of approximation we please. Such a set of enclosure-volumes is called by Professor Whitehead a 'convergent set'. In no case do we reach a volume than which no volume could be smaller. In other words, we do not reach an *absolute minimum*. But this is what we need if a point is to be without parts and without magnitude. There can be no doubt that Euclid's definition expressed the general idea of a point, although he did not say how such an idea is possible. If, now, we consider the three properties of the set of enclosure-volumes, we see that this set is a route of approximation to a point; it *converges to a point* in virtue of these three properties. The relations of these enclosure-volumes have all the logical properties required of points for their use in mathematics. Hence, we reach a provisional definition of a point as a series of volumes that would be commonly said to converge to a point. This definition certainly seems queer at first sight, and must be further discussed. But it is first necessary to show that this definition is not quite correct, and must be emended.

We saw that our set of enclosure-volumes might be spheres, or cubes, or alternate spheres and cubes. Any such set will be a convergent set providing a route of approximation. But we cannot define a point in terms of one route rather than of another. Consider, for instance, a set of alternate concentric cubes and spheres. Let us call the set consisting only of the cubes, the set C, and the set consisting only of the spheres, the set S. Then every member of C will enclose some members of S, and every member of S will enclose some members of C. Such sets are said to *cover* each other,

29

to the same point ". We then obtain the required definition, viz. *A moment is the class of all convergent sets converging to the same moment.*[1]

It must not be supposed that the method of extensive abstraction is confined to what has the *part-whole* relation. On the contrary, it is used frequently in the theory of number. Thus an irrational number, for example, $\sqrt{2}$, can be defined in this way. Thus $\sqrt{2}$ *is the series of all rational numbers whose squares are less than* 2. [2] It is not necessary for our purpose to discuss this definition. The examples we have given suffice to indicate the nature of the method, so far as that is possible without technical details that would be unsuitable in a book of this kind.

The question that we have now to consider is what is the value of this method. Its value consists in showing how it is possible to proceed from the world of common sense to the world of the physicist and back again. Thus Professor Whitehead referring to the extensive definition of a moment says : ' The difficulty is to express our meaning in terms of the immediate deliverance of sense-awareness, and I offer the above explanation as a complete solution of the problem.' [3]

It is of the utmost importance to remember that physics is an empirical science which has been extraordinarily successful in elaborating constructive descriptions which guide experiment and permit the prediction of what will be observable under certain conditions. This success of physics in dealing with the sensible world is inexplicable *unless* such expressions as " point ", " line ", " moment ", " instantaneous space ", " momentary configurations " *can* be expressed in terms of what is sensible. For this purpose it is necessary to *exhibit in detail* how the exact and tidy world of the physicist is connected with the fragmentary and untidy world of common sense. To do this is to demonstrate the applicability of abstract deductive systems to the world given in sense-experience. There is no necessity to be found within the abstract system itself that would guarantee its applicability. The value of the method of extensive abstraction can be gauged by the fact that it shows *how* abstract deductive systems can be applied to the world presented in sense. Hence its importance for the student of scientific method.

[1] For a detailed discussion see Whitehead, *Concept of Nature*, Chap. III ; and cf. N. Wiener, " A Contribution to the Theory of Relative Position " (*Proc. Camb. Phil. Soc.*, XVII, 5).

[2] For a discussion of this definition see C. D. Broad, *Scientific Thought*, pp. 39–44.

[3] op. cit., p. 62.

§ 3.   ABSTRACTION AND OCCAM'S RAZOR

In this section we shall be concerned with a question that is strictly philosophical rather than logical. Nevertheless, it may usefully be considered by the student of logic since it indicates the importance of *logical method* for the solution of philosophical problems. Moreover, this question raises a problem that is likely to have occurred to the student whilst reading the last section. The question is : Do *points, moments, irrational numbers*, etc., exist ? It will be sufficient for our purpose to consider the case of points, since what is said about them will apply, *mutatis mutandis*, to other entities defined by means of extensive abstraction.

The simplest way of answering this question will be to ascertain what *kind* of entity a point is supposed to be if it is not necessary that it should be defined by extensive abstraction. Consider, for instance, the view taken with regard to the nature of points by a philosopher who accepts a theory of absolute space. He will regard a point as a particular, or individual, of the *same kind* as a finite volume, for example, a Chinese box, differing from it only because it is imperceptible. But this difference is very difficult to understand. The point, on this view, will be imperceptible, not only because it is very small, but also because it is unextended and utterly unlike anything that we *can* perceive. Hence, *what* it is, as well as its existence, remains hypothetical. Consequently, many philosophers have refused to admit that points exist. The difficulty of denying the existence of points is that such a view renders inconceivable the *success* of physics which *uses* points in the formation of constructive descriptions of what is perceptible. We have now to ask whether the definition of points obtained by the method of extensive abstraction, which, as we saw, resolves this difficulty, justifies us in saying that points exist. Before attempting to answer this question we must consider an alternative way of dealing with the problem, which is much favoured by Mr. Russell.

It is granted that points can be *defined* by extensive abstraction. Suppose, now, that points *exist*. They will have the properties laid down in the definition, since the definition was constructed to secure these properties. Suppose, again, that points do not exist. Then the definition provides us with the *same set of logical properties*. On either hypothesis, then, the definition yields everything for which points are required in mathematics. Hence, no reasoning into which a point enters would be invalidated if there were no points. We shall then be *safer* if we neither assert nor deny that points exist, and we shall gain no advantage by *assuming* their existence. It seems reasonable, it is urged, to refrain from making any assertion.

between logic and mathematics. But although every one grants that logic is *necessary* to mathematics only in quite recent times has it been seen to be *sufficient*. Mathematics has been traditionally defined as "the science of discrete and continuous magnitude", or as "the science of quantity". Even Leibniz, who saw in the theory of the syllogism 'a kind of universal mathematics', followed the tradition in confining what was properly to be called "mathematics" to the science of quantity. Nor is it surprising that this definition of mathematics should for so long have seemed satisfactory. Arithmetic and algebra regarded as sciences concerned with *number*, geometry regarded as a science concerned with *points, lines, planes*, and *volumes*, would all appear to be exactly described as concerned with discrete and continuous quantity. It is true that *points* are not quantities, but, since the relations between points can be expressed by means of geometrical quantities, the case of points did not appear to make the definition unsuitable ; it merely caused trouble with regard to the nature of points. When, however, projective geometry, the theory of abstract groups, and the algebra of logic—to mention only a few departments of mathematics—were developed, it became obvious that there is no essential relation between mathematics and quantity.

The study of mathematics, as in the case of the other sciences, had its origin in the attempt to render sensible experience orderly. We saw in Chapter VIII how difficult must have been the advance in abstractness of thinking when it was first realized that a set of days, a set of fish, and a set of apples, might all have *the same number*. This degree of abstraction is now so familiar to us that we take it for granted, and believe that we know what *number* is. It is possible that we mistake familiarity for understanding. Since the numbers with which we are familiar are the finite, or inductive numbers to which the process of counting is applicable, the common-sense notion of number is to a considerable extent based on intuitions derived from counting, whilst the operation of counting remains unanalysed. Consequently our conception of number is unduly restricted and unclear. We have seen that counting consists in establishing a one-one correlation, the objects counted being taken in a certain order. Counting, therefore, presupposes the notion of similarity, and is less logically simple, since counting requires an order but similarity does not. Hence, the definition of number by means of similarity leads to greater generality. In this way arithmetic is freed from its dependence upon intuition. In spite of unclear ideas with regard to the relation between number and counting, most educated people would probably admit that the properties of number which yield the rules of arithmetic are independent of what actually exists. This is to admit that the propositions of arithmetic are *a priori*, i.e. capable of being known independently of any given subject-matter. It is likely that there would be some hesitation in admitting that there is a science, rightly called *geometry*, which is equally independent of intuitions given in experience. There is some justification for such hesitation. What is ordinarily called geometry is to be sharply distinguished from arithmetic, since it is a science as entirely empirical as dynamics and is thus a branch of natural science. This branch of natural science—which, for convenience, we may call " empirical geometry "— has been traditionally confused with geometry as pure mathematics. To this confusion was due the belief that geometry was a science of quantity, concerned with the properties of space.[1] It was assumed that the axioms of geometry were descriptive of our space and that the theorems of geometry were necessarily true, since they were taken to be demonstrated by means of the axioms alone. This view, as we saw in Chapter X, is now known to be mistaken. We have seen that the attempt to deduce Euclid's theorems from his axioms showed that his deductions were lacking in logical rigour, since they required assumptions which were not included in the axioms but which were in conformity with our spatial intuitions.[2] The axiom of parallels was recognized to be less *plausible* than Euclid's other axioms, so that many attempts were made to derive the parallel axiom from the others. These attempts failed, and mathematicians began to construct geometrical systems based upon the denial of Euclid's axiom. In this way arose the non-Euclidean geometries which have played so great a part in the development of mathematics and mathematical physics. This development cannot be followed here.[3] It must be sufficient to observe that the result of this development was to establish the fact that every geometry is rigidly deductive, and does not employ any form of reasoning that is not found in arithmetic. That is to say, a pure geometry is a deductive system constructed by means of primitive concepts and primitive propositions in the manner explained in Chapter X.

Every branch of mathematics consists of assertions that such and such primitive propositions imply such and such consequences. Thus a mathematical proposition is of the form : *If a set of elements x, y, z, ... satisfy such and such conditions, then these elements will*

---

[1] Thus, for example, de Morgan, having asserted that ' space and time are the only necessary matters of thought ', adds, ' and these form the subject-matter of the mathematics '. (*Proc. London Mathematical Society*, Vol. I, p. 1.)

[2] The theorem that the sum of the angles of a triangle is equal to two right angles follows from the parallel postulate, and is conformable to our ordinary spatial intuitions. The denial of the postulate led on the one hand to hyperbolic, on the other to elliptic geometry.

[3] See Cajori : *History of Mathematics*.

matics. Mr. Russell asserts : ' If there are still those left who do
not admit the identity of logic and mathematics, we may challenge them to indicate at what point, in the successive definitions
and deductions of *Principia Mathematica*, they consider that logic
ends and mathematics begins. It will then be obvious that any
answer must be quite arbitrary.' [1] This must be granted. [2]

We must now consider to what extent the ideal of logical
rigour has been attained. A difficulty arises with regard to the
concept of a *class*. In the attempt to carry out a strictly rigorous
deduction of the general properties of classes and relations from the
fundamental logical premisses certain contradictions became
apparent. We shall begin by considering Mr. Russell's contradiction with regard to classes that are not members of themselves.
Ordinarily we should not suppose that a class is a member of itself.
For example, the class of all *tables* would not itself be regarded as a
table, nor the class of all *men* as a member of itself, that is, a *man*.
But it might be natural to suppose that the class of all things that
are not men is itself not a man and, therefore, a member of itself.
This supposition, however, leads to contradiction. This contradiction may be easily shown if we call a class which does not contain
itself as a member an *ordinary class*. Then let O be the class consisting of all ordinary classes. We have now to consider whether
O is a member of itself, or not. If O is a member of O, it follows
from the hypothesis that O *is an ordinary class* that O is not a member
of O ; if O is not a member of O, it follows *from the hypothesis* that
O is a member of O. Thus either supposition, viz. that O is a member of itself, and that it is not a member of itself, leads to contradiction. Mr. Russell met this contradiction by distinguishing different logical types. We saw in Chapter IX that a class consisting
of individuals is not itself an individual. If we were to say that
both the class *and* the individuals are " entities " we should be
using the word " entity " in two different senses. Thus we have

---

[1] op. cit., p. 194.

[2] It should be observed that what is required for mathematics is that the
axioms should be consistent. We saw in Chapter X that consistency could be
established only by finding an interpretation for which the axioms are true.
These objects cannot be taken from the real world, since that would leave
the method open to the uncertainties of the experimental method ; they must
therefore be taken from other branches of mathematics. So far as geometry
is concerned, it is possible to take the real numbers and show that they
satisfy the axioms. For example, " point " may be interpreted as applying
to an ordered triad of numbers (x, y, z) ; " plane " may be interpreted as
applying to the set of such ordered triads satisfying a linear equation, and so
on. But when we attempt to investigate the consistency of the axioms formulated by Peano for real numbers, we can find no *simpler* branch of mathematics
which could provide an interpretation. Hence the necessity for the reduction
of these concepts to logic.

to recognize that objects are of different logical types, and that any given predicate can be significantly asserted only of one type of subject. For example, it is significant to assert that " Socrates is a man ", but it is *meaningless* to assert that " A class is a man ". Accordingly we must recognize that propositions about individuals are not of the same form as propositions about *classes of individuals*. Similarly we must recognize that propositions about *classes* are not of the same form as propositions about *classes of classes*, and so on. These various propositions will be of different orders, the order depending upon the *type*. Thus, if we say that propositions about individuals are of the first order, then propositions about classes of individuals will be of the second order, and so on. In accordance with this theory of logical types we must admit that both the statements " A class is a member of itself " and " A class is not a member of itself " are strictly meaningless. Our failure to realize that such statements are not false but *meaningless* is due to our inveterate habit of supposing that every grammatically correct sentence must be significant.

We have further to distinguish between different orders of properties applicable to the same type of subject. On Mr. Russell's view propositions about classes are propositions about the properties which define the classes. Thus a proposition about a class (e.g. great poets) will be a proposition about all the properties which define the class. We must then consider whether there are any difficulties with regard to propositions about *all properties*. It is clear that there are. For example, given an object A, we can ask whether A has any property of the kind Φ. If A has such a property, then that A has this property will be another property of A. Call this property F. Then we can ask whether F can be a property of the kind Φ. It seems clear that it cannot. For example, if we say "Shakespeare had all the characteristics which belong to a great poet ", then " characteristics " must not be understood in such a way that it could include such a property as *having all the characteristics of a great poet* ; since this property presupposes the totality of such characteristics. Thus, if A has a property of the kind Φ, then the property F, viz. *having a property of the kind Φ*, cannot itself be a property of the kind Φ. Thus F is a property of a higher order than Φ. Any property which is defined by means of *all properties* of a certain order must then be a property of a higher order.[1]

This theory of types enables us to avoid the contradiction with

---

[1] The principle involved in the theory of types is called " the vicious-circle principle ", and is thus stated by Mr. Russell : ' Whatever involves *all* of a collection must not be one of the collection.' Violation of this principle results in illegitimate totalities. (See *Principia Mathematica, Introduction,* Chap. II,

process of mathematical discovery is confined to deductive reasoning. On the contrary, the mathematician uses all the resources of scientific insight. He imagines, he relies on analogies, he is guided by geometrical intuition and by a feeling for pure form that leads him to important discoveries. But mathematical theorems, however they may have been discovered, must be capable of being formulated abstractly and demonstrated by purely logical methods. A branch of mathematics is a set of propositions capable of abstract formulation in such a way that every proposition can be demonstrated to follow from the primitive concepts and the primitive propositions. Mathematics may then be regarded as consisting of all completely abstract deductive systems.

CHAPTER XXIV

THE CHARACTERISTICS OF LOGICAL THINKING

' If a man can play the true logician, and have as well judgement as invention, he may do great matters.'—*Francis Bacon.*

§ 1. PERSUASION AND CONVICTION

THE purpose of logical thinking is to reach conclusions. The process of reaching conclusions is reasoning. Ordinarily we reason from something we know to something which, prior to our reasoning, we did not know, but which we now know as the result of our reasoning. Strictly speaking we cannot be said to *know* anything unless it is the case. Thus, in order that a proposition should be *known* it is necessary both that the proposition should be believed and that it should be true. Although *to believe* a proposition and *to believe it to be true* are one and the same thing, yet we believe many propositions which are in fact false. Sometimes we discover their falsity by reasoning from the propositions we believe to conclusions which we recognize to be false. When we reason we desire to ascertain what is true, or what must be true if something else is true. We can *know* our conclusions to be true only when we know both that the premisses are true and that these premisses imply the conclusion. Sometimes we can recognize that we *believe* a proposition, and therefore believe it to be *true*, although we recognize that we do not yet *know* it to be true. Often, however, we fail to distinguish between our *beliefs* and our *knowledge*. When our belief is challenged then we may come to recognize that, after all, we did not *know* but only *believed* that so-and-so was the case. Doubting is a mental state clearly distinguishable from belief. We *doubt* a proposition when with regard to it we know that we do not *know* whether it is true or whether it is false. The state of doubting is usually unpleasant ; hence, we desire to resolve a doubt. Reasoning from true premisses, or from premisses believed to be true, is a method of resolving doubt. But we may be persuaded to believe by other methods than reasoning. Also many of our beliefs are due neither to persuasion nor to reasoning. Were this not the case we could have but few beliefs, since neither our mental power nor our length of days permit us to inquire into the

30   465

foundation of all that we believe. Thus many of our beliefs are not *well-founded* beliefs even though what we believe may happen to be true.

There are at least five different ways in which belief may be attained. First, we may believe a proposition because we always have believed it. How we first came to believe it we need not here inquire. We are concerned only to notice that we believe some propositions only because we have never seen fit to doubt with regard to them. Such beliefs are usually pleasant, that is to say, the truth of the propositions thus believed seems to us to be conducive to our interests ; were this not the case we should be tempted to doubt, since unpleasantness is a stimulus to activity. The fact that some people, of a melancholy cast of mind, may believe a proposition that something unpleasant is the case, for no other reason than its unpleasantness, does not contradict this contention. For it is just this unpleasantness that satisfies their melancholy, hence, their *belief* that something unpleasant is the case is not *itself* unpleasant. This way of attaining belief may be called, by a perhaps permissible metaphor, *the way of the limpet*. The thinker sticks to his belief as the limpet to its rock, without taking note of its connexion with anything else in the neighbourhood. Thus, for instance, the ardent hunter may believe that foxes enjoy being hunted ; the wealthy old lady, tender-hearted but unimaginative and conservative, may believe that the unemployed are " the won't-works ".[1] The chief advantage of this way of belief is its comfortableness. Its disadvantage is due to the fact that beliefs thus attained may be upset by the pressure of facts, and that this upset may have disastrous consequences.

The second way of attaining belief may be described as the way of authority. Two different types of authority may be distinguished. To accept a proposition on authority is to accept it on the ground that some one whose opinion we respect has asserted it to be true. Our respect may be due to the office occupied by this person or to our recognition that he is an expert with regard to the subject-matter of our belief. The first case is exemplified in the acceptance of the authority of a church, or of a parent, or of a teacher whom we have not learnt to doubt.[2] The disadvantage of acquiring beliefs

---

[1] There is a difficulty in giving examples of this way of belief, since the writer is bound to give examples which appear to her to be baseless beliefs, whereas, with regard to any example chosen, the reader may have sources of knowledge, unknown to the writer, which would justify these beliefs. In that case, the reader will have no difficulty in finding examples, supplied by other peoples' beliefs, which seem to him baseless. To recognize that a belief is after all only a *prejudice* is to recognize that it was attained by the way of the limpet.

[2] It is not unreasonable to suppose that a teacher (in the educational sense) whose pronouncements are *never* doubted is a bad teacher.

in this way is that the acceptance of authority stifles inquiry. Moreover, authorities may be mistaken. The advantages resemble the advantages of the way of the limpet. The second case is exemplified in the acceptance of expert testimony. When a man has made a careful study of a subject, and has come to conclusions for which he is prepared to offer evidence that seems to him conclusive, then it is not unreasonable to believe that his opinion has more weight than that of one who has made no such study. When there is a consensus of expert opinion with regard to a given proposition it is reasonable to accept the opinion of these experts if we have not ourselves examined the evidence upon which the proposition is asserted to be based. Thus it is reasonable for the layman to accept the authority of the expert. With regard to the greater part of our beliefs we are all in the position of laymen. It follows that to believe a proposition on authority is often the wisest course to pursue. The danger of this way of belief is that we are liable to confuse one kind of authority with another and to be confident that experts cannot err. But even a consensus of experts is not infallible.

Thirdly, we may attain belief by the way of self-evidence. We cannot disbelieve what is self-evident, for to say that a proposition is self-evident is to say that its truth is obvious. But what is obvious may nevertheless not be the case. If there are propositions which no one *can* doubt, then they are in fact indubitable. But propositions that have been accepted by many careful thinkers as self-evident have finally been found not to be indubitable. Thus we must distinguish between the assertion that a given proposition is psychologically self-evident, in the sense that no one doubts it, and the assertion that it is self-evident in some *other* sense, strictly relevant to logic. Whether there are any propositions self-evident in the latter sense is a matter for investigation.[1] To recognize that self-evident propositions may require investigation is already to have abandoned the way of self-evidence. The danger of this way of belief is that it checks inquiry and may encourage erroneous beliefs. To avoid this danger it is well to form the habit of suspending judgement, and hence of being prepared to doubt whatever can be doubted.

The fourth and fifth ways of attaining belief are to be distinguished from the first three in that they involve a process of inquiry the purpose of which is to resolve a state of doubt. This process may be terminated either by persuasion or by conviction. Here " persuasion " is used in opposition to " conviction ", although no doubt they are sometimes used as synonyms. The way of persuasion is to be distinguished from the way of conviction by the nature of the process whereby doubt is resolved. Even if ration-

[1] See Chap. X, pp. 175–7.

ality is the distinguishing characteristic of human nature, it must be admitted that few of our beliefs are based upon rational grounds. Moreover, not only do we tend to believe what we wish to believe but, further, this wish to believe often operates in making us suppose that what we believe is a logical consequence of something else that may be taken for granted. Rhetoric is a means of persuasion. The aim of the orator is to induce belief, not to demonstrate a conclusion ; his art consists in persuading others to accept a conclusion for which there is no adequate evidence. Since our beliefs are determined to such a small extent by logical considerations the orator employs various devices to persuade us. If his hearers were clear thinkers, free from the bias of special interest, and if his conclusions were susceptible of demonstration, then he would need no other method of producing belief than the method of logical argument. Seldom, however, is either of these conditions satisfied. Consequently, the orator substitutes persuasion for conviction, appealing to emotion rather than to reason. The speech of a great orator is a work of art ; as such, it has nothing to do with logic, and, as such it can be admired by those whom it does not persuade. But the way of persuasion is not confined to great orators ; it is employed with considerable success by advertising experts, whose insight into practical psychology makes them adepts in persuading those who do not think to buy goods which are either useless or harmful. Possibly in this case there is action without belief so that this topic lies outside the scope of our discussion.

The way of conviction is by reasoning. This is the method of science and the proper business of the logician. It might be supposed that as logicians we have no concern with any other way of attaining belief. In a sense this is so, but it is often difficult to determine *how* a belief has been attained although the ways of attainment are distinct. Not all thinking is logical thinking, nor all reasoning good. We may more easily apprehend the characteristics of good reasoning when we have recognized the various ways in which we attain our beliefs. A well-constructed argument the purpose of which is to produce conviction exhibits the characteristics of clearness, connectedness or relevance, freedom from contradiction or consistency, demonstrativeness or cogency. Throughout our discussion of logical method we have laid stress upon relevance as an essential characteristic of logical thinking. To know what is relevant to a situation is to apprehend connexions. The discovery of relevance requires judgement, for not all relevance is logical. But in connected thinking certain logical principles are implicit, upon which the cogency of the argument depends. These principles will be considered in the next section.

§ 2. LOGICAL PRINCIPLES AND THE TRADITIONAL "LAWS OF THOUGHT"

All logical thinking exemplifies certain abstract principles in accordance with which such thinking takes place. It is extremely difficult to determine what these principles are, and which, if any, are independent of the rest. Three of these principles have been singled out by the traditional Logicians and described as "Laws of Thought". This description is unfortunate, since it suggests a reference to uniformities of thinking, i.e. to psychological laws, which was probably not intended.[1] But the chief objection to the traditional treatment lies not in the description but in the conception of what it was that was thus described. For "*the* laws" must mean *all* the laws; but it is absurd to suppose that there are only three. There has been considerable difference of opinion as to how these "laws" should be stated. The starting-point of the traditional theory of logic is to be found in the Aristotelian category of substance-attribute. Assertions with regard to the attributes of a substance can be most naturally expressed in singular propositions of the subject-predicate form, viz. *This S is P*. Accordingly the "laws" have often been expressed in a manner appropriate only to propositions of this form. An affirmation with regard to *This S* was held both by Plato and Aristotle to be an affirmation with regard to a definite thing, or individual, having a determinate nature. From this point of view the Laws may be stated as follows:

(1) *The Law of Identity*. Everything is what it is; or, A is A.

(2) *The Law of Contradiction*. A thing cannot both be and not be so and so; or, A is not both B and not B.

(3) *The Law of Excluded Middle*. A thing either is or is not so and so; or, A either is or is not B.

The formulation of (1) as " A is A " may be regarded as expressing an important principle of symbolism, but it is not usually so regarded. From the point of view of a principle concerned with the use of symbols, the principle of identity can be formulated as follows : *Sameness of symbol indicates sameness of referend*. Clearly symbols which refer to different referends are different symbols. Hence, it must always be non-significant to write ' A = A '. It is true that it is convenient in practice to say that a name is identical with a given description (e.g. ' Scott is identical with the author of *Waverley* '), or that two descriptions are identical (e.g. ' The author of *Waverley* is identical with the author of *Marmion* '). But in these cases analysis reveals that what is meant by " is identical with " involves the notion of *applying to*. But neither the traditional Law of Identity nor any principle of identity concerning the use of

[1] See Sir William Hamilton, *Lectures on Logic* (Sect. V).

symbols has ever been interpreted in terms of *applying to*. Consequently, these expressions cannot be regarded as exemplifications of the law of identity. The traditional inter-relation of this law is metaphysical. If " A " be regarded as symbolizing a subject of attributes, then the formula may be interpreted as expressing the permanence of substance, or as the persisting of something through change. Such an interpretation is clearly metaphysical ; it expresses a theory with regard to the nature of persistent individuality. This could not properly be regarded as a fundamental principle of logical thinking, so that this interpretation need not be discussed here. Aristotle did not himself formulate any " law of identity ", but such a law might be extracted from his assertion, ' Everything that is true must in every respect agree with itself.' [1]

It is worth while to consider briefly how Aristotle was led to formulate the law of contradiction. He was in search of an indemonstrable principle which could be regarded as the basis of all demonstration. For, as he points out, ' it is impossible that there should be demonstration of absolutely everything ; for there would be an infinite regress, so that there would still be no demonstration '. [2] Now, he argues, ' the most certain principle of all is that regarding which it is impossible to be mistaken '. Such a principle is ' that the same attribute cannot at the same time belong, and not belong to the same subject in the same respect. . . . This, then, is the most certain of all principles, since it answers to the definition given above. For it is impossible for any one to believe the same thing to be and not to be, as some think Heraclitus says '. [3] This statement suggests the formulations given of (2) above. But Aristotle was aware that contradiction is a relation that holds between two propositions which are such that one must be true one false. In discussing the relations between propositions he formulated both the laws of contradiction and excluded middle as follows :

' If it is true to say that a thing is white, it must necessarily be white ; if the reverse proposition is true, it will of necessity not be white. Again, if it is white, the proposition stating that it was white was true ; if it is not white, the proposition to the opposite effect was true. And if it is not white, the man who states that it is is making a false statement ; and if the man who states that it is white is making a false statement, it follows that it is not white. It may therefore be argued that it is necessary that affirmations or denials must be either true or false '. [4]

---

[1] *Anal. Priora.*, 47a, 9.   See Sigwart, *Logic*, I, pp. 83–9, for a discussion of the principle of identity.
[2] *Metaphysica*, 1006a, 7.
[3] *ibid.*, 1005b, 17.   Cf. Socrates' attempt to express this principle in *Republic*.
[4] *De Interpretatione*, 18b, 1–5.

It is not difficult to extract from this passage the formulations : (i) *This S is p* and *This S is not p* cannot both be true ; (ii) Either *This S is p* is true or *This S is not p* is true.   These are respectively the laws (2) and (3).   This passage also brings out clearly that *both* these laws, or principles, are required in order to define the *relation of contradiction* between propositions, since contradictory propositions cannot *both* be true and *one* must be true.

With regard to these three Laws there has been considerable discussion as to whether they are laws of *thought* or of *things*.   They are clearly not laws of thought in the sense that they express ways in which we always *do* think, since we sometimes fall into contradiction.   If it be maintained that on such occasions we are *not thinking*, then " thinking " must be taken as equivalent to " logical thinking ". In that case these " laws " cannot be regarded as uniformities, or generalizations derived from experience.[1]   Probably few, if any, logicians to-day would take this view.   Mr. Joseph says : ' Now though these are called laws of thought, and in fact we cannot think except in accordance with them, yet they are really statements which we cannot but hold true about things.   *We cannot think* contradictory propositions, because we see that *a thing cannot have* at once and not have the same character ; and the so-called necessity of thought is really the apprehension of a necessity in the being of things '.[2]   This passage suggests that Mr. Joseph holds both that these laws are laws of *thought* and that they are laws of *things*.   There seems nothing to be said in favour of this view.   We have already seen reason to reject the view that these " laws " are laws of *thought*. It is also misleading to describe them as laws of *things* since such an expression suggests that they in some way determine what is *actual*, or *given*.   They are, however, purely *formal* principles which are independent of what is given ; they are negative determinations of what is *possible*.   Only in the sense that what is *actual* must also be *possible* could these principles be regarded as determining what is *actual* ; they do not determine what is actual *in so far as it is actual* ; they in no sense limit the *actual* to be *so-and-so*.

Dr. J. N. Keynes says : ' The so-called fundamental laws of thought . . . are to be regarded as the foundation of all reasoning in the sense that consecutive thought and coherent argument are impossible unless they are taken for granted '.[3]   It is certainly true that ' consecutive thought and coherent argument ' must exemplify these principles, but it would be incorrect to suppose that they are

[1] The view that these laws are generalizations from experience was held by Mill.

[2] *Introd.*, p. 13.   It is clear that Mr. Joseph supposes that all *thinking* is *logical* thinking.

[3] *F.L.*, p. 450.   Appendix B to the *Formal Logic* contains a long discussion of the traditional laws.

sufficient to constitute 'the 'foundation of all reasoning'. We cannot here attempt to state all the principles that would together be sufficient ; we shall select those which are most obviously exemplified in ordinary reasoning.[1] We may first restate the 'three laws' in the form of principles exemplified in the relations between propositions. We shall, as usual, employ p, q, to stand for any propositions.

(1) *Principle of Identity.* If p, then p.

(2) *Principle of Contradiction.* p cannot be both true and false.

(3) *Principle of Excluded Middle.* Either p is true or p is false.

This formulation brings out the essential relation of the three principles. They cannot, however, be reduced to a single principle, since the deduction of, for instance, (3) *Either p is true or p is false* from (1) If p, then p, or from (2) Not both p true and p false, requires the independent notion of *falsity*, or of *negation*, which cannot be defined without using the principles themselves.[2]

We require principles of implication and of deduction. These may be stated as follows :

(4) *Principle of Syllogism.* If p implies q, and q implies r, then p implies r.

(5) *Principle of Deduction.* If p implies q, and p is true, then q is true.

This principle is required in order that conclusions should be drawn : the principle permits the omission of an implicans provided that the implicans is *true*.

There is further required a principle permitting the substitution of any *given* member of a class in an assertion about *every* member of the class. This might be expressed as follows :

(6) Whatever can be asserted about *any instance* however chosen, can be asserted about *any given instance*.

This principle may be described as the " principle of substitution " since it is in virtue of this principle that we can substitute constant values for the variables in a functional expression. Mr. Johnson calls this the 'Applicative Principle' and says that it 'may be said to formulate what is involved in the intelligent use of " every "'.[3] This principle together with the principle of deduction is exemplified in all chains of reasoning.

There are three principles relating to the conjunctive use of *and* which are important.[4] These are :

(7) *Principle of Tautology.* p *and* p is equivalent to p. This principle asserts that the reiteration of a proposition adds nothing to the original assertion.

(8) *Principle of Commutation.* p *and* q is equivalent to q *and* p.

[1] See Chap. X, § 5, for a fuller statement of these principles.
[2] See p. 191 above.   [3] W. E. J., II, p. 9.   [4] W. E. J., I, pp. 29–30.

This principle asserts that the order in which propositions are asserted is indifferent. This principle follows from the fact that *and* is a symmetrical relation.

(9) *Principle of Association.*   *p and q and also r* is equivalent to *p and also q and r*. This principle asserts that the order in which propositions are grouped is indifferent. These principles also relate to the alternative *or*. They can be restated by substituting *or* for *and* in each case.

(10) There is a *Principle of Distribution* relating to the combination of propositions connected by *and* and by *or*. This may be stated in the form: *p or q, and also r* is equivalent to *p and r, or q and r*.

It is not likely to be denied that these principles are all psychologically self-evident. Within a given deductive system these principles may be deduced from logically more primitive principles. But these primitive principles will not be self-evident in any sense in which the derived principles are not also self-evident; they will be *primitive*, or *underived*, only because they are taken for granted, and thus form the basis of the given system. Fundamental logical principles cannot be *proved* in any absolute sense, for all proof must presuppose them. To think logically *some* principles must be assumed, since logical thinking is thinking in accordance with logical principles. The notion of proof is relative to something unproved; what is taken as unproved determines what *can* be proved. The principles can be used so that they can be proved by themselves. Such proof is circular. This circularity is a test of self-consistency. Those principles which appear in every deductive development from given principles, *either* as unproved principles *or* as deductions from these principles, may be regarded as fundamental logical principles. The three principles selected by the traditional Logicians have this characteristic only in a more obvious manner than the other principles we have stated.

§ 3.   THE NORMATIVE ASPECT OF LOGIC

Logicians have been wont to raise the question whether logic is a science or an art. Presumably, a science is a systematic study, whilst an art is a set of rules the learning of which may fit some one to do something. If this be so, there seems little doubt that logic is not an art, but a science. There may be an art of thinking. Not a few public men have recently written books professing to deal with such an art. But the art of thinking must not be confused with logic. No doubt the man who sets out to instruct us how to think must be conversant with the logical principles of reasoning as well as with the ordinary workings of the human mind. The logician also may have to take note of psychological processes, but

CHAPTER XXV

A SKETCH OF THE HISTORICAL DEVELOPMENT
OF LOGIC

'Everything of importance has been said before by somebody who did not discover it.'—*A. N. Whitehead.*

§ 1. ORIGIN OF LOGIC IN THE ANALYSIS OF
REFLECTIVE THINKING

AT the present day there is considerable diversity of opinion with regard to the proper definition and scope of logic. Traditionally logic has been regarded as essentially concerned with thinking regarded from the regulative, or normative, point of view. Yet, as we have seen, the generalization of logic has resulted in a science of pure form not to be distinguished from mathematics. One of the ablest modern writers on mathematical logic declares, 'It really should be clear that those who say mathematics is logic are not meaning by "logic" at all the same thing as those who define logic as the analysis and criticism of thought.' [1] This is true. Logic as the science of order, capable of expression in a symbolic system, is certainly quite different from logic as the analysis and criticism of thought. So, too, are practical land surveying and geometry quite different. But just as geometry originated in practical land surveying and only by a long process of development became a purely formal science, so logic originated in the analysis and criticism of thought, and only by a long process of development became the purely formal science of order. The development of a science is an historical process dependent upon the ways in which men think. The development of geometry from reflection upon the operations involved in practical land surveying, and the development of generalized logic from reflection upon the operations involved in reflective thinking, has in each case been one of continuous generalization and consequent abstraction, with the result that the two lines of development have met together in the science of pure form, which is the general science of order.

The collection of doctrines that have been gathered together at various times under the one name "logic" is not, then, a mere

[1] See F. P. Ramsey, *Proc. London Mathematical Association, Series* 2, Vol. 25, Pt. 6, p. 353*a.*

haphazard collection, although no doubt the *selection* of certain of these doctrines within the covers of a single book claiming the comprehensive title of " logic " has often been haphazard. These various doctrines may be grouped as follows : (1) psychological discussion of the nature of the thinking process ; (2) linguistic discussion with regard to the use of words, sometimes including historical information with regard to their etymological derivation ; (3) epistemological considerations with regard to the nature of knowledge ; (4) metaphysical discussions with regard to problems such as the nature of universals, and the relation of thought to sense ; (5) discussion of formal validity and the principles of reasoning ; (6) discussion of the ' methods ' employed by scientists ; (7) discussion of rhetorical arguments with an examination of certain ancient fallacies. It must be granted that (3) and (4) form no part of logic ; that (7) is in the nature of an appendix ; that (1) and (2) are in the nature of prolegomena. But (5) and (6) both properly belong to logic. Their precise relation is seldom stated with any approach to clearness, but, since scientific method is essentially logical, and since the validity of reasoning depends upon its form, it follows that these topics are closely connected.

In this chapter we shall attempt to indicate the way in which logic has developed from the science of reflective thinking, or reasoning, to the science of form.

For our purpose it is not necessary to seek the origins of the science of logic farther back than the age of the sophists in Greece. The contribution of the sophists lies in their development of the art of argumentative discussion. No doubt they sought rather to instruct than to demonstrate, so that they were content with persuasion instead of rational conviction. Their starting-point was provided by customary opinions accepted without criticism and held without clearness.   To reasoning ' from opinions that are generally accepted ' Aristotle gave the name ' dialectic '.[1] Thus understood, dialectic is an art, not a science concerned with principles. In this art Socrates, as we pointed out in Chapter XXII, was proficient. But he was not content to accept customary opinion ; he sought to be clear as to the grounds on which a given conclusion was to be accepted. Thus he sought to know *what* it is concerning which conclusions are drawn. In this way, as we saw, Socrates was led to seek for definitions regarded as expressing the essence of that which was defined. ' It was natural ', says Aristotle, ' that Socrates should seek the essence. For he was seeking to syllogize and the essence is the starting-point of syllogisms. . . . For two things may be fairly ascribed to Socrates—inductive arguments and universal definition, both of which are concerned with the starting-

[1] *Topica*, Bk. I, 100*a*, 30.

from, the first as in or from a whole, the extremes must be related
by a perfect syllogism. I call that term middle which is itself contained in another and contains another in itself : in position also
this comes in the middle. By extremes I mean both that term
which is itself contained in another and that in which another is
contained. If A is predicated of all B, and B of all C, A must be
predicated of all C. . . . Similarly also, if A is predicated of no B,
and B of all C, it is necessary that no C will be A.' [1] From this point
of view Aristotle was led to limit the premisses and conclusion of
a syllogism to one or more of the four A E I O forms. [2]

We have now to inquire why Aristotle should have been led to
restrict the syllogism to this form. The answer has to be found
in the mode of reasoning which Aristotle selected for analysis. We
saw that the answer to the question what makes an act to be just,
or courageous, or holy, takes the form that it is an act of such and
such a sort. This is an assertion that such and such characteristics
belong to all of a certain set of acts. The given act is judged to
belong to this set because it has those characteristics. We see,
therefore, how Aristotle was led to analyse the syllogism into three
and only three terms connected by the relation *is*. In spite of his
reliance upon linguistic forms he saw that the number of *words* has
no relevance to the number of *terms*. For example, in " All who are
fit to govern are reluctant to govern ; this man is fit to govern ;
therefore, this man is reluctant to govern ", the conclusion is demonstrated of the minor through the middle. In attempting to exhibit
the *validity* of such an argument Aristotle was led to recognize that the
set of words preceding the verb must be *taken as a whole*, and likewise the set of words following the verb. This is not because the
same set of words occurs twice (either in both premisses, or in one
premiss and the conclusion), but because the connexion asserted in
the conclusion is established only because the two sets of words
have each been related *as a whole* to the set of words that occur
in each premiss. It follows that each set of words must be symbolized by a *single* symbol, since what is symbolized is taken as
a unit. Thus the argument is symbolized by : All B is C, This
A is B ; therefore, This A is C. Thus A, B, and C are taken each
as a single term about the whole or part of which a predication is
made. [3] The result of this analysis yields the four forms of the
traditional schedule.

---

[1] *Anal. Priora*, 25*b*, 32–26*a*, 1. It will be noticed that Aristotle's first
example is a syllogism in *Barbara*, the second of one in *Celarent*.

[2] Thus the major, A, is predicated of all, or of no, or of some, or of not all,
the minor, B. It should be noticed that Aristotle writes the *major* term first,
since he expresses the proposition in the form " A is predicated of all B ".

[3] It should be observed that Aristotle reached this symbolism from an
analysis of the whole argument. If he had attempted to analyse a sentence

The discovery of the syllogism as a *form* of reasoning necessitated the use of symbols *to express the form*. This point should require no further discussion.[1] Whatever may be the defects of Aristotle's logic it cannot be denied that his treatment of the syllogism was formal. His main error lay not in any failure to realize the importance of form but in his failure to carry the analysis far enough. Thus he did not attempt to symbolize the *relation* connecting the terms of a proposition; consequently he did not realize that the subsumptive syllogism is only *one* form of demonstrative reasoning, and that its validity depends upon the formal properties of the relations that enter into the reasoning. Had he done so he could hardly have failed to recognize that the propositional form *All S is P* is different from the propositional form *This S is P*. To recognize this distinction is to admit that *All S is P* is not a simple proposition. It is to be regretted that Aristotle did not attempt to analyse the method of mathematics before he had developed his theory of the syllogism. Had he done so he might have been led to the discovery of the logical variable. His great merit is to have generalized a common form of reasoning by exhibiting it in symbolic form. There is some foundation for Leibniz's view that the syllogism 'is like a universal mathematics'.[2] But it was not given to Aristotle to apprehend it from this point of view.[3]

Before considering Leibniz's attempt to develop a universal mathematics we must refer briefly to Aristotle's conception of mathematical reasoning. In the *Analytica Posteriora*, in which he discusses this subject, he says: ' All instruction given or received by way of argument proceeds from pre-existent knowledge. This becomes evident upon a survey of all the species of such instruction. The mathematical sciences and all other speculative disciplines are acquired in this way, and so are the two forms of dialectical reasoning, syllogistic and inductive ; for each of these latter make use of old knowledge to impart new, the syllogism assuming an audience that accepts

expressing a definition it is extremely unlikely that he would have analysed it into *two* terms connected by the verb *to be*. Such a sentence as " Every just act has such and such characteristics " would be naturally symbolized by " AX is BCD ". It is in the use of " AX is BCD " as a premiss in a syllogism that ' AX ' and ' BCD ' must be taken as single wholes.

[1] See above, Chap. VI, § 6 ; Chap. X, § 1.

[2] *New Essays on the Human Understanding*, Bk. IV, Chap. XVII, § 9.

[3] Aristotle's logical works have been grouped together by his successors under the title *Organon* ("the Instrument"). They consist of : (1) *The Categories*, dealing with names for the fundamental ideas involved in all thinking ; (2) *De Interpretatione*, dealing mainly with the structure of thought as revealed in language ; (3) *Prior Analytics* ; (4) *Posterior Analytics*. The last two discuss the nature of demonstration, and of induction, regarded as a means of deriving general principles. (5) The *Sophistici Elenchi*, dealing with the refutation of sophistical fallacies ; (6) The *Topica*, dealing with dialectical argument.

must be precise, exact, and universal. His project differed in two important respects from present conceptions of mathematical logic, since (1) he failed to realize that the *relations* involved must be analysed in precisely the same way as the terms ; and (2) he supposed that the primitive concepts would necessarily result from a correct analysis since they would be given by means of the alphabet of human thought. This is a mistake. We have seen that the primitive concepts of a deductive system are, to some extent at least, arbitrarily chosen, so that many different deductive systems are possible.

Leibniz did not publish his researches on these topics so that his work has not directly affected the subsequent development of the subject. This development followed two main lines, the one being in accordance with Leibniz's project of a calculus of reasoning, the other in accordance with his conception of a universal mathematics. Each of these developments must be very briefly considered.

The development of a calculus of reasoning leads directly to the conception of a symbolic system whose significance is independent of its interpretation. The foundations of symbolic logic were laid down by George Boole.[1] He says : ' Those who are acquainted with the present state of the theory of symbolic algebra are aware that the validity of the processes of analysis does not depend upon the interpretation of the symbols which are employed but solely upon the laws of their combination. Every system of interpretation which does not affect the truth of the relations supposed is equally admissible, and it is thus that the same process may under one scheme of interpretation represent the solution of a question or the properties of number, under another that of a geometrical problem, and under a third that of optics '.[2] Boole recognized that ordinary language is not a perfect medium for the expression of thought, and he accordingly attempted to devise a symbolic language in terms of which he could exactly express ' the laws of thought '. He was mistaken in supposing that he was concerned with *thinking* ; he was in fact constructing a symbolic logic. The elements of language are, he said, signs ; signs are arbitrary marks to which are assigned fixed interpretations, and which are susceptible of combination with other signs in accordance with fixed laws dependent upon their mutual relations.[3] These signs are of three kinds, namely, (1) literal symbols, x, y, . . . which represent the objects of our conceptions ; (2) signs of operations such as $+$, $-$, $\times$, by means

---

[1] Boole (1815–64). His chief works are *The Mathematical Analysis of Logic*, and *The Laws of Thought*. See also " The Calculus of Logic " in the *Cambridge Mathematical Journal*, 1848.

[2] *The Mathematical Analysis of Logic* (1847), p. 3.

[3] See *The Laws of Thought*.

of which literal signs are combined ; (3) the sign of identity, $=$, which Boole regarded as the fundamental relation.

Boole's contemporary, Augustus de Morgan,[1] began a thorough analysis of *relations* and *operations*. This work was of the greatest importance. He used a symbolism much less adapted to the needs of a calculus than was the algebraical symbolism of Boole, so that he remains somewhat outside the main line of development. Nevertheless, de Morgan may be said with Boole to have laid down the lines of subsequent research. Their work was continued by Ernst Schroeder,[2] Mrs. C. Ladd-Franklin, and Hugh MacColl. The most elaborate development of Boole's system was due to Schroeder, whose work was a continuation of Leibniz's conception of a calculus of reasoning, in the form of an *algebra of logic*.

The second line of development was concerned with the construction of a deductive system which should be a ' universal mathematics ', such as Leibniz foresaw but did not work out in detail. This development was not a little aided by the discovery of non-Euclidean systems of geometry, which made clear, for the first time, the independence of the axioms of the characteristics of spatial intuitions.[3] We saw in Chapter X that this discovery led to a more rigorous analysis of the fundamental concepts, which resulted in making explicit all the assumptions involved in the construction of a deductive system. The foundations of this logical analysis were laid down by Frege[4] in his *Grundlagen der Arithmetik*, and the *Grundgesetze der Arithmetik*. Since Frege's purpose was not to develop a calculus by means of which logical problems could be accurately and rapidly solved, but to analyse the logical relations involved in arithmetic, he found it necessary to invent non-algebraical symbols. His purpose was to stress the *differences* rather than the *analogies* between logical relations and the operations of ordinary mathematics. He succeeded in developing arithmetic from purely logical premises, and thus showed that the fundamental conceptions of mathematics are capable of being defined in terms of relations that enter into any complicated process of thought. Thus Frege achieved the complete separation of deductive systems from intuitions derived from counting or from perceptions of spatial relations. Frege's symbolism, however, was so cumbersome and difficult that his work was left unnoticed, so that much of it had to be done over

---

[1] de Morgan (1806–78) wrote a great many papers on mathematical methods in logic (see *Bibliography*, p. 495).   He also made important contributions to the subject in his *Formal Logic* (1847), *Syllabus of a Proposed System of Logic*.

[2] See *Vorlesungen über die Algebra der Logik* (3 vols., published 1890–95) ; *Der Operationskreis des Logikkalkuls* (1877) ; *Abriss der Algebra der Logik*, Hrsg. v. E. Muller.

[3] Cf. Chap. X above.

[4] Frege's books were published in 1884, and 1893–1903.

time of Bacon until the present day, and to point out how this development has affected the statement of the second problem.

(1) Rival conceptions of scientific method can be most clearly distinguished by considering the function assigned to hypothesis in scientific investigation. To admit that hypothesis is indispensable is to admit the union of theory and observation in scientific theory. To admit that the most fruitful hypotheses are those which are susceptible of mathematical development is to admit that the most satisfactory theories are those which transcend *in exactness* any possible verification of them by observation of what happens. Modern theories of scientific method make both these admissions. Bacon's conception is based upon the refusal to admit either. His view is clearly indicated in four *Aphorisms* in Book I of the *Novum Organum* :

Aph. I. 'Man, being the servant and interpreter of Nature, can do and understand so much and so much only as he has observed in fact or in thought of the course of nature : beyond this he neither knows anything nor can do anything.'

Aph. XIX. 'There are and can be only two ways of searching into and discovering truth. The one flies from the senses and particulars to the most general axioms, and from these principles, the truth of which it takes for settled and immoveable, proceeds to judgement and to the discovery of middle axioms. And this way is now in fashion. The other derives axioms from the senses and particulars, rising by a gradual and unbroken ascent, so that it arrives at the most general axioms last of all. This is the true way, but as yet untried.'

Aph. XXII. ' Both ways set out from the senses and particulars, and rest in the highest generalities ; but the difference between them is infinite. For the one just glances at experiment and particulars in passing, the other dwells duly and orderly among them. The one, again, begins at once by establishing certain abstract and useless generalities, the other rises by gradual steps to that which is prior and better known in the order of nature.'

Aph. XXVI. ' The conclusions of human reason as ordinarily applied in matter of nature, I call for the sake of distinction *Anticipations of Nature* (as a thing rash and premature). That reason which is elicited from facts by a just and methodical process, I call *Interpretation of Nature.*' [1]

These passages express Bacon's distrust of hypothesis as anticipations of nature. He completely failed to see that experimental observation must be guided and controlled by hypothesis.[2] His failure to grasp the importance of hypothesis is partly due to his reaction against excessive reliance upon syllogistic reasoning based upon premises too rashly assumed to be ' truths that cannot be shaken ', and partly to the fact that he immensely underestimated the complexity of nature. There is no doubt that he was right in insisting upon the importance of experiment, for, as we have seen, scientific theories are based upon observable facts and return to them. He was also right in insisting that theories must be tested by " descending " again to the particulars. But it was an error

---

[1] Translation by Ellis and Spedding.   [2] Cf. Bk. I, *Aph.* 104.

to suppose that theories can be ' read off ' from a collection of facts. This, however, is exactly what Bacon did suppose. He believed that the work of science was to discover what he called " Forms ". In Bk. II, *Aph. IV*, Bacon says :

'For the Form of a nature is such, that given the form the nature infallibly follows. Therefore it is always present when the nature is present, and universally implies it, and is constantly inherent in it. Again, the Form is such, that if it be taken away the nature infallibly vanishes. Therefore it is always absent, when the nature is absent, and implies its absence, and inheres in nothing else. Lastly, the true Form is such that it deduces the given nature from some source of being which is inherent in more natures, and which is better known in the natural order of things than the Form itself. For a true and perfect axiom of knowledge then the direction and precept will be, that another nature be discovered which is convertible with the given nature, and yet is a limitation of a more general nature, as a true and real genus.' [1]

By a *Form* Bacon seems to mean what a given thing really is, and he conceived that this would always be ' a limitation of a more general nature ', i.e. a species of a more generic nature. For example, *heat* is one species of motion, *colour* another species ; hence, the *form of heat* and the *form of colour* would be limitations of the same more general nature. For the discovery of these Forms induction by simple enumeration is useless. It is necessary to draw up three ' Tables of Investigation ' as follows : (1) *Table of Essence and Presence* containing all known instances in which the simple nature is present ; (2) *Table of Absence* containing instances corresponding to those in the first Table except that the simple nature is absent ; (3) *Table of Degrees* containing instances in which the simple nature is present in varying degrees. By comparison of these tables what is not the Form can be excluded. What remains is the Form. Bacon was fully aware of the difficulty of this method of exclusion. Thus he says : ' In the process of exclusion are laid the foundations of true Induction, which however is not completed till it arrives at an affirmative. Nor is the exclusive part itself at all complete, not indeed can it possibly be so at first. For exclusion is evidently the rejection of simple natures ; as if we do not yet possess sound and true notions of simple natures, how can the process of exclusion be made accurate ? ' [2] He suggested various devices for strengthening the method of exclusion by the use of what he calls ' Prerogative Instances ', which cannot, however, be discussed here. Although Bacon recognized the difficulty of carrying out satisfactorily an investigation in accordance with the three Tables owing to our inadequate knowledge of simple natures, it never occurred to him to suppose that the method itself is inadequate. Its inadequacy is due to the fact that he failed to grasp the importance of hypothesis and of mathematical deduction in scientific investigation. As Mr.

[1] See C. D. Broad, loc. cit., p. 33.   [2] *Nov. Org.*, Bk. II, *Aph. XIX.*

ment of a constructive theory into a more and more comprehensive
theory is made possible only by the union of exact mathematical
deduction and accurate observation. It is now generally admitted
that only hypotheses which are stated in precise quantitative terms
can yield satisfactory theories with regard to the order of nature.
The physical sciences at all events have reached a stage of development in which the inductive methods of Bacon and Mill have ceased
to be useful. The marvellously exact experiments of modern science
are suggested by mathematical deductions and are at every stage
controlled by theoretical considerations. We saw in Chapter XX that
such a procedure results in theories which are fragile because they
are exceedingly comprehensive. The development of physical science
from Galileo to Einstein justifies this conception of scientific method.

(2) The problem of the logical justification of induction is not
one that need concern the scientist. He may be content to proceed
step by step satisfied if his theories be verified, knowing that at best
they are but approximations. The logician, however, must ask
what are the grounds upon which these theories are to be accepted.
Little remains to be added to the discussion of this problem in Chapter
XXI. We saw that Hume raised the question of the validity of
induction, and that his critics have failed to answer him. As Mr.
Keynes says : ' Hume's statement of the case against induction has
never been improved upon ; and the successive attempts of philosophers, led by Kant, to discover a transcendental solution have
prevented them from meeting the hostile arguments on their own
ground and from finding a solution along lines which might, con-
ceivably, have satisfied Hume himself.' [1] Nevertheless, not Bacon
only but also Mill believed that inductive conclusions are capable
of yielding certainty. Their belief was no doubt based upon the
unrecognized assumption of the principle of limited independent
variety. Dr. Broad has pointed out that Bacon ' asserts at least
two different forms of this principle. In the first place, he definitely
asserts that the same simple nature, e.g. heat, cannot be reduced
in some cases (e.g. in fires) to one form, and in other cases (e.g. in
the heavenly bodies or in dunghills) to another form. He thus
definitely denies that there can be a plurality of forms for a given
simple nature. Secondly, Bacon says that " the forms of simpler
natures, though few in number, yet in their communications and
co-ordinations make all this variety " '.[2] Mr. Keynes points out
that Mill assumes ' that every event can be analysed into a limited
number of ultimate elements ',[3] although he does not make this
assumption explicit. Certainly without such an assumption Mill's
methods are unworkable ; with it they have some approach to

[1] A *Treatise on Probability*, p. 272.
[2] op. cit., pp. 35-6.   [3] op. cit., p. 272.

cogency. Both Bacon and Mill assumed what might be called an *alphabetic* view of the universe, although neither of them realized that this was an assumption which stands in need of justification, or at least of explicit statement. Mr. Keynes and Dr. Broad have stated very clearly what exactly must be assumed with regard to the constitution of the existent world if inductive conclusions are to be regarded as more likely to be true than to be false. Every modern logician recognizes that the foundation of the theory of induction is to be found in the theory of probability.

The development of the conception of scientific method is of interest to the logician since the scientist is concerned with the discovery of types of order by means of which conclusions can be drawn. It has been the purpose of this chapter to show that the traditional Aristotelian logic and the recent development of logic as the science of pure form have had a common origin in reflection upon the nature and conditions of valid reasoning. Reflection upon scientific method has also aided the development of logic. We saw that the generalization of logic as the science of pure form resulted from the attempt to make explicit all the premisses that enter into the construction of a system of geometry. In making a similar attempt with regard to the analysis of scientific method the logician has been led to emphasize the distinction between pure and empirical science. In the former, demonstration is possible; in the latter, it is not. The impossibility in the latter case is due to the dependence of empirical science upon sensible facts. Yet even an empirical science as it becomes highly developed tends to become deductive in form, in spite of the demand that it must fit the facts. In its final stage scientific method takes the form of constructive description.

It is true that the discovering of an hypothesis which will serve to render intelligible the connexion between sensible facts is extra-logical. So, too, is the flash of insight by means of which the mathematician is led to see *how* his problem can be solved. But the statement of the hypothesis as a construction capable of ordering the facts, as well as the statement of the mathematical problem, exhibits form. Only when the form of the reasoning is thus exhibited can the validity of the reasoning in either case be tested. In so far as scientific method exhibits form it is the proper concern of the logician.

BIBLIOGRAPHY

THIS bibliography is not intended to be exhaustive. Its purpose is to suggest further reading along various lines of approach to the subject. Books of an advanced nature mentioned in the second and third sections are marked by an asterisk.

I. GENERAL INTRODUCTORY BOOKS

CARVETH READ. *Logic, Deductive and Inductive.* (Simpkin Marshall.)

J. E. CREIGHTON. *An Introductory Logic.* (Macmillan.)

S. H. MELLONE. *An Introductory Textbook in Logic.* (Blackwood.)

A. WOLF. *Textbook of Logic.* (Allen & Unwin.)
> Any one of these would provide the student with an elementary treatment of logic along traditional lines.

H. W. B. JOSEPH. *An Introduction to Logic.* (Oxford University Press.)
> This is by far the best systematic exposition of the traditional Logic. It is written from an Aristotelian point of view, and affords the best introduction to philosophical logic.

II. FORMAL LOGIC AND MATHEMATICAL LOGIC
A. LESS ADVANCED WORKS

J. N. KEYNES. *Formal Logic.* (Fourth Edition.) (Macmillan.)
> This is an exhaustive study of Aristotelian logic in its purely formal aspect, and is the best book written from this point of view. It contains a valuable *Appendix* dealing with a generalization of logical processes, in their application to complex inferences, without the aid of symbols of operation. (1st Ed., 1884; 4th Ed., 1906.)

J. ROYCE. "The Principles of Logic" in *Encyclopaedia of the Philosophical Sciences,* Vol. I, *Logic.* (Macmillan, 1913.)
> This is a masterly introduction to the general principles of logic, written from the modern point of view. The student who is interested in the generalization of logic would be well advised to read this essay.

L. COUTURAT. "The Principles of Logic" (*in the same volume as the preceding*).
> This is a brief introductory exposition of the nature of symbolic logic.

> *Algebra of Logic.* (Paris, 1905; Eng. Trans. by *Robinson*, 1913. Open Court Publishing Company.)

*C. I. LEWIS. *A Survey of Symbolic Logic.* (University of California Press. Berkeley. 1918.)
> This is the most comprehensive and simplest exposition of the various systems of symbolic logic. Chapter I contains an excellent historical survey, and there is a very full bibliography.

*R. M. EATON. *Symbolism and Truth. An Introduction to the Theory of Knowledge.* (Harvard University Press, 1925.)
> This is a discussion of the rôle of symbols in knowledge. It contains a useful chapter on 'Formal Deduction'.

*B. A. W. RUSSELL. *Introduction to Mathematical Philosophy.* (Allen & Unwin, 1919.)
> This is the standard introduction to the subject.

L. ROUGIER. *La Structure des Théories Déductives.* (Paris. Alcan. 1921.)

B. CLASSICAL WORKS IN CHRONOLOGICAL ORDER

G. BOOLE. 1847. *The Mathematical Analysis of Logic.* (Macmillan.)
1848. "The Calculus of Logic", *Cambridge Mathematical Journal.*
1854. *An Investigation of the Laws of Thought.* (Reprinted in 1916 as Vol. 2 of *Boole's Collected Logical Works*; ed. by Jourdain. Open Court Publishing Company.)

A. DE MORGAN. 1847. *Formal Logic :* or *The Calculus of Inference, Necessary and Probable.* (Edited by A. E. Taylor in 1926. Open Court Publishing Company.)
1846–1863. *Five papers, "On the Syllogism, etc."* (Transactions of the Cambridge Philosophical Society.)
1860. *Syllabus of a Proposed System of Logic.* (Walton.)

*B. PEIRCE. 1870. *Linnear Associative Algebras.* (Republished, with notes by C. S. Peirce, in *American Journal of Mathematics,* 1881.)

*C. S. PEIRCE. 1870. " Description of a Notation for the Logic of Relatives." (*Memoir of the American Academy of Arts and Sciences,* Vol. 9.)
1880. " On the Algebra of Logic." (*American Journal of Mathematics,* Vol. 3.)

*E. SCHROEDER. 1877. *Der Operationskreis des Logikkalkuls.* (Leipzig, Teubner.)
1890–1895. *Vorlesungen über die Algebra der Logik.* (Leipzig, Teubner.)

*G. FREGE. 1884. *Die Grundlagen der Arithmetik, eine logischmathematische Untersuchung über den Begriff der Zahl.* (Breslau, Koebner.)
1893–1903. *Grundgesetze der Arithmetik.* (Jena, Pohle.)

*G. PEANO. 1895–1908. *Formulaire de Mathématiques.* (Turin, Bocca.)
These five volumes contain writings by a set of Italian logicians ; the successive volumes are in fact revised and enlarged editions of the preceding ones.

*A. B. KEMPE. 1886. " Memoir on the Theory of Mathematical Form." (*Phil. Trans. Roy. Soc.,* Vol. 177.)
1890. " On the relation between the logical theory of classes and the geometrical theory of points." (*Proc. London Math. Soc.,* Vol. 21.)
1890. "The Subject-matter of exact thought." (*Nature,* Vol. 43.)

*B. A. W. RUSSELL. 1903. *Principles of Mathematics.* (Cambridge University Press ; only Vol. I published.)
1905. " On Denoting." (*Mind,* N.S., 14.)
1906. "The Theory of Implication."
1908. " Mathematical Logic as based on the Theory of Types." (Both in *American Journal of Mathematics.*)
1913. " The Philosophical Importance of Mathematical Logic." (*Monist,* Vol. 23.)

*A. N. WHITEHEAD and B. A. W. RUSSELL. 1910–1926. *Principia Mathematica.* (Vol. I, 1st Ed., 1910 ; 2nd Ed., 1925 ; Vol. II, 1912, Vol. III, 1912.)

*L. WITTGENSTEIN. *Tractatus Logico-philosophicus.* (Kegan Paul, 1922.)

III. SCIENTIFIC METHOD, INCLUDING STATISTICAL METHODS, AND PROBABILITY

A. D. RITCHIE. *Scientific Method.* (Kegan Paul, 1923.)
An elementary treatment of methodology.

F. WESTAWAY. *Scientific Method.* (Blackie.)
This is also an elementary treatment ; it contains some useful detailed examples of scientific method.

Printed in Great Britain by
Butler & Tanner Ltd.,
Frome and London